Design Liability in the Construction Industry

Fourth Edition

David L. Cornes
BSc(Eng), AKC, FICE, CEng, FCIArb
Solicitor of the Supreme Court

D1393945

OXFORD

BLACKWELL SCIENTIFIC PUBLICATIONS

LONDON EDINBURGH BOSTON

MELBOURNE PARIS BERLIN VIENNA

Copyright © D. L. Cornes 1983, 1985,
1989, 1994

Blackwell Scientific Publications
Editorial Offices:
Osney Mead, Oxford OX2 0EL
25 John Street, London WC1N 2BL
23 Ainslie Place, Edinburgh EH3 6AJ
238 Main Street, Cambridge,
    Massachusetts 02142, USA
54 University Street, Carlton,
    Victoria 3053, Australia

The right of D. L. Cornes to be identified as the
author of this work has been asserted in
accordance with Sections 77 & 78 of The
Copyright, Designs and Patents Act 1989.

First published in Great Britain by
Granada Publishing 1983
Second edition published by
Collins Professional and Technical Books 1985
Third edition published by
BSP Professional Books 1989
Fourth edition published by
Blackwell Scientific Publications 1994

Set by DP Photosetting, Aylesbury, Bucks
Printed and bound in Great Britain by
Hartnolls Ltd, Bodmin, Cornwall

DISTRIBUTORS

Marston Book Services Ltd
PO Box 87
Oxford OX2 0DT
(*Orders:* Tel: 0865 791155
        Fax: 0865 791927
        Telex: 837515)

USA
Blackwell Scientific Publications, Inc.
238 Main Street
Cambridge, MA 02142
(*Orders:* Tel: 800 759-6102
            617 876-7000)

Canada
Oxford University Press
70 Wynford Drive
Don Mills
Ontario M3C 1J9
(*Orders:* Tel: (416) 441-2941)

Australia
Blackwell Scientific Publications Pty Ltd
54 University Street
Carlton, Victoria 3053
(*Orders:* Tel: 03 347-5552)

British Library
Cataloguing in Publication Data

A Catalogue record for this book is
available from the British Library

ISBN 0–632–03261–8

Library of Congress
Cataloging in Publication Data

Cornes, David L.
    Design liability in the construction
industry/David L. Cornes.—4th ed.
        p.   cm.
    Includes index.
    ISBN 0-632-03261-8
    1. Architects—Malpractice—Great
Britain.   2. Engineers—Malpractice—
Great Britain.   3. Construction contracts—
Great Britain.   I. Title.
KD2978.C67   1994
346.4203'6—dc 20
[344.20636]   94-2181
                                       CIP

Contents

Preface

Since the First Edition of this book, there has been dramatic change in the law of tort and limitation. By the time the Third Edition of this book was published, the House of Lords' decision in *Anns* v. *Merton* was coming under serious pressure in other cases. It is now well known that *Anns* has been overruled by the House of Lords in *Murphy* v. *Brentwood District Council* in 1990. That development has involved an almost complete rewriting of the sections of this book dealing with the law of tort. The fear of designers that they could incur liability in tort, many years after they had completed projects, to many different categories of people has become very much less of a problem for them. However, those fears have to some extent been replaced by the concerns over the use of collateral warranties and their terms. The opportunity has been taken in this Fourth Edition to set out some basic information about collateral warranties in Chapter 7. The law of contract is now paramount in construction cases; tort still remains as a remedy in construction but in a fairly narrow set of circumstances.

In 1993, the House of Lords was faced with a dilemma following the changes in the law of tort. How could they hold a contractor liable to the subsequent owner of a building in circumstances where there was no contractual relationship and no collateral warranty: *Linden Gardens Trust Ltd* v. *Lenesta Sludge Disposals Ltd* and *St Martin's Property Corporation Ltd* v. *Sir Robert McAlpine*. In a remarkable legal development, the House of Lords decided that the original employer under the building contract could recover the costs of making good defects incurred by the subsequent owner. This decision appears to cut across the usual contract rule that only parties to a contract can sue and be sued on the contract. There is a lengthy discussion of these cases and some of the possible consequences of the decisions in Chapter 7.

Given that design and build contracts (and their variants) are now achieving a very substantial share of the market in the UK, it seemed appropriate to expand the discussion on this subject in this Fourth Edition. I have tried to show how the position of a design and build contractor differs from that of a professional designer. I have also endeavoured to deal with the particular problems that arise on design and build in relation to insurance and collateral warranties.

I have aimed to state the law applicable in England and Wales as at 1 January 1994. I have also included some cases from outside of England and Wales which, although they are not binding on the English courts, are likely to be of persuasive influence. Whilst I have sought to explain the law as I see it, a book is no substitute for good legal advice when a problem arises.

In the text of this Fourth Edition, I have continued, as in previous editions to use the word 'designer' wherever possible to mean *anyone* who undertakes design work and only where necessary have I been more specific by referring to architects or engineers or contractors.

I owe a debt of gratitude to Ann Hockin who typed the lengthy alterations for the Third Edition and to Kay Oliver who has, without any complaint, produced the typescript for this edition. My thanks also go to my partners, Richard Winward, Adrian Luto and Roger Doulton who have assisted me with their views on parts of this edition. I am also grateful to Zak Mulla who assisted me on the table of cases, and to David Bridge and Tracey Perrett who gave me great assistance with research. Notwithstanding all this assistance, it goes without saying that in the end, the views expressed in this book are my own. My thanks also go to Julia Burden of Blackwell Scientific Publications for her kindness, professionalism and, most of all, her patience.

David L. Cornes
Winward Fearon & Co.
35 Bow Street
LONDON
WC2E 7AU   1 January 1994

For Katrina, Charlotte, Oliver and Edward

Chapter 1

The problems of design

Architects, engineers, quantity surveyors and others involved in the design of buildings and structures quite properly wish to do just that; after all, that design process is the end result of many years of studying, training and experience. It is easy enough to see that when a design is faulty in some way, the presence of that fault strikes at the very reason for existence of the designer and he is likely to find himself in a new and unfamiliar world inhabited by insurers, solicitors, barristers and expert witnesses, judges and arbitrators.

1.1 Areas of risk

The areas of work in which designers are most at risk are difficult to establish with any certainty; the reason for this is probably twofold. Firstly, not every dispute related to design results in a legal action and a reported case; the vast majority of disputes are settled. The second reason is that insurers who provide professional indemnity insurance are understandably reluctant to produce details of the claims in which they have been involved. However, some information has been given following an analysis of settled claims on professional indemnity insurance policies, which is helpful in showing the areas in which there has tended to be negligence.

The Royal Institute of British Architects (RIBA) conducted a professional indemnity insurance survey and the results were set out and analysed in PR/83/27 'Confidential Report to the RIBA Practice Committee', 13 July 1983 and PR/83/31, 'Report on the Analysis of Individual Claims'. Based on the survey, an article appeared in *Construction Law Journal* ((1986) 2 Const LJ 167). In that article, the following information is given:

'The value of insurance claims against architects is wide ranging from under £100 to £9m. Virtually 60% of claims are for amounts up to £10,000 with 25% of them being for sums up to £50,000 and relate to contracts of similar value. Yet there are a significant number of claims amounting to over a quarter, where the amount exceeds the original value of the contract and which may be the result of the continuous inflation of building costs since a contract was started. The type of claims reflect the general composition of work carried out by architects. Thus 50% of insurance claims arise from housing schemes, whilst 25% are related to industrial and commercial buildings such as factories, warehouses, offices and shops. The single major cause of claims, amounting to 25% of the total results from the failure of roofs, both pitched and flat equally, the external superstructure accounts for about 20% whilst 16% of claims relate to the general sub-structure. In over 80% of the cases against architects, the claimant is the building owner.'

The designer of today has a greater chance of being involved in such problems than he had a few decades ago. The increased risk is for a variety of reasons of which some of the most important are as follows.

1.2   Reasons for increased risk

1.2.1   Technical developments

Many modern buildings and structures are extremely complex in their conception. Their design involves knowledge and techniques that were not available a few decades ago. In some cases, the design is at the very frontiers of technical knowledge, such as box girder bridges and cylindrical television masts: *IBA* v. *EMI Electronics and BICC Construction* (1980). Innovation necessarily involves greater risk than traditional, tried and tested methods. The same can be said of new methods of construction and the use of new materials. Examples of this can be found in the difficulties encountered in high-rise and prefabricated buildings, where there have been many examples of structural and water penetration problems. Another example is to be found in the early use of mastic, when it was regarded by some designers as being the only material necessary to protect a junction of two different materials from water penetration.

1.2.2   Claims consciousness

This is the age of the consumer; if an employer spends a lot of money on a building, he does not expect it to be full of defects on completion. If there are such defects, he is likely to look to the contractor and the designer to sort out the problems, without cost to himself.

Contractors and sub-contractors are nowadays better informed as to their rights and remedies than they used to be. This also leads to more claims.

1.2.3   Changes in the law

Designer's liability, as will be seen, has been altered in time and transformed in character although the onward march of the law of tort has been stopped and there has been clear retrenchment. Designers need to be aware of their duties and liabilities in carrying out the design so that they can take steps in their procedure and their practice to minimise the risk of an action being brought against them for negligence, and, should they become involved in a dispute, to be aware of what to expect.

1.3   Design procedure

In the latter part of the eighteenth century and the first half of the nineteenth century, the bulk of Britain's railways and canal systems were built. As many as 200,000 men are believed to have been involved in canal construction at its peak. The majority of the excavation for canals, railway cuttings and tunnels was by hand. Initially, the procedure for design and construction of the works bore little relation to that used today.

For example, on the railways, it was usual for a railway company wishing to construct a new line to commission an engineer. He would then survey the proposed line and design the gradients, thereby determining where embankments and cuttings would be located, and assist in the obtaining of the necessary authority from Parliament. He would then obtain assistant engineers who would in their turn engage labour directly for the construction works. It was not until the vast expansion of works that occurred during the canal and railway building boom that a system of contractors and sub-contractors developed in response to the enormous demands for construction works in the industrial revolution. This development sowed the seeds of the arrangements that exist today for the design and execution of construction work.

1.4 The construction professions

Those professions most closely involved in construction today are architecture, civil, mechanical, electrical and structural engineering, heating and ventilating engineering, and quantity and building surveying. All have their own professional bodies which regulate the training and conduct of their members. Of all these professions, only those who desire to call themselves 'architects' are subject to statutory registration, although there are controls over those engineers permitted to be involved in the design of dams. It is essential to consider these professions, their functions and the standard terms and conditions of engagement on which they are likely to carry out their design work for the employer in order to understand the differences between the professions in relation to design.

1.4.1 Architects

The architect is the designer of buildings and landscape. In addition to his function as the designer, the architect may undertake many other tasks. For example, he is likely to be dealing with town and country planning applications and Building Regulation approval, advising the employer as to the building contract, certifying money to be paid to the contractor and issuing various other certificates that are required under the standard forms of contract. It follows that the architect is not only required to have artistic and architectural skill but, in addition, considerable skill in administration and management.

The standards for the education and training of architects are determined by two factors. Firstly, a person who wishes to practise under the title of 'architect' in the United Kingdom is required by law to be registered and the registering body, the Architects' Registration Council of the United Kingdom (ARCUK), has power to determine those educational standards that it thinks are appropriate before permitting a person to register. Secondly, the main voluntary professional organisation for architects, the Royal Institute of British Architects (RIBA), has its own rules and regulations as to admission of members.

1.4.2 The Architects' Registration Council

The government announced in 1993 that they wished to de-regulate architects.

This announcement created a debate within and without the profession as to the merits of registration but by November of 1993, the government appeared to drop its plans for de-regulation. Unless and until the government take action, the Architects (Registration) Acts of 1931, 1938 and 1969 require the registration of those who wish to describe themselves as architects in the United Kingdom, including Scotland. Others can practise architecture and call themselves something other than 'architect' without infringing the Acts; further, the use of the word 'architect' with an adjectival qualification, as in 'naval architect' or 'landscape architect', is also excluded from the operation of the Acts. On the other hand, a partnership, not all of whose members are on the register, or a limited or unlimited company, can call itself 'architects' provided that the work of architecture is under the supervision of one superintendent who is on the register: section 17 of the Architects (Registration) Act 1931. The system is administered by ARCUK which was set up under the 1931 Act. Unless a person is registered by ARCUK, he is forbidden by statute to carry on his business or practice under the title 'architect' (section 1, 1931 Act).

The 1931 Act also creates powers under which the Registration Council can remove names from the Register. These are set out in section 7 of the 1931 Act where a registered person is convicted of a criminal offence, or where the registered person has been found guilty of 'conduct disgraceful to him in his capacity as an architect'.

The procedure in a case of alleged disgraceful conduct, if there is a complaint, is that an inquiry is held by a Disciplinary Committee who, if they find disgraceful conduct, report the fact to the Council. The Council then has power under section 7(1) of the Act to order that the name of that person be removed from the Register for such period as the Council may determine.

The Disciplinary Committee consists of persons nominated by various bodies: four registered persons by the Council (including one practising as an architect in Scotland), one by the Commissioners of Works, one by the Minister of Health and two by the President of the Law Society. There are certain safeguards to ensure that at least one member of the Disciplinary Committee is in the same kind of employment or practice as the person against whom the complaint is made (section 7(2), 1931 Act).

ARCUK produce a booklet *Conduct and Discipline* (approved by the Council on 17 June 1981) which sets out a 'standard of conduct for architects'. This deals with integrity, misleading statements, ousting another architect from engagement, general points on terms of architects' engagements, and conflicts of interest. This standard of conduct has no statutory force in the sense that ARCUK is not specifically authorised by statute to issue such a code. The booklet contains an appendix as to the procedure to be adopted when a complaint is to be made to ARCUK. If the government proceed with de-regulation, it is thought that ARCUK may no longer exist for any of its present functions.

The European Union Commission has been working for many years on mutual recognition of qualifications throughout the EU. In relation to architects, a system has been arrived at. The Architects (Registration) Act 1931 has been amended by the addition of a new section 6A (under Architects' Qualifications (EEC Recognition) Order 1987 SI 1987 No. 1824, and SI 1988 No. 2241). This section provides that if an architect from another member state of the EU can satisfy the qualification requirements and pays the fee, he can apply for registration in the UK. The qualification requirements are stated in the section. By section 1A, Architects (Registration) Act 1938, (inserted under the same Order and Statutory Instruments as mentioned above), an architect from another member state may call himself an architect whilst on a business visit to the UK without being registered, provided he is on the list of visiting architects.

1.4.3   The Royal Institute of British Architects

The RIBA is the largest professional organisation for architects and its objectives are described in the Royal Charter of 1837 as 'the general advancement of Civil Architecture, and for promoting and facilitating the acquirement of knowledge of the various Arts and Sciences connected therewith'. The RIBA has by-laws, regulations and its own code of professional conduct, which is in addition to that produced by ARCUK. The Code of Conduct has been altered considerably as to advertising by architects and the carrying on of practice by way of limited liability companies since 1 January 1981. This subject is discussed in Chapter 11 in so far as limitation of liability is concerned.

The Code of Conduct consists of three principles, and rules relevant to each principle. The three principles relate to the faithful carrying out of duties, conflicts of interest and reliance only on ability and achievement as the basis for advancement. Some of these rules have great relevance to the design process and the most important of these are (July 1991 reprint):

Rules (made under Principle One):
'1.1   A member shall when making an engagement, whether by an agreement for professional services by a contract of employment or by a contract for the supply of services or goods, have defined beyond reasonable doubt and recorded the terms of the engagement including the scope of the service, the allocation of responsibilities and any limitation of liability, the method of calculation of remuneration and the provision for termination.'

The wording and phraseology of this rule is more closely akin than it used to be to the Standard of Conduct for Architects (ARCUK, approved on 17 June 1981, re-printed: September, 1990 – see section 11.1.1). Members of the RIBA are therefore required to define their terms of engagement 'beyond reasonable doubt'. That is a heavy responsibility – indeed it is the test that is applied for a guilty verdict in criminal law cases; it is at least arguable that some of the conditions contained in the standard forms of engagement produced by the RIBA ('Architect's Appointment' and 'Standard Form of Agreement for the Appointment of an Architect') may not comply with rule 1.1 in this respect. There are distinct dangers in not setting out the terms of an engagement in writing (see section 1.5).

The Code also contains 'Notes' which are said to 'explain particular applications of a Principle or Rule, in some cases laying down conditions under which certain activities are permitted, or indicate good practice and how best to observe a Principle or Rule.'

Note 1.1.1
'A member proposing or making an agreement for an engagement as an

independent consulting architect should make use of the RIBA Architect's Appointment to define the terms of the engagement.'

The word 'should' is probably not mandatory. The Note makes no reference to the new Standard Form of Agreement published in 1992 (SFA/92).

'1.2   A member shall arrange that the work of his office and any branch office insofar as it relates to architecture is under the control of an architect.

1.3   A member shall not sub-commission or sub-let work without the prior agreement of his client or without defining the changes in the responsibilities of those concerned.

Rules (made under Principle Two):
2.9   ...a member who employs architects shall define their conditions of employment, authority, responsibility, and liability.'

Whilst it is not too difficult to define conditions of employment, authority and responsibility, there may be considerable difficulty in defining 'liability'. The RIBA publishes a *Guide to Employment Practice* which may be of some assistance.

Rules under Principle Three permit fee negotiation and advertising subject to some detailed rules set out in rule 3.6.

The principles and rules are binding on members of the RIBA and members can be reprimanded, suspended or expelled from membership under by-law 5.1 if the Disciplinary Committee finds that there is a contravention of the Code. It follows that, where an architect is involved in a dispute as to design involving any contravention of the principles or rules, he may not only be liable to his client and third parties but can also face disciplinary action by his own professional body.

The Architect's Appointment has been replaced since July 1992 with the 'Standard Form of Agreement for the Appointment of an Architect' known as SFA/92 (published for the RIBA by RIBA Publications Limited). This is an extensive document and the conditions which apply to an architect's appointment are substantially revised from those contained in the previous Architect's Appointment. SFA/92 is in the following parts:

- *Part One* is common to all commissions, and relates to the proper law of the contract – the agreement is approved for use by the RIBA, the Royal Incorporation of Architects in Scotland, the Royal Society of Ulster Architects and the Association of Consultant Architects so it is necessary to have additional provisions dealing with the laws of England and Wales, Scotland and Northern Ireland; assignment and sub-contracting; payment; suspension, resumption and termination; copyright and dispute resolution.
- *Part Two* relates to design under work stages A–H of the RIBA's model *Plan of Work.*
- *Part Three* relates to administration and inspection under work stages J–L of the RIBA's model *Plan of Work*
- *Part Four* relates to the appointment of consultants and specialists where the architect is the lead consultant.

There are four Schedules provided with SFA/92:

- *Schedule One* sets out the information to be supplied by the client to the architect.
- *Schedule Two* sets out the services to be provided by the architect.
- *Schedule Three* deals with payment (calculation, charging and payment).
- *Schedule Four* is used to deal with the appointment of other consultants, specialists and site staff.

Additional Schedules are available (but not as part of the standard form) for use in relation to commissions involving historic buildings and community architecture.

The RIBA also publish special versions of SFA/92 for use in design and build projects. There is one for use where the architect is engaged by the design and build client: '*Employer* Client Version.' There is another for use where the architect is engaged by the contractor: '*Contractor* Client Version.'

RIBA members are now subject to rules in relation to the keeping of clients' accounts (Code of Professional Conduct). These include the keeping of full books of account recording all money received and spent for clients as well as keeping all clients' money in separate bank accounts.

1.4.4   *The Association of Consultant Architects*

The Association of Consultant Architects is an organisation comprising members who are in private practice. As a result of general dissatisfaction with the 1980 JCT Standard Form of Building Contract, the ACA produced their own 'ACA Form of Building Agreement 1982' now in its Second Edition (1990 Revision), together with a sub-contract. The ACA have also prepared a modified edition of their building contract to be used with the British Property Federation system.

1.4.5   *Engineers*

Professional engineers in the United Kingdom are not as high in the public esteem as they are in most of Europe where 'engineer' is used as a title to the surname in the same way as 'doctor' is in this country. One reason for this may be the lack in this country of any substantial statutory registration or control which means that anyone may call himself an 'engineer'. However, there are very strict controls over training and membership of the major engineering institutions. The first institutions to be formed were the three Institutions of Civil, Mechanical and Electrical Engineers. There are now many more institutions. In addition to the three already mentioned, the ones most likely to be encountered in the construction world are the Institution of Structural Engineers and the Chartered Institution of Building Services.

Each of these bodies has its own admission and membership requirements. By way of example, the Institution of Civil Engineers requires applicants for admission to be at least 25 years of age, to be actually engaged in the profession of civil engineering, to have obtained an academic standard not less than that of a degree of engineering, to have had at least three years' practical experience and responsibility as an engineer and to have passed the professional interview. The professional interview is arranged in such a way that the Institution can be satisfied that the applicant for membership has acquired an adequate knowledge of the profession. All the members are bound by the rules of professional conduct and there are disciplinary regulations contained in the by-laws.

1.4.6   The Association of Consulting Engineers

The Association of Consulting Engineers (ACE) exists to promote the advancement of the profession of those engineers who practise as consulting engineers. The ACE does not deal with educational standards or the like. It used to require its members to be Fellows (that is the senior grade of membership) of one of the institutions referred to above, or some other specified institution but now, since January 1993, the membership basis has been changed to firms rather than individuals. The ACE has its own rules for professional conduct dealing with a great many aspects of a consulting engineer's practice. Two aspects of these rules of conduct deal with insurance and limiting liability. These are discussed in Chapters 10 and 11.

The ACE also publish Conditions of Engagement which are widely used by consulting engineers. There are different forms each of which is appropriate in different circumstances:

- **Agreement 1** – for report and advisory work.
- **Agreement 2** – for civil, mechanical and electrical work and for structural engineering work where an architect is not appointed by the client.
- **Agreement 3 (1984)** – for structural engineering work where an architect is appointed by the client – harmonised with the Architect's Appointment.
- **Agreement 4A(i) Full Duties** – for engineering services in relation to sub-contract works.
- **Agreement 4A(ii) Abridged Duties** – for engineering services in relation to sub-contract works.
- **Agreement 4A(iii) Performance Duties** – for engineering services in relation to sub-contract works.
- **Agreement 4B** – for engineering services in relation to direct contract works.

1.4.7   Quantity Surveyors

Quantity surveyors are to be found both in private practice and in contractors' organisations. They are the people who have the most intimate relationship with money and the cost of projects. They can have wide responsibilities, as well as particular responsibilities under the JCT contracts. Some of the tasks that they carry out are the measurement of quantities from the designer's drawings, preparation of bills of quantities, preparation of cost estimates from feasibility studies, analysis of contractors' tenders, valuation of work in progress on site for the purposes of interim payments, preparation of final accounts and general advice on cost and cost control for architects and employers. Indeed, some quantity surveyors nowadays describe themselves also as 'building cost consultants'. They have also become involved in being appointed as the 'Employer's Agent' under the JCT with Contractor's Design form of building contract.

As with engineers, there are no statutory registration requirements for quantity surveyors. However, it is usual for quantity surveyors to be members of the Royal Institution of Chartered Surveyors (RICS). A member of the RICS is entitled to call himself a 'Chartered Quantity Surveyor'. The RICS has education, training and entry requirements and a code of conduct.

The RICS have their own disciplinary procedure which includes a professional practice committee and a disciplinary board and its own appeals procedure to an appeals board. The disciplinary powers of the RICS enable it, amongst other things, to reprimand a member, require him to give an undertaking, suspend him from membership, and expel him from membership.

The Institution of Civil Engineering Surveyors is designed to serve the needs of land surveyors and quantity surveyors in the civil engineering industry. There are various grades of membership including Associates whose membership requirements are set out in regulations published by the Institution. This Institution has its own code of conduct and by-laws.

1.5   Conditions of engagement

Architects may use the Standard Form of Agreement for the Appointment of an Architect (SFA/92) or the Architect's Appointment in their contracts with their clients; members of the ACE are likely to use the appropriate Conditions of Engagement published by the ACE. In law, these conditions of engagement are contracts and the ordinary rules of contract apply to them. They contain detailed terms in relation to the obligations of the parties including the services that the designer will carry out and the terms of payment of the designer. In order that these standard conditions of engagement can become part of the contract between the parties, those conditions must be expressly referred to in the document forming the contract. One simple method of achieving this aim is to have a memorandum of agreement which is signed by the parties and refers to and expressly incorporates the conditions of engagement.

The ACE Conditions of Engagement contain such a memorandum whereas the RIBA Architect's Appointment merely contains a sample of a Memorandum of Agreement and Schedule of Services and Fees. These samples have the words 'for information' printed across them and the intention is that there should be a separate memorandum and schedule completed in respect of each project and indeed these documents are available separately for that purpose. (For the risks of not using these documents see below.) There are further risks if the memorandum and schedule are not used in conjunction with the Architect's Appointment. Firstly, it is the schedule that sets out precisely what services the architect is to provide; how the architect's remuneration is to be calculated; what consultants and site staff are to be appointed by the client and what site staff are to be appointed by the architect. Secondly, there are *alternative* clauses in the Conditions of Appointment in Part 3. These appear at condition 3.26 (English and Welsh arbitration), 3.26S (Scottish arbitration). Furthermore, in clause 3.28 there are alternative provisions as to which law governs the application of the conditions: England and Wales (clause 3.28), Scotland (clause 3.28S) and Northern Ireland (3.28NI). Provision is made in the Schedule of Paragraph S3 for those clauses which are not to apply to be set out. It is essential that this should be done or, alternatively, the inoperative clauses be deleted by the conditions in Part 3.

The Standard Form of Agreement for the Appointment of an Architect (SFA/

92) comes with two memorandums of agreement. One is for use where the agreement is to be signed as a simple contract (six year period of limitation). The other is to be used where the intention is to create a deed (12 year period of limitation). Clearly, both must not be used in the same agreement. It is very important that all the schedules to this form are also properly completed and included. Consideration should be given as to whether any of the alternative schedules or one of the design and build versions should be used (see 1.4.3). SFA/92 comes in loose leaf form. It would be a sensible precaution to bind the completed document before it is signed. This will avoid the possibility of the various parts becoming separated over a period of time and the difficulties that would otherwise arise in any dispute as to what was in fact incorporated into the legal agreement.

Where a contract is not clear as to which country's law should govern the interpretation of the conditions the courts will usually try to overcome the difficulty, but much time will have been lost and much expense incurred in the process. An example of these difficulties arose in *Miller (James) & Partners* v. *Whitworth Street Estates* (1970), where it was held that the law of one country applied to the interpretation of the contract and the law of another country applied to the procedure to be adopted in the arbitration. These matters are particularly important where, as in the *Miller* case, the architect has his office in England and carries out work in Scotland for a client in Scotland, or vice versa.

The incorporation of conditions into the contract can be done either by a memorandum of agreement or by an exchange of letters. It would be possible for the conditions to be part of the contract by a course of dealing: that is to say where the architect and his client had been engaged on a number of projects over a period of time where the conditions had been used, thus giving rise to the implication that the parties intended to use them on the project in question. These points were discussed by the Court of Appeal in *Sidney Kaye, Eric Firmin & Partners* v. *Leon Joseph Bronesky* (1973). It follows that designers wishing to use standard conditions of engagement should see that they are properly incorporated into the contract.

1.6 Design and build

There is no need to set out the traditional methods of designing and executing construction work; these are well known. However, it is appropriate to look at design and build contracts, which are becoming widely used.

Under this arrangement, the designer occupies a position completely different from those in either traditional building or civil engineering projects. The person for whom the works are to be undertaken goes directly to a contractor who provides a complete service of both design and construction of the works. Where this arrangement involves building or civil engineering works, it is usually known as a package deal or design and build project; where it is desired that the contractor supplies not only the building but also the machinery and ancillary works, then the arrangement is known as a turnkey project – the building owner has simply to turn the key of the door and he will immediately be able to put his new buildings into full productive use. Some use is being made of 'build, operate and transfer', or 'bot' on major projects such as power generation.

These types of project can vary in size and style from a house extension to complete factories, power stations and petrochemical plants, covering an enormous range in value from a few hundred pounds to many tens of millions of pounds. It is unlikely that at the bottom end of the scale, the building owner would employ his own designer to advise him; however, it is not unusual in the case of industrial projects of this type for the building owner to employ his own adviser to produce some sort of document containing the building owner's proposals so that the contractor can be given his brief. However, the majority of the detailed design will be carried out either in the contractor's own organisation by his own designers, or by architects' firms and consulting engineers in private practice engaged by the contractor specifically for the project. In the latter case, the role of the designer is substantially different in that he will be in contract with the contractor and not with the building owner, as he would have been if the traditional method had been adopted.

These types of arrangement for contracting are less criticised than they used to be by those who prefer the traditional methods. The usual basis of this criticism is that the building owner does not normally have the same independent professional advice that he would have if he were to adopt the traditional method. Proponents of the system argue that it enables the building owner to be in a position to deal with only one party, the contractor, and not separately with architects, engineers, quantity surveyors and contractors. They argue that this leads to more efficiency, economies and a shorter period from inception of the design to completion of the works. In the case of major projects, there is now a substantial amount of competitive tendering on this basis in the United Kingdom.

1.6.1   Contracts for design and build

There are many different types of contract used for such projects; construction companies have their own forms. There are, however, some standard forms of contract.

The most widely used standard form is that produced by the Joint Contracts Tribunal (JCT) and known as the 'Standard Form of Building Contract with Contractor's Design, 1981 Edition'. This contract runs to 73 pages and is based in part on the JCT Standard Form of Building Contract, 1980 edition, that is used in the traditional arrangements. This contract envisages that a building owner will produce a document setting out his requirements known as the 'Employer's Requirements' so as to enable tendering contractors to prepare their proposals and an analysis of the price that they require, known respectively as the 'Contractor's Proposals' and the 'Contract Sum Analysis'. The Employer's Requirements, the Contractor's Proposals and the Contract Sum Analysis all become incorporated in the contract.

The JCT 'Contractor's Designed Portion Supplement' has been drafted for use with the JCT Standard Form of Building Contract, 1980 Edition, where the contractor is to design part only of the works.

The ACA Form of Building Agreement has alternative provisions such that the architect is only obliged to prepare certain information and that the contractor prepares all further drawings and details beyond those which the architect is to provide. There is another version of this contract produced by the British Property Federation.

In 1993, the Department of the Environment published 'GC/Works/1(Edition 3) – General Conditions of Contract for Building and Civil Engineering – Standard Form of Contract – Single Stage Design and Build Version'. The contract is substantially based on the pre-existing form of GC/Works/1 (Edition 3), Lump Sum with Quantities, but amended to take account of the needs of a lump sum design and build version. It is itself a lump sum contract and can cope with varying amounts of input to design from the contractor. As drafted, however, it is only suitable for use on government contracts where the procurer is a government department.

The Institution of Civil Engineers have also produced a design and build contract: the 'ICE Design and Construct Conditions of Contract' in association with the Association of Consulting Engineers and the Federation of Civil Engineering Contractors. This form relies for its starting point on the ICE Conditions of Contract for use where an engineer is appointed by the employer but amended to take account of the design and build procedure.

The Institution of Chemical Engineers have produced the 'Model Form of Conditions of Contract for Process Plants' in two forms: firstly, for use on lump sum contracts where it is known as the 'Red Book', and secondly, for use on reimbursable contracts where it is known as the 'Green Book'. Neither is suitable without amendments for design and build but the forms are included here because, with amendments, they are used for design and build work.

The Institution of Mechanical Engineers and the Institution of Electrical Engineers and the ACE have also produced a contract with a design and build element: 'Model Form of General Conditions of Contract for use in connection with home or overseas contracts – with erection', known as MF/I.

Chapter 2

Principles of law

Designers will usually have a contract that governs their relationship with the employer. These can be in a variety of forms including conditions of engagement or package deal contracts. However, whether or not a designer can incur liability to persons who are not parties to the contract is decided by the law of tort. It follows that the laws of contract and tort are of fundamental importance when considering a designer's duties and liabilities.

2.1 Law of contract

2.1.1 The essentials of a simple contract

A contract comes into being where one person makes an offer, the offer is accepted and there is consideration for the promise made in the offer; or in other circumstances where, although no specific offer and acceptance can be identi-fied, the court is satisfied that the parties have assumed contractual obligations to one another.

A contract for design work does not have to be in writing to be enforceable (although some contracts, e.g. hire purchase contracts, are required to be in writing). It follows that a contract can be created orally, such contracts being known as parol contracts. Sometimes a contract can be formed which is partly oral and partly in writing. For example, a designer might write to the employer saying: 'I am writing to confirm the agreement reached at our meeting today for us to carry out the design work that was discussed at the meeting, payment for which will be made on our scale of fees.' In such a case, there is consideration by way of the promise to pay on the scale of fees and the promise to undertake the design. There is also agreement as to the work that is to be carried out even though it is not described in the letter; it would be necessary in any proceedings for evidence to be given as to what the design work was. Clearly, there is scope for misunderstanding and uncertainty in such arrangements.

2.1.2 Memorandum of agreement

The agreement may be evidenced in the shape of a formal memorandum of agreement which should contain the following:

(1) The names and descriptions of the parties must be set out.
(2) The subject matter of the contract and its conditions must be clearly stated. So far as the subject matter is concerned, this will be a description

of the design work to be carried out. Insofar as the terms and conditions of the contract are concerned, these may either be referred to and attached to the memorandum, or alternatively, referred to in such a way as to clearly identify the terms that are to be incorporated into the contract.

(3)   The consideration should be stated. In designers' contracts, the consideration will usually be the fee; the rate, amount, and method of calculation of the fee should be set out.

A court will only be concerned to see that there was consideration and it will not look into whether that consideration was adequate; in other words, courts do not exist to put right a bad bargain that a party may have made. There merely has to be some consideration for the promises that are made in the agreement. Even if it is not expressly stated, the courts will imply a term that the designer be paid a reasonable sum.

(4)   The memorandum must be signed by the parties. It is only by signing the memorandum that a party to it demonstrates that he accepts its terms. Usually, therefore, unless evidence can be brought that there was a pre-existing contract which the memorandum merely set out in writing, it will not be possible to sue on a memorandum that is unsigned by the party to be sued.

2.1.3   *Difficulties with contract formation*

It sometimes happens that one of the parties thinks that a contract has one meaning whilst the other party has a different meaning in mind. Indeed, it can happen that a concluded contract in the legal sense never comes into existence: this may result in an obligation on the party who made the request to pay a reasonable sum for such work that has been done, sometimes called a *quantum meruit*. This can even be the result where one substantial commercial organisation has carried out extensive work for another (see, for example, *British Steel Corporation* v. *Cleveland Bridge and Engineering Co. Limited* (1982)). It is, therefore, of the utmost importance when entering into contracts that they should be clear as to their meaning and intent. Many difficulties can arise where there are inconsistencies between different parts of the contract and more than one interpretation is possible to resolve that inconsistency. There are particular dangers where parties seek to modify a document containing standard terms and conditions. The case of *Sidney Kaye, Eric Firmin & Partners* v. *Leon Joseph Bronesky* (1973) is an example of such difficulties.

In that case, architects entered into a contract with a property developer by terms of contract in a letter of 28 May 1971. Clause 9 of the letter stated 'the RIBA Conditions of Engagement so far as it is consistent with the foregoing shall apply.' The previous parts of the letter related to calculation of fees and matters of copyright. The RIBA Conditions of Engagement contained an arbitration clause. The architects claimed substantial sums in the proceedings; the developer sought to have the proceedings stayed and the dispute referred to arbitration (under section 4 of the Arbitration Act 1950) on the basis that there was an arbitration clause in the contract. The architects, on the other hand, argued that the Conditions of Engagement only applied to matters not covered by the first eight clauses of the letter and that, as the dispute between the parties arose under the terms of the letter, there was no agreement to refer the dispute to arbitration.

The Court of Appeal upheld the judge's decision that the dispute should be referred to arbitration. They also held that the RIBA Conditions of Engagement did not of themselves form a contract unless they were incorporated into the contract. In this case they were so incorporated. One judge held that they were incorporated by a necessary implication because the architects had been carrying out work for three years for the same property developer on the RIBA terms.

Similar problems arose in *Richard Robert Holdings Limited* v. *Douglas Smith Stimson Partnership and Others* (1988). Here, the architect had worked for the company since 1960. The architect thought that he had at some time provided a copy of the RIBA Conditions of Engagement to the chairman of the company, who was a close friend. The chairman, on the other hand, could not remember ever having seen any standard terms. On these facts, no standard terms could be incorporated in law.

These cases amply illustrate the problems which can arise where the terms agreed between the parties can bear two meanings, and show that clear words must be used to incorporate conditions of engagement into the contract, in the absence of a formal memorandum of agreement.

In *Davies* v. *Land and Commercial Assets Limited* (1983), there was conflicting evidence as to an oral contract; the client alleged the architect had agreed to work on a contingency basis: no planning permission, no fee. After a hearing in the Court of Appeal, the architect was given judgment on a quantum meruit basis.

In *Edwin Hill & Partners* v. *Leakcliffe Properties Limited* (1984), it was held that there has to be an express agreement to terminate an architect's services before completion of the project in hand. If there is no such provision, a client who terminates the engagement will have to pay a reasonable sum for the work that has been done and damages for the loss of profit which the architect has been prevented from earning on the balance of the work to complete the project. However, it should be noted that there is a provision for termination on reasonable notice in the Architect's Appointment (condition 3.23), and in SFA/92 (condition 1.6.5).

2.1.4 Terms of the contract

2.1.4.1 Express terms

These are the terms that were agreed by the parties either in writing or orally. Where there is a written contract, there will not be any difficulty, subject to any ambiguity or inconsistency in the terms, in establishing what the parties had agreed. In the case of oral contracts, evidence would have to be given to the court by the parties so as to establish the terms of the contract; clearly this can give rise to difficulty where there is conflicting evidence.

The terms of a contract do not have the same weight in their effect; some terms are vital and go to the root of the contract – such terms are known as conditions. Other terms are of lesser importance and are subsidiary to the main purpose of the contract – these terms are known as warranties. The distinction is of great importance in that a breach of condition enables the innocent party to treat the contract as discharged and to claim damages for breach of a contract. A breach of warranty, on the other hand, enables the innocent party to claim damages only. Whether any particular term is a condition or a warranty does not depend on whether the parties have used either of those words in their contract, but rather, it is determined by reference to what the parties intended, viewed in the light of commercial practice.

It is possible to include exclusion or exemption clauses into contracts for the purposes of limiting the liability of a party who is in breach and this subject is discussed in Chapter 11.

2.1.4.2   Implied terms

Terms may be part of a contract, although not mentioned or considered by the parties at the time that they entered into their contract. These terms are known as implied terms and the implication can be made in one of three ways.

Firstly, a term can be implied by reason of statute and examples are to be found in the Sale of Goods Act 1979 by reason of which certain conditions of warranty are implied into contracts for the sale of goods. These include terms as to title, description, merchantable quality and fitness for purpose.

Contracts for the provision of professional services are not contracts for the sale of goods and hence no such implications are made into those contracts by reason of that Act. Likewise, package deal contracts are contracts for work and materials and not for sale of goods and, similarly, no such implication is made into those contracts by reason of that Act; similar terms may be implied by the courts by operation of law into such contracts. However, the Supply of Goods and Services Act 1982 provides terms to be implied by statute into contracts for the supply of a service (both where goods are supplied with the service and where goods are not supplied with the service). Details of this Act and its effect will be found at section 2.3.1.

Secondly, terms can be implied by course of dealing; this could arise, for example, where a designer had carried out many projects for an employer where the basis of the contract had been the same in each case; it might be possible to establish that those conditions applied to a subsequent contract, where there was no express agreement: *Sidney Kaye, Eric Firmin & Partners* v. *Bronesky* (1973).

Thirdly, a court can imply a term into a contract to give effect to the presumed intention of the parties. This does not mean that the court will correct mistakes in the contract or correct any nonsense that the parties may have agreed upon, although the courts will normally strive to give commercial effect to what the parties have agreed. The term can only be implied when it is necessary to do so. It is usually said that this necessity arises for the purpose of giving business efficacy to the contract:

> 'The implication which the law draws from what must obviously have been the intention of the parties, the law draws with the object of giving efficacy to the transaction and preventing such a failure of consideration that cannot have been within the contemplation of either side; and I believe if one were to take all the cases, and there are many, of implied warranties or covenants in law, it will be found that in all of them the law is raising an implication from the presumed intention of the parties with the object of giving to the transaction such efficacy as both parties must have intended that at all events it should have. In business transactions such as this, what the law desires to effect by the implication is to give such business efficacy to the transaction as must have been intended at all events by both parties who are businessmen; not to

impose on one side all the perils of the transaction, or to emancipate one side from all the chances of failure, but to make each party promise in law as much, at all events, as it must have been in the contemplation of both parties that he should be responsible for in respect of those perils or chances': Lord Justice Bowen in *The Moorcock* (1889).

It has been said in the House of Lords that the term must have been a term that went without saying, a term necessary to give business efficacy to the contract, a term which, though tacit, formed part of the contract which the parties made for themselves: *Trollope and Colls Limited* v. *North West Metropolitan Regional Hospital Board* (1973).

2.1.4.3   Implied terms: presence of express terms

Where the parties have dealt expressly with a particular subject in the contract, a term will not be implied by law to deal with that subject. The ACE Conditions of Engagement contain an express term as to care and diligence: 'The consulting Engineer shall exercise all reasonable skill, care and diligence in the discharge of the services agreed to be performed by him' (clause 5.1). The Architect's Appointment provides, similarly, 'the Architect will exercise reasonable skill and care in conformity with the normal standards of the architect's profession' (clause 3.1), as does SFA/92, 'The Architect shall in providing the Services exercise reasonable skill and care in conformity with the normal standards of the Architect's profession.'

On the other hand, if conditions of engagement contain no such express term, the absence of such term will not usually give rise to any difficulty because, it is submitted, a court would have no difficulty in implying a term that the designer should use reasonable skill and care in carrying out his duties. In any event, a term is to be implied by statute that the service will be carried out with reasonable care and skill (Supply of Goods and Services Act 1982, section 13). An injured party might seek to have a term implied that the designer's duty was higher than that of reasonable skill and care, namely that the design should be fit for its purpose (see, for example, *Greaves* v. *Baynham Meikle & Partners* (1975) at section 4.1.2). In such circumstances, the express term as to reasonable skill and care in the ACE Conditions of Engagement, the Architect's Appointment and SFA/92 would be likely to operate in such a way as to prevent implication of a term for fitness for purpose. The absence of a term dealing with the standard of duty would leave the way clear for the implication of such a term in an appropriate case.

Where there is a breach of a term in the contract, whether express or implied, to use reasonable skill and care, that breach is known as professional negligence, even though it is a breach of contract and not negligence as defined in the law of tort.

2.1.5   Privity of contract

The basic rule of English law is that of privity of contract (although proposals have been put forward for change by the Law Commission). No one can sue or be sued on a contract to which he is not a party. Where a contract is made between a designer and his employer, the general rule, therefore, is that only the designer and his employer can sue or be sued on that contract. Neither the contractor nor any other third party has any right to sue or be sued on the contract between a designer and the employer. The Law Commission are presently engaged on a review of privity of contract. This is concerned, for example, with the point that a consumer has to sue the retailer, not the manufacturer, if a product is defective (but has not caused personal injury). How any suggested reform of the law will affect the construction professions is not yet clear.

The most important exception to the basic rule of privity is in the case of agency. A person who has actual, or presumed or apparent authority can make contracts on behalf of a principal which are binding on that principal. This can arise where an agent does not disclose the existence of the principal for whom he is acting. In such a case, the principal can sue on the contract and the third party, on discovering the principal, can sue either the agent or the principal. This exception is not of great importance in designers' contracts.

There have been many attempts to avoid the rules as to privity of contract and one such method is the use of a device called the collateral contract. It works in this way. A manufacturer may advertise the benefits of his product to an employer. The employer, relying on what he has been told by the manufacturer, instructs his contractor to use the manufacturer's product. The product fails. A collateral contract is said to have arisen between the employer and the manufacturer in that, in consideration for the employer specifying the use of the manufacturer's product, the manufacturer warranted that his product was suitable for its purpose: *Shanklin Pier Limited.* v. *Detel Products Limited* (1951).

The use of collateral warranties (in writing) has become widespread in construction and this is discussed in Chapter 7.

2.2   Tort

The law of tort is separate and distinct from the law of contract. A breach of contract arises from the failure to perform an obligation undertaken by the parties. Liability in tort arises independently of contract.

Every book on tort begins by explaining how difficult it is to define a 'tort'. It is a fact that a definition covering every aspect is extremely difficult. A simple, and rather simplistic, definition is that a tort is any act or omission that infringes an obligation imposed by the law which gives the injured party the right to bring an action for damages.

A simple example of tortious liability is that arising in cases of car accidents where there is no contractual arrangement between the parties: a liability arises on the part of the party at fault to make good the damage to the innocent party. Designers can, therefore, have a liability to make good damage suffered by persons who are not parties to their design contract.

2.2.1   Liability and parties in tort

It is beyond the scope of this book to consider in detail those who could possibly be parties to an action in tort. However, the most common parties are likely to be companies and partnerships as well as individuals.

Insofar as companies are concerned, they can sue for all torts committed against them. There are, of course, some torts that cannot be committed against a company by reason of the fact that it is an artificial legal entity. For example, a company cannot be assaulted.

All the partners of a firm are liable for a tort committed by a partner who committed the tort in the ordinary course of the firm's business or with the express or implied authority of his co-partners. This liability arises on the basis of vicarious liability (see below) because each partner is the agent of his co-partners.

2.2.1.1 *Vicarious liability*

A person who commits a tort is liable for the damage that he causes. Another person can also be liable in respect of the same tort even though he did not commit it. This can arise, for example, where an employee commits a tort in the course of his employment; his employer will be liable for the tort of his employee. This is known as vicarious liability.

In considering vicarious liability, lawyers normally use the terminology of 'masters' and 'servants'. Thus a master is liable for the tort of his servant not only when he authorises it or ratifies it, but also when the tort is committed in the course of the servant's employment. This raises two important issues: who is a servant and what is the meaning of 'course of employment'.

A person is a servant in circumstances where his employer has the right to control the work that he does and the way in which he does it *Hewitt* v. *Bonvin* (1940). The test is whether there is a right of control and not whether control was in fact exercised in the particular case. It follows that where people are employed to carry out design work by a partnership or by a company, the partnership or the company will be responsible for the torts of their employed designers provided the tort was committed in the course of the employee's employment.

The position of an employee or servant must be carefully distinguished from the position of an independent contractor. The term 'independent contractor' is a legal term meaning a person whose work is not under the control of the person for whom he carries it out. The employer of an independent contractor will not be liable for the tort of that independent contractor. It follows that, subject to the terms of any contract that may be relevant, if a designer delegates work to another party, he will be liable for that other party's tort if he has the right to control the work and the way in which it is done (master and servant) but he will not be liable if he has not retained that right of control (independent contractor).

A resident engineer who is employed by, and has his salary paid by, the building owner is a servant and not an independent contractor: *Morren* v. *Swinton and Pendlebury Borough Council* (1965). There are some exceptions to the rule that an employer is not liable for the tort of an independent contractor, but these exceptions are not likely to be of great importance when considering design liability.

'In the course of employment' means within the scope of those categories of work which the employee was employed to carry out. It follows that where a designer is employed to carry out design and he is negligent in his work, then provided an action can be brought in tort, the employer, as well as the employee, will be liable in respect of that negligence. An injured party in such circumstances can elect to sue the employer or the employee, or both. In cases where the employer's contract with the innocent party has a clause excluding or limiting the employer's liability, provided there is a cause of action in tort, there is nothing to prevent the injured party suing the employee, who cannot rely upon the exclusion clause in his employer's contract, since he is not a party to that contract: *Adler* v. *Dixon* (1955).

Furthermore, it has been held by the House of Lords in *Lister* v. *Romford Ice and Cold Storage Co. Limited* (1957) that an employee has a duty to perform his work with reasonable care and skill and that where he, by his negligence, causes his employer to be vicariously liable for his tort, he will be liable in damages to his employer for breach of contract. The basis of this finding was that the House of Lords held that a term is to be implied into the contract of employment that an employee will indemnify his employer in respect of the employer's loss that arises from the employee's negligence. In the *Lister* case, a lorry driver employed by a company negligently reversed a lorry into his father who was also employed by the same company. The company's insurers paid damages to the father and then sued the lorry driver to recover what they had paid to the father. The court held that they could recover damages by reason of breach by the lorry driver of his duty to perform his work with reasonable skill and care.

In such a case, the damages awarded against an employee are likely to be the full amount of the employer's loss. Where the employer is insured for his loss, there will be nothing to prevent the insurance company making use of their rights of subrogation, bringing an action against the employee to recover the sums that they have paid (but see 10.3.5). Nor is there anything in law or practice which prevents an employer, who has suffered loss as the result of the conduct of an employee, from recovering his loss from the employee: *Janata Bank v. Ahmed* (1981).

2.2.2   Negligence

The tort of negligence is concerned with breach of a duty to take care. This duty arises independently of any contractual relationship. In order to succeed in an action for negligence, a plaintiff must prove:

- the defendant owed to the plaintiff a legal duty of care, and
- the defendant was in breach of that duty, and
- the plaintiff has suffered damage as a result of that breach.

Whether there is or is not a duty of care in any particular case is a question of law; the courts now have a long series of cases to guide them in deciding whether there is a duty of care.

In 1932, the celebrated case of *Donoghue (or McAlister)* v. *Stevenson* reached the courts. A young lady was bought a bottle of ginger beer by a friend. She had drunk some of the ginger beer, which was in an opaque bottle, before she discovered that there was a decomposing snail in the bottle. It was alleged that she became ill as a result. There was no question in this case of the friend bringing an action in contract under the Sale of Goods Act against the retailer from whom the ginger beer had been purchased because the friend had not suffered any damage. The plaintiff could not sue the retailer because she had no contract herself with him.

The House of Lords were asked whether she had a cause of action in negligence against the manufacturer. The House held that a manufacturer who sold products in such a form that they were likely to reach the ultimate consumer in the state in which they left the manufacturer, with no possibility of intermediate examination, owed a duty to the consumer to take reasonable care to prevent injury. In order to understand what a radical departure and important step this was for the development of the law of England, it is only necessary to look at the dissenting judgment of Lord Buckmaster in that case:

> 'There can be no special duty attaching to the manufacture of food apart from that implied by contract or imposed by statute. If such a duty exists, it seems to me it must cover the construction of every article, and I cannot see any reason why it should not apply to the construction of a house. If one step then why not 50? If a house be, as it sometimes is, negligently built and in consequence of that negligence the ceiling falls and injures the occupier or anyone else, no action against the builder exists according to English law, although I believe such a right did exist according to the laws of Babylon.'

That dissenting judgment would be well received in the courts today – such is the recent movement in the law. However, Lord Buckmaster's view did not prevail and the majority in the *Donoghue* case reached a different conclusion; Lord Atkin formulated a principle so as to test whether a duty of care exists. In summary form: there must be personal injury or there must be damage to the injured party's property, other than the product itself and there must have been no reasonable opportunity for intermediate examination which would have enabled the injured party to realise the possibility of harm before it occurred.

Lord Atkin put the test this way:

> 'The liability for negligence whether you style it such or treat it, as in other systems, as a species of *culpa* is no doubt based upon a general public senti-ment of moral wrong doing for which the offender must pay. But acts or omissions which any moral code would censure cannot in a practical world be treated so as to give a right to every person injured by them to demand relief. In this way rules of law arise which limit the range of complaints and the extent of their remedy. The rule that you are to love your neighbour becomes in law, you must not injure your neighbour; and the lawyer's question who then is my neighbour? receives a restrictive reply. You must take reasonable care to avoid acts or omissions which you can reasonably foresee would be likely to injure your neighbour. Who, in law, is my neighbour? The answer seems to be persons who are so closely and directly affected by my act that I ought reasonably to have them in contemplation as being so affected when I am directing my mind to the acts or omissions which are called into question.'

The law then remained fairly static but in the 1960s, the 1970s and the early 1980s, the law of tort developed at a fast pace and the categories of negligence and the persons and parties capable of being liable were greatly extended by the courts. There is now massive retrenchment by the courts in these fields but in order to understand that retrenchment, it is necessary to trace some of the history of the development of the law following the *Donoghue* case.

2.2.2.1 *1932–1964: Historical perspective*
It took from *Donoghue* in 1932 until 1964 to extend the principles of *Donoghue* to

statements which were given negligently (as opposed to acts or omissions). This was the case of *Hedley Byrne & Co. Limited* v. *Heller & Partners Limited* (1964). Advertising agents, Hedley Byrne, needed a reference from a banker as to the credit-worthiness of a potential customer. They approached their bankers who sought the advice of merchant bankers who in turn reported to Hedley Byrne. The report, which was headed 'without responsibility', said that the potential customer was good for ordinary business arrangements. Hedley Byrne proceeded with their contract and by reason of the customer not being good for ordinary business arrangements, lost a considerable sum of money. They sued the merchant bankers. The merchant bankers escaped liability by reason of having expressed their report to be without responsibility but the House of Lords held that a professional man is liable for statements made negligently in circumstances where he knows that those statements are going to be acted on, and they were acted on.

This important decision is ignored by designers at their peril. It could lead a designer into liability for statements given to a contractor at a pre-tender stage as to the design, or nature of the sub-soil, or the possibility of constructing the works in a certain order, and so on. Likewise, the designer could incur liability to the building owner, sub-contractors, suppliers and so on. Indeed, *Hedley Byrne* may have assumed greater importance since *Murphy* v. *Brentwood District Council* (1990).

2.2.2.2   1972–78: Historical perspective

The next major extension of Lord Atkin's test is to be found in a case in 1972, *Dutton* v. *Bognor Regis Urban District Council and Another*, (now overruled by *Murphy*). In Bognor Regis, there was a rubbish tip which had been filled in. In 1958 a builder bought land in the area that included the filled rubbish tip and developed the site as a housing estate. One of the houses that he built was sold to Mr Clark. He only lived there a short while and then sold the house to Mrs Dutton. In due course, the walls and ceiling cracked, the staircase slipped and the doors and windows would not close: the damage was caused by inadequate foundations. Mrs Dutton sued the builder and the local authority. She, of course, had no contractual relationship with either. Before the hearing, the action against the builder was settled. It was held by the Court of Appeal that the Council, through their building inspector, owed a duty of care to Mrs Dutton to ensure that the inspection of the foundations of the house was properly carried out and that the foundations were adequate and the Council were liable to Mrs Dutton for the damage caused by the breach of duty by their building inspector in failing to carry out a proper inspection of the foundations.

Lord Denning MR said in his judgment that the case was entirely novel because no such claim had ever been made before against a council or its surveyor for negligence in inspecting the foundations. The application of the test of Lord Atkin to the facts of the *Dutton* case is best seen in the following extract from the judgment:

'... the foundations of a house are in a class by themselves. Once covered up they will not be seen again until the damage appears. The inspector must know this or, at any rate, he ought to know it. Applying the test laid down by Lord Atkin in *Donoghue* v. *Stevenson*, I should have thought that the inspector ought to have had subsequent purchasers in mind when he was inspecting the foundations – he ought to have realised that, if he was negligent, they might suffer damage.'

The *Dutton* case not only had great implications for local authorities; builders who developed their own land found the previously existing law radically changed. Until that time, the seller of a house owed no duty to the purchaser of the house or to a visitor to the premises: *Otto* v. *Bolton and Norris* (1936); *Bottomley* v. *Bannister* (1932). This was known as 'let the buyer beware' or *caveat emptor*. Builder developers thought they were in the same position prior to the *Dutton* case. The Court of Appeal held that where the seller of a house is also the builder, he would be liable for negligence in constructing a house in a defective manner. The *Dutton* case was followed on this point in many subsequent and important cases: *Sparham-Souter* v. *Town and Country Developments (Essex) Limited* (1976); *Sutherland and Sutherland* v. *C.R. Maton & Son Limited* (1976); *Anns* v. *Merton London Borough Council* (1978); and *Batty and Another* v. *Metropolitan Property Realisations Limited and Others* (1978).

The law developed after *Dutton* but it is now seen as ironical that the basis for the later destruction of these developments is to be found in the judgment of Lord Justice Stamp in the *Dutton* case which shows another approach:

'I may be liable to one who purchases in the market a bottle of ginger beer which I have carelessly manufactured and which is dangerous and causes injury to person or property; but it is not the law that I am liable to him for the loss he suffers because what is found inside the bottle and for which he has paid money is not ginger beer but water. I do not warrant, except to an immediate purchaser, and then by the contract and not in tort, that the thing I manufacture is reasonably fit for its purpose. The submission is, I think, a formidable one and in my view raises the most difficult point for decision in this case. Nor can I see any valid distinction between the case of a builder who carelessly builds a house which, though not a source of danger to personal property, nevertheless, owing to a concealed defect in its foundations, starts to settle and crack and becomes valueless, and the case of a manufacturer who carelessly manufactures an article which, though not a source of danger to a subsequent owner or to his other property, nevertheless owing to hidden defect quickly disintegrates. To hold that either the builder or the manu-facturer was liable except in contract would be to open up a new field of liability the extent of which could not, I think, be logically controlled and since it is not in my judgment necessary to do so for the purposes of this case, I do not more particularly because of the absence of the builder express an opinion whether the builder has a higher or lower duty than the manufacturer.'

It is those seeds sown by Lord Justice Stamp in his judgment that have now developed to be the law, and *Dutton* itself is overruled *(Murphy)*.

2.2.2.3   1978: Anns
In 1978, the position altered again with *Anns* v. *Merton London Borough Council*. In this case, lessees of flats claimed against the local authority in negligence in relation to the local authority's powers of inspection under the by-laws in that, it

was said, they had allowed the contractors to build foundations in breach of the by-laws, with resulting damage to the flats. Lord Wilberforce in a passage of crystal clarity, which later became the excuse for a far reaching and dramatic expansion of the circumstances in which a duty of care might be held to exist, said the following in the House of Lords:

> 'Through the trilogy of cases in this House, *Donoghue* v. *Stevenson* (1932), *Hedley Byrne & Co. Limited* v. *Heller & Partners Limited* (1964) and *Home Office* v. *Dorset Yacht Co. Limited* (1970), the position has now been reached that in order to establish that a duty of care arises in a particular situation it is not necessary to bring the facts of that situation within those of previous situations in which a duty of care has been held to exist. Rather the question has to be approached in two stages. First one has to ask whether, as between the alleged wrong doer and the person who has suffered the damage there is a sufficient relationship of proximity or neighbourhood such that, in the reasonable contemplation of the former, carelessness on his part may be likely to cause damage to the latter in which case a *prima facie* duty of care arises. Secondly, if the first question is answered affirmatively, it is necessary to consider whether there are any considerations which ought to negative, or to reduce or limit the scope of the duty or class of person to whom it is owed or the damages to which a breach of it may give rise.'

This passage became known as 'the two stage test'.

Again, the House of Lords were concerned with a claim against a local authority in an action to which the builder was not a party. However, they felt obliged, as they had in *Dutton* to consider the position of the builder, if he had been sued, on the basis that it would be unreasonable to impose liability on the council if the builder, whose primary fault it was, was immune from liability. Lord Wilberforce, having considered *caveat emptor* (buyer beware) and other similar propositions, said:

> 'I am unable to understand why this principle or proposition should prevent recovery in a suitable case by a person who has subsequently acquired the house, upon the principle of *Donoghue* v. *Stevenson*; the same rules should apply to all careless acts of a builder, whether he happens also to own the land or not. I agree generally with the conclusions of Lord Denning MR on this point in *Dutton* v. *Bognor Regis Urban District Council* (1972). In the alternative, since it is the duty of the builder (owner or not) to comply with the by-laws, I would be of the opinion that an action could be brought against him, in effect, for breach of statutory duty by any person for whose benefit or protection the by-law was made. So I do not think there is any basis here for arguing from a supposed immunity of the builder to immunity of the council.'

When *Anns* came to be considered in the House of Lords in *D & F Estates Ltd* Lord Bridge said of that passage in *Anns*:

> 'It is particularly to be noted that Lord Wilberforce founded his view of the builder's liability on the alternative grounds of negligence and breach of statutory duty and that his opinion as to the nature of the damages recoverable

is strictly applicable to the liability of the local authority and perhaps also to the liability of the builder for breach of duty under the by-laws, but it is *obiter* in relation to the builder's liability for the common law tort of negligence. It is, moreover, difficult to understand how a builder's liability, whatever its scope, in respect of a dangerous defect in a building can arise only when there is imminent danger to the health and safety of occupiers.'

The approach of the House of Lords in *D & F* to *Anns* is considered further below.

However, the *Anns* decision was of fundamental importance at the time for many reasons. Firstly, there appeared to be a clear acceptance of the principles set out in *Dutton*, namely that a contractor may be liable for negligence in building a house to a party with whom he is not in contract, not only in respect of personal injury but also in respect of damage to the property itself (the latter point now having been decided differently in *D & F*). Secondly, *Anns* appeared to place the main emphasis for establishing a duty of care on the foreseeability of harm rather than giving emphasis to proximity and/or neighbourhood. Thirdly, the judges tended to perceive the policy restrictions (the second part of the two stage test) as being restrictions which should only be applied in fairly exceptional circumstances. Fourthly, and very importantly, lawyers and judges, in particular, had at last a clear test which they could apply with a measure of ease to almost any factual background in order to establish whether or not a duty of care existed.

In *Batty and Another v. Metropolitan Realisations Limited and Others* (1978), a development company and a builder had inspected land on the side of a valley. There was nothing on the land forming the site to show it unsuitable for building; however, on the other side of the valley and on adjoining land, there were signs that a soil investigation was necessary. One of the plots of land on which a builder built a house was on a plateau above a steep slope. Some three years after the house had been sold, there was a severe landslip below the house, damaging the garden but not the house. The Court of Appeal held that the developer and the builder were liable to the purchasers in negligence in addition to the developer's liability in contract. Although the house itself was undamaged by the landslip, the court treated it as 'doomed' and as falling within the 'present or imminent danger' test in *Anns*.

The *Batty* decision now has to be regarded as having been overruled by *D & F*. Lord Bridge in *D & F* and *Murphy* was also a judge in the Court of Appeal in the *Batty* case and of his decision in that case he says (in *D & F*):

'My own short extemporary judgment, which treats the issue of the builder's liability in damages and the fundamental question raised by Stamp LJ in *Dutton v. Bognor Regis Urban District Council* (1972) as settled by the speech of Lord Wilberforce in *Anns v. Merton London Borough Council* (1978) was, I now think, unsound.'

2.2.2.4   1983: Junior Books

The development and extension of the law of tort during the period up to 1988 probably reached its climax in the House of Lords in *Junior Books Limited v. Veitchi Co. Limited* (1983). In that case, on appeal from Scotland, specialist flooring sub-

contractors had laid a floor at the employers' factory and it was said by the
employers that that floor was defective. The employers, who were not in contract
with the sub-contractor, brought an action in delict, which is substantially the
same cause of action in Scotland as negligence in England. There was no allegation made by the employers in these proceedings that there was a present or
imminent danger to the occupier.

Notwithstanding the potential difficulties, the employers succeeded in their
argument that the sub-contractor owed them a duty of care in negligence and
that the sub-contractor was in breach of that duty. It was said in this case that
there was a close commercial relationship between the employers and the sub-
contractors. Lord Brandon, the dissenting judge, drew attention to the fact that
Donoghue was based on a danger of personal injury or damage to the plaintiff's
property other than the product itself. Since the decision in that case, it has been
reconsidered in other cases and is beginning to be treated as a case on its own.
For example, in *Muirhead* v. *Industrial Tank Specialist Limited* (1986), it was said by
Lord Justice Goff after having outlined some of the difficulties with the *Junior
Books* decision:

'Faced with these difficulties it is, I think, safest for this court to treat *Junior
Books* as a case in which, on its particular facts, there was considered to be such
a very close relationship between the parties that the defenders could, if the
facts as pleaded were proved, be held liable to the pursuers.'

Junior Books was again considered in *D & F*, where Lord Bridge said of the
decision in that case:

'The consensus of judicial opinion, with which I concur, seems to be that the
decision of the majority is so far dependent upon the unique, albeit non-
contractual relationship between the pursuer and the defender in that case and
the unique scope of the duty of care owed by the defender to the pursuer
arising from that relationship that the decision cannot be regarded as laying
down any principle of general application in the law of tort or delict.'

It is now clear that *Junior Books* lays down no principles of general application in
the law of tort; however, the apparent assumption in this judgment and in the
judgment in *Muirhead* that the relationship between the defender and the pursuer in *Junior Books* was unique is surely, with respect, misplaced. There can
hardly be a more common relationship than that between an employer and a
nominated sub-contractor.

2.2.2.5   1985–1988: The retreat
At the time of the *Junior Books* decision in 1983, many people in the construction
industry and its professions were beginning to think that the flood gates were
now fully open and that almost anything that they did was capable of creating a
liability to someone. The first major step on the road of retrenchment came with
Governors of the Peabody Donation Fund v. *Sir Lindsay Parkinson & Co. Limited*
(1985). This case concerned drains which had to be reconstructed when they
were found to be unsatisfactory. In discussing the issue as to whether or not the
local authority owed a duty in tort to *Peabody*, Lord Keith said:

'The true question in each case is whether the particular defendant owed the particular plaintiff a duty of care having the scope which is contended for, and whether he was in breach of that duty with consequent loss to the plaintiffs. A relationship of proximity in Lord Atkin's sense must exist before any duty of care can arise, but the scope of the duty must depend on all the circumstances of the case.'

He also said the following of Lord Wilberforce's judgment in *Anns* (the so called 'two stage test'):

'There has been a tendency in some recent cases to treat these passages as being themselves of definitive character. This is a temptation which should be resisted.'

This tentative step down the route of retreat from *Anns* was followed in the case of *Leigh and Sillivan Limited* v. *Aliakmon Shipping Co. Limited* (1986) where Lord Brandon made the following comment in relation to Lord Wilberforce's test in *Anns*:

'The first observation which I would make is that the passage does not pro- vide, and cannot in my view have been intended by Lord Wilberforce to provide, a universally applicable test of the existence and scope of a duty of care in the law of negligence.'

In the same case, Lord Brandon drew the courts attention to Lord Keith's com- ment in the *Peabody* case above and then went on:

'The second observation which I would make is that Lord Wilberforce was dealing, as is clear from what he said, with the approach to the questions of the existence and scope of a duty of care in a novel type of factual situation which was not analogous to any factual situation in which the existence of such a duty had already been held to exist. He was not, as I understand the passage, suggesting that the same approach should be adopted to the existence of a duty of care in a factual situation in which the existence of such a duty had repeatedly been held not to exist.'

In *Curran and Another* v. *Northern Ireland Co-ownership Housing Association Limited and Others* (1987), it was held that the Northern Ireland Housing Executive, which had exercised its statutory power to pay an improvement grant for the building of an extension to a house, but had no power of control of the building operation, did not owe a duty of care to future owners of the house to see that the extension had been properly constructed. In this case, it was said that *Anns* represented the high water mark of a trend in the development of the law of negligence towards the elevation of the 'neighbourhood' principle into one of general application from which a duty of care might always be derived unless there were clear countervailing considerations to exclude it. It is important to note that Lord Bridge referred in this case, with approval, to a case in the High Court of Australia where that court specifically refused to adopt the two stage *Anns* approach.

These three cases, *Peabody*, *The Aliakmon* and *Curran*, have often been referred to as the 'Retreat from *Anns*' but the retreat continued. In the case of *Yuen Kun-Yeu* v. *Attorney General of Hong Kong* (1987), the two stage test of Lord Wilberforce in *Anns* was put to rest by Lord Keith in these words (although *Anns* was not then overruled):

'Their Lordships venture to think that the two stage test formulated by Lord Wilberforce for determining the existence of a duty of care in negligence has been elevated to a degree of importance greater than it merits, and greater perhaps than its author intended. Further the expression of the first stage of the test carries with it a risk of mis-interpretation. As Gibbs CJ pointed out in *Sutherland Shire Council* v. *Heyman* there are two possible views of what Lord Wilberforce meant. The first view, favoured in a number of cases mentioned by Gibbs CJ, is that he meant to test the sufficiency of proximity simply by the reasonable contemplation of likely harm. The second view, favoured by Gibbs CJ himself, is that Lord Wilberforce meant the expression 'proximity or neighbourhood' to be a composite one, importing the whole concept of necessary relationship between plaintiff and defendant described by Lord Atkin in *Donoghue* v. *Stevenson*. In their Lordships' opinion, the second view is the correct one. As Lord Wilberforce himself observed in *McLoughlin* v. *O'Brien* (1982), it is clear that foreseeability does not of itself, and automatically, lead to a duty of care. There are many other statements to the same effect. The truth is that the trilogy of cases referred to by Lord Wilberforce each demonstrate particular sets of circumstances, differing in character, which were adjudged to have the effect of bringing into being a relationship apt to give rise to a duty of care. Foreseeability of harm is a necessary ingredient of such a relationship but it is not the only one. Otherwise there would be liability in negligence on the part of one who sees another about to walk over a cliff with his head in the air and forebears to shout a warning.'

In *Simaan General Contracting Co.* v. *Pilkington Glass* (1988), it was held that a supplier of glass units for a new building who had no contractual relationship with the main contractor, and had not assumed responsibility to that contractor, was not liable in tort for foreseeable economic loss caused by defects in the units where there was no physical damage to the units, and the contractor had no proprietary or possessory interest in the property. In this Court of Appeal case, many of the authorities referred to above were discussed. In particular, some emphasis was laid by Lord Justice Bingham on words of Lord Keith in *Peabody*:

'So in determining whether or not a duty of care of particular scope was incumbent upon a defendant, it was material to take into consideration whether it was just and reasonable that it should be so.'

2.2.2.6   1988: D & F Estates Limited and Others v. Church Commissioners for England and Others

In *D & F Estates Limited and Others* v. *Church Commissioners for England and Others*, judgment was given in the House of Lords in 1988. The case concerned defective plastering carried out by sub-contractors to a main contractor. The non-occupying leaseholder, which was a company, claimed against the main contractor (with whom it did not at any time have a contract) in respect of costs of repair to plastering actually carried out, future repair costs and loss of rent.

The case was heard by five judges, Lord Bridge delivering the main speech; Lord Oliver delivering a shorter concurring speech; and the remainder agreeing with Lord Bridge and Lord Oliver. Accordingly, this decision is not a majority decision and no substantial dissent between the judges appears in the report of the case.

The non-occupying leaseholder plaintiff had no option but to bring its case in tort against the main contractors for the simple reason that it had no contract with them. It was not an easy case to frame in tort for the reason that a contractor has no liability in law for the torts of his independent contractors (namely the sub-contract plasterers). Accordingly, the case could not be put on the simple basis that the contractor owed the same duty of care to the plaintiff as did the plastering sub-contractors had they been sued. The duty was put by the plaintiff as a duty to adequately supervise the work of the plasterers. As a matter of fact, it was found that the plasterers had failed to follow the plaster manufacturers' instructions and the judge at first instance had found that the contractors were in breach of their duty to provide adequate and proper supervision of the plastering work and that they were liable in negligence to the plaintiffs for that breach of their duty. The House of Lords found differently on this point and their reasons are of great and fundamental importance in the area of negligence liability in the construction industry.

Lord Bridge, having reconsidered many previous cases (and relevant comments where appropriate have been included above), took the view that it was more profitable to examine the issues in this case from first principles on the basis that the authorities '... speak with such an uncertain voice that, no matter how searching the analysis to which they are subject, they yield no clear and conclusive answer'. He went on:

> 'It is, however, of fundamental importance to observe that the duty of care laid down in *Donoghue* v. *Stevenson* was based on the existence of a danger of physical injury to persons or their property. That this is so is clear from the observations made by Lord Atkin at pages 581–582 with regard to the statements of law of Brett MR in *Heaven* v. *Pender* (1883). It has, further, until the present case, never been doubted so far as I know that the relevant property for the purpose of the wider principle on which the decision in *Donoghue* v. *Stevenson* was based was property other than the very property which gave rise to the danger of physical damage concerned.'

Lord Bridge then turned to the second part of the two stage test put forward by Lord Wilberforce in *Anns*, namely the question as to whether there are any considerations which ought to limit the scope of the duty which exists. He said:

> 'To that second question, I would answer that there are two important considerations which ought to limit the scope of the duty of care which it is common ground was owed by the appellants to the respondents on the assumed facts of the present case. The first consideration is that, in *Donoghue* v. *Stevenson* itself and in all the numerous cases in which the principle of that decision has been applied to different but analogous factual situations, it has

always been either stated expressly, or taken for granted, that an essential ingredient in the cause of action relied on was the existence of danger, or the threat of danger of physical damage to persons or their property, excluding for this purpose the very piece of property from the defective condition of which such danger, or threat of danger, arises. To dispense with that essential ingredient in a cause of action of the kind concerned in the present case would, in my view, involve a radical departure from long established authority.'

Lord Bridge, in *D & F*, regards these passages as receiving powerful support from the unanimous decision of the Supreme Court of the United States of America in *East River Steamship Corporation* v. *Transamerica Delaval Inc.* (1986) which he regarded as in turn undermining the earlier American authorities relied on in the New Zealand case of *Bowen* v. *Paramount Buildings (Hamilton) Limited* (1977). Lord Bridge then goes on to set out the important part of the House of Lords' decision in relation to tortious liability:

'If the hidden defect in the chattel is the cause of personal injury or of damage to property other than the chattel itself, the manufacturer is liable. But if the hidden defect is discovered before any such damage is caused, there is no longer any room for the application of the *Donoghue* v. *Stevenson* principle. The chattel is now defective in quality, but is no longer dangerous. It may be valueless or it may be capable of economic repair. In either case the economic loss is recoverable in contract by a buyer or hirer of the chattel entitled to the benefit of a relevant warranty of quality, but is not recoverable in tort by a remote buyer or hirer of the chattel.'

Lord Bridge then considered whether or not the issues may be different in a complex building project where the whole project is an entire series of separate pieces brought together. He considered a garden wall, as a simple structure, and came to the clear view that there is no reason in principle why an action should lie in tort against the builder for the cost of either repairing or demolishing a damaged garden wall in circumstances where no personal injury had occurred and there was no damage to property other than the wall itself. He went on to say:

'However, I can see that it may well be arguable that in the case of complex structures, as indeed possibly in the case of complex chattels, one element of the structure should be regarded for the purpose of the application of the principles under discussion as distinct from another element, so that damage to one part of the structure caused by a hidden defect in another part may qualify to be treated as damage to 'other property', and whether the argument should prevail may depend upon the circumstances of the case. It would be unwise and it is unnecessary for the purpose of deciding the present appeal to attempt to offer authoritative solutions to these problems in the abstract. I should wish to hear fuller argument before reaching any conclusion as to how far the decision in the New Zealand Court of Appeal in *Bowen* v. *Paramount Builders (Hamilton) Limited* should be followed as a matter of English law. I do not regard *Anns* as resolving that issue.'

On this basis, it was easy for the House of Lords in *D & F* to come to the view that the plaster, being the damaged thing itself, had not caused damage to persons or property (other than the *de minimis* cleaning of carpets £50) and that the non-occupying leaseholder was not entitled, therefore, to succeed against the con-tractor.

Clearly, the House of Lords had great difficulty in trying to reconcile their decision in *D & F* with their previous decision in *Anns*. In truth, such a recon-ciliation was not possible and it became inevitable that someone, sometime, would mount a concerted attack on *Anns* in the House of Lords. It is open to the House of Lords to depart from its own previous decision: *Practice Statement (Judicial Precedent)* (1966). However, in the meantime, it was clear that pur-chasers, tenants and funding institutions could place no reliance whatsoever on being able to recover losses in respect of defective design and construction through the law of tort. This gave a compelling and urgent boost to the use of collateral warranties in construction: the creation by a collateral warranty of *contractual* relationships where previously *tort* had provided a remedy.

The final assault on *Anns* was not long in coming: 1990 saw the decision in *Murphy* v. *Brentwood District Council*.

2.2.2.7   *Murphy* v. *Brentwood District Council*

The decision in *Murphy* was given in July of 1990. It had been very widely known that *Anns* was under attack in the argument before their Lordships. They care-fully reviewed in their speeches the law of negligence as it had developed since 1932 and gave consideration to cases from the Commonwealth as well as America. They had also to look again at *Anns* and *D & F*. In particular, Lord Keith expressly approved a passage from an Australian case in which the High Court of Australia had refused to follow *Anns*: *Council of the Shire of Sutherland* v. *Heyman* (1985). In that case, the Australian court had decided that the proper approach to the extension of the duty of care in novel situations was an incre-mental one. Lord Keith went on to say:

'In my opinion, there can be no doubt that *Anns* has for long been widely regarded as an unsatisfactory decision. In relation to the scope of the duty owed by a local authority it proceeded upon what must, with due respect to its source, be regarded as a somewhat superficial examination of principle and there has been extreme difficulty, highlighted most recently in the speeches in *D & F Estates*, in ascertaining upon exactly what basis of principle it did proceed. I think it must now be recognised it did not proceed on any basis of principle at all, but constituted a remarkable example of judicial legislation. It has engendered a vast spate of litigation, and each of the cases in the field which have reached this House has been distinguished. Others have been distinguished in the Court of Appeal. The result has been to keep the effect of the decision within reasonable bounds, but that has been achieved only by applying strictly the words of Lord Wilberforce and by refusing to accept the logical implications of the decision itself. These logical implications show that the case properly considered had potentiality for collision with long estab-lished principles regarding liability and the tort of negligence for economic loss. There can be no doubt that to depart from the decision would establish a degree of certainty in this field of law which it has done a remarkable amount to upset.'

Lord Keith then pointed out that *Anns* had stood as law for 13 years and that the House of Lords should be cautious in overturning its own previous decisions but he nonetheless went on to overrule *Anns* in a robust manner:

'My Lords, I would hold that *Anns* was wrongly decided as regards the scope of any private law duty of care resting upon local authorities in relation to their function of taking steps to secure compliance with building by-laws or regulations and should be departed from. It follows that *Dutton v. Bognor Regis Urban District Council* should be overruled as should all cases subsequent to *Anns* which were decided in reliance on it.'

It is not difficult to see that this was a landmark decision of enormous importance in the field of professional liability and other fields. However, the manner of the overruling of *Anns* has left considerable doubt as to which cases, precisely, have also been overruled. This problem will be with us for some time as further cases test the boundaries of *Murphy*.

It may be that it is now necessary to look at the nature of the damage rather than the type of plaintiff. In the *Sutherland* case, which was referred to in *Murphy*, Mr Justice Brennan, said:

'Liability in tort is for damage done, not merely foreseeable or threatened or imminent.... The corollary is that a postulated duty of care must be stated in reference to the kind of damage that a plaintiff has suffered and in reference to the plaintiff or a class of which the plaintiff is a member.... The question is always whether the defendant was under a duty to avoid or prevent that damage, but the actual nature of the damage suffered is relevant to the existence and extent of any duty to avoid or prevent it.'

That passage seems to have been approved in the House of Lords in *Caparo Industries plc* v. *Dickman and Others* (1990), a case concerned with whether it was reasonably foreseeable that shareholders and potential investors might rely on an auditor's report when dealing in the shares of the company. It was found that there was no such duty owed by auditors to that class of persons.

The real effect of *Murphy* is to remove a basis of claim that had been relied on in construction cases for many years. Indeed, the House of Lords in *Murphy* went on to decide that the damage suffered by the plaintiff in *Anns* was properly to be characterised as economic loss. The consequence of this case and *D & F* is that claims based on tort in construction are now very restricted. In many ways the law has gone full circle back to 1932. This retrenchment of tortious claims has come as something of a relief to the designers in the construction field and their professional indemnity insurers. However, with the advent of the widespread use of collateral warranties to create contractual duties, this relief has been short-lived, at least on major commercial projects.

It is important to note that the decision in *Hedley Byrne & Co. Limited* v. *Heller & Partners Limited* survives the decision in *Murphy*. This appears to mean that economic loss can be recovered arising out of negligent mis-statements of facts or opinions (*Hedley Byrne*) but if the loss is caused by, say, defective workmanship and suffered by a subsequent owner, nothing can be recovered in tort and the damage is said to be irrecoverable economic loss (*D & F* and *Murphy*). If this

analysis is right, then claims brought on the basis of *Hedley Byrne*, such as negligent advice, are likely to assume greater importance. An example of such a
claim is to be found in *IBA* v. *EMI and BICC* (1980). BICC wrote in a letter to IBA:
that they were '...well satisfied that the structures will not oscillate dangerously....' IBA relied on that assurance. A structure later collapsed and BICC
were held liable for negligent mis-statement.

However, it is often difficult in practice to distinguish between negligent
design advice, when economic loss is apparently recoverable, and damage
caused to a building by negligent design, when economic loss is not recoverable.
This difficulty was confronted in *Preston and Another* v. *Torfaen Borough Council*
(1993). Here, the Court of Appeal decided that an expert, Norwest Holst Soil
Engineering Limited, who had advised the local authority as to the requirements
for the foundations of a house, did not owe a duty of care to a subsequent owner
or occupier who did not rely on the expert's advice. It was said that at the time of
the negligent act, there was no complainant who could be identified other than a
'class of potential purchasers.' There was no reliance by the complainant on the
advice. There was no public policy reason to allow such claims. The court distinguished this case from *Ross* v. *Caunters* (1980) where solicitors were found
liable to a beneficiary, even though the beneficiary had not relied on the solicitors' advice on the basis that there were not comparable features; the court had in
mind that the category of complainants in *Ross* was small and identifiable at the
time of the negligent act. Indeed, *Ross* has been applied in cases since *Murphy*:
Keeskemeti v. *Rubens Rabin & Co.* (1992) and *White* v. *Jones* (1993). In the first case,
at first instance, and in the second case in the Court of Appeal, it was said that
Ross was left intact as precedent, notwithstanding *Caparo* and *Murphy*.

At the same time, *Murphy* has apparently left untouched the decision in *Junior
Books* in ways which are inconsistent and probably unsupportable in the context
of the new orthodoxy created by *Murphy*. In *Murphy*, *Junior Books* was said by
Lord Keith to be an application of the principle set out in *Hedley Byrne*. It is hard
to see any justification for such a statement and if it were right, the decision in
Murphy would be of little effect. Lord Bridge, on the other hand, said that *Junior
Books* could only be understood on the basis of a so-called 'special relationship of
proximity' between the owner and the nominated sub-contractor. With respect
to his Lordship, such a relationship is ordinary in the extreme in construction; it
is very difficult, therefore, to understand the survival of *Junior Books* on that basis
either. It remains to be seen how this conundrum is to be resolved. In the
meantime, it will be a very brave litigant indeed who seeks to rely on *Junior Books*
in preference to *Murphy* – such a litigant would probably receive short shrift in
the present climate in the courts on this issue.

On the same day as the *Murphy* decision, the House of Lords also decided
Department of the Environment v. *Thomas Bates and Son Limited* (1990). The builders
of offices were sued by under-lessees of part of the building to try to recover the
costs incurred in strengthening columns which did not carry their design load.
Having decided *Murphy*, they had to find that this was economic loss and that it
could not be recovered.

2.2.2.8 The 'complex structure' theory after Murphy

In *D & F*, Lord Bridge had raised the possibility that one element of a structure
could be regarded as distinct from the other elements, so that damage to one part

of the structure caused by a hidden defect in another part, could qualify as damage to 'other property.' This raised the possibility of using this so-called 'complex structure' theory to pursue cases in tort that might otherwise have been hopeless. The theory was revisited in *Murphy*.

Lord Bridge in *Murphy* said:

'A critical distinction must be drawn here between some part of a complex structure which is said to be a 'danger' only because it does not perform its proper function in sustaining the other parts and some distinct item incorporated in the structure which positively malfunctions so as to inflict positive damage on the structure in which it is incorporated. Thus, if a defective central heating boiler explodes and damages a house or a defective electrical installation malfunctions and sets the house on fire, I see no reason to doubt that the owner of the house, if he can prove that the damage was due to the negligence of the boiler manufacturer in the one case or the electrical contractor in the other, can recover damages in tort on *Donoghue* v. *Stevenson* principles. But the position of the law is entirely different where, by reason of the inadequacy of the foundations of the building to support the weight of the superstructure, differential settlement and consequential cracking appears. Here, once the first cracks appear, the structure as a whole is seen to be defective and the nature of the defect is known. Even if, contrary to my view, the initial damage could be regarded as damage to other property caused by a latent defect, once the defect is known, the situation of the building owner is analogous to that of the car owner who discovers that the car has faulty brakes. He may have a house which, until repairs are effected, is unfit for habitation, but the building no longer represents a source of danger and as it deteriorates will only damage itself.'

It was the situation of an exploding catastrophic failure in a pipe, damaging other parts of the plant, that led to liability for that damage in *Nitrigin Eireann Teoranta and Another* v. *Inco Alloys Limited and Another* (1991).

Lord Keith said this of the complex structure theory, in *Murphy*:

'I think that it would be unrealistic to take this view as regards a building the whole of which had been erected and equipped by the same contractor. In that situation, the whole package provided by the contractor would, in my opinion, fall to be regarded as one unit rendered unsound as such by a defect in the particular part. On the other hand, where, for example, the electric wiring had been installed by a sub-contractor and due to a defect caused by lack of care a fire occurred which destroyed the building, it might not be stretching ordinary principles too far to hold the electrical sub-contractor liable for the damage.'

It can be seen that there are fairly close parallels in the speeches of Lord Keith and Lord Bridge as to the principles involved. However, Lord Jauncey said this of the only context in which the complex structure theory might operate:

'... where one integral component of the structure was built by a separate contractor and where a defect in such a component had caused damage to other parts of the structure, e.g. a steel frame erected by a specialist contractor which failed to give adequate support to floor or walls. Defects in such ancillary equipment as central heating boilers or electrical installations would be subject to the normal *Donoghue v. Stevenson* principles if such defects gave rise to damage to other parts of the building.'

These speeches taken together raise as many questions as they answer. It is unfortunate that the law in this important area should have been so left by the House of Lords in a case where opportunity could have been taken to establish clear precedent. Lords Keith and Bridge appear to associate the complex structure theory with catastrophic failure, explosions and fires. They appear also to say that a building is otherwise to be regarded as 'one unit' (Lord Keith) and foundations and superstructure are indivisible (Lord Bridge). That might be regarded as the majority decision of the House of Lords. On the other hand, a steel frame erected by a specialist sub-contractor is divisible from the floors and walls (Lord Jauncey). It is difficult, if not impossible, to justify an apparent distinction between, on the one hand, structure and foundations being indivisible and, on the other hand, steel structure and walls and floors being separable albeit on the assumption that the steel frame work was sub-contracted. Clearly, the complex structure theory is not dead, but it is much restricted. The need now is to resolve whether the test for its applicability, outside the area of catastrophic failures, is whether a building is one unit, where it will not apply, or specialist sub-contracting, where it may apply. It has yet to be decided what application, if any, this has to the liability of designers.

2.2.2.9   Tort: Summary

These recent developments in the law of tort leave some difficulty in coming to simply explained propositions by way of summary. However, the following is an attempt to put the present position in short form, with all the risk that such a difficult area of law is really incapable of being so contained:

(1)   Where defects are discovered before they cause either or both personal injury or damage to property other than the 'thing itself', damages are not recoverable. Those damages (even if they are, for example, the cost of rectification of defects) are to be categorised as economic loss.

(2)   Economic loss cannot generally be recovered in tort in building cases except where:

   (a)   the cause of action falls within the principles of *Hedley Byrne*, for example, negligent advice. The extent to which 'design' is 'advice' for this purpose is likely to be explored in future cases. (It has been suggested, for example, that the first purchaser of a new house places such reliance on the builder to sell to him a satisfactory house that the purchaser could, on the basis of *Hedley Byrne*, claim for economic loss as a result of the house being defective: *Hoskisson and Another v. Donald Moody Limited*).

   (b)   the 'complex structure' argument can be used. This does not appear to be a promising area for potential plaintiffs.

   (c)   personal injuries arise.

(3) Local authorities are not likely to be liable if they perform their building
     control responsibilities negligently (but see 4.3.4).
(4) The Defective Premises Act 1972 provides a statutory remedy in the case
     of dwellings provided the claim can be brought within the cases detailed
     at 2.3.4 and the dwelling is not covered by an Approved Scheme.
(5) There is the possibility of claims for breach of statutory duty (Building
     Regulations) but see 4.3.2 and 4.3.3.

2.2.3   Contributory negligence

It used to be the law that if the injured party were guilty of negligence that
contributed to the injury that he suffered, then he could recover nothing from the
other party. Since the Law Reform (Contributory Negligence) Act 1945, the
injured party's claim will not be defeated but the court has power to reduce the
damages to an amount that it considers just and equitable. In making that
assessment, the court has to have regard to the injured party's responsibility for
the damage.

The Act does have application to breaches of contract since the case of
Forsikringsaktieselskapet Vesta v. *Butcher & Others* (1988): it is possible for a court to
reduce the damages in contract where it considers it just and equitable so to do,
at least in circumstances where the defendant's liability in contract is the same as
his liability in the tort of negligence independently of the existence of any contract. An example of this arose in *Barclays Bank plc* v. *Fairclough Building Limited*
(1993). The case arose out of asbestos contamination of a building following the
cleaning down of corrugated asbestos roof sheets by pressure jetting with water.
The slurry had entered the building and then dried. His Honour Judge Richard
Havery, Official Referee, held that there was a claim both under the contract and
in tort. He further held that the fact that the contractor was also in breach of
contractual obligations which did not depend on negligence on the part of the
contractor does not prevent the 1945 Act operating because those were the very
acts and omissions which constituted the failure to exercise reasonable skill and
care.

2.2.4   Joint and several liability

If two or more people cause different damage to the same person, the claims of
that person are separate and distinct. That person can only recover damages
from each of those people for the damage that they have caused.

However, if two or more people cause the same damage to the same person,
then they are both liable to that person. It used to be the case that those liable
could not claim contribution as between themselves but that is now changed: see
9.2.2.

This joint and several liability has been felt to be a great evil by the construction professions for many years. So much so that an important report
recommended changing the law in this respect: 'Professional Liability: Report of
the Study Teams' – Department of the Environment, November 1989. The Study
Team suggested to the government that joint and several liability should be
altered in commercial transactions not involving personal injury and where the
claim exceeds £50,000. In those cases, they recommended that a defendant whose

actions are partly the cause of damage to the plaintiff, but such actions were not carried out jointly with another defendant, should be responsible to the plaintiff only for damage equivalent to that part of the plaintiff's loss fairly attributable to his or her breach.

2.2.5   Trespass

Designers can by their design cause a trespass to be committed. They can do so by, for example, designing their new building in such a way that it encroaches on another person's land. This would include foundations that protruded on to another's land even though the wall, sitting upon that foundation, was within the boundary. The courts have held that an advertising sign fixed to a wall, but overhanging another person's land, is a trespass: *Kelsen* v. *Imperial Tobacco Co. Limited* (1957).

Trespass is a direct interference with the possession of another person's land in the absence of lawful authority. It is a tort for which an action can be brought even though there is no damage; put in lawyers' language, it is a tort that is said to be actionable *per se*. If there is damage, then there may be an additional liability in the tort of nuisance.

The aggrieved party has several remedies available to him, the most usual of which is to bring an action for recovery of the land. In appropriate cases, an injunction may be given restraining the offending party from continuing or repeating the trespass. The designer who causes a trespass to be committed by his design is at risk of being a party in such proceedings or, at the very least, at risk of being sued in respect of the building owner's costs arising from the design error. Such a claim might include the cost of altering the work on site, a claim made by the contractor against the building owner for loss and expense, damages for delay in completion, and the costs and damages incurred in the trespass action.

2.3   Liability arising by statute

There are many statutes that affect the construction world; of these, the most important insofar as designers are concerned are the Supply of Goods and Services Act 1982, the statutes under which Building Regulations and by-laws are made, and the Defective Premises Act 1972.

2.3.1   The Supply of Goods and Services Act 1982

This Act amends the law in relation to terms to be implied in certain contracts; amongst the contracts that are affected are contracts for the supply of a service and contracts where property in goods is transferred in contracts that are not solely contracts for the sale of goods. In the former category are, for example, designers' services; in the latter category are, for example, building contracts.

2.3.1.1   Supply of services

The definition of a contract for the supply of service in the Act is a contract 'under which a person ('the supplier') agrees to carry out a service'. This is so whether or not goods are also transferred or to be transferred under the contract (sections 12(1) and (3)). The effect of these provisions is therefore that the sections relating to supply of services will apply to architects, engineers, designers in general, nominated sub-contractors and design and build contractors.

The Act provides that, where a designer acting in the course of a business supplies a service, there is to be an implied term that the service will be carried out with reasonable care and skill (section 13). This section provides for a term to be implied by statute into such contracts. That particular implication by statute is the same as that to be implied at common law (see 3.1.1).

Where there is already an express term in the contract as to carrying out the service with reasonable skill and care, that express term will not negative the term to be implied by the Act *unless inconsistent with it* (section 16(2)). Furthermore, the contents of the Act do not prejudice any rule of law which imposes on the supplier of the service a duty which is stricter than that of reasonable skill and care (section 16(3)(a)). It therefore follows, for example, that where a design and build contractor is operating under a contract which impliedly or expressly imposes upon him an obligation that his design will be fit for its purpose, he will not be able to argue that his stricter duty is cut down by the implied term of the Act. The same applies to architects and engineers.

The Secretary of State has power to provide that section 13 shall not apply to certain services (section 12(4)); by statutory instrument, the Secretary of State has ordered that section 13 shall not apply to the services of an advocate in court, or before any tribunal, inquiry or arbitrator and in carrying out certain preliminary work, or to services rendered by a company director to his company (SI 1982/1771). There are also terms to be implied by the Act providing that, where no time is fixed for the completion of the service, the obligation will be to complete the service within a reasonable time, and where the consideration for the service has not been fixed, the supplier will be paid a reasonable sum. The Act provides that what is a reasonable time and what is a reasonable charge are to be questions of fact (sections 14 and 15).

As to whether the rights, duties and liabilities which arise by reason of the provisions of the Act can be negatived or varied, the Act provides that in respect of suppliers' services and suppliers' goods they can be negatived or varied by

- express agreement or
- course of dealing between the parties or
- such usage as binds both parties to the contract.

Such exclusion of liability is expressly made to be subject to the Unfair Contract Terms Act 1977 (sections 11(1) and 16(1)).

2.3.1.2   *Supply of goods*

Parts of the Act apply to contracts for the transfer of property in goods and these contracts are defined as contracts under which one person transfers or agrees to transfer to another the property in goods, other than an excepted contract. The exceptions do not include or extend to a design and build contract. Accordingly the provisions in the Act as to the supply of goods apply to design and build. There are provisions in relation to the selection, quality and the like of the goods. Section 3 provides that there will be an implied condition that the goods will correspond with the description where there is a contract for the transfer of goods by which the transferor transfers or agrees to transfer the property and the goods by description (sections 3(1) and (2)).

Where there is a contract for the transfer of goods and the transferor transfers the property in the goods in the course of a business, then there is to be implied a condition that the goods supplied are of merchantable quality (section 4(1) and (2)). That condition will not be implied where defects were specifically drawn to the transferee's attention before the contract was made or the transferee examined the goods before the contract was made as regards defects which that examination ought to have revealed (section 4(3)).

As to fitness for the purpose, the Act provides that where the property in the goods is transferred in the course of business and the transferee makes known to the transferor a particular purpose for which the goods are being acquired, then there will be an implied condition that the goods are reasonably fit for that purpose, whether or not that is a purpose for which the goods are commonly supplied (section 4(4) and (5)). However, as with contracts for the sale of goods and the term implied by the common law, no implied condition that the goods are reasonably fit for their purpose will be made where the transferee does not rely, or it would be unreasonable for him to rely, on the skill and judgment of the transferor. This position substantially puts in statutory form the existing common law position in building contracts: where the architect or the employer selects particular materials and instructs the contractor to use them, they will not be relying on the contractor's skill and care and a condition that those goods will be fit for their purpose will not usually be implied in the building contract (see 4.1.1 and *Young and Marten* v. *McManus Childs* (1969)).

2.3.2   *Building Regulations and by-laws*

It used to be the case that each local authority in England and Wales produced its own by-laws governing building works. The Building Regulations 1965, which were made under the Public Health Acts, came into force in 1966 and were from time to time amended.

However, a whole new scheme of things now applies to the regulation of building construction in England and Wales. The new Building Regulations (SI 1985 No. 1065) and the Building Regulations (Amendment) Regulations 1989 (SI 1989 No. 1119) have been made by the Secretary of State pursuant to powers under section 1 and Schedule 1 of the Building Act 1984. This Act consolidates all the previous statutory provisions relating to local authority control over the building work although in relation to drains and sewers, the Public Health Act 1936 is still in force.

Furthermore, and importantly, unlike the previous system of building control, these same regulations also apply to Inner London and have done so since 1 April 1986.

This system is different in many respects to the old system. For example, the regulations themselves are made on a basis which, in general, requires a particular type of performance, rather than specifying how that performance is to be achieved. A system of approved inspectors has been set up. It is now the case that either the local authority or an approved inspector (engaged and paid for by the building owner) can carry out the supervision and control of building operations under the legislation. The National House-Building Council (NHBC) is likely to be a leader in the field of approved inspectors. A useful discussion of the potential liability of approved inspectors and of the new building regulations can be found in two articles in *Construction Law Journal* (1984–85) 1 Const LJ 264 and (1986) 2 Const LJ 262.

There are three possible ways in which these regulations and by-laws can bring about civil liability on the part of designers and contractors.

The first is contractual. The ICE Conditions of Contract for civil engineering works, all the editions of the JCT Contract, and the ACA Contract contain express provisions that the contractor will comply with statute. The Building Regulations in England and Wales are part of the statute law and it follows that any breach of those Regulations and by-laws during construction by the contractor will be a breach of contract entitling the employer to damages. The position of a designer in such circumstances is considered in Chapter 7 and the position of a design and build contractor in Chapter 8.

The second way in which civil liability can arise where Building Regulations or by-laws are not complied with is that the affected building owner may be able to bring an action for breach of statutory duty against a builder who failed to comply with the Building Regulations or by-laws. The third way is under section 38 of the Building Act 1984. This is discussed further in Chapter 4.

2.3.3   The Defective Premises Act 1972

The Defective Premises Act was brought into being by Parliament in 1972, within a few months of the decision in the *Dutton* case but not in any way connected with the finding in that case. The Act came into force on 1 January 1974 and its provisions only apply to dwellings built after that date. In broad terms, the scheme of the Act is to impose a duty contained in section 1(1) of the Act:

'1(1)   A person taking on work for or in connection with the provision of a dwelling (whether the dwelling is provided by the erection or by the conversion or enlargement of the building) owes a duty

       (a)   if the dwelling is provided to the order of any person, to that person; and

       (b)   without prejudice to paragraph (a) above, to every person who acquires an interest (whether legal or equitable) in the dwelling;

to see that the work which he takes on is done in a workmanlike or, as the case may be, professional manner, with proper materials and so that as regards that work the dwelling will be fit for habitation when completed.'

It follows that any person who takes on 'work for or in connection with the provision of a dwelling' will owe this duty and it is submitted that the wording is wide enough to include a designer of a 'dwelling' which includes blocks of flats. If it is right that the section imposes a duty on designers, then that duty will be to provide a design that enables the dwelling to be fit for habitation on completion and includes seeing that the work is done with proper material; this wording therefore makes it clear that the duty encompasses the specifying of materials. The view that section 1 imposes a duty on designers is reinforced by section 1(2) which provides a defence to any person who takes on work in connection with the provision of a dwelling on terms that he will do so in accordance with instructions given by or on behalf of the person for whom he is carrying out the work.

Two further points should be noted in relation to section 1(1). Firstly, it is limited to the provision of dwellings, including dwellings that are created by conversion or enlargement. It follows that the Act does not apply to other categories of construction. Further, the duty that is owed is not only owed to the person for whom the work is carried out, but to every person who acquires an interest in the dwelling; in other words, the duty is owed to all subsequent purchasers of the property.

The question arises as to what is the nature, extent and scope of the duty. The Court of Appeal in *Alexander and Another* v. *Mercouris* (1979) had to consider when the duty arose, not its scope, but some observations are helpful, even though they may be *obiter dicta* (although an Official Referee regarded them as binding in *Thompson*, see below):

> 'The reference to the dwelling being fit for habitation indicates the intended consequence of the proper performance of the duty and provides a measure of the standard of the requisite work and materials. It is not, I think, part of the duty itself' – Lord Justice Buckley.
> '...the concluding words of the section do not state the duty but the measure of the duty imposed by the earlier words, that is to say, to do the work in a workmanlike, or as the case may be, professional manner and to do it with proper materials, so that the result may be produced that the dwelling will be fit for habitation when completed.' – Lord Justice Goff.
> '...the duty starts when the person takes on and continues while the work is done, and the test of the manner in which the work is done is that when the building is completed, it is fit for human habitation.' – Lord Justice Waller.

These words have been considered in two subsequent cases. In the first case, *Andrews* v. *Schooling* (1991), the Court of Appeal were concerned with penetrating damp in a cellar in a house converted into flats by the third defendant developers. The court found that a dwelling could be unfit for habitation even though the problem was not manifesting itself: for example, a missing damp course, even though damp was not yet apparent. They also held that section 1(1) of the Act imposed a liability not only for misfeasance but also for non-feasance. It follows that the section applies to a failure to carry out necessary work as well as to carrying it out badly.

In *Miles Charles Thompson* v. *Clive Alexander & Partners (A Firm) and Another* (1992), an Official Referee had to grapple with the question:

(1) Is it sufficient to prove merely that the defect arose out of a failure by the other party to carry out their work in a professional manner or with proper materials; or
(2) is it also necessary to prove that the defect rendered the dwelling unfit for habitation when completed?

The Official Referee decided that the duty imposed by section 1(1) is limited to the kind of defect in the work done and the materials used whether by a builder or by a professional man, such as an architect or engineer, which makes the dwelling unfit for habitation on completion. He said it was not enough to prove that the defects arose solely from a failure on the part of a party to carry out their work in a professional manner and with proper materials. This finding is, of course, based on the express words of the Act. It may be that the Law Commission had intended that the obligations in the Act should be disjunctive and not conjunctive (Law Commission Working Paper No. 40: 'Civil Liability of Vendors and Lessors for Defective Premises').

There is an exception to the imposition of the duty; where an 'approved scheme' is in operation, in relation to the dwelling, then the Act provides that no action can be brought in respect of the duty in section 1 of the Act (see section 2(1)). The National House-Building Council operate a scheme. Under this the builder or developer has to be on the register of the NHBC and the NHBC inspect the dwellings during construction; it is not at all unknown for developers and contractors to be removed from registration in cases where their workmanship or materials do not meet the NHBC standards. The nub of the NHBC scheme is a contract between the developer or the builder and the purchaser of the dwelling and it contains a warranty on the part of the builder or developer 'to build in an efficient and workmanlike manner and of proper materials and so as to be fit for habitation'.

The NHBC did, for many years, have their schemes approved under section 2 of the Act. However, some confusion was created because it seems that the 1979 scheme, although the subject of a statutory instrument, was never effective as an approved scheme under the Act. In detail, the position appears to be as follows. The House Building Standards (Approved Scheme) Orders 1973 (1973 SI No. 1843), 1975 (1975 SI No. 1462) and 1977 (1977 SI No. 642) were effective to make the NHBC schemes to which they referred approved schemes under the Act. It followed that owners of dwellings built under those schemes could not bring claims under the duty created by section 1 of the Act.

At the beginning of 1979, there was a proposed change to the NHBC scheme. A new House Building Standards (Approved Scheme) Order was laid before Parliament but the NHBC realised that certain of the documents referred to were incorrect and told the Department of the Environment that the Order should not be published. Some documents in the 1979 Order (1979 SI No. 381) were therefore not published. It appears to be the case that the 1979 Order is ineffective and it follows that the relevant NHBC scheme is not an approved scheme under section 2 of the Act. No approval under the Act has been sought by the NHBC for any subsequent schemes, such as the Buildmark scheme, which commenced on 1 April 1988. Owners of dwellings built under that scheme therefore have the ability to claim under the scheme as well as under section 1 of the Act. This is a benefit to owners because, for example, the NHBC scheme cover, in some respects, might be seen as more restrictive than the remedy available under the Act. One example of this is that the NHBC ten year cover has to come within the words 'major damage caused by defects in the structure' (see section 3 of the policy). The Act is not so restrictive. Further, there are divisions in the NHBC policy as to who takes responsibility (vendor/NHBC) depending on whether the claim falls under the two year or the ten year cover.

The Act makes void any provision in an agreement which purports to exclude or restrict the operation of the Act (section 6(3)); the Act also provides its own rules for limitation of action. Any cause of action in respect of breach of duty is deemed to have accrued at the time when the dwelling was completed (section 1(5)). It follows that six years after completion of the dwelling, there will be a defence to any action brought in respect of breach of the duty imposed by the Act.

The Act makes clear that the duty that it imposes is in addition to any duty that may be owed by any person apart from the Act (section 6(2)).

2.4 Copyright

The matter of copyright is of great importance to designers. It is an area of law designed to protect the designer's rights in ideas and creativity from exploitation by others. It can give rise to an element of security for fees: making a licence for use of the copyright by the developer conditional on the payment of the designer's fees.

2.4.1 Copyright, Designs and Patents Act 1988

The Copyright, Designs and Patents Act 1988 is of great importance to designers. There are transitional provisions that distinguish between works of copyright prior to and after 1 August 1989 but the discussion here deals with works after that date. Under the Act, copyright arises automatically in original artistic works provided the author is a 'qualifying person' or if the work was first published in the United Kingdom or a country to which the Act has application by reason of a statutory instrument. Each of the factors is now considered separately.

Architecture and civil engineering design are almost certainly to be regarded as 'artistic' works. Even though there is no statutory definition as such or any English authority on the point, Commonwealth authority suggests, albeit on different statutory wording, that this view is correct: *Hay and Hay Construction* v. *Sloan* (1957), Canada; *Ownit Homes Proprietary Limited and Others* v. *Manusco Investments Proprietary Limited and Others* (1990), Australia. On the other hand, 'artistry' may have to have a sense of 'uniqueness' rather than just 'originality': *Viceroy Homes Limited* v. *Ventury Homes Incorporated*, (1991), Canada. Under section 175 of the Act, construction of a building is 'publication'. 'Originality' probably means nothing more than the artistic work is not copied; there is no need for subjective originality: *University of London Press Limited* v. *University Tutorial Press Limited* (1916). The incorporation of standard components will not of itself prevent a design being original for this purpose: *Hay and Hay Construction* v. *Sloan* (1957), Canada, and neither will the constraint of the site plan: *Kaffka* v. *Mountain Side Development* (1982). In a New Zealand case, skill was said to be a necessary ingredient: *Beazley Homes Limited* v. *Arrowsmith* (1978). Although there is no authority on the point, it is likely that 'publication' will include the public exhibition of scheme designs during or after an architectural competition. Under section 175 of the Act, construction of the building does act as 'publication' for the purposes of the Act.

The period of copyright created by the Act is 50 years from the end of the year in which the designer dies and vests in the author who is the person who creates the design (section 9 of the Act).

Under section 16 of the Act, an infringement is created by copying the whole or a substantial part of the building, as is the copying of plans but the copying of plans in brochures, such as estate agents particulars, is not an infringement if it is for the purpose of sale or letting of the building (section 63). An architect who is engaged to design an extension to an existing building, which was designed by another architect. will infringe the first architect's copyright if the extension is in substantially the same style: *Chabot* v. *Davies* (1936).

The remedies for an infringement are damages and/or an account of profits and/or, possibly, an injunction. Prior to this Act, injunction was not available as a remedy: section 17(4), Copyright Act 1956. However, on usual principles, an injunction will not be granted if damages are an adequate remedy: *American Cyanamid Co.* v. *Ethicon Limited* (1975). The Act also provides for a remedy where the copyright owner refuses to grant a licence on reasonable terms, known as a 'Licence of right' procedure. An architect, not a company, now has the 'moral right' to be identified on the building he has designed provided he follows the procedure in the Act (section 78). Another moral right created by the Act enables an architect to have his name removed from a building if his work is being exploited in a derogatory manner: for example, the building is being altered by another architect in a derogatory manner.

2.4.2   Copyright under SFA/92

Most of the standard conditions of engagement contain provisions as to copyright, as do most collateral warranties. For example, SFA/92 contains:

'1.7.1   Copyright in all documents and drawings prepared by the Architect and in any work executed from those documents and drawings shall remain the property of the Architect.'

That provision should be sufficient to prevent an argument that the building owner or the contractor, not the architect, is the 'author' of the design for copyright purposes. Such a proposition is, in any event, supported by authority: *Meikle* v. *Maufe* (1941). Further provisions deal with other aspects of copyright:

'2.3.1   Notwithstanding the provisions of condition 1.7.1, the Client shall be entitled to reproduce the Architect's design by proceeding to execute the Project provided that:

- the entitlement applies only to the Site or part of the Site to which the design relates, and
- the Architect has completed a scheme design or
- has provided detail design and production information, and
- any fees, expenses and disbursements due to the Architect have been paid.

This entitlement shall also apply to the maintenance repair and/or renewal of the Works.

2.3.2   Where the Architect has not completed a scheme design, the Client shall not reproduce the design by proceeding to execute the Project without the consent of the Architect.

2.3.3   Where the Services are limited to making and negotiating planning applications, the Client may not reproduce the Architect's design without the Architect's consent, which consent shall not be unreasonably withheld, and payment of any additional fees.'

It is to be noted that these provisions set out reasonably clearly the position on copyright in various typical situations and that there is a linking of copyright and fees so as to give the architect some element of security for his fees.

Chapter 3

Professional negligence and designers' general duties

The profession of civil engineer is defined in the charter of the Institution of Civil Engineers as being 'the art of directing the great sources of power in nature for the use and convenience of man'. This is a grand turn of phrase and certainly a desirable objective; no designer would consciously design a bridge or a multi-storey block of flats liable to collapse or an office block that has leaking windows. Sometimes the effects of a design or construction problem come to light in a most dramatic way such as the partial collapse of the flats at Ronan Point and the collapse of the 1250 foot high Elmley Moor television mast. The vast majority of failures in buildings are nothing like so dramatic but the consequences of the problems, both in human terms and in cost, can be severe nonetheless.

What happens in those cases where a designer falls short of the desirable in his design and where the cost of making that design desirable can run into millions of pounds? Is the designer liable for the cost of making good the damage simply because his design is less than desirable? To answer these questions it is necessary to look at the nature of liability for professional negligence, the duties the designer may undertake to the employer and the application of the tests for liability to particular aspects of those duties and other aspects of construction that can lead to a liability on the part of the designer.

3.1 Nature of liability for professional negligence

The phrase 'professional negligence' is used in a generic sense to cover all situations in law where a professional person is being pursued for some act or omission, irrespective of the precise nature of the legal right being used. This rather imprecise language can lead to confusion. It is important in the law to be very precise as to the nature of the case being made. For example, is the claim in respect of the breach of an obligation (either express or implied) in contract to use reasonable skill and care, or is it a claim in the tort of negligence? Is it both, concurrently or in the alternative? Is it a claim for breach of statutory duty or is a claim for breach of the duty set up by the Defective Premises Act? In particular, contract and tort are now considered as the basis of claims, together with what is meant by reasonable skill and care, and what effect the existence of a contract may have on a claim in tort.

3.1.1 Reasonable skill and care – generally

There will usually be a contract arising out of the relationship between designer and employer. This contract can take many forms including an agreement by word of mouth, or a simple written agreement such as an exchange of letters, or the more detailed ACE or RIBA conditions of engagement. The terms of such a contract may consist of express and implied terms.

The person who holds himself out as being a designer, whether he possesses qualifications or not, impliedly warrants that he is reasonably competent to carry out the task he undertakes. Indeed, 'the failure to afford the requisite skill which has been expressly or impliedly promised is a breach of legal duty': *Harmer* v. *Cornelius* (1858). 'Every person who enters into a learned profession undertakes to bring to the exercise of it a reasonable degree of care and skill': *Lanphier* v. *Phipos* (1838). It is not difficult to see that a designer who proves in the event not to have the necessary skill may be liable for the damage that he causes to the employer; but in order that an employer may establish that his designer has liability he must show that there has been a breach of duty by the designer that has caused the damage. In order to establish that there has been a breach of duty, it must be shown that the designer was negligent. 'Negligence' in this sense is analogous to the standard of care in the law of negligence. In the ordinary case of negligence, outside the field of professional negligence, the test that is applied in order to decide whether there has been a breach of duty amounting to negligence was set out in 1856 in *Blyth* v. *Birmingham Water Works Co:*

'Negligence is the omission to do something which a reasonable man, guided upon those considerations which ordinarily regulate the conduct of human affairs, would do, or doing something which a prudent and reasonable man would not do.'

3.1.2 Reasonable skill and care – the test

This leaves open the difficulty of defining the reasonable man. Lawyers were known in long gone days to refer to the ordinary man on the Clapham omnibus in relation to duties. It was his view that was said to be the test of the standards expected of professional designers who exercise every day special skills of which the ordinary man is usually ignorant. The courts have therefore evolved a special way of looking at the professional man's special obligations. In a leading medical negligence case, it was put this way by the court:

'How do you test whether this act or failure is negligence? In an ordinary case it is generally said that you judge that by the action of the man in the street. He is the ordinary man. In one case it has been said that you judge it by the conduct of the man on the top of a Clapham omnibus. He is the ordinary man. But where you get a situation which involves the use of some special skill or competence, then the test whether there has been negligence or not is not the test of the man on top of the Clapham omnibus, because he has not got this special skill. A man need not possess the highest expert skill at the risk of being found negligent. It is well established law that it is sufficient if he exercised the ordinary skill of an ordinary competent man exercising that particular art.' Mr Justice McNair in *Bolam* v. *Friern Hospital Management Committee* approved in *Whitehouse* v. *Jordan* (1981), House of Lords, and in *Greaves* v. *Baynham Meikle* (1975), a construction case in the Court of Appeal.

This test is to be applied to all professions requiring special skill, knowledge and experience: *Gold* v. *Haringey Health Authority* (1988).

3.1.3 Application of the test

In deciding whether there is negligence in a particular case, it is necessary to look at what an ordinary competent designer exercising the particular skill would do and to compare that with the actions of the person against whom the negligence is alleged. One way that this can be done in practice is to seek the views of other designers as to the action that was taken by the designer whose actions have been questioned. It is for this reason that it is usually necessary for expert evidence of such matters to be given to a court hearing such a dispute: *Worboys* v. *Acme Investments* (1969).

There are some cases in relation to the construction professions which are useful in this context. For example, in a case involving civil engineers arising out of personal injuries incurred when a pumping station exploded during a visit by members of the public, (*Eckersley and Others* v. *Binnie & Partners and Others* (1988)) Lord Justice Bingham said:

'... a professional man ... must bring to any professional task he undertakes no less expertise, skill and care than other ordinarily competent members would bring but need bring no more. The law does not require of a professional man that he be a paragon combining the qualities of polymath and prophet.'

An Australian case, *Voli* v. *Inglewood Shire Council* (1963), gives assistance with architects:

'An architect undertaking any work in the way of his profession accepts the ordinary liabilities of any man who follows a skilled calling. He is bound to exercise due care, skill and diligence. He is not required to have an extraordinary degree of skill or the highest professional attainments. But he must bring to the task he undertakes the competence and skill that is usual among architects practising their profession. And he must use due care. If he fails in these matters and the person who employed him thereby suffers damage, he is liable to that person. The liability can be said to arise either from a breach of his contract or in tort.': Mr Justice Windeyer.

It is necessary to look beyond the professional man's contract to find all his duties. Take the position of an architect operating with a JCT 80 contract for the building works. In carrying out his design, he will have to provide information and details to the contractor in accordance with the requirements of the building contract. Many other examples can be given of such obligations being incorporated by reference to contracts other than the conditions of engagement themselves. It should be understood that 'reasonable skill and care' is not an all embracing obligation in the sense of describing all the designer's obligations but rather a convenient framework against which to assess particular and precise points.

Greaves v. *Baynham Meikle* (1975) is discussed in the next chapter in relation to whether or not there is an implied term in a designer's contract that the result of his design will be fit for the employer's purpose. That would, of course, be a higher duty than that of exercising reasonable skill and care; however, not-withstanding the *Greaves* case, it is submitted that the test for negligence in design is that of the *Bolam* case, although in the circumstances of any particular case it may be that 'special steps [are] necessary in order to fulfil the duty of care': Lord Denning in *Greaves*. It follows from this that a designer's liability is not usually strict or absolute and he will not be liable as if he had guaranteed that the design would produce a particular result, unless, of course, he has expressly agreed to do so. Different considerations apply to design and build contracts and this subject is discussed in Chapter 8.

3.1.4   The test and different professional practices

It follows that in the usual case, provided the designer can show that he acted in accordance with the usual practice of his profession, then he will usually be able to escape liability. The same principles would apply where there were several accepted but differing practices within the profession and the designer acted in accordance with one of those practices.

This last point is by analogy with the finding in the *Bolam* case which was concerned partly with the question as to the scope for genuine difference of opinion in the medical profession in relation to different methods of treatment adopted by different doctors. The adoption by a doctor of one, out of several, methods of treatment does not imply negligence, provided that his belief is based on reasonable grounds. It will not necessarily be sufficient to establish negligence for the plaintiff to show that there was a body of competent profes-sional opinion that considered the decision had been wrong, if there was also a body of professional opinion, equally competent, that supported the decision as having been reasonable in the circumstances: *Maynard* v. *West Midlands Area Health Authority* (House of Lords, 1984).

The application of this principle to the construction industry is difficult to reconcile with the finding of the Court of Appeal in the *Greaves* case where evidence had been given that competent designers might have formed the same view as the designer in the dispute, and yet the designer in that case was held liable in negligence. One conclusion that can be drawn from these cases is that each dispute must be viewed in the light of its own facts and it must always be borne in mind that the court takes great account of the merits of the parties in dispute. For example, in a surveyor's negligence case it was held that although failure to discover damp in one particular place might not automatically be negligent, the surveyor could not have failed to find the damp if he had inves-tigated as thoroughly as he should have done; thus he had fallen below the standard of care to be expected of a reasonably competent surveyor exercising skill and care appropriate to his duties: *Fryer* v. *Bunney* (1982). Furthermore, although a surveyor carrying out a building society valuation was not under a general duty to move carpets and furniture, if his suspicions had been aroused as to a defect in the property, he was under a duty to follow the trail of suspicion, by moving carpets and furniture if necessary, until he had all the information which it was reasonable for him to have before making his valuation: *Roberts & Another* v. *J Hampson & Co* (1988).

The question sometimes arises whether the general practice of the profession is the right practice and whether in those circumstances a designer could escape liability by saying that he merely did what everyone else in his profession was doing. This point has been considered both in relation to solicitors' duties and doctors' duties. A firm of solicitors has been held negligent for failing to make a commons registration search in a conveyancing transaction and their defence that they made all the searches that solicitors usually make was rejected by the court: *Ladenbau* v. *Crawley and de Reya* (1978).

In *Sidaway* v. *Governors of Bethlem Royal Hospital*, the Court of Appeal (1984), and the House of Lords (1985), were concerned amongst other things with the extent of a surgeon's duty to inform a patient of risks to such an extent that the patient is able to give full consent. Although there were clearly policy decisions in this case which was in any event a medical negligence case, and which may not be appropriate in the average building negligence problem, it is clear that it is open to the court to reject expert evidence as to the practice of a profession, at least in certain circumstances. In the Court of Appeal, Sir John Donaldson MR had suggested that:

'In an appropriate case, a judge would be entitled to reject a unanimous medical view if he was satisfied that it was manifestly wrong and that the doctors must have been mis-directing themselves as to their duty in law.'

He went on to say that he thought his view could be best expressed in this way:

'The duty is fulfilled if the doctor acts in accordance with a practice rightly accepted as proper by a body of skilled and experienced medical men.'

This point was considered again in the House of Lords where Lord Templeman said:

'In the case of a general danger, the court must decide whether the information afforded to the patient was sufficient to alert the patient to the possibility of serious harm of the kind in fact suffered. If the practice of the medical profession is to make express mention of a particular kind of danger, the court will have no difficulty in coming to a conclusion that the doctor ought to have referred expressly to this danger as a special danger unless the doctor can give reasons to justify the form or absence of warning adopted by him. Where the practice of the medical profession is divided or does not include express mention, it will be for the court to determine whether the harm suffered is an example of a general danger inherent in the nature of the operation and if so whether the explanation afforded to the patient was sufficient to alert the patient to the general dangers of which the harm suffered is an example.'

These cases indicate that in an appropriate case a court may have the right to reject expert evidence where that evidence is of a general practice in a profession which is not a rightful practice. It may well be, for example, that these cases will open up the possibility of calling expert evidence as to the practice in countries outside the United Kingdom in fields where the professional experience may be different or more extensive.

3.1.5   Contract and tort concurrently?

What is the position where there is a contract but there is also, *prima facie*, a duty of care owed in tort? Is it possible to bring proceedings both in contract and tort? This issue which had been thought to be tolerably clear at the time of previous editions of this book is another area of the law where developments have taken place.

This issue is important and difficult.

It is important because of the difference between tort and contract in limitation and damages. A cause of action in contract is barred six years (12 if a deed or under seal) after the cause of action accrues. In tort, the date on which the claim will be barred is also six years from the date on which the cause of action accrues. However, for reasons explained in Chapter 12, the accrual of the cause of action in tort is usually later than in contract. Further, if the Latent Damage Act 1986 applies only to claims in negligence as a tort, then there is another distinction with contract because such tort claims can be brought for up to three years from the 'date of knowledge.' It follows that in tort, claims are likely to be statute barred at a later date than contractual claims.

It is also important because in tort a designer may have available a defence not available to him in contract: the delegation of work to an independent contractor.

It is difficult because the cases do not speak with a clear voice and because the ability to bring claims in tort for economic loss in construction cases is now so restricted (see Chapter 2).

There have, historically, been a great number of cases where the liability of professional men has been held, and in many cases assumed, to arise both in contract and tort concurrently. For example, in *Donoghue* v. *Stevenson* (1932) Lord Macmillan, in a passage which must be *obiter dicta* but also highly persuasive, said:

> 'The fact that there is a contractual relationship between the parties which may give rise to an action for breach of contract does not exclude the co-existence of a right of action founded on negligence as between the same parties, independently of the contract, though arising out of the relationship in fact brought about by the contract. Of this the best illustration is the right of the injured railway passenger to sue the railway company either for breach of the contract of safe carriage or for negligence in carrying him.'

On the face of it, therefore, there would appear to be no reason why actions in tort should not be brought where there is a tortious duty, even in cases where there is a contract. The starting point in this aspect of the law is *Bagot* v. *Stevens Scanlan & Co.* (1964) and which case has not been expressly overruled even though the basis for the judgment has been strongly criticised in many subsequent leading cases. It may well be, however, that this case would find favour with the judges in the more recent cases of the late 1980s.

In the action, an employer of a firm of architects sought damages for breach of contract and for the tort of negligence. The court held that duties owed by professional men arose only in contract and not in tort. That case was followed in *Higgins* v. *Arfon Borough Council* in 1975 (since itself overruled).

Lord Denning MR in *Esso Petroleum Co. Limited* v. *Mardon* (1976) had to

consider whether there was tortious liability in respect of pre-contract negotiations in circumstances where a contract was ultimately entered into. It had been
argued in the case that the fact that there was a contract excluded any tortious
liability. In referring to the *Bagot* case, Lord Denning suggested that the decision
was in conflict with decision of higher authority to which that court was not
referred in coming to its decision, and he quoted passages from two old House of
Lords cases:

> '... wherever there is a contract, and something to be done in the course of the
> employment which is the subject of that contract, if there is breach of duty in
> the course of that employment, the plaintiff may either recover in tort or in
> contract': *Boorman* v. *Brown* (1844).

> '... the solicitor contracts with his client to be skilful and careful. For failure to
> perform his obligation he may be made liable at law in contract or even in tort,
> for negligence in breach of a duty imposed on him': *Nocton* v. *Lord Ashburton*
> (1914).

The Court of Appeal again doubted the *Bagot* decision in 1978 but did not
overrule it, in *Batty* v. *Metropolitan Realisations Limited*, on the basis of Lord
Denning's comments in the *Esso* v. *Mardon* case. Those criticisms were such that
in another case in 1978, *Midland Bank Trust Co. Limited* v. *Hett, Stubbs and Kemp*, a
judge, sitting alone, felt able to satisfy himself that he was not bound by the *Bagot*
decision. He said of the argument in *Bagot*, that the cause of action there was
necessarily in contract alone because the architects in that case had failed to do
the very thing which they contracted to do: 'well, so they had, but the form of the
breach cannot affect the nature of the duty, nor does an obligation imposed by
law become an obligation different in quality simply because the obligee agrees
to accept money for its performance.'

In *Junior Books*, Lord Brandon expressed serious reservations as to the legal
position where there is a contract with an exclusion clause and a parallel duty in
tort, and what the effect is, if any, of an exclusion clause in a contract in relation
to the duty in tort. It may be that the words of Lord Roskill in that case have led to
discussion in other cases and to what can now be perceived as a general trend in
the direction of denying concurrent remedies in tort where there is a contract, at
least in certain situations. In *Tai Hing Cotton Mill Limited* v. *Liu Chong Hing Bank
Limited* (1986), the Privy Council gave consideration to a claim by a company
against a bank for paying on cheques which had been forged by an accounts
clerk. Lord Scarman, in delivering the judgment of the Privy Council said:

> 'Their Lordships do not believe that there is anything to the advantage of the
> law's development in searching for a liability in tort where the parties are in a
> contractual relationship. This is particularly so in a commercial relationship.
> Though it is possible as a matter of legal semantics to conduct an analysis of
> the rights and duties inherent in some contractual relationships including that
> of banker and customer either as a matter of contract law when the question
> will be what, if any, terms are to be implied or as a matter of tort law when the
> task will be to identify a duty arising from the proximity and character of the
> relationship between the parties, their Lordships believe it to be correct in

principle and necessary for the avoidance of confusion in the law to adhere to the contractual analysis: on principle because it is a relationship in which the parties have, subject to a few exceptions, the right to determine their obligations to each other and for the avoidance of confusion because different consequences do flow according to whether the liability arises from contract or tort e.g. in limitation of action.'

Lord Scarman then considered and agreed with part of a dissenting speech in *Lister* v. *Romford Ice and Cold Storage Co. Limited* (1957) and went on:

'Their Lordships do not, therefore, embark on an investigation as to whether in the relationship of banker and customer, it is possible to identify tort as well as contract as a source of the obligations owed by the one to the other. Their Lordships do not, however, accept that the parties' mutual obligations in tort can be any greater than those to be found expressly or by necessary implication in their contract. If therefore, as their Lordships have concluded, no duty wider than that recognised in *McMillan* (1918) and *Greenwood* (1933) can be implied into the banking contract in the absence of express terms to that effect, the banks cannot rely on the law of tort to provide them with greater protection than that for which they have contracted.'

Indeed, in a case involving a ship owner, mortgagees and insurers, the court decided, following *Tai Hing*, that where a duty of care was claimed to arise as an implied term under a tripartite agreement and also in tort, if the plaintiff failed in contract, he must also necessarily fail in tort: *Bank of Novia Scotia* v. *Hellenic Mutual War Risks Association (The Good Luck)* (1988).

It does seem likely that the courts will look much more carefully at situations where concurrent remedies in contract and tort are pleaded, and by reason of the other developments in negligence law, courts will look much more carefully as to whether there is a duty of care in any event. It must follow, if this trend continues, that contractual relationships and the definition of the terms governing that relationship, will become more and more important.

In *Ernst & Whinney* v. *Willard* (1987), the decision was given by Judge John Davies QC, Official Referee. In this case, assignees of a long lease of an office development brought a claim against engineers, nominated mechanical sub-contractors and ductwork sub-contractors in respect of alleged deficiencies in the air conditioning system. The Official Referee decided that it would not be just and reasonable to impose liability in negligence on the defendants for a variety of reasons. The case had been put on the basis that the ventilation system was defective; its defects caused physical damage to the building which was thereby caused by the defendants' failure to do the work with due care and skill; that failure was a breach of their duty to the plaintiffs as subsequent purchasers of the building. In other words the argument was put principally on the basis in *Junior Books* and *Anns. Anns* of course, since been overruled.

In *Greater Nottingham Co-operative Society* v. *Cementation Piling and Foundations Limited* (1988), the plaintiffs were building owners and the defendants, sub-contractors for piling. The sub-contractors had executed a JCT collateral warranty agreement in the then form. By reason of negligent piling, there was damage to an adjoining property. In this action, the employers claimed the additional cost of executing a revised piling scheme, the sums paid to the main contractor for loss and expense and the consequential economic loss due to delay. The employer's claim was brought in tort notwithstanding the direct contract (which was not apposite to deal with the particular issues). In considering whether there should be a concurrent but more extensive liability in tort as between the two parties arising out of the execution of the contract, Lord Justice Purchas in the Court of Appeal said:

'... it was relevant to bear in mind:

(a) the parties had an actual opportunity to define their relationship by means of a contract and took it; and
(b) the general contractual structure as between [the employer], the main contractor and Cementation provided a channel of claim which was open to [the employer]. It would not be in accordance with present policy to extend *Junior Books* rather than to restrict it.'

The Court of Appeal went on to decide that there was no liability in tort in this case. This case indicates that a contract can have the effect of limiting, but not excluding, tortious duties. In an insurance case, a tort claim was not allowed where plaintiffs had made a claim against the errors and omissions insurers of their brokers. The brokers were insolvent and the plaintiff had no contract with the insurers: *Abrahams* v. *Nelson Hurst and Marsh Limited* (1989).

Recent construction cases indicate that judges are adopting different approaches to the issue as to concurrent liability in tort and contract. Three relevant decisions are as follows.

In *Hiron and Hiron and Legal and General Assurance* v. *Pynford Southern and Others* (1991), Mr and Mrs Hiron had subsidence problems with their house. They, and Legal & General, their insurers, sued Pynford, underpinning contractors, Leo Lewis & Co. (Surveyors) and Peter M. Olley & Associates. Leo Lewis were assumed to have approved on behalf of the Hirons a scheme produced by Pynford which had been checked by Peter M. Olley & Associates, who had been retained by Legal and General, the Hirons' insurers. The Hirons sued Pynford and Leo Lewis in contract. Legal and General sued Peter M. Olley in contract. Both the Hirons and Legal and General also alleged that all the defendants owed them a duty of care at common law. Judge Newey QC, Official Referee, held that the mere existence of the contracts here did not preclude liability in tort. The correct approach when there was a contract was that it was an important consideration in deciding whether there was sufficient proximity between the parties and whether it was just and reasonable that a duty in tort should be owed. In the event, it was found that no duty was owed at common law by Peter M. Olley to the Hirons or to Legal and General. It seems to be the case that the judge was heavily influenced by the existence of contracts and by the fact that the Hirons had retained their own advisers, Leo Lewis.

In *Barclays Bank plc* v. *Fairclough Building Limited* (1993), which is discussed in section 2.2.3, another Official Referee found that the fact that there was a contract did not prevent the existence of a duty of care in tort.

Judge Michael Kershaw QC had to deal with concurrent liability in *Lancashire and Cheshire Baptist Churches Incorporated* v. *Howard and Seddon Partnership* (1993).

Howard and Seddon were architects for a church sanctuary completed in 1980. It was alleged that there was condensation and inadequate ventilation. The claim in contract was out of time for limitation purposes and the action proceeded on the claim in tort, which was not out of time. The judge had no difficulty in holding that the architect owed duties in tort – there is a long line of authority for the proposition that professional men owe duties in contract and tort. In *Tai Hing*, it had been suggested that in commercial relationships, the contractual relationship should determine rights and obligations. The judge dealt with this point by saying that *Tai Hing* was authority for a narrow proposition, namely: where there is a contract, the tortious duties cannot be more extensive than the duties in the contract. He also found that there was no objection that could be taken about a party relying on the longer limitation period in tort where the contractual claim was barred out.

Perhaps we should all look with a new eye at the New Zealand case of *Rowe* v. *Turner Hopkins & Partners* (1980), where it was suggested that the duty of a professional man is in contract only. In the ordinary case, there may well be no difficulty, provided there is a contract. However, there are many circumstances where difficulties may be created, particularly in relation to direct warranty agreements where the direct warranty agreement does not cover the claim sought to be made.

The present position appears to be as follows but the law continues to develop and short summaries must be treated with caution. There will usually be concurrent rights against a designer in contract and tort. The existence of the contract provides the necessary proximity for the tortious claim. The existence of the contract may be relevant in deciding the nature and extent of the tortious duty. However, it may also be that the tortious duty cannot be any more extensive than the contractual duty. It is submitted that careful and clear words (such as the use of the word 'negligence') would have to be included in the contract to exclude or restrict the tortious duty, which restrictions or exclusions may fall to be considered under the Unfair Contract Terms Act 1977. The debate in the cases will, no doubt, continue but probably at a slower pace in construction because of the effect on tort claims of *Murphy* and *D & F*.

3.2 General duties of a designer

The particular obligations that a designer undertakes in any particular case will be governed by the arrangements between the designer and the employer. It may be that the designer is engaged for a limited function of, say, obtaining planning permission only. It may be that the employer only requires a feasibility study in order to decide whether or not he should proceed with the construction work. It is, therefore, necessary in any particular circumstances to look at precisely what obligations the designer has undertaken. For design work which is to be undertaken on the ACE or RIBA Conditions, those conditions should be referred to.

In any case, where there is any doubt as to the obligations undertaken by the designer, it would be necessary to call members of the same profession to give evidence as to what a reasonably competent member of their profession would do in the circumstances that had given rise to the dispute. It follows that it is impossible to give a detailed and accurate list of the duties that would fit every possible case. Judge Stabb QC made some observations as to the general duties of an architect to his employer in the case of *Sutcliffe* v. *Clippendale and Edmondson* (1971) which subsequently went to the Court of Appeal, but not on this point:

'It can be said that when a person engages an architect in relation to the building of a house, he is entitled to expect that the architect will perform his duties in such a manner as to safeguard his interest and that he will do all that is reasonably within his power to ensure that work is properly and expeditiously carried out, so as to achieve the end result as contemplated by the contract. In particular the building owner is entitled to expect his architect so to administer the contract and supervise the work, as to ensure as far as is reasonably possible, that the quality of the work matches up to the standard contemplated.'

In *Hudson's Building and Engineering Contracts* the duties of architects and engineers to advise, design, make plans and supervise as they are generally carried out in the United Kingdom are set out. *Hudson's* list of duties (excluding those matters not related to design and supervision of the construction of that design) are as follows:

'(1) To advise and consult with the employer (not as a lawyer) as to any limitation which may exist as to the use of the land to be built on, either (*inter alia*) by planning legislation, restrictive covenants, or the rights of adjoining owners or the public over the land, or by statutes and by-laws affecting the works to be executed.

(2) To examine the site, sub-soil and surroundings or to make arrangements for such an examination, including advising on the need for the employment of specialists or consultants.

(3) To consult with and advise the employer as to the proposed work.

(4) To prepare sketch plans and a specification, having regard to all the conditions known to exist and to submit them to the employer for approval, with an estimate of the probable cost, if requested.

(5) To elaborate and, if necessary, modify or amend the sketch plans, and then, if so instructed, to prepare drawings and a specification of the work to be carried out as a first step in the preparation of contract documents including advising on the need for the employment of any specialists or consultants.

(6) To consult with and advise the employer as to the form of contract to be used (including whether or not to use bills of quantities) and as to the necessity or otherwise of employing a quantity surveyor (engineers usually do not employ an independent quantity surveyor) to prepare bills and carry out the usual valuation services during the currency of the contract.

(7) To bring the contract documents to their final state before inviting tenders, with or without the assistance of quantity surveyors and structural engineers, including the obtaining of detailed quotations from and arrangement of delivery dates with any nominated sub-contractors or suppliers whose work may have to be ready or available at an early stage of the main contractor's work.'

(For the full list see *Hudson's Building and Engineering Contracts* 10th Edition at page 103, and the Supplement to the 10th Edition.)

In the Standard Form of Agreement for the Appointment of an Architect (SFA/92) there are clauses dealing expressly with the architect's authority:

> '1.2.2   The Architect shall act on behalf of the Client in the matters set out or necessarily implied in the Appointment.
>
> 1.2.3   The Architect shall at those points and/or dates referred to in the Timetable obtain the authority of the Client before proceeding with the Services.'

Condition 1.2.2 gives the architect authority in respect of those matters 'set out or necessarily implied' in the appointment; it is submitted that where an architect was engaged to perform services in relation to, for example, a JCT 80 Form of Contract, he would have implied authority to carry out the functions ascribed to the architect under that contract. However, the conditions do not give express authority to an architect to delegate any of his functions and no such term will be implied (see 5.5). Accordingly, the architect has no authority to delegate any of his functions without express authority.

It is convenient now to consider the duties and the other problems that can arise in relation to design during the construction process by reference to specific obligations and liabilities.

Chapter 4

Detailed duties and liabilities of designers

The general principles of law and general duties of a designer are now considered in detail by reference to particular duties and areas where liability can be incurred by designers.

4.1 Fitness for purpose

4.1.1 Generally

Does the obligation imposed on a designer to use reasonable skill and care mean that there is an obligation to see that the design is fit for its purpose? Fitness for purpose is a greater obligation than the use of reasonable skill and care in the design. This aspect of the design process has been touched on in two cases, *Greaves (Contractors) Limited* v. *Baynham Meikle & Partners* (1975) and *IBA* v. *EMI and BICC* (1980). Both these cases were on particular facts and were not cases that arose out of the commonly found relationship between designers, contractors and employers; in the *Greaves* case, the contract was a package deal and in the *IBA* case, it was the contractor's sub-contractor who carried out the design. Before looking at these cases, it is necessary to look at the development of the law in relation to fitness for purpose in construction.

Where there is a contract for sale of goods, then the Sale of Goods Act 1979 implies a condition that the goods shall be reasonably fit for any purpose made known to the seller by the buyer. The Sale of Goods Act, as its name implies, only applies to contracts for sale of goods and does not, therefore, apply to building contracts, which are contracts for work and materials. It follows that terms are not implied into building contracts by reason of the Sale of Goods Act. However, it has been held that a person contracting on the basis of work and materials impliedly warrants that the materials will be reasonably fit for the purpose for which he is using them unless he can show that the purchaser did not rely on his skill and judgment: *Myers* v. *Brent Cross Service Company* (1934). This principle was approved by the House of Lords in *Young and Marten* v. *McManus Childs* (1969). In other words, the position of a builder supplying materials as part of his work under the building contract, will usually be much the same as it would be if the Sale of Goods Act applied to the transaction, provided the employer relied on the skill and judgment of the contractor. A similar term will be implied under the Supply of Goods and Services Act 1982 (section 4 and see 2.3.1).

Similarly, where a contractor is employed to build a house, there is a term implied by law that the contractor will do his work in a good and workmanlike manner and that the house will be reasonably fit for human habitation on completion. In other words, a contractor's duty in such circumstances is not limited to using reasonable skill and care; he is obliged to ensure that the finished work is reasonably fit for the purpose of human habitation: *Miller* v. *Cannon Hill Estates Limited* (1931); *Hancock* v. *B. W. Brazier (Anerley) Limited* (1966); and *Test Valley Borough Council* v. *GLC* (1979). It is on this basis that it is said that, where there is no express obligation to the contrary, a contractor who undertakes to design and build on a package deal basis is under an implied obligation to provide a building fit for the purpose for which it was required (see *Viking Grain Storage Limited* v. *T. H. White Installations Limited and Ano*ther (1985) and Chapter 8).

Is there any reason why a similar term should not be implied into a designer's contract? The implied term as to reasonable skill and care under the Supply of Goods and Services Act does not prejudice any rule of law which imposes a duty stricter than that of reasonable skill and care (section 16(3)(a)); so that Act does not of itself prevent the implication of a fitness for purpose term.

4.1.2 *Greaves (Contractors) Limited* v. *Baynham Meikle & Partners*

The case of *Greaves (Contractors) Limited* v. *Baynham Meikle & Partners* (1975), which arose out of a design and build contract, is important. Contractors by a contract agreed to design and construct a warehouse and office for a company which intended to use the warehouse for storage of barrels of oil. The contractor engaged structural engineers to design the structure of the warehouse and in the course of giving instructions to those structural engineers, the contractor told them that the first and upper floors of the warehouse would have to take the weight of fork-lift trucks carrying heavy barrels of oil. The warehouse, which was built following the structural engineers' design, was brought into use and the floors began to crack. It was found at the trial that the cracks were the result of vibration of the fork-lift trucks. The Court of Appeal held that there was a term to be implied in the designer's contract that they should design a warehouse fit for the purpose for which it was required, namely reasonably fit for the use of fork-lift trucks carrying barrels of oil. As the structural engineers had not produced such a design, they were liable to the contractor for the cost of the remedial works required by the building owner. In the alternative, if there was no such term to be implied, the structural engineers were in breach of their duty to use reasonable skill and care because they knew or ought to have known that the purpose of the floors was to carry fork-lift trucks laden with barrels of oil.

Lord Denning in his judgment in the *Greaves* case drew the distinction between a term which is to be implied *by law* and a term which is to be implied *in fact*. Where the *presumed intention* of the parties is clear, then the term will be implied *by law*; where the parties *actual intention* is clear, the term is said to be implied *in fact*. The decision in the *Greaves* case was based on a term that was found to have been implied in fact and does not therefore give rise to any general assumption that there is to be implied into a designer's contract a term that his design will be fit for its purpose. Lord Denning put it this way:

'The law does not usually imply a warranty that he will achieve the desired result but only a term that he will use reasonable skill and care. The surgeon does not warrant that he will cure the patient. Nor does the solicitor warrant that he will win the case. But, when a dentist agrees to make a set of false teeth for a patient, there is an implied warranty that they will fit his gums, see *Samuels* v. *Davis* (1943).

What then is the position when an architect or an engineer is employed to design a house or a bridge? Is he under an implied warranty that, if the work is carried out to his design, it will be reasonably fit for the purpose or is he only under a duty to use reasonable skill and care? This question may require to be answered some day as a matter of law. But, in the present case I do not think we need answer it. For the evidence shows that both parties were of one mind on the matter. Their common intention was that the engineer should design a warehouse which would be fit for the purpose for which it was required. That common intention gives rise to a term implied in fact.'

By way of emphasis, Lord Justice Browne in the same case said that the decision in the case laid down no general principle as to the obligations and liabilities of professional men; it was a case that depended on the special facts and circumstances that had arisen.

4.1.3   *IBA* v. *EMI and BICC*

The fitness for purpose issue again came close to being decided in a House of Lords case, *Independent Broadcasting Authority* v. *EMI Electronics Limited and BICC Construction Limited* in 1980. The case is of such importance that the facts and findings are worth setting out in some detail.

On 19 March 1969, a 1250 foot high television mast at Elmley Moor in Yorkshire collapsed. The owner of the mast, IBA, sued EMI, as main contractors and BICC, their sub-contractors, for damages. IBA alleged breach of the contract, which was in the form of the Model Conditions of the IMechE/IEE for home contracts with erection, and negligence against EMI, and negligence, breach of warranty and negligent mis-statement against BICC. The judge who originally heard the case had determined that the reason for the failure was the fracture of a flange at 1027 feet above ground level and that this failure had been caused primarily by vortex shedding (induced by wind) and to a lesser extent by the asymmetric loading of ice on the mast. The House of Lords held:

(1) BICC had been negligent in the design of the mast
(2) a statement in a letter from BICC to IBA that 'We are all well satisfied that the structures will not oscillate dangerously' was, in the state of BICC's then knowledge, a negligent mis-statement
(3) that assurance had no contractual effect
(4) EMI were under contractual liability to IBA for the design of the mast; at its least, that responsibility extended to responsibility for a negligent design.

Since the design was negligent it was unnecessary further to consider the full extent of that responsibility.

As in the *Greaves* case, the House of Lords, because of their findings on other issues, did not decide whether there was to be a term implied in law that the television mast should be fit for its purpose. This is because they found that EMI had a contractual responsibility for the design of the mast and that at the very least that responsibility must have extended to seeing that the design would not be carried out negligently. They found that the design had been carried out negligently so it follows that it was not necessary for them to consider the fitness for purpose issue. However, there are some comments in that case that are highly relevant. Viscount Dilhorne, for example, said:

'In the circumstances it was not necessary to consider whether EMI had by their contract undertaken to supply a mast reasonably fit for the purpose for which they knew it was intended and whether BICC had by their contract with EMI undertaken a similar obligation but had that been argued, I would myself have been surprised if it had been concluded that they had not done so.'

Lord Fraser in the *IBA* case considered the *Young and Marten* case in relation to materials and said that he thought the same principle should be applied in this case in respect of the complete structure, including its design; he appears to have adopted this argument on the basis that the implication of a warranty as to fitness for purpose would be reasonable in most cases because the main contractor, liable to the employer for defective material, would generally have a right of redress against the person from whom he bought the material. In other words, there should be a chain of responsibility. Lord Fraser said:

'In the present case, it is accepted by BICC that if EMI are liable in damages to IBA for the design of the mast, then BICC will be liable in turn to EMI. Accordingly, the principle that was applied in *Young and Marten Limited* in respect of materials ought in my opinion to be applied here in respect of the complete structure, including its design. Although EMI had no specialist knowledge of mast design, and although IBA knew that and did not rely on their skill to any extent for the design, I can see nothing unreasonable in holding that EMI are responsible to IBA for the design seeing that they can in turn recover from BICC who did the actual designing.'

Lord Scarman in the same case referred to *Samuels* v. *Davis* (1943) in which case the Court of Appeal had held that where a dentist agrees to make false teeth for a patient for a fee, then there will be an implied term of the contract that the false teeth will be reasonably fit for their intended purpose. He drew the distinction between a dentist's obligation to use reasonable care in taking out a tooth and the entirely different case where false teeth are to be delivered. Lord Scarman, therefore, formed the view that in the absence of any term negativing the obligation, a person 'who contracts to design an article for the purpose made known to him undertakes that the design is reasonably fit for the purpose. Such a design obligation is consistent with the statutory law regulating the sale of goods.'

4.1.4 *Norta Wallpapers (Ireland)* v. *Sisk & Sons (Dublin)*

The Supreme Court of Ireland considered the implication of a term as to fitness for purpose of a sub-contractor's design into a main contractor's contract in 1978: *Norta Wallpapers (Ireland)* v. *Sisk & Sons (Dublin)*.

The employer contracted with a contractor to build a factory and specified that the roof was to be supplied and erected by a particular sub-contractor who manufactured and supplied superstructures. The sub-contractor under the sub-contract indemnified the contractor against any liability which might arise under the main contract as a result of the sub-contractor's breach of the sub-contract. After completion, the roof leaked and was unsuitable for its purpose. An arbitrator found that the problem was 85% due to the defective design of roof lights.

It was held on appeal that there is normally implied in a building contract a term making the contractor liable to the employer for any loss suffered by him as a result of the sub-contractor's goods, materials or installations not being fit for their purpose, but that such an implied term cannot be held to exist unless it comes within the presumed intention of the parties and should not be read into the contract unless it would be reasonable to do so; no such term could be implied in relation to the fitness of the roof's design.

At first sight, the *Norta* case appears to be inconsistent with the *IBA* case, although both are similar on their facts. Lord Fraser in the *IBA* case explained the apparent inconsistency by pointing out that before the main contract in the *Norta* case was made, Norta had already approved the sub-contractor's design, specification and price.

Thus, Sisk were given no option but to use the sub-contractor, his design and his price. In the *IBA* case, EMI had no option but to appoint BICC but they were not bound to accept any particular design at any particular price. In this way, it is possible to argue that there is no inconsistency between the *IBA* and the *Norta* cases.

The importance of the distinction between the use of reasonable skill and care and an obligation as to fitness for purpose is that in the former case negligence has to be shown whereas in the latter case there is an absolute obligation which is independent of negligence: negligence does not have to be proved where there is an obligation as to fitness for purpose. The cases set out above indicate that the English courts are not yet bound by a precedent that an obligation should be implied *in law* as to fitness for purpose in a professional designer's contract. However, it is quite clear that where a particular purpose is made known to a designer, he may be in breach of his obligation to use reasonable skill and care if he did not take those matters sufficiently into account such as to amount to negligence.

4.1.5 *George Hawkins* v. *Chrysler (UK) Limited and Burne Associates*

The dicta of Lord Denning in *Greaves* were considered in a case in 1986: *George Hawkins* v. *Chrysler (UK) Limited and Burne Associates* (1986), a case in the Court of Appeal. The plaintiff was an employee of Chrysler who slipped on water in a shower room after using a shower. He sued Chrysler, his employer and Burne Associates (who had designed, specified and supervised the installation of the showers) in respect of his injuries. Further, Chrysler also claimed against Burne. Chrysler settled the action with the injured employee but continued the proceedings against Burne Associates. Chrysler alleged:

(1) that it was an implied term of the contract that Burne would use reasonable care and skill in selecting the material to be used for the floor of the showers, and

(2)   there was an implied warranty that the material used for the floor would be fit for use in a wet shower room.

The Court of Appeal applied the dicta of Lord Denning in *Greaves* to the effect that a warranty can be implied either as a matter of fact (to give effect to the actual intentions of the parties) or as a matter of law (to give effect to the presumed intention of the parties). They decided that in this case there was nothing to give rise to the inference of any warranty other than to take reasonable care; further that such a warranty would only be implied where it was necessary to give business efficacy to the contract. The Court of Appeal therefore found that no warranty was to be implied beyond that of reasonable skill and care and that whilst there may be anomalies between the positions of contractors and sub-contractors in this respect (i.e. fitness for purpose), as opposed to professional people, in the absence of special circumstances it was not open to the court to extend the responsibilities of a professional man beyond the duty to exercise reasonable care and skill in accordance with the usual standards of his profession. It may well be that this case now settles the point (in a way which *Greaves* expressly did not).

4.2   Negligent mis-statements

It used to be thought that no claim could be founded on a statement that was made negligently where there was no contractual relationship. However, the law of tort has extended its arm into this field; where a statement is made by one party to another party and there is a 'special relationship' between the parties, the legal duty of care arises and breach of that duty gives rise to a claim for damages. This legal doctrine is known as negligent mis-statement and arises from *Hedley Byrne & Co Limited* v. *Heller & Partners Limited* (1963) in which case merchant bankers gave a reference as to the credit worthiness of a third party to advertising agents by saying that the third party was respectably constituted and considered good; the merchant bankers said the statement was made without responsibility on their part. The House of Lords was quite clear that the duty of care could arise in such circumstances but in that particular case it held that the disclaimer was adequate to exclude such duty. Do statements made by designers to employers give rise to liability in the tort of negligent mis-statement?

The *IBA* case is an example of how this liability on the part of designers can arise. As to negligent mis-statement, the only issue before the court in that case was whether the statement that had been made by the designer was negligent; the designer never disputed that when making the statement that was made he owed a duty of care to the employer. What happened was this. When another television mast that the IBA were having erected reached 851 feet in height, it began to oscillate, so much so that the workmen refused to work on it. IBA were naturally concerned and wrote to BICC expressing their concern and suggesting that the oscillating television mast should be fitted with various instruments to provide data for design purposes. BICC replied that 'we are well satisfied that the structure will not oscillate dangerously.' IBA contended that, but for that assurance, they would not have been satisfied that the masts were safe. The House of Lords found that the assurance had been given negligently and it followed that the designer was liable to the employer for his negligent mis-statement. There was, of course, in that case, no direct contractual relationship between BICC and IBA.

The importance of the approach in *Hedley Byrne* has been highlighted by the decisions in *D & F* and *Murphy*. In cases involving negligent design, will the claim fall within:

(1) *Hedley Byrne* as negligent advice, in which case damages will be reco-verable, including economic loss, or
(2) *D & F* and *Murphy* in which case where defects are discovered before they cause either or both personal injury or damage to property other than 'the thing itself', no damages will be recoverable because they are economic loss?

Owners of defective buildings who wish to pursue claims in tort will be seeking to frame their cases on the basis of *Hedley Byrne*. It will be of interest to see how such attempts work out over the next few years.

The importance of this extension of potential liability in tort is considered further in Chapter 5 in relation to designers' duties of care to third parties, such as the contractor.

4.3   Statutes, by-laws and Building Regulations

4.3.1   *Generally*

Everyone is deemed to have knowledge of the general law. As a general prin-ciple that cannot be doubted, although Parliament makes it increasingly difficult for even lawyers to find quickly relevant sections of Acts of Parliament and statutory instruments made under powers given to Ministers by statute. Indeed, there are many sections of modern Acts of Parliament that are not brought into force upon the act receiving the royal assent in the usual way. It is now quite common for powers to be reserved to a particular Secretary of State to bring into force sections of statutes on days to be appointed by him by way of statutory instrument. This is how the Building Regulations 1985 were brought into effect by the Secretary of State. However, notwithstanding all these difficulties, it will be no excuse for a designer to plead ignorance of such requirements as are in force at any particular time.

It will usually be part of a designer's duty to obtain the necessary planning permission for the construction of the works from the local planning authority and the designer's duty will extend to providing proper information and drawings to support such an application. A designer should have knowledge of any particular government controls by statute relating to particular develop-ments. Failure by a designer to comply with statutory provisions can have very serious consequences indeed for the employer. For example, if work to which Building Regulations are applicable contravenes those regulations, the local authority can require the owner to pull down or remove the works (section 36, Building Act 1984). In such circumstances the designer will be liable to the employer for the costs that he incurs by reason of a designer's default.

The designer's duty does not extend to that of having the detailed knowledge of a lawyer but he has to have knowledge of the general law and it is likely that he must know sufficient of the law to enable him to know when to advise the employer of the need to obtain expert legal opinion. The case of *B.L. Holdings Limited* v. *Robert J. Wood & Partners* (1979), which went to the Court of Appeal, demonstrates the problems inherent in this area. The judge found the designer had been negligent and yet the Court of Appeal reversed his decision. The facts of the case are as follows.

In 1970, designers were engaged in relation to the development of an employer's derelict site in Brighton. At that time, it was necessary for planning permission to be effective for an Office Development Permit (ODP) to be issued. An ODP was not required if the office space did not exceed 10,000 square feet. The local planning authority told the designer that the largest building that would be permitted on the site would be about 15,000 square feet and that it would be necessary to provide car parking. The local authority further told the designer that they would not take the area set aside for car parking into account in determining whether or not an ODP was necessary. The designers were surprised at this but they did not mention their surprise to the employer. After further discussion with the local authority, the designers put in an additional floor to their design and the local authority said that if the top floor were a self-contained residential unit, it would not be counted for the purposes of ODP calculations. Planning permission was granted in respect of the designer's design which had a gross area of 16,100 square feet, of which the office space comprised 10,000 square feet. No ODP was granted and the building was completed in 1972. Thereafter, a prospective tenant queried the absence of an ODP but the employer was unable to get the matter put right until 1976 when the exemption from ODPs was raised from 10,000 square feet to 50,000 square feet. The building remained unoccupied throughout that period. The employer alleged that the designer was in breach of duty and negligent in failing to advise that an ODP was required. The Court of Appeal, reversing the judge's decision, held that the designers were not negligent or in breach of their duty.

The judge who heard the case originally, before it went to the Court of Appeal, said: 'It may be thought by some to be hard to require of an architect that he know more law than the planning authority.' But he went on to say:

'I am left with the clear conviction that I have not on the facts set too high a standard of care of judgment for an ordinarily competent architect who in 1970 was undertaking to advise in planning matters relating to office development. Indeed, I am convinced that the standard which the law sets, namely that of the ordinarily competent and skilled architect certainly requires of [the designer] that he should at least have given that advice and warning to his clients.'

The judge felt that the wording of the Act of Parliament was sufficiently clear to make it plain to any competent architect that the planning application would be ineffective if an ODP had not been obtained. However, when the action reached the Court of Appeal, the Court of Appeal held that the designer was not negligent or in breach of his duty. The Court of Appeal did not disagree with the judgment of the judge as to the principles governing the duties owed by a designer to an employer but they clearly felt that the issue of law involved in the granting of the particular ODP was a difficult one; even so they did not hold that the designer was not negligent in not advising the employer of the need to obtain independent legal advice.

This case has emphasised, particularly in the different approach between the judge and the Court of Appeal, that this is a particularly difficult area of law for designers. The one lesson that can be clearly drawn from the case is that where circumstances arise where a decision needs to be made by a designer and where that decision involves risk attaching to the employer, the designer would be well advised to draw the risk to the attention of his employer and where appropriate advise that independent legal opinion should be sought. In this way, the designer will probably discharge his duty to his employer and at the same time put the commercial decision in the lap of the party who carried the commercial risk. In giving advice on such matters, the designer should use plain and clear language in specifying the problem, such that a layman not experienced in these matters is able to appreciate and understand clearly and precisely the point that is being put to him.

It is commonplace for defects in design to also constitute breaches of the Building Regulations. The designer can incur liability to the employer in respect of his failure to see that the building complies with the Building Regulations in three possible ways. Firstly, for breach of duty under his contract; the employer is entitled to have a design that complies with the law. Secondly, liability may arise for breach of statutory duty and, this being a tortious liability, the employer may be able to argue that the start of the period for limitation of action is later than that in contract and thus be able to bring a successful claim against the designer some time after the limitation has expired in a contractual claim. Thirdly, under section 38 of the Building Act 1984, liability can arise. These points are now considered in more detail.

4.3.2   Breach of statutory duty

In order to bring a claim for breach of statutory duty, it is necessary to look at the particular statute to ascertain whether the duty that the statute imposes is intended to give rise to a claim for breach of statutory duty at all and, if so, whether the duty is intended to be absolute or merely a duty to take reasonable skill and care. The authorities speak with a mixed voice on the possibility of claims for breach of statutory duty arising out of the Building Regulations. Indeed, some of the cases were decided before the Building Act 1984 which contains express provisions dealing with civil liability for breach of the Building Regulations (see 4.3.3). It may be the position that because that Act provides expressly a remedy, then a proper legal construction of the statute is that no other civil remedy should be permitted. However, the regulations to make section 38 effective have not been made as yet. That absence of regulations may mean that a claim for breach of statutory duty can be brought but the position is very unclear.

It was in *Anns* v. *London Borough of Merton* (1978), now overruled on the scope of the duty to take reasonable care, that Lord Wilberforce said in the House of Lords:

'Since it is the duty of the builder, owner or nor, to comply with the by-laws, I would be of the opinion that an action could be brought against him in effect for breach of statutory duty by any person for whose benefit or protection the by-law was made.'

In *Eames London Estates* v. *North Hertfordshire District Council and Others* (1980), a contractor was held liable in respect of foundations that did not comply with the by-laws (the then equivalent of Building Regulations). Judge Fay QC, Official Referee, followed Lord Wilberforce's view in *Anns* as to duties and took the matter further by holding that the contractor was 'liable for breach of statutory duty irrespective of negligence'. The effect of this finding was that the duty to comply with the by-laws was absolute; in other words, there is strict liability and no need to prove any negligence on the part of the contractor.

In *Worlock* v. *Saws and Rushmoor Borough Council* (1981), when the case was before Mr Justice Woolf he held that contractors were not liable for breach of duty imposed by Building Regulations on the basis that it would be wrong to regard those regulations as giving rise to a statutory duty creating an absolute liability. This case went on appeal to the Court of Appeal where the appeals were dismissed but the judgments of the Court of Appeal are consistent with the view that the duty was not an absolute duty independent of fault: *Worlock* v. *Saws and Rushmoor Borough Council* (Court of Appeal 1982). However, the point is not dealt with expressly in the judgments, and the issue remained open for further consideration by the courts.

In *Taylor Woodrow Construction (Midlands) Limited* v. *Charcon Structures Limited and Others* (1982), where there had been reference to *Eames* and *Worlock* (at first instance), the Court of Appeal did not have to, and did not, decide the issue but Lord Justice Waller said that whether or not a breach of the regulations in that case gave rise to an action for damages without proof of negligence is 'to say the least, doubtful.'

In *Perry* v. *Tendring District Council* (1984), Judge Newey QC found that the Building Regulations did not *per se* give rise to a liability in damages.

Lord Oliver in *Murphy* v. *Brentwood District Council* (1990) said that: 'There is nothing in the terms or purpose of the statutory provisions which supports the creation of a private law right of action for breach of statutory duty.' Against the background of such a statement in a recent case in the House of Lords, breach of statutory duty is unlikely to be a successful contender in the courts, although there is clearly scope for argument.

4.3.3 Section 38 of the Building Act 1984

The Building Act 1984 has a section dealing with civil liability for breach of the Building Regulations. Section 38 provides:

'(1) Subject to this Section:

    (a) breach of a duty imposed by building regulations, so far as it causes damage, is actionable, except in so far as the regulations provide otherwise, and,

    (b) as regards such a duty, building regulations may provide for a prescribed defence to be available in an action for breach of that duty brought by virtue of this sub-section.'

This section will come into force on a date to be appointed by the Secretary of State (section 134). The effect of the section is to provide that certain Building Regulations will be actionable as a breach of duty and that there may be prescribed defences in the regulations. This section could be of great importance to designers and any liability they may incur under the Building Regulations. Indeed, the wording of the section itself may cause some difficulty in respect of the date from which the limitation period is said to run: the liability is subject to the words 'so far as it causes damage' and it will almost certainly be argued that these words mean that the cause of action does not arise, and hence the period of limitation does not begin to run, until the damage has occurred. However, no use can be made of this section until a regulation is made to bring it into use.

4.3.4   Local authority: approval of plans and inspection

Since *Murphy* a local authority cannot be held liable for damages, being the cost of repair, arising from breach of the Building Regulations. However, it may still be an open question as to whether a cause of action would lie in negligence if a local authority passed plans or inspected negligently. Some caution must be exercised in relying on pre-*Murphy* decisions but for some assistance in this area some cases are relevant.

Local authorities may be under a duty to take reasonable care in deciding whether plans required by Building Regulations were defective, at least insofar as inspection is necessary thereafter, such as a plan saying 'Foundations – to approval according to site conditions': *Dennis* v. *Charnwood Borough Council* (1983); *Lyons* v. *F. W. Booth (Contractors) and Maidstone Borough Council* (1982). This duty may extend to a local authority's failure to insist on details of steelwork and calculations being provided: *Cynat Products Limited* v. *Landbuild (Investments and Property) Limited and Others* (1984), subject to the principles set out in *Peabody*.

If there is a duty, it is clear that the duty is not owed by the building inspectors themselves but by the local authority: *Worlock* v. *Saws and Rushmoor Borough Council* (1982). In *Haig* v. *London Borough of Hillingdon* (1980), there had been a failure by the local authority to inspect building works in circumstances where a builder had omitted an RSJ and used instead two softwood joists strapped together. The court considered the practice of the local authority as to inspection and found it wanting; the Official Referee also considered that the claim against the local authority was not defeated by reason of there having been a reasonable opportunity for intermediate inspection which would have disclosed the defect, namely, a survey by the purchaser of the lease: the judge had doubted whether such a survey would have involved inspecting the particular failure that occurred here.

4.3.5   Health and safety

The Health and Safety at Work Act 1974, and regulations made under it, have provided a large part of the modern framework for health and safety on construction projects. Designers tend to assume that such matters are only the responsibility of the employer and the contractor. That is an erroneous assumption. For example, designers have duties under sections 2 and 3 of the Act. Section 3 requires that employers and the self-employed conduct their undertakings in a way such as to ensure that persons *not in their employment* are not exposed to risks to their health and safety.

The European Union is beginning to move into this area of construction operations. For example, Council Directive 92/57/EC of 24 June 1992 deals with 'the implementation of minimum safety and health requirements at temporary or mobile construction sites'. The Directive requires member states to implement laws and regulations to comply with the Directive by 31 December 1993. In order to comply with the UK's obligations under the Treaty of Rome by implementing the Directive, the Health and Safety Commission have published 'Proposals for Construction (Design and Management) Regulations and Approved Code of Practice' which invited comments by 29 January 1993. The final version of the new regulations had not been published in time for the Fourth Edition of this book; it follows that the details now set out are by reference to draft proposals and the Regulations when implemented must be studied for their exact words and effect. However, their effect is so important that it is felt appropriate to deal with them before they have become law.

The draft Construction (Design and Management) Regulations, which will be made under delegated power created by the Health and Safety at Work Act, suggest the following in relation to designers:

'*Requirements on Designer*
10.(1)   Any employer or self-employed person who prepares the design of a structure or part of a structure shall

   (a)   ensure, so far as is reasonably practicable that the design he prepares is such that, if the structure conforms to the design, persons at work who are building, maintaining (including re-pointing, redecorating or cleaning) or repairing the structure will not be exposed to risks to their health and safety;
   (b)   ensure, so far as is reasonably practicable that the design includes adequate information about any aspect of the design or materials (including articles and substances) which might affect the health and safety of any contractor or any other person carrying out construction work on that structure:
   (c)   co-operate with the planning supervisor so far as is necessary to enable each of them to comply with their duties under the relevant statutory provisions.

   (2)   For the purposes of this Regulation 'design' includes design details, specification, bill of quantities (including specification of articles and substances) and documents on which any person is intended to rely when submitting a tender, and 'designer' shall be construed accordingly.'

In that extract, it should be noted that, under these draft regulations, every client has to appoint a planning supervisor, separately on each project, who is 'a competent person (who shall be appointed from among the employers and self-employed persons who are responsible to the client for the design of the project) . . . .' (draft Regulation 4.(1)(a)). It should also be noted that 'structure' is also defined to include the normal range of building, civil engineering projects and large manufacturing plants but also temporary works, such as scaffolding and falsework (draft Regulation 2.(1)). Amongst the matters that have to notified to the Health and Safety Executive on every project are the name and address of the planning supervisor and a declaration by him that he has been so appointed (draft Schedule under Regulation 5(3)).

The draft Regulations are accompanied by a draft Code of Practice. This Code contains guidance on the duties of designers, preparation of the design, design information, co-operation with the planning supervisor and limitations on the designer's duty. Every designer should read this draft Code and apply it in practice. When they are brought into force, breach of the Code will be *prima facie* evidence of a breach of the Regulations. The thrust of the draft Code is to make risk assessment of health and safety issues a central part of the design function when decisions are being taken about fitness for purpose or aesthetics or other developments in the design. This assessment goes to the construction phase as well as after completion on maintenance and repair, including safe means of access. It also goes to 'substances and equipment'. There is an obligation to communicate with and discuss various matters with the 'planning supervisor'.

The Code indicates that the Regulations will have 'no formal effect' in relation to feasibility studies unless and until 'a project is confirmed', at which time the designer will have to see that his design complies with the draft Regulations (Code of Practice, Paragraph 10.12).

4.3.6   Contractual provisions

The designer can also incur liability in respect of breach of the Building Regulations to the contractor; for example, under clause 6.1.1 of the 1980 JCT Contract, clause 26(3) of the ICE Conditions of Contract (6th Edition), and the 1984 edition of the ACA Form of Building Agreement 1982, the contractor undertakes to comply with statutes which includes the Building Regulations.

Clause 6.1.1 of JCT 80 provides:

'Subject to clause 6.1.5 the Contractor shall comply with, and give all notices required by, any Act of Parliament, any instrument rule or order made under any Act of Parliament, or any regulation or byelaw of any local authority or of any statutory undertaker which has any jurisdiction with regard to the Works or with whose systems the same are or will be connected (all requirements to be so complied with being referred to in the Conditions as "the Statutory Requirements").'

Clause 26(3) of the ICE Conditions provides:

'The Contractor shall ascertain and conform in all respects with the provisions of any general or local Act of Parliament and the Regulations and Bye-laws of any local or other statutory authority which may be applicable to the Works and with such rules and regulations of public bodies and companies as aforesaid and shall keep the Employer indemnified against all penalties and liability of every kind for breach of any such Act Regulation or Bye-law. Provided always that:

(a)   the Contractor shall not be required to indemnify the Employer against the consequences of any such breach which is the unavoidable result of complying with the Contract or instructions of the Engineer;

(b)   if the Contract or instructions of the Engineer shall at any time be found not to be in conformity with any such Act Regulation or Bye-law the Engineer shall issue such instructions including the ordering of a variation under Clause 51 as may be necessary to ensure conformity with such Act Regulation or Bye-law;

(c)   the Contractor shall not be responsible for obtaining any planning permission which may be necessary in respect of the Permanent Works or any Temporary Works specified or designed by the Engineer and the Employer hereby warrants that all the said permissions have been or will in due time be obtained.'

Clause 1.7 of the 1984 edition of the ACA contract provides:

'Unless the Architect instructs the Contractor to the contrary, the Contractor . . . shall fully comply with the provisions of the Statutory Requirements. Subject to clause 1.6, the Contractor shall indemnify the Employer against all damage, loss and/or expense which may be incurred by the Employer in respect of any breach by the Contractor of this clause 1.7. . .'

Clause 1.6 provides for any discrepancies between the contract documents and the statutory requirements to be dealt with by way of an architect's instruction.

The contractor will incur liability to the employer for any breach of these obligations subject only to the exception in the JCT contract at clause 6.1.5 (which provides that the contractor shall not be so liable where and to the extent that the contractor has carried out the works in accordance with the contract) and the ICE Conditions at clause 26(3)(a), (b) and (c) above.

The designer may render himself liable to the contractor in tort where the design is in breach of the law; this arises because of the custom in the construction industry that the designer is responsible for seeing that the work complies with the law: *Townsend Limited* v. *Cinema News* (1959). However, a contractor will not escape liability for breach of Building Regulations even where he follows the designer's design to the letter: *Street* v. *Sibbabridge* (1980).

Early on a spring morning in 1968, there was progressive collapse of part of a block of flats known as Ronan Point. The collapse was triggered by a gas explosion in a flat on the eighteenth floor of a 22 storey block of flats. The explosion blew out the non-loadbearing walls of the kitchen and living room of the flat and the external loadbearing flank wall of the living room and bedroom. This had the effect of removing the support for the floor slabs of the flat above, which collapsed, and subsequently there was a progressive collapse of all the floors and walls of the corner of the block down to the level of the podium on which the block was built. The Court of Appeal had to consider in due course the effect of the design and build contract that the contractor had with the local authority for the design and erection of the flats: *London Borough of Newham* v. *Taylor Woodrow Anglian Limited* (1981). The form of building contract was a modified JCT Standard Form (1963 Edition). Condition 4(1) of the contract, which was unamended from the JCT Standard Form, provided an obligation on

Taylor Woodrow to comply with the by-laws. Those by-laws included, in particular, by-law 21 which provided:

> 'The load bearing structure of a building above foundations shall be capable of faithfully sustaining and transmitting the dead load and imposed loads and the horizontal and inclined forces to which it may be subjected without exceeding the appropriate limits and stresses for the materials of which it is constructed and without undue deflection.'

The court held that this by-law meant more than simply getting the arithmetic right; Taylor Woodrow were found to have failed to comply with the by-law. On the other hand, the Court of Appeal could find no sufficient reason to disagree with the trial judge in his finding that Taylor Woodrow, through their designers, had not been negligent. Indeed, the trial judge had found that the consulting structural engineers had been both competent and conscientious.

4.4   Examination of the site above and below the ground

It is hard to imagine that a designer would design a project without visiting the site; this examination will probably fall into two parts.

Firstly, the designer will look for all the things that are readily apparent on the site which may affect his design; he will be able to see whether there are buildings adjacent to the site that give rise to problems relating to party walls or rights of light. There may be footpaths which would cause the designer to make enquiries as to the possibility of the existence of rights of way. It is also essential to know the exact area of the site and the location of all the boundaries to some degree of accuracy and this may itself require a survey to be carried out to produce a plan and a grid of levels of the site. It probably will not assist the designer to say the he relied on information produced by the Ordnance Survey even though this is a common practice amongst designers: *Columbus* v. *Clowes* (1903); or that he relied on information provided by the employer or his agent: *Moneypenny* v. *Hartland* (1826).

Secondly, the designer will need to ascertain the nature and load bearing capacity of the soil underneath ground level. He will not be able to do so by visual inspection alone. It may be that the designer is familiar with the character and nature of the soil in that particular location and it is not, therefore, necessarily negligent to fail to take bore holes or excavate to trial pits. Both the ACE and RIBA conditions of engagement refer to soil 'investigations' and it is the usual practice nowadays for a company specialising in soil mechanics to take cores, by drilling, and to produce from the cores a section drawing showing the strata at various depths and to test the cores in order to produce the information that engineers need in order to determine the appropriate foundations for the site. That this is the usual way to proceed is shown by expert evidence given to and accepted by the court in the *Eames* case:

> 'I consider it normal practice for an architect to draw his client's attention to the need for ground conditions to be investigated. Also, that the client be advised of the possible need to carry out a detailed site investigation, if the architect was uncertain in any way of the type and bearing capacity of the

ground': *Eames London Estates* v. *North Hertfordshire District Council and Others* (1980).

It will not assist the designer in a claim brought against him that he agreed the bearing capacity of the ground with the local authority's building inspector or district surveyor, at least where no soil investigation has been carried out: again in the *Eames* case, a designer agreed with the local authority's building inspector that three quarters of a ton per square foot bearing capacity was the load that the local authority wanted for this particular site. The whole of the site of the building was on made-up ground and in part of the site there had been an old railway embankment, which was well consolidated being more than 100 years old. The designer did not obtain boreholes or advise that boreholes should be taken or that specialist engineering advice be obtained. Although the site was filled, the 25 inch Ordnance Survey map showed that a railway crossed only part of the site. Evidence was given at the trial that a proper investigation would have indicated that simple shallow foundations would be bound to lead to serious, uneven and continuing settlement. It was held that the designer could not shed his responsibility by ascertaining what the local authority would accept; specifying three quarters of a ton per square foot indicated that he appreciated the inferior nature of the ground and he was put on inquiry that further investigation or specialist design was required. The designer was held to have been negligent.

A designer who accepts the results of borings taken by someone engaged by his employer previously will not necessarily escape liability if his design is inadequate but based on those borings: *Moneypenny* v. *Hartland* (1826).

Sometimes, the alternative foundation designs that may be available carry with them different cost implications and different risks. It is usually, but not always, the case that the more expensive the design the less the risk. This is a matter of designer's skill and judgment in providing the most economical safe solution for his employer. Where there are these alternative approaches, then the designer would be well advised to discuss them with the employer so that he is in a position to understand and to make any commercial decisions that should be made in the light of the risks that have been ascertained. The responsibility should be on the employer; the designer makes these decisions for the employer at his peril. A designer designing a cheaper method of construction involving risk, without discussing the alternative of a more expensive safe scheme, will be liable in negligence if the design fails: *City of Brantford* v. *Kemp and Wallace-Carruthers & Associates Limited* (1960), Canada. Furthermore, structural engineers engaged by an architect who warned the architect of the need for further soil reports and the risk of proceeding without such reports, were held liable in negligence to the employer for failing to give that warning to the employer, notwithstanding the fact that there was no contract between the engineer and the employer: *District of Surrey* v. *Carroll-Hatch & Associates* (1979), Canada.

Does the designer have to look beyond his employer's land when he is examining the site before carrying out his design? Does he have to look at and investigate neighbouring land? This point arose in the *Batty* case (since overruled but not, it is submitted, on the following points); the developer and the builder had inspected the site but they had not inspected adjoining land, or land on the other side of the valley, where there were signs that a detailed inspection by experts might have revealed the possibility of a landslip on the site. Although the case is relevant to a builder's duty when examining site before building on it, certain conclusions can be drawn in respect of designer's responsibility. The court held that the builder's duty to examine the land before building on it was to be determined by reference to what a careful and competent builder would have done in the same circumstances.

A designer's duty is similar: *Bolam* v. *Friern Hospital Management Committee* (1957). The court also held that the builder's duty was not limited to defects that could be observed on the land owned by the builder in circumstances where a careful and competent builder would have observed defects on adjoining land or where he would not have built until there had been a further site investigation or an expert's report on the condition of the subsoil. Designers should, therefore, ensure that they not only examine the site but also look for problems on neighbouring land and obtain a soil investigation or an expert's report in circumstances where a competent designer would do so.

The designer should also consider the effect of trees on the site; it has been published knowledge since about 1971 that the felling of trees, for the purposes of a development, can result in substantial heave of clay subsoil. This is because the trees, before they were felled, absorbed moisture from the clay, which moisture is taken up again by the soil when the trees have gone. This issue arose in *Balcomb and Another* v. *Wards Construction (Medway) Limited and Others* (1980), where an engineer who failed to make enquiries as to whether there had been trees on the site was held liable to his client, the builder, in contract for failing to exercise professional skill and in tort for breach of duty of care; the engineer was also found liable to the owners of the house in tort, although this part of the decision may not have survived the overruling of *Anns* by *Murphy*. It was said in that case:

'I find the conclusion inescapable that in 1971, a competent engineer encountering London clay, as in this case, would have made enquiries whether there had been trees on the site and, finding that there had been, would have caused moisture content and plastic limit tests to be carried out. Had that course been taken it is not disputed, and there can be no doubt that [the designer] would have advised, that the proposed foundations were inadequate.'

In *Acrecrest Limited* v. *W.S. Hattrell & Partners and Another* (1983) owners of flats, where there had been structural movement, brought an action against the architect for negligence and against the local authority for negligent inspection. There had been heave of the clay subsoil following the removal of trees. It was held that the primary responsibility lay with the architect but that the local authority should contribute 25%. Although this case has now been overruled by the House of Lords, it will remain a useful indicator as to the court's approach to apportionment of damages between a number of parties, each of whom has been held liable to the injured party.

4.5   Public and private rights

It is the designer's duty to find out from the employer whether there are any restrictions on the use to which his site may be put. This could arise, for example, by way of a restrictive covenant in the sale of the land to the employer which could involve a limitation as to the type of building that could be erected and the nature of the materials that may be used in its construction. There may be easements affecting the land, such as the right of adjoining owners to carry wires over the land or drainage or other services underneath the land. It is for this reason that the designer should specifically ask the employer to tell him of any such restrictions or easements. Additionally, the designer should, when examining the site, carefully have regard to any evidence of such rights that are apparent on visual inspection. His design must take such matters into account.

A question as to the rights of light of adjoining owners may also arise and it is essential that the designer should not design in such a way that those rights are affected because by so doing he will put the employer at risk of an action by the adjoining owner which may be an action for damages or an action for a mandatory injunction requiring the employer to pull down that part of the building that infringes the rights. Infringement of such rights is, of course, a matter of expert evidence and where such evidence cannot establish on the balance of probabilities that the neighbour's rights are in fact infringed, then the designer may escape liability: *Armitage* v. *Palmer* (1960).

An action for trespass can be brought by an adjoining owner without the need to prove any damage, in other words trespass is actionable *per se*. A designer is, therefore, at risk of an action for trespass should his design necessitate a trespass. This could arise if a means of escape in case of fire from the roof of a building involves those escaping from the fire passing over an adjoining owner's roof without that owner's consent. Where a designer is in the position that his design must necessarily involve a trespass, then he should immediately draw the problem to the employer's attention so that either the design can be varied or the employer can seek the necessary consents.

The designer must comply with the building lines set down by local authorities and, in particular, the designer will be liable if he does not, by the exercise of reasonable care and diligence, prevent the encroachment of a building under construction over the street line *Siegel* v. *Swartz* (1943), Canada.

A case in relation to damage, both actual and prospective, to adjoining property by construction work provides a useful summary of both the law in relation to rights of support and the liability of designers in such circumstances: *Midland Bank plc* v. *Bardgrove Property Services Limited and Others* (1992). The Midland Bank were lessees and occupiers of premises next to land which was developed by Bardgrove Property Services Limited. Their contractors were John Willmott. Marshall Botting Associates were structural engineers retained to advise Bardgrove and/or Willmott on and design temporary works of shoring to the boundary with Midland's property. Structural Design Partnership were retained by Bardgrove to advise on and design the temporary and permanent works in connection with the excavation. The Midland asserted that the work on the adjoining site had caused damage to their property (subsidence, broken roadway and unsafe gas pipe) and this meant that they had to carry out their own works, including the construction of a sheet piled retaining wall on their own land to restore its stability. However, the sheet piling was put in to deal with future stability issues, not the previous damage. The cost was about £318,000 including professional fees.

Midland Bank brought proceedings in negligence against all the other parties. In addition, they claimed against Bardgrove and Willmott for interference with a natural right of support. At first instance Judge Thayne-Forbes QC, Official Referee (as he then was), decided that Bardgrove did not owe a duty of care because they were entitled to carry out their excavation on their own land. He decided that mere loss of stability was not sufficient to constitute the actual damage that is required to give rise to an actionable claim for wrongful interference with a natural right of support to the land. He also decided that the other defendants could not owe a wider duty than Bardgrove. As there was no special relationship and the claim was for economic loss, the claim in negligence failed.

The Court of Appeal was only concerned with Bardgrove and Willmott. They decided that the occurrence of physical damage was a necessary ingredient in the tort of interference with rights of support. The future potential damage here was insufficient for that purpose.

4.6   Plans, drawings, specifications and changes

4.6.1   *Generally*

It is a necessary part of the design process that the design is committed to paper. This is usually done by means of drawings which show the dimensions and positions of all the elements of the building in sufficient detail to enable them to be located in three dimensions and a specification which, largely, deals with the quality and type of materials and goods to be supplied. This process is often a continuous one and it is quite likely that drawings will continue to be prepared whilst the contractor is constructing the works. The drawings and specifications must take into account the other aspects of design including the examination of the site, the subsoil conditions, private and public rights, and the employer's requirements. It is usually said that the design must be comprehensive, and it should include everything necessary in order that the works may be properly completed: see, for example, *Wilkes* v. *Thingoe RDC* (1954).

A case arising out of the construction of Rhyl Hospital gives some assistance as to the amount of detail that should appear on drawings, in particular as to whether sealants used in windows should be shown. The windows were designed by a nominated sub-contractor; nominated sub-contractors usually prepare their design, submit it to the architect for approval and, once approved, the architect issues those approved drawings so that they become drawings issued under the main contract; thereby the work shown on those drawings becomes part of the main contract works. In this particular case, the window company failed to submit details of the sealants for the architect's approval; the trial judge said that the nominated sub-contractor:

'... should have submitted full particulars of their designs, including details of sealants, to [the architect] for approval. Inevitably that approval would have been of a somewhat formal character, since [the sub-contractor] and not [the architect] were the experts with regard to sealants as they were with regard to windows generally, but the effect would have been to make quite certain that the sealants become part of the contract works': *Holland Hannen and Cubitts*

(Northern) Limited v. *Welsh Health Technical Services Organisation and Others* (1981).

Although it is usual for the employer's approval of drawings to be obtained, that approval will not usually absolve the designer from liability for negligence; the employer is relying on the skill and care of the designer in a specialist field in which the employer may have no detailed knowledge whatsoever. The giving of Building Regulation approval by a local authority does not prevent the local authority from bringing proceedings against the employer, before the expiry of 12 months from the date of completion of the work, to pull down or remove the works where there is a breach of the Building Regulations. This power given to the local authority applies notwithstanding the fact that they may have approved the plans or failed to reject them within the prescribed period. It should, however, be noted that the local authority can be required to pay to the employer compensation if the local authority requires works to be altered when that local authority has previously passed the plans, or failed to reject them within the prescribed period and the work has been constructed in accordance with the deposited plans (see Building Act 1984, section 36).

It often happens that an employer puts considerable pressure on a designer to cut short the period of design in order to secure early tenders from contractors. This can result in the design not being complete in detail at the time that a contractor begins on the site. These are the circumstances in which a contractor may become delayed by lack of information, and make a claim against the employer for an extension of time for completion and the loss and expense caused by the delay to the project. These contractual remedies are to be found in the JCT forms and in the ICE Conditions of Contract. The designer should, therefore, guard against this possibility and he would be well advised to point out to his employer the difficulties of shortening the period before the contractor is appointed so that he becomes aware that any time saved may be lost later, and, in addition that he may face extensive claims from the contractor.

Where the contractor is delayed by reason of necessary instructions not being given to him in due time, and this delay results from action by the employer in, for example, changing his requirements, then the employer will not usually be able to seek to pass on to the designer the claims that he receives from the contractor for delay. However, where the delay has arisen by reason of the designer's delay then the employer may be able to recover from the designer the damages that he has to pay to the contractor in respect of that particular delay, provided there is a direct connection between the designer's default and the contractor's damages.

An example of these difficulties arose in the case of *Holland Hannen and Cubitts (Northern) Limited* v. *Welsh Health Technical Services Organisation* (1981). The contractor had been engaged to construct a hospital at Rhyl under a 1963 JCT contract. There were nominated sub-contractors for the supply and installation of window assemblies and the sub-contract was in the Green Form. The sub-contractor had also entered into the direct warranty agreement with the employer to exercise all proper skill and care in the design of the sub-contract works and the selection of materials and goods so far as such matters were designed or selected by them.

There was considerable leakage of rainwater through the window assemblies and the architects issued an instruction requiring that the windows be made weathertight before internal finishes were applied. In the event, there were very great delays on the project and very great costs were incurred. The Official Referee held that in circumstances where the project was being so delayed, the architect ought to have issued the contractor with a variation order to enable him to overcome the design defects in the sub-contract works either under clause 3(4) of the main contract or by reason of the implied obligation that the architect would do all things necessary to enable the contractor to carry out and complete the works. It also followed that the contractor should have been granted an extension of time for completion under the main contract and been paid loss and expense. Under the direct form of warranty, the employer was entitled to be reimbursed in respect of that loss and expense by the sub-contractor.

It was held that the architect had failed to act properly and was liable to the employer in both contract and tort; in this particular case, the sub-contractor indemnified the employer against the contractor's claim for loss and expense and the architect's damages were nominal. This case provides a classic example of the fact that, whilst a nominated sub-contractor may carry out design under the standard form of building contract, the architect remains responsible for that design *vis à vis* the contractor.

It sometimes happens that a employer states a cost which must not be exceeded by the designer in his design. If the designer does not produce a design capable of being constructed within the cost limit, he is not necessarily precluded from obtaining a proper fee for his services. The test will be whether the architect, having genuinely exercised reasonable skill and care, produced a design which was capable of being constructed within or approximating to the specified cost. If the employer brings evidence that the design was incapable of being so constructed within the cost, that evidence is admissible but will not be conclusive: *Nemer* v. *Whitford* (1984), South Australia Supreme Court. It is often exceedingly difficult in practice to show what the damage is that the designer's client has suffered in such circumstances: the client will usually have received value in the building works for what he has paid, and in many cases he will be unable to show that he has suffered a loss and, if he has suffered no loss, he will be unable to prove negligence. Each case of this kind has to be considered on its own particular facts.

4.6.2   Architect's Appointment

The Architect's Appointment has provisions dealing with variation in the work and the cost:

> '3.3   The architect shall not make any material alteration, addition to or omission from the approved design without the knowledge and consent of the client, except if found necessary during construction for constructional reasons in which case the architect shall inform the client without delay.
>
> 3.4   The architect will inform the client if the total authorised expenditure or the building contract period is likely to be materially varied.'

The meaning of 'material alteration' in condition 3.3 may cause difficulty in some cases; clearly some minor routine matter would not fall within the definition but where is the line to be drawn? Each case will have to be considered on its own facts and merits. The risk to the architect is that if he has no authority from the client to vary the work in a particular way, then whilst it is likely his client will have to pay the contractor for that work, the client may be able to recover the costs of that work from the architect. Clearly it is preferable for architects to err on the side of caution and keep the client informed and obtain his consent to any matter which might even arguably be a material alteration in design, time or cost.

4.6.3   SFA/92

The Standard Form of Agreement for the Appointment of an Architect (SFA/92) has different provisions to those set out above:

'1.2.4.   The Architect shall make no material alteration to or addition to or omission from the Services without the knowledge and consent of the Client except in the case of emergency when the Architect shall inform the Client without delay.

1.2.5.   The Architect shall inform the Client upon its becoming apparent that there is any incompatibility between any of the Client's Requirements; or between the Client's Requirements, the Budget and the Timetable; or the need to vary any part of them.

1.2.6.   The Architect shall inform the Client on its becoming aware that the Services and/or the fees and/or any other part of the Appointment and/or any information or approvals need to be varied. The Architect shall confirm in writing any agreement reached.'

In SFA/92, the word 'Budget', which appears above, is defined as 'the sum the client proposes to spend on the Project inclusive of professional fees and expenses, disbursements, statutory charges and the Construction Budget but excluding site acquisition costs, client's legal and in-house expenses and any VAT thereon'. 'Timetable' is defined as the timetable for completion of the architect's services. If those services include administering the building contract, the architect under this agreement has a clear duty to the client to keep him informed as to time and budget. This is a more precise and detailed obligation than that under the Architect's Appointment.

4.6.4   Life expectancy and codes of practice

The issue as to recommending particular materials and warning of life expectancy arose in the case of *Imperial College of Science and Technology* v. *Norman and Dawbarn* (1986). The defendants were architects of a 12-storey block at Imperial College, London. The block was clad with glazed ceramic tiles of Swedish manufacture, obtained through an English supplier. Some 80 tiles fell from the building in October 1977, and an investigation revealed the need for substantial remedial work. Although the architects were found negligent in relation to lack of supervision, the design aspects of this case are of great interest. Expert evidence was given to, and accepted by, the court that the primary causes of failure of the tiling were the entry of excessive water between the tiles and the substrate, differential thermal and moisture movements, inadequate key between concrete and render, and excessive overall thickness of bed and render, setting up shear stresses on interfaces. The judge came to a clear view on the expert evidence that the avoiding of excessive water penetration was paramount and he said that:

'... the criticisms that are made of the [architects] in regard to design and supervision in this respect relate principally to the inadequacy of the weathering strips immediately beneath the cills at the top of the tiling in each panel and the failure to require waterproof grout.'

Later in his judgment, he said:

'Manful efforts have been made to explain to me that the difficulties originated because the architects did not pay sufficient attention to the relationship between the tiling, which necessitated precision, and the concrete frame, which was not capable of similar precision, it may be so. Nonetheless the evidence appears equally likely to indicate that the fault lies not in the inadequacy of the design or in the architect's periodical supervision but rather in the inability of the operatives to execute the design with the care and skill that the architects reasonably anticipated. And so however this matter is put, I reach the conclusion that the negligence of the architects does not extend beyond:

(a) the failure to take reasonable steps to protect adequately against excessive water penetration, and
(b) permitting bad workmanship of the tilers to remain uncorrected whereby the effect of water penetration exacerbated what, in the event, was a dangerous situation.'

It is clear that in cases of professional negligence in the building and civil engineering industry, the court will put great weight upon relevant codes of practice and indeed, the knowledge generally available to the profession (at the time of the design). An example of this arose in *Kalizewska* v. *John Clague & Partners* (1984). The case concerned the construction of a bungalow on an orchard site from which trees had to be grubbed up in order for the bungalow to be built. The defendant architect did not consider the removal of the trees to be a potential hazard and gave no advice or warning to the plaintiff about the risk of settlement and heave. The design of the foundations also failed to comply with the then Building Regulations and failed to meet the standard set generally by the then current British Standard codes of practice. Expert evidence was given to the court as to the breaches by the actual design of the Building Regulations and the current code of practice CP 101:1963. The latter warned:

'The depth to which foundations should be carried depended, *inter alia*, in the case of clay soils on penetration below the zone where shrinkage and swelling due to seasonal weather changes and due to trees and shrubs, are likely to cause appreciable movement.'

The judge, having found that the defendant's design did not comply with the code of practice said:

> 'I am sure the truth simply was that the defendant did not pay any or sufficient regard to the trees on this particular site. He said as much in the course of his evidence: "I did not think that the trees were a problem, that is why I did not take them seriously. I do not think I considered the trees large enough to be of any concern." He was patently in error; this had nothing to do with local practice. If, which I doubt, he made any allowance for the trees as opposed to the sloping site, either in going deeper than usual or in using reinforcement, there was no attempt to deal with the problem in a methodical way and to bring to his aid the current knowledge available to him. In using his judgment he was, as Dr Weeks [the plaintiff's expert] so neatly said, acting by guess and by God. This was not good enough for this site, as he should have been aware, and his design inevitably failed.'

4.7 Materials

In a building contract, there will usually be an implied warranty on the part of the contractors that materials supplied by them for use in the work will be reasonably fit for their purpose and of good quality: *Young and Marten Limited* v. *McManus Childs* (1969). However, where the building owner relies on his own judgment rather than that of the contractor, the warranty as to fitness for purpose will not be implied and the contractor will have no responsibility to supply materials that are fit for their purpose. In such circumstances, the warranty of quality will still usually be implied. A designer who selects materials and specifies them, so that the contractor has no choice as to what materials to buy, will remove the employer's cause of action against the contractor in respect of an implied warranty for fitness for purpose. The employer can still usually rely on the implied warranty as to good quality, at least in cases where the defect complained of is one of quality rather than fitness for purpose.

However, circumstances can arise where the implied warranty as to fitness and the implied warranty as to quality are both excluded. In *Gloucester County Council* v. *Richardson* (1968), Richardson had a main contract in the 1939 RIBA Form of Building Contract, 1957 Revision. There was a prime cost sum for concrete columns to be supplied by a nominated supplier. Richardson was to erect the columns. There was no right of reasonable objection to the nomination in the contract in this respect. Further, there was no right to make reasonable objection on grounds that the supplier would not indemnify Richardson in respect of his main contract obligations in respect of the columns. The architect instructed Richardson to place an order with a supplier whose standard terms of trade restricted their liability for defects. On those facts, the House of Lords held that neither the warranty of fitness nor the warranty of quality should be implied.

The designer cannot get round this problem by specifying a particular material and then adding words such as 'or other approved' because it has been held that such words do not give the contractor a choice but merely permit the designer to specify some other material: *Leedsford Limited* v. *Bradford Corporation* (1956). The designer should be aware of the effect that his specification of particular materials will have on the contractual relationship between the employer and the contractor.

Recent years have seen designers adopting a great many materials for use in construction that have proved, with the benefit of hindsight, to have properties that were inadequate for the task. Designers are under the same duty in selecting materials as they generally are in relation to design and they will incur liability to their client if they select materials without reasonable skill and care.

Designers should make their own enquiries as to the suitability of materials or products and should not rely on manufacturers' literature or recommendations. If they do not do so, they risk being in breach of duty. In the case of *Sealand of the Pacific* v. *Robert C. McHaffie Limited* (1974), Canada, Robert McHaffie advised the use of a material to produce lightweight concrete; the material was not suitable. The court held McHaffie's company liable on the basis that they should not have relied on the manufacturers and should have made their own enquiry and examination.

In *Richard Roberts Holdings Limited* v. *Douglas Smith Stimson Partnership and Others* (1988), RRH claimed damages against the architect for breach of contract and negligence in recommending or permitting a method of lining an effluent cooling tank, which had been designed and supplied by Erosion and Corrosion Control Limited. ECC were engaged direct by RRH. The architects, who charged no fee for this part of their work, asserted that they had no legal responsibility in relation to the lining of the tank. RRH, who knew that the architects had no knowledge of linings, had themselves sought independent advice from the Wool Industries Research Association (WIRA) and the Cement & Concrete Association (C&CA). The architects said they were acting informally in seeking quotations for the lining in order to be helpful, not as experts or in a professional capacity. The architects were said by RRH to have been architects for the whole dyeworks project and if they had wanted to limit their duties in the way they now asserted, they should have done so expressly, which they did not. Judge John Newey QC, Official Referee, found that the architects were responsible for the design of the whole dyeworks and the lining, which was an inherent part of the tanks that had been designed by the architects. He also found that they should have made their own investigations as to possible alternatives for the lining and cost (in the context of effectiveness, cost and expected life) and put proposals to RRH. The architects did not, but should have, sought help from other architects, and from the WIRA and the C&CA. Indeed, the judge found that when they received ECC's quotation, which was suspiciously cheap, it was not properly considered; no alarm bells rang as they should have done and the architects merely passed on the quotation to RRH without any warning. The architects were found to be in breach of contract and of their duty in tort.

The case of *Greater London Council* v. *Ryarsh Brick Co. and Others* (1985) is a salutary lesson for architects relying on brochures. The case arose out of the construction of boundary walls and stores on the GLC estate at Thamesmead. Some of the walls collapsed and some were demolished. The GLC sued Ryarsh, the manufacturers of the calcium silicate bricks, for breach of warranty and negligent mis-statement and also the main contractor for breach of contract. The essence of the GLC's complaint was that they had specified the bricks to be supplied by Ryarsh after their architect had read the Ryarsh brochure and been in contact with them. The bricks would not adhere properly to the mortar. The evidence in the case was that, at a meeting between Ryarsh's representative and the GLC architect, Ryarsh learned of the intended use of these bricks to build walls and stores, but not about the proposed thickness of the structure nor any other information in relation to the design. Ryarsh did not expect any problems with regard to adhesion. The judge was able to conclude from this that no express warranty or representation as to adhesion of the bricks had ever been given to the GLC and on that basis, he was able to dismiss the GLC's claim against the manufacturer.

In *Hill Samuel* v. *Frederick Brand and Another* (1993), a dispute concerning glass reinforced cement ('grc') cladding panels, a decision had to be made as to where liability should fall in circumstances where the architect had chosen grc panels but the panels were designed by an engineer. It was held that the architect owed a duty to the original building owners to exercise reasonable skill and care in recommending the use of grc panels, in selecting the consultant to design them and in carrying out any other duties in relation thereto. They were not relieved from liability by the fact that they had been relieved from responsibility for work undertaken by consultants under their conditions of engagement. It was also held that if an architect chooses properly a specialist designer, he does not owe a further duty to conduct independent research as to the design produced beyond what would be done by an ordinary competent architect. As to the engineer, the court found that if he undertakes to check 'the structural performance of proprietary cladding as specified by the architect', he must exercise 'the skill and care to be expected of an ordinarily competent engineer to review or carry out such calculations, and to review or procure such testing, as would be necessary to satisfy such an engineer, exercising such degree of care and skill, that the panels would over their expected projected life safely withstand the stresses and loads that such an engineer would think it reasonable to assume might be imposed on them'.

See also 'Novel and risky designs' below at 4.8.

4.8 Novel and risky designs

Where an ordinary and routine piece of design fails in practice, this may provide evidence of the designer's negligence, although it will in practice usually be necessary to call expert evidence. What is the position where a designer is operating at the frontiers of knowledge where there is no fund of knowledge or codes of practice upon which he can rely?

There is a very old case which indicates that failure by a designer to succeed with a new method, of which he had professed no expertise, was not negligence: *Turner* v. *Garland and Christopher* (1853), *Hudson's Building Contracts*, 4th Edition, Volume 2, page 1.

A designer was employed to prepare plans and superintend the erection of model lodging houses for an employer who instructed him to put in a new patent concrete roofing, which was much cheaper than lead or slate. The concrete roofing proved a failure and had to be removed and replaced. The employer brought an action for negligence against the designer. The judge told the jury that although failure in an ordinary building was evidence of want of competent skill, yet if out of the ordinary course a designer is employed in some novel thing in which he has no experience and which has not the test of experience, failure may be consistent with skill.

That case was decided well over 100 years ago and conditions in the construction industry and the law have changed out of all recognition since then. It is probable that the result of that case would be different if it were to be heard today. This aspect of design was touched upon in the case of *IBA* v. *EMI and BICC*. In that case a 1250 foot high television mast collapsed, and it was accepted that the design of such a cylindrical mast was 'both at and beyond the frontier of professional knowledge' at that time. It was also accepted that although subsequent to the collapse of the mast, the reasons for the collapse were known to designers, such knowledge was not available at the time of the design. It was therefore agreed that it could not have been negligent to design the mast without having regard to the factors that did cause the collapse. One of these factors was asymmetric loading caused by ice on the stays. It had been assumed in the design that such excessive deposits of ice would crack and fall away in fluctuating winds. Viscount Dilhorne said of that assumption, in his judgment in the House of Lords:

'Was it right to make such an assumption with regard to a design which was at and beyond the frontiers of professional knowledge? I see no justification for doing so. BICC's experience with lattice masts, where vortex shedding was no problem, may have led them to believe that ice would be shaken off the stay ropes in strong winds but when they knew that the critical wind speeds were so low, they should surely have considered whether at such wind speeds the ice would crack and fall from the stays. No consideration was, it appears, given to asymmetric icing on the stays then I am at a loss to understand why it would have been assumed that the ice loading would be symmetric; [the designer] was asked in cross-examination whether it was not obvious that there might be additive stresses caused by vortex shedding and ice loading. He said it was not obvious because it had never been considered.'

Lord Edmund-Davies said in the same case:

'What is embraced by the duty to exercise reasonable care must always depend on the circumstances of each case. They may call for particular precautions: *Readhead* v. *Midland Railway Co.* (1869). The graver the foreseeable consequences of failure to take care, the greater the necessity for special circumspection: *Paris* v. *Stepney Borough Council* (1951). Those who engage in operations inherently dangerous must take precautions which are not required of persons engaged in the ordinary routine of daily life: *Glasgow Corporation* v. *Muir* (1943). The project may be alluring. But the risks of injury to those engaged in it, or to others, or to both, may be so manifest and substantial and their elimination may be so difficult to ensure with reasonable certainty that the only proper course is to abandon the project altogether. Learned Counsel for BICC appeared to regard such a defeatist outcome as unthinkable. Yet circumstances can and have at times arisen in which it is plain common-sense and any other decision foolhardy. The law requires even pioneers to be prudent.'

It is clear that the judges in this case did not regard the fact that there was no precedent for a design of such a tall cylindrical mast as being any reason for excusing the designers when the mast collapsed. Indeed, the court took the view that the designer needs to take added precautions in order to discharge his duty of reasonable skill and care in the circumstances of a novel design.

4.9   Employer's interference in the design

It often happens that the employer becomes increasingly concerned during the construction of a project with its cost. It is usual nowadays for building and civil engineering contracts to be let on the basis that the contractor is entitled to recover the increased cost of materials and labour, known in the trade as fluctuations. As a result the contract price can escalate over a two or three year contract period. The employer may find that the project may cease to be financially viable if the costs continue to escalate. In order to try to prevent the project losing its viability, the employer may request or even insist on the designer reducing the quality of the works by both omissions and variations.

Where these changes are likely to lead to a job that is unsatisfactory, then the designer's duty is to tell the employer in clear language of the likely outcome of his instructions. That warning by the designer may be sufficient to discharge him from further liability. However, where the employer insists upon changes that would result in a defective construction or a breach of the law, for example of the Building Regulations, then the position is much more difficult. On the one hand, the designer is obliged to have regard to his employer's wishes and on the other hand he has a duty to use reasonable skill and care, probably to produce a design that is reasonably fit for any purpose made known to him, and to comply with the general law. It may well be that, if the designer cannot discharge his duty to use reasonable skill and care by giving a warning that carrying out the employer's wishes would produce a defective building in breach of the obligations that he has undertaken or in breach of statutory requirements, the designer may have no alternative but to resign. Such a course of action should not be undertaken lightly because of the consequences that can flow from the employer treating that resignation as a repudiation of the contract. Where a serious matter of this sort arises, a designer would be well advised to seek legal advice.

4.10   Revision of design during construction

A designer's duty to see that his design will work does not end when he has completed his design. In *Brickfield Properties* v. *Newton* (1971), it was said:

> 'The [designer] is under a continuing duty to check that his design will work in practice and to correct any errors which may emerge. It savours of the ridiculous for the architect to be able to say, as it was here suggested that he could say, "true my design was faulty, but of course I saw to it that the contractor followed it faithfully" and be enabled on that ground to succeed in the action.'

The continuing duty probably extends both as to the designer's particular design and to any matters which become known to the construction industry in general. An example of this was a commonly used brickwork detail where brick slips were stuck to the face of concrete slabs in order to give the appearance that brickwork was continuous above and below a concrete floor slab. It was in the late 1960s that journals within the industry began to record failures of this detail and suggest means of overcoming it by the introduction of movement joints. Although it may not have been negligence to specify brick slips without a movement joint prior to the knowledge becoming generally available to the industry, it would be negligent to permit construction to proceed on the basis of such a detail in circumstances where the designer had discovered or ought to have discovered after design, but before construction, that the detail would be likely to fail. The problem should be immediately drawn to the employer's attention together with proposals for overcoming the difficulty.

The decision in *Brickfield* was followed in *Equitable Debenture Assets Corporation Limited* v. *William Moss Group Limited and Others* (1984) where Judge Newey, Official Referee, held that an architect's obligation in respect of the design was not a once and for all obligation performed when a complete set of working drawings was concluded. The architects had both the right and the duty to check their initial design as work proceeded and to correct it if it was necessary. Their obligation to design a satisfactory building ended only when the building reached practical completion. Furthermore, the judge held that the duty in negligence extended to design, supervision and inspection which like the obligations in contract continued until practical completion.

Notwithstanding what was said in that case, it is to be doubted whether the duty ceases at practical completion. For example, there are obligations on the contractor as to defects within the defects liability period under the JCT contracts and it is highly likely that any investigation of defects which become apparent during that period could extend the architect's duty to see that his design is working. In *London Borough of Merton* v. *Lowe and Pickford* (1981), the court held that the architects had a duty to undertake a proper investigation into defective ceilings at a time prior to the issue of the final certificate. The decision of Judge Stabb QC, Official Referee, was upheld by the Court of Appeal. In his judgment he had said:

'I am now satisfied that the architect's duty of design is a continuing one, and it seems to me that the subsequent discovery of a defect in the design, initially and justifiably thought to have been suitable, reactivated or revived the architects' duty in relation to design and imposed upon them the duty to take such steps as were necessary to correct the results of that initially defective design.'

Architects within local authorities are probably under an even greater duty than those in private practice in this respect. The Court of Appeal decision in *Rimmer* v. *Liverpool City Council* (1984) shows how this can arise. The original project for a block of flats in Liverpool had been designed in the council's architect's department in or about 1959 and that design had involved, originally, the installation of Georgian wired glass in the fully glazed lounge door. However, at some time prior to construction the architect in charge had altered the glass to ordinary glass, one eighth of an inch thick. Mr Rimmer had fallen through the glass panel, seriously injuring himself in 1975. Mr Rimmer had made complaints at various times during the previous year about the thinness of the glass and of the possible danger to his five year old son. It was held that the local authority, not as landlord but as their own architects and builders, owed a common law duty of care to see that Mr Rimmer was reasonably safe from personal injury caused by the glass; the court did not accept that Mr Rimmer's own knowledge of the danger could exonerate the local authority. It is therefore the case that a decision by an architect in 1959 to change the specification of the glass from Georgian wired to plain formed the first link in a chain of liability to proceedings being started in 1978 and liability being found in 1984. The decision in *Rimmer* has been followed in another case which was heard after *Murphy: Targett* v. *Torfaen Borough Council* (1991).

It often happens that a design error is not discovered until after construction has begun. In such a case, there will not only be redesign to be carried out but also additional work on site to put right the design error. Where the design error is a breach of duty by the designer, then the employer will be able to recover from the designer all those costs which flow naturally and directly from the breach of duty: *Leslie R. Fairn & Associates* v. *Colchester Developments Limited* (1975), Canada.

The continuing duty to revise design during construction arose again in *Hubert Leach Limited and Another* v. *Norman Crossley & Partners* (1984). In this Court of Appeal case, it was held that a consulting structural engineer engaged to design a car deck on a warehouse, ought to reappraise his calculations to see whether a heavier material could safely be used when the original material is found unsuitable. This case provides an interesting assessment of the differences of approach between CP 114 and CP 110 in relation to the design of the reinforced concrete car deck. At the time of the design of this project, in 1973, both codes of practice were available: CP 114 since 1957 (amended in 1965), and CP 110 since 1972. Interestingly, even on the facts of this case, it was not suggested during the trial that in 1973 the defendant's use of CP 114 in his design was in any way negligent. In any event, the Court of Appeal found that the defendant was liable, because when he learned that the original material to be used was unsuitable, he should have appreciated that a significantly heavier material would have to be used. If he had reappraised his figures in the light of this as he should have done, he would have got a different figure. By not carrying out the appraisal, he inevitably limited the plaintiffs in the type of materials they could use.

There are two further cases that should be considered in relation to this continuing duty. The first is the case arising out of the Abbeystead explosion and the second is a case arising out of the construction of buildings at the University of Glasgow.

Mr Justice Rose who heard the Abbeystead case, (*T. E. Eckersley and Others* v. *Binnie & Partners and Others* (1988)) at first instance caused enormous concern amongst the professions when he appeared to find that there was a continuing duty on an engineer after completion, to check and recheck his design. He found that the engineers had been 'to some slight degree negligent in not keeping abreast with, passing on to the [water authority] and considering, in relation to design, developing knowledge about methane between handover and 1984'.

It was in 1984 that the explosion occurred which caused death and serious injury to visitors to the pumping station on the completed project. Whilst the Court of Appeal found liability attaching to the engineer for other reasons, and they did not have to make a decision on this point, the Court of Appeal both by a majority and in the dissenting judgment, went to some lengths to say that they did not agree with the decision at first instance in this respect. Lord Justice Bingham in his dissenting judgment referred to the finding of the judge causing serious concern amongst professional indemnity underwriters and he found the whole concept of a continuing duty in these circumstances as being surprising, novel and burdensome. On the other hand he accepted that there were some examples that were persuasive where there might be a danger to life or health and where some response by a professional man might well be called for. However, he said that if any such duty was to be imposed, its nature, scope and limits required to be very cautiously defined and that the development of the law on this point, if it occurred, should be gradual and analogical.

The authorities, in relation to the continuing duty to check the design were reviewed by Judge Peter Bowsher QC, Official Referee, in *University of Glasgow* v. *W. Whitfield and John Laing Construction Limited* (1988). He referred to the *Brickfield Properties* v. *Newton* (1971) decision and also referred to *Merton* v. *Lowe and Pickford* (1981), where the Official Referee, Sir William Stabb, had said:

'... that the subsequent discovery of a defect in the design ... reactivated ... the architect's duty.'

He then went on to consider whether or not the duty extended only until practical completion of the building works. He decided that the judgments in *Equitable Debenture* and *Victoria University of Manchester* were not authorities for the proposition that the continuing duty extended only to practical completion and he found that there was no reason in principle why the duty should be so limited despite the fact that the architect's right to require work to be done altered at that point. However, on the issues in this case, it was not necessary for the court to decide for how long the duty might continue or indeed what factors might be concerned with an evaluation of that issue.

4.11   Duty to warn

4.11.1 The origins of the duty

It is the case that there is no general duty imposed by the law upon a party to a contract who is in breach of it to inform the other party of his breach. However, such a duty can arise in particular circumstances. In *Stag Line Limited* v. *Tyne Shiprepair Group Limited and Another* (1984), a ship repairer had used the wrong material in relining a tube in the other contracting party's ship. Mr Justice Staughton held that in the circumstances of this case the court would imply into the contract a term imposing a duty on the party who was in breach to inform the other party of the breach. The factors that were said to give rise to the duty in this case were that the tube was unlikely to be examined for four years, the rules of the applicable classification society had been infringed and there was a possible danger to life and to very valuable property. This duty was said to be a contractual duty. It is not difficult to see that the three reasons given in this ship repairing case could easily arise in construction and there is no difference in principle between the duties under the contract in this case and the duties of a designer under his design and inspection contract.

The issue also arose in *Equitable Debenture Assets Corporation Limited* v. *William Moss Group Limited and Others* (1984) where the judge held that Moss, who were large and experienced builders, having formed the view that part of the architect's design would not work, had a duty to immediately pass their concern to the architect and that there was, therefore, an implied term in the building contract to warn of design defects. The Official Referee in this case found that this duty was both an implied term in contract and a duty in tort. This duty arose, notwithstanding the fact that Moss had no design obligation in their building contract.

Contractors were found to have been under a duty to warn the house owner of bad house design where the designer was not retained to supervise construction: *Brunswick Construction* v. *Nowlan and Others* (1974), Canada.

4.11.2 The development of the duty

The whole area of the duty to warn has been considered in a number of later cases. For example, in *Victoria University of Manchester* v. *Hugh Wilson and Lewis Womersley and Pochin (Contractors) Limited* (1984), the same judge who heard the *Equitable Debenture* case, Judge John Newey QC, Official Referee, decided that the contractors owed a duty to warn the architects, as agents of the University, of defects in the design of the architect. The case arose out of problems with the failure of ceramic tiles to adhere to the external walls of two new complexes built for the University. The contract between the contractor and the employer was in the JCT 1963 form. The allegations in negligence had been abandoned against the contractor so the judge's finding in this case was limited to contract. He put his decision in this way:

> 'The University alleged that a duty to warn was to be implied. The contractor did not admit the allegation, but the matter was not argued at length because in *Equitable Debenture Assets Corporation Limited* v. *William Moss and Others* I had decided that such a term could be implied. My conclusion in *EDAC* was based upon *Duncan* v. *Blundel* (1820), and *Brunswick Construction Limited* v. *Nowlan* (1974), both construction cases, and on the application of *The Moorcock* (1889), *Reigate* v. *Union Manufacturing Co.* (1918) and *Liverpool City Council* v. *Irwin* (1977), which deal with implication of terms.
>
> In this case I think that a term was to be implied in each contract requiring the contractors to warn the architects as the University's agents, of defects in design, which they believed to exist. Belief that there were defects required more than mere doubt as to the correctness of the design, but less than actual knowledge of errors.'

In a medical negligence case, the duty to warn has also been considered: *Thake* v. *Maurice* (1985). The plaintiffs, Mr and Mrs Thake, decided that they should have no more children and they agreed that Mr Thake would have a vasectomy performed privately by the defendant surgeon for £20 under local anaesthetic. The operation was carried out entirely properly, but unfortunately after an initial successful period of infertility, Mr Thake became fertile again and Mrs Thake became pregnant. A child was born and they sued the surgeon for the costs of the birth and maintaining the child as being their losses arising from the unsuccessful vasectomy. They succeeded in their claim both before the judge and in the Court of Appeal. The Court of Appeal said that the surgeon was a general surgeon with his professional qualifications whose competence was not in question. On this occasion, he had failed to give his usual warning that there was a small risk of the operation failing by the tissues rejoining and restoring fertility. This constituted an inadvertent breach of duty amounting to negligence both in contract and in tort.

In *Holland Hannen and Cubitts (Northern) Limited* v. *Welsh Health Technical Services Organisation and Others* (1985) (an appeal by Alan W. Marshall and Partners arising out of this lengthy litigation) again a duty to warn was considered. The principal issue was whether or not it was the duty of the engineers to foresee and warn their clients of the visual appearance the floor of a hospital building might have when the tiles were laid on it. The Court of Appeal held that there was no such duty on the engineer in these particular circumstances to warn of the visual appearance of the floor.

In another case, where it was accepted that, as a matter of law, a duty to warn could arise, it was held that the architects were not in breach of the duty: *Imperial College of Science and Technology* v. *Norman and Dawbarn* (1986). In 1956, during the course of preparation of the design, the architects included Swedish ceramic tiles amongst many other materials for consideration for external cladding. In due course, the architects recommended the tiles. No warning was given to Imperial College that the life expectancy was less than 60 years. Evidence was given to the court that in the mid-1950s, atmospheric pollution took precedence in deciding the cladding system for a building and that the self-cleansing properties of Swedish ceramic tiles had many advantages. Evidence was accepted that by the 1960s it was thought generally that life expectancy of external ceramic tiling was between 30 and 40 years, but that it was not until 1963 that there were widespread failures of external tiling. Judge David Smout QC found:

> 'Having regard to the state of the art when the recommendation was made by Norman and Dawbarn, and as it was between then and the construction of the building and to the apparent success at that time of tall buildings so clad in other countries, I do not conclude that the architects were in error in failing to warn the client that the life of the tiling was likely to be less than 60 years, still less that they thereby fell below the standard of care of a competent practitioner. Even if a breach of duty had been established in this respect, it is difficult to understand how the damage suffered could be categorised as other than economic loss.'

4.11.3 Re-consideration of the duty

However in a more recent case in 1988, considerable doubt has been cast on the existence and/or the scope of a duty to warn: *University of Glasgow* v. *W. Whitfield and John Laing Construction Limited* (1988). In this case Judge Peter Bowsher QC, Official Referee, reviewed many of the authorities referred to above in this section, but he did so in the context of the development of the law of tort and the retrenchment that has taken place in very recent times. There were, in fact, two different categories of duty to warn considered in this case. There was the duty considered above, namely a duty on the part of the contractor, owed to the employer, to warn the employer/the employer's architect of errors in the design (the purpose of this allegation being to enable there to be an order for contribution against the contractor). Secondly, it was argued that the contractor was in breach of a duty of care to the architect to inform him of defects in the design of which he as contractor knew or ought to have known.

As to the first type of duty alleged, namely to the employer or to the architect of the employer as agent, the judge found that where there was a detailed contract as here (JCT 1963, 1971 Revision with Scottish appendix), there was no room for the implication of a duty to warn about possible defects in design: it was said that this followed from *Tai Hing Cotton Mill Limited* v. *Liu Chong Hing Bank Limited* (1986).

As to the duty being put as a duty in tort, it was said that there was a clear contractual duty governing the relationship between the parties in relation to the damage arising out of the defective building, and counsel for the contractor suggested that whilst there might conceivably be a concurrent duty in tort, it was limited to a duty of care to avoid acts or omissions which are liable to cause damage to persons or to some property other than the defective building being created. In the judge's view, that submission was well-founded on the present state of the law, and he referred in that respect to *Simaan General Contracting Co.* v. *Pilkington Glass* (1988). That finding is consistent with *D & F* and *Murphy*, which came later. It followed from this that there was no duty to warn the employer of design defects.

As to the architect's allegation that the contractor owed a duty to the architect, again, having reviewed the recent cases and also concluding that the architect was not relying on the contractor for design advice, the court came to the view that no such duty was owed. It therefore followed that the architect in this case was not entitled to any contribution whatsoever from the contractor.

The decision in the *University of Glasgow* case does therefore distinguish the decisions in *Equitable Debenture Assets Corporation* v. *William Moss* and *Victoria University of Manchester*; in view of the recent developments in tort law which were considered in the *University of Glasgow* case, it may well be that *University of Glasgow* is to be preferred to the pre-existing decisions which were made prior to the most recent developments in tort law. The judge in *University of Glasgow* said:

'The decisions in *Equitable Debenture* and *Victoria University of Manchester* could stand with more recent decisions if they were read as cases where there was a special relationship between the parties, but not otherwise, and bearing in mind the difficulties in analysing, the meaning of the words "special relationship" and "reliance" demonstrated by Robert Goff LJ in *Muirhead* v. *Industrial Tank Limited* (1986).'

Indeed, Judge Esyr Lewis QC, Official Referee, preferred the decision in *University of Glasgow* in *Chancellor, Masters and Scholars of the University of Oxford (Trading as Oxford University Press)* v. *John Stedman Design Group (A Firm) and Others* (1991). The judge said that in *Equitable Debenture*, reference had been made to *Duncan* v. *Blundell* (1820) where the following had been said:

'Where a person is employed in a work of skill, the employer buys both his labour and his judgment; he ought not to undertake the work if he cannot succeed, and he should know whether it will or not; of course it is otherwise if the party employing him choose to supersede the workman's judgment by using his own.'

Judge Lewis went on to say that the proviso in that statement was important; Oxford University Press had relied on the architects so it could not be said they had relied on the contractors. He could therefore see no basis for finding on the part of the contractor a duty, in tort, to warn of design defects, unless they might give rise to danger to the safety of persons or damage to some property other than that which was the subject of the defect. There was also a detailed building contract and he could see no basis for the implication of a term in contract either. He pointed out that it would give rise to difficulties in practice if a contractor had to warn his employer about matters of design where that employer had engaged an architect to be responsible for that design.

A potentially massive extension of the duty to warn has been overturned in the Court of Appeal: *T. E. Eckersley and Others* v. *Binnie and Partners, Edmund Nuttall Limited and the North West Water Authority* (1988). This case concerned the explosion at the Abbeystead pumping station in the spring of 1984 due to the presence of methane gas. Nuttalls were the main contractors and the judge, at first instance, decided that although they had no design obligation, had they had a proper system of testing for methane during construction, there was a possibility that they would have discovered the seepage of methane and if they had, they would have reported that to the engineer who would have redesigned the pumping chamber in such a way as to avoid the danger of methane being pushed into it, with the consequent risk of explosion. It was a tortuous route to a duty to warn. The Court of Appeal decided that the purpose of testing during construction was to ensure, for the benefit of the workforce, that the concentration of methane was such that there would be no explosion. There was nothing in the relationship between Binnie and Nuttalls to put Nuttalls on notice that testing had to be continued upon their ceasing to occupy the site. Nuttalls were never requested by Binnie to test for the safety of the permanent works and it was therefore found that there was no duty on Nuttalls as had been found by the judge at first instance.

More recently, in 1992, the case of *Lindenberg* v. *Joe Canning and Others* was heard by Judge Newey QC, the same judge who heard *Equitable Debenture* and *Victoria University of Manchester*. This case was concerned with walls shown on a drawing as non-loadbearing which turned out to be loadbearing. Damage occurred when demolition of these walls began. The judge found that the fact that the chimney breast was shown as non-loadbearing but had 9 inch brick walls ought to have caused Canning 'to have grave doubts about the plan.' He went on:

'Mr Canning should I think have proceeded with the very greatest caution. At the very least, he should have raised with [Mr Lindenberg's surveyor] doubts as to his plan and asked whether [he] was sure the 9 inch walls were not load bearing. Even if [he] had given assurances, Mr Canning would, I think, have been prudent to have put in temporary propping, but in the absence of such an assurance, he should undoubtedly have done so. Instead, without taking any precautions whatsoever, Mr Canning proceeded to demolish the walls. I think he behaved with much less care than was to be expected of the ordinary competent builder and that he therefore acted in breach of contract'.

In the course of his judgment the judge referred to *Equitable Debenture Assets Corporation* v. *William Moss* but it is apparent that he preferred (although he did not express the preference) in this case to put the point as breach of an implied term that the contractor would exercise the care to be expected of an ordinary competent builder, rather than a duty to warn.

4.11.4   The present position

The cases therefore leave uncertainty in resolving whether or not there exists a duty to warn of defective design. The following analysis is put forward very tentatively:

(1)   Where there are extensive contractual provisions (for example JCT 80), a duty to warn will be unlikely to be found.
(2)   Since *Murphy* the cases above, where the duty has been found in tort, should perhaps be treated with caution as to liability in tort because the damage may be economic loss and irrecoverable.
(3)   Some cases of this type may still arise but are perhaps more likely to be characterised as either:

(a)   breach of a duty to exercise reasonable skill and care, or
(b)   a *Hedley Byrne* case that is to say , there has been some kind of statement on which reliance has been placed.

4.12   Special skills

Where a designer holds himself out as having special skills, the question as to what is the appropriate test for negligence will arise. This has been considered in two cases, one in construction and one in medicine.

The test, approved in the House of Lords, is that set out in *Bolam* (see 3.1.1), which is the ordinary skill of an ordinary competent man exercising that particular art. In *Wimpey Construction (UK) Limited* v. *Poole* (1984), the court had to consider what the effect of that test was in circumstances where a professional man held himself out as having especially high skills and had been retained on that basis. It was held that you judge that professional man by the standards of an ordinary skilled man exercising and professing to have the special professional skill. The court rejected the view that the test should be that of a man exercising or professing to have especially high professional skills. If such a man had as a matter of fact a higher degree of knowledge of awareness and acted in a way which, in the light of that actual knowledge, produced damage which he ought reasonably to have foreseen, then he would be liable in negligence; that would be so even though the ordinary skilled man would not have had that knowledge. In *Ashcroft* v. *Mersey Regional Health Authority* (1983), a medical negligence case, it was said that the more skilled a person is, the more is the care which is to be expected of him but that that test should be applied without gloss either way.

4.13   State of the art

It will usually be the case that the courts will judge the standard against which negligence will be assessed by reference to the state of the art of that design at the time when the design was carried out. Most cases will proceed on that basis. In other words, the standards to apply to the alleged negligent design will be the professional standards of the time at which it was designed and not any later standards which may be different or higher: *Wimpey Construction (UK) Limited* v. *Poole* (1984), *Kensington and Chelsea and Westminster Area Health Authority* v. *Adams Holden & Partners and Another* (1984). This has become known as the 'state of the art defence' to a claim for professional negligence.

However, it is possible to discern three methods by which a state of the art defence might be challenged. The first is by reason of the designer's continuing duty to revise his design and check that it will work. The second is the possibility that in exceptional cases the court might take the view that the practice of the profession at the time that the design was carried out was not a rightful practice: *Sidaway* v. *Board of Governors of the Bethlem Royal Hospital and the Maudsley Hospital and Others* (see 3.1.1) The third area is where a design is novel or at the frontiers of knowledge, where the court may take the view that it would be foolhardy even to try to construct such a structure and that even pioneers must be prudent: *IBA* v. *EMI and BICC* (1980).

4.14   Cost inflation

Amongst architects and quantity surveyors it is a well-known fact that a 'fixed price' under many of the standard forms of contract may well have a different meaning to them, when compared with the meaning that might be understood by an employer not experienced in these matters. For example, under the JCT standard forms, there can be increases (and in theory decreases), in that price as a result of variations, delay and/or disruption involving loss and/or expense and fluctuations; the latter head, which is more often than not these days calculated on a NEDO formula basis, is nothing more nor less than a reflection of the fact that inflation is usually positive and not negative, and is always present, the only issue being the rate of inflation.

Whether or not an architect who fails to warn of the risks of inflation on a building contract is negligent was considered by the Court of Appeal in *Nye Saunders and Partners* v. *Alan E. Bristow* (1987). In this case, the architects as plaintiffs, started proceedings for unpaid fees amounting to £15,581.59. The defendant employer defended the claim on the basis that the architects had failed in their duty to take due care in providing a reliable approximate estimate in 1974 and that they had failed to draw the employer's attention to the fact that since inflation would increase the cost, the total cost of the project would rise to a figure beyond the amount which the employer had said was at his disposal for the purposes of the building works. In detail, the employer had told the architects that he had about £1m to spend on the work. Before the planning application had been granted, the employer asked the architect to provide a written estimate of the cost of the works; the architects brought in a quantity surveyor and thereafter they wrote to the employer setting out a schedule of costs totalling some £238,000 but they did not show any figure as to inflation, nor did they include any sum whatsoever for contingencies. After the architects had been engaged, and planning permission granted, an up-to-date estimate was provided amounting to some £440,000 which included for the first time a figure for the likely increase in costs over the estimated 18 month contract period. The employer terminated the architect's employment.

Mr Recorder Donald Keating QC, sitting as a Deputy Official Referee, dismissed the architect's claim and the Court of Appeal dismissed the architect's appeal. The Court of Appeal found that the cause of the massive increase in cost which led the employer to cancel the project was inflation, and in respect of that element of cost, he had not been warned. Further, the Court of Appeal accepted that at the time the services were performed, there was no practice accepted as proper by a reasonable body of architects that no warning as to inflation needed to be given when providing an approximate estimate of the cost of a project and that, therefore, the architects were in breach of their duty to the employer. Finally, the architect was found not to have discharged his duty by consulting a quantity surveyor and providing the quantity surveyor's estimate to the employer. Indeed, Lord Justice Stephen Brown went so far as to say that, although it may have been prudent for the architect to consult a quantity surveyor, the architect could not thereby avoid responsibility for not drawing to the attention of the employer the fact that inflation was not taken into account. It was said that that duty rested upon the architect and it could not be avoided by seeking to move the responsibility to the quantity surveyor.

The employer's argument in this case was, of course, that he would not have permitted the architect's fees to have been incurred had he had a more accurate estimate of the cost at the outset. It followed that the defence went to the whole of the architect's claim for fees and he was not entitled to any fee whatsoever. This is another aspect of the older case of *Moresk Cleaners Limited* v. *Hicks* (1966) where an architect did not avoid liability to the employer by delegating part of his design function to a sub-contractor.

A similar decision was reached in a Canadian case: *Fidias Consulting Engineering Limited* v. *Thymaras* (1985), Alberta Queen's Bench, Canada. In this case, the employer engaged Fidias to perform architectural, engineering and general professional services in connection with the renovation of the restaurant of Thymaras. Thymaras advised Fidias that the total renovation costs must not exceed $500,000. Fidias' plans produced an estimated construction cost of $896,830. It was held that the architect had a duty to design plans within the monetary limits imposed by the client and that as Fidias had failed to perform the task it had agreed to perform, it was not entitled to recover further payment for services rendered which were of no value to Thymaras.

It is the case that the Standard Form of Agreement for the Appointment of an Architect (SFA/92) contains express obligations as to keeping the client informed about such matters. An architect engaged on that form should not abandon that responsibility to a quantity surveyor.

4.15   Recommending contractors

A Canadian case in 1980 considered the liability that can arise for negligent mis-statement in making a recommendation: *Nelson Lumber Co. Limited* v. *Koch*. Here a manufacturer of prefabricated timber homes recommended a contractor to a potential home purchaser. In fact, the manufacturer knew that the contractor was an undischarged bankrupt and when the contractor did not finish the construction work, owing to financial problems, the court held that the purchaser of the prefabricated home had relied on the recommendation of the manufacturer and he was awarded damages against the manufacturer.

The point also arose in an English case in the Court of Appeal: *Valerie Pratt* v. *George J. Hill Associates* (1987). Miss Pratt suffered greatly in her attempts to build a bungalow from 1976 onwards. Her architects, the defendants in this action, had obtained tenders from builders including two who were stated by the architects to be 'very reliable'. Miss Pratt entered into a building contract with one of those recommended contractors, Swanmore Builders Limited. Swanmore failed to carry out their work properly and in due course the architect's retainer was terminated, but before it was terminated those architects had issued a certificate which Miss Pratt had paid. The contractors continued to carry out the work and were paid a further sum of money on the certificate of a new architect; however the contractor failed to complete the work and in due course was required to leave the site of the bungalow. Swanmore commenced an arbitration which ended with the removal of the arbitrator by the court on the grounds of misconduct (see *Pratt* v. *Swanmore Builders Limited* (1980)). Thereafter, Swanmore became insolvent.

Miss Pratt began these proceedings against the architect, seeking amongst other things, damages for negligence in recommending Swanmore. At first instance, the court found that the architect was in breach of duty but did not allow Miss Pratt's claims for the amount paid to Swanmore and the cost incurred in the arbitration proceedings for the reason that those sums were lost by reason of Swanmore's insolvency and that there was no duty of care on the part of the architect to protect her from that insolvency. The court said that the architects had no duty to protect her from insolvency and that she knew that small builders were financially risky. The Court of Appeal allowed Miss Pratt's appeal and her claims in those two respects on the basis that those losses arose directly from the misrepresentation negligently given by the architects and which led directly to her making a contract with highly unreliable builders. Lord Justice Parker put it this way:

'The arbitration was an inevitable result of an incompetent builder who was not prepared to pay up for the consequences of his incompetence. The arbitration inevitably resulted in the expenditure of money; costs therefore are recoverable as a head of damage. The fact that had the arbitration gone ahead and had costs been awarded, they might or would not have been recoverable owing to insolvency, is neither here nor there. With regard to the two interim payments, it appears to me, with all respect to [Counsel for the architects] who struggled manfully to make bricks without straw, that they are as plain an expense resulting from the employment of an incompetent builder as it would be possible to find.'

Failing to put work out to competitive tender can of itself lead to successful claims for professional negligence: *Hutchinson* v. *Harris* (1978).

Chapter 5

Delegation of design duties

Modern buildings are technically complex; even small commercial warehouse developments now involve so many skills that it would be unlikely to find all the necessary skills in one designer's office. At the other extreme, there is the modern hospital with its multi-storey buildings, its complex mechanical services ranging from the supply of multiple medical gases to air conditioning and air purification for its operating theatres. It is precisely because of these complexities that it has become commonplace, and necessary, for designers to pass specialist design work to those who are specialist in that particular field. A designer taking on a project impliedly warrants that he has the necessary skill and he would, of course, be in breach of his duty if he were to fail in his attempt to design something that was not within his sphere of competence. It follows that a designer could be held negligent because he failed to delegate in such circumstances. The delegation of design duties can also put the employer at risk and this area of the designer's work is a potential minefield waiting to trap the unwary.

5.1   The general issues

It is always as well to remember that, in general, a contractor on JCT 80 (unless there is performance specified work under Amendment 12) will not have any obligation in relation to design. Difficulties often arise in this area and in particular in relation to performance specifications included in bills of quantities and in relation to sub-contractors, usually nominated sub-contractors.

In *John Mowlem & Co. Limited* v. *British Insulated Callenders Pension Trust Limited and S. Jampel & Partners* (1977), it was held by Judge William Stabb QC, Official Referee, that usually work carried out under a JCT 63 contract does not include design as part of the contractor's obligation. A further and important point arose in this case. The bills of quantities contained a performance specification in relation to watertight construction in these terms: 'retaining walls forming external walls to buildings and basement slabs are to be constructed so that they are impervious to water and damp penetration, and the contractor is responsible for maintaining these in this condition.' Cracks and water penetration occurred and litigation ensued.

It was held that, insofar as the performance specification purported to impose a design liability on the contractor, it was ineffective by virtue of the provision of clause 12(1) of JCT 63 which provides that nothing contained in the contract bills shall override, modify or affect the conditions of the contract. Similar wording is used in JCT 80 and it is submitted that the result on a similar point on JCT 80 would be the same. However, the position is different in relation to performance Specified Work under JCT 80 (see 8.4).

In relation to nominated sub-contractors, an enormous number of problems abound in almost every aspect of the nominated sub-contractor system. With respect to design, the problems are substantial. Usually, there will be a direct warranty agreement in the form of NSC/W between the sub-contractor and the employer in relation to the design aspects of the nominated sub-contractor's work (see under 'Designer causes sub-contractor to design' in 5.4 below). Any nomination of a sub-contractor to a contractor which purports to include design would be likely, it is submitted, to enable the contractor to refuse the nomination (see clause 35.4.1 of JCT 80 which reads 'No person against whom the contractor makes a reasonable objection shall be a nominated sub-contractor'). Indeed, clause 35.21 of JCT 80 provides:

'Whether or not a Nominated Sub-contractor is responsible to the Employer in the terms set out in ... NSC/W the Contractor shall not be responsible to the Employer in respect of any Nominated Sub-Contract works for anything to which such terms relate. Nothing in clause 35.21 shall be construed so as to affect the obligations of the Contractor under this Contract in regard to the supply of workmanship, materials and goods.'

The effect of this clause will normally be, therefore, that the contractor has no obligation to the employer in respect of the matters in the direct warranty agreement which do, of course, include warranties as to design, selection of material and goods and the satisfaction of any performance specification in the sub-contract; however the main contractor remains liable for breaches by the sub-contractor of obligations in relation to workmanship and materials, subject to the restrictions set out in *Fairclough* v. *Rhuddlan* (1985).

All these points were considered in *John Jarvis Limited* v. *Rockdale Housing Association Limited* (1985), where there are extensive observations on the structure of JCT 80 and the main contractor's liability for nominated sub-contractor's defaults generally, and in particular in relation to design. If, however, the contractor does not take a point of reasonable objection when he receives a nomination of a sub-contractor whose tender contains design obligations or even an obligation as to the production of installation drawings, the position may be different and, in particular, it will not be open to the main contractor to argue that the nominated sub-contractor's failure to supply drawings amounted to a breach by the employer of his obligation as and when it may reasonably be necessary to supply drawings to the contractor under clause 3(4) of JCT 63: *H. Fairweather & Co. Limited* v. *London Borough of Wandsworth* (1987).

It should not be forgotten that a contract for design work may be a personal contract. The employer may have engaged that particular designer because he values his reputation and in such circumstances, unless there is express agreement, a designer is not entitled to assign any part of his duties to another designer. This situation could arise, for example, where a firm of designers has achieved such a good reputation that it can no longer cope with the volume of work which it has taken on. Delegation of some of this work to firms of designers might be considered in such circumstances. However, it should not be forgotten that there is no right to assign a personal contract. An example of this is to be found in *Southway Group Limited* v. *Esther Wolff and Morris Wolff* (1991).

However, the most usual reason for delegation is that the designer requires the benefit of specialist skills which he does not possess himself. All designers should consider carefully their terms of engagement because, in the absence of express agreement giving the designer authority to delegate, there is no implied authority that a designer can delegate any part of his duties to anyone.

In the case of *Moresk* v. *Hicks* (1966), an architect asked a sub-contractor to design the reinforced concrete frame of a building. He approved the drawings prepared by the sub-contractor, which erected the reinforced concrete frame to its own design. The design was defective in two respects: the purlins were not strong enough to support the roof, and the portal frames should have been tied together either at knee level or at ground level. The architect sought to argue that there was an implied right to delegate the duty of design. It was held that there could be no such implied term.

The judge in *Moresk* said:

'In my view if a building owner entrusts the task of designing a building to an architect he is entitled to look to that architect to see that the building is properly designed. The architect has no power whatever to delegate his duty to anybody else. Certainly not to a contractor who would in fact have an interest which was entirely opposed to that of the building owner.'

These principles were reaffirmed in *Equitable Debenture Assets Corporation Limited* v. *William Moss Group Limited and Others* (1984) and *Southern Water Authority* v. *Duvivier and Others* (1984).

Although the ACE Conditions of Engagement, the Architect's Appointment and the Standard Form of Agreement for the Appointment of an Architect (SFA/92) all contemplate delegation, which is considered below in some detail, architects and engineers should not assume that these conditions are impliedly incorporated into the terms of their engagement. Unless these standard form terms are expressly incorporated into the agreement, a court will not hold that they are impliedly incorporated: *Sidney Kaye, Eric Firmin & Partners* v. *Leon Joseph Bronesky* (1973). In other words, if a designer wishes to delegate, he must have the employer's express agreement so to do.

In practice, a designer usually delegates in one of three ways:

(1)   The designer engages a specialist designer and the designer, out of his own fees, pays the specialist.
(2)   The designer advises the employer to engage a specialist designer direct.
(3)   The designer obtains a design, usually free of charge, from a sub-contractor, who usually later becomes a nominated sub-contractor.

Each of these aspects is now considered separately on the assumption that the designer has the employer's authority to delegate.

5.2   Designer engages specialist designer direct

This is probably the least common in practice of the three methods of delegation.

There will be a chain of contracts: there will be one between the employer and the designer, and another between the designer and the specialist designer. In this way, if there is a failure in the specialist design, the employer will be able to sue the designer in contract and the designer will in turn be able to sue the specialist designer in contract. In normal circumstances therefore, neither the employer nor the designer is seriously at risk in respect of the failure in the specialist design, in the sense that both are in a position to recover their loss. This does depend on the specialist designer having sufficient funds, or professional indemnity insurance, to meet the claim made against him. It also depends on there being no break in the chain of liability such as a clause in the specialist designer's contract that seeks to exclude or limit his liability. It follows that any designer delegating on this basis should satisfy himself that the chain of liability is not broken by any of the terms of this contract with the specialist designer, and that his specialist designer has adequate professional indemnity insurance, or sufficient resources to meet any possible claim.

In such an arrangement, there is no contract between the employer and the specialist designer. It follows that any claim by the employer against the specialist designer direct would have to be in tort. Although each case would have to be viewed on its particular facts, in general, a specialist designer in such circumstances may owe a duty of care to the employer but the existence and the extent of that duty will be open to considerable argument unless it can be brought within *Hedley Byrne* principles, for example: advice and reliance. One particular duty was discussed in a Canadian case where a structural engineer had been engaged by an architect. The structural engineer, who was not a soils specialist, had recommended that further soil investigation should be carried out. The architect told the engineers that the employer would not authorise such work. The structural engineers designed the building. Differential settlement occurred. The architect was held liable in contract to the employer, and the consulting engineer was held liable in tort to the employer: *District of Surrey* v. *Church* (1977), and *District of Surrey* v. *Carroll-Hatch & Associates* (1979), Canada. In that case, it was held that the fact that the structural engineer had advised the architect of the need to carry out further investigations did not discharge him from his duty to the employer. In order to discharge his duty to the employer, he should have made certain that the employer was aware of the difficulty. It follows from this that specialist designers engaged by designers should bear in mind the need to see that any fundamental points in their design are drawn to the employer's attention direct.

On the other hand, in *Kensington and Chelsea and Westminster Area Health Authority* v. *Adams Holden & Partners and Another* (1984) it was held that an engineer discharged his duty by notifying the architects of their knowledge of unsatisfactory fixings of precast concrete mullions. This case is probably to be distinguished on the grounds that the court found that the engineer's duty would not ordinarily extend to the supervision of the fixings of mullions which in 1964–5 was an area for which the architect's profession were ordinarily responsible. Further, the law report does not make clear whether or not the engineers were in contract with the architects or with the employer.

In *Equitable Debenture Assets Corporation Limited* v. *William Moss Group Limited and Others* (1984), the defects that were complained about were in curtain walling. The architects who had been sued by the building owner had engaged curtain walling consultants themselves. Those curtain walling consultants were also in the proceedings. The design work was suspended in 1971 and not reactivated until a later date. The court found that the architect had exercised all reasonable skill and care until the date of suspension but that, when the scheme was reactivated, the architects had allowed haste to prevail over care and, in particular, they had not given the curtain walling consultant an opportunity to revise his details and specifications before seeking new tenders. It was the case that standards for curtain walling had improved between the date when the project was suspended and when it was reactivated. On those facts, the court found that the architect was liable in negligence to the building owner. As to the consultants in curtain walling, it was said that they owed such a duty both to the architects and to the building owners but on the facts of this particular case they were never given proper opportunities or facilities to provide their services efficiently; they were able to shelter behind their lack of instructions and, accordingly, were not in breach of their duties to either the architect or to the building owner.

5.3 Employer engages specialist designer direct

Here the designer recommends to the employer that specialist designers should be engaged by him. The designer will usually retain overall control of the co-ordination of the various designers, rather like the conductor of an orchestra. The legal position is, of course, different. There will be a direct contract between the employer and the specialist designer, and the employer has recourse both in contract and in tort against the specialist in respect of any defects in his design. The designer, in making such recommendations to the employer as to who should be employed, should bear in mind that the employer, who may have no knowledge in the field, will be relying on the designer's representations and skill and care in entering into such contracts on such advice. The designer should, therefore, be careful in making such recommendations because, if the specialist designer turns out to be incompetent, the designer could then be held liable on the principle of negligent mis-statement: *Hedley Byrne* v. *Heller & Partners*, (see section 2.2.2.1). An example of how this liability can be incurred arose in a Canadian case: *Nelson Lumber Co. Limited* v. *Koch* (1980).

A manufacturer of prefabricated timber homes recommended a contractor to a potential home purchaser. The manufacturer knew that the contractor was an undischarged bankrupt. The contractor did not finish the construction work, due to his financial problems. The court held that the manufacturer knew that the recommendation by them of a suitable contractor was likely to induce the purchaser to purchase one of their prefabricated homes.There was therefore a special relationship, and the purchaser had relied on the recommendation. The purchaser was awarded damages against the manufacturer.

A further case in relation to liability incurred by architects in making recommendations of contractors is *Valerie Pratt* v. *George J. Hill Associates* (1987), which is discussed at section 4.15.

The Court of Appeal have had the opportunity of considering the effect of an architect, engaged on the former RIBA Conditions of Engagement, where he passes work to engineers. In findings which are *obiter dicta*, the Court of Appeal decided that clauses 1.20, 1.22 and 1.23 of the RIBA Conditions of Engagement contemplated that, where part of the work involves specialist knowledge or skill beyond that which an architect of ordinary competence may reasonably be expected to possess, the architect is at liberty to recommend to his client that a reputable independent consultant, having the relevant specialist knowledge and skill, should be appointed by the client to perform the task. Lord Justice Slade went on to say:

'If, following such a recommendation, a consultant with these qualifications is appointed, the architect will normally carry no legal responsibility for the work to be done by the expert, which is beyond the capability of an architect of ordinary competence; in relation to the work allotted to the expert, the architect's legal responsibility will normally be confined to directing and coordinating the expert's work in the whole. However, this is subject to one important qualification. If any danger or problem arises in connection with the work allotted to the expert, of which an architect of ordinary competence reasonably ought to be aware and reasonably could be expected to warn the client, despite the employment of the expert, and despite what the expert says or does about it, it is in our judgment the duty of the architect to warn the client. In such a contingency, he is not entitled to rely blindly on the expert,with no mind of his own, on matters which must or should have been apparent to him': *Investors in Industry Commercial Properties Limited* v. *The District Council of South Bedfordshire and Others* (1985).

In *Richard Roberts Holdings Limited* v. *Douglas Smith Stimson Partnership and Others* (1988), RRH claimed damages against the architect for breach of contract and negligence in recommending or permitting a method of lining an effluent cooling tank, which had been designed and supplied by Erosion and Corrosion Control Limited. ECC were engaged direct by RRH. The architects, who charged no fee for this part of their work, asserted that they had no legal responsibility in relation to the lining of the tank. RRH, who knew that the architects had no knowledge of linings, had themselves sought independent advice from the Wool Industries Research Association (WIRA) and the Cement & Concrete Association (C&CA). The architects said they were acting informally in seeking quotations for the lining in order to be helpful, not as experts or in a professional capacity. The architects were said by RRH to have been architects for the whole dyeworks project and if they had wanted to limit their duties in the way they now asserted they should have done so expressly, which they did not. Judge John Newey QC, Official Referee, found that the architects were responsible for the design of the whole dyeworks and the lining, which was an inherent part of the tanks that had been designed by the architects. He also found that they should have made their own investigations as to possible alternatives for the lining and cost (in the context of effectiveness, cost and expected life) and put proposals to RRH. The architects did not, but should have, sought help from other architects, and from the WIRA and the C&CA. Indeed, the judge found that when they received ECC's quotation, which was suspiciously cheap, it was not properly considered; no alarm bells rang as they should have done and the architects merely passed on the quotation to RRH without any warning. The architects were found to be in breach of contract and of their duty in tort.

5.4   Designer causes sub-contractor to design

It is common practice nowadays, particularly with electrical and mechanical services, for a sub-contractor to carry out detailed specialist design and then to prepare a price for the proposed sub-contract works based on his own design. If his tender price is eventually accepted, he will become a nominated sub-contractor to a main contractor who is in contract with the employer. Without more, the employer is left in a difficult position in the event that the sub-contract design is defective. He may not be able to sue his designer if that designer has excluded liability for a sub-contractor's design in his terms of engagement. He will not be able to sue the main contractor because, since the employer has not relied on the main contractor's skill and care, the contractor will not be liable for his sub-contractor's design: *Norta Wallpapers (Ireland) Limited* v. *John Sisk (Dublin) Limited* (1977) see 4.1.4. The position may be different, and the employer may be able to sue the main contractor, where the contract incorporates a clear chain of responsibility from the sub-contractor to the contractor and the contractor to the employer.

Sometimes, the employer may be able to set up a collateral warranty, not in writing, separate from the main contract. This concept is best explained by looking at the case of *Shanklin Pier Limited* v. *Detel Products Limited* (1951).

A paint manufacturer told an employer, who was about to build a pier, that his paint was suitable for use below water level and was resistant to salt water. The employer, relying on what the manufacturer had said, specified the paint in a contract for the building of the pier. The paint failed. It was held that there was a contract directly between the employer and the manufacturer, completely separate and distinct from the building contract, and the employer was entitled to recover from the manufacturer. It was said that in consideration of the employer specifying the paint, the manufacturer undertook that the paint was suitable for the purpose required.

It would of course be entirely unsatisfactory for the employer to have to rely on such representations as being his only redress for a default in the specialist designer's obligations. On the other hand, the House of Lords appeared to extend tortious liability in this field very considerably in the case of *Junior Books Limited* v. *Veitchi Limited* (1982), although more recent cases cast very serious doubt on the general applicability of this case (see 2.2.2.4). In this Scottish case, the building owners brought an action in delict (the Scottish name for tort) against specialist flooring sub-contractors. Those sub-contractors had been engaged by a contractor and there was no contractual relationship between the building owner and the sub-contractor. The action had been brought in relation to floor cracking and in particular the remedial work costs and various items of economic and financial loss consequential on replacement, such as the cost of removal of machinery and loss of profits while the floor was being relaid. It was not alleged in the proceedings that there was a risk of any danger of injury or safety or health to people or property in the factory. The House of Lords held that there was a duty in such circumstances not only to avoid causing foreseeable harm to persons or property but also a duty to avoid causing pure economic loss consequential on defects in the work. This case has not been overruled by *D & F* or *Murphy* but is impossible to reconcile with those decisions.

It is now common in the construction industry for collateral warranties to be formalised into a written agreement between a sub-contractor and the employer. The JCT publishes a form of agreement, NSC/W, between an employer and a nominated sub-contractor, whereby the sub-contractor gives certain warranties and undertakings to the employer. The importance of this is that a contractual relationship is established directly between the employer and the sub-contractor.

Some of the warranties given by the sub-contractor are set out in clause 2 of NSC/W:

'2.1   The Sub-Contractor warrants that he has exercised and will exercise all reasonable skill and care in:

.1   the design of the Sub-Contract Works insofar as the Sub-Contract Works have been or will be designed by the Sub-Contractor; and

.2   the selection of the kinds of materials and goods for the Sub-Contract Works insofar as such kinds of materials and goods have been or will be selected by the Sub-Contractor: and

.3   the satisfaction of any performance specification or requirement insofar as such performance specification or requirement is included or referred to in the description of the Sub-Contract Works included in or annexed to the numbered tender documents enclosed with NSC/T Part 1.'

The ICE do not publish a similar form of collateral warranty and this is discussed at 5.6.2.

The Court of Appeal have considered the effect of a direct warranty agreement in a building contract: *Greater Nottingham Cooperative Society* v. *Cementation Piling and Foundations Limited and Others* (1988). In this case, there were problems with the piling which resulted in a revised piling scheme having to be adopted. The Society claimed damages in tort against Cementation, the piling contractor, for the cost resulting from the revised piling scheme, for the sums paid to the main contractor arising out of the delay and the Society's consequential economic loss due to the delayed completion. The Court of Appeal had to consider whether there was a duty in tort in circumstances where the parties (an employer and a sub-contractor) had chosen to enter into a contract in which they had an actual opportunity to define their relationship and took the opportunity, and the fact that there was a chain of contracts through from the employer to the main contractor to the sub-contractor. They took the view that it would not be in accordance with present policy in this area of the law to extend the *Junior Books* decision rather than to restrict it. Having also considered the question of economic loss, they came to the view that the damages claimed were not recoverable in tort. The other important aspect of this case is that, following the changes in the law of tort and the more restricted nature of duties that are likely to be found nowadays by the court, the precise wording of direct warranty agreements becomes of paramount importance.

In view of the protection that can be given to the position of the employer by such collateral warranties, designers would be well advised to recommend the use of such written contracts to the employer in the light of more recent developments in the law of tort. The certainty of a contract is to be preferred to reliance on tort.

The positions of architects and engineers under the RIBA and ACE Conditions of Engagement and JCT and ICE Conditions of Contract are now considered separately.

5.5   Architects

5.5.1   *The Architect's Appointment*

The Architect's Appointment provides:

'3.5   Consultants may be appointed by either the client or the architect, subject to acceptance by each party.

3.6   Where the client employs the consultant, either directly or through the agency of the architect, the client will hold each consultant, and not the architect, responsible for the competence, general inspection and performance of the work entrusted to that consultant, provided that in relation to the execution of such work under the contract between the client and the contractor nothing in this clause shall affect any responsibility of the architect for issuing instructions or for other functions ascribed to the architect under that contract.

3.7   The architect will have the authority to co-ordinate and integrate into the overall design the services provided by any consultant, however employed.'

There is no express authority to delegate here and none is implied; express authority is therefore required to delegate. It follows that an architect engaged under the Appointment must seek express authority from the employer in respect of any delegation and he would be well advised to have such authority in writing: see *Moresk* v. *Hicks* (1966) and *Investors in Industry Commercial Properties Limited* v. *The District Council of South Bedfordshire and Others* (1985). There is nothing that requires architects to advise the employer as to the need for employer/sub-contractor warranty agreements. There is, however, little doubt that it is part of an architect's duty to his employer to advise him of the difficulties and problems of nomination and to advise that such direct warranties should be entered into. If he does not so advise him then he risks a claim by the employer for breach of duty. This is particularly so in the light of the purported exclusion of liability.

Clause 3.6 purports to exclude the architect's liability 'where the client employs the consultant, either directly or through the agency of the architect'. Where the client employs the consultant directly, there will not usually be problems but liability could arise on the architect in respect of negligent mis-statement in recommending a particular consultant; the wording of the clause would not be sufficiently wide to exclude the architect's liability in such circumstances.

The words 'through the agency of the architect' may apply to two separate and distinct legal arrangements; firstly, where the architect was an agent, in the legal sense, then it is likely there will be a contract between the client and the consultant, and the architect could not be sued on that contract. Secondly, it might be argued that the words apply where the architect has employed his own consultant under a contract.

Is the clause effective·to exclude the architect's liability for breach of contract or negligence by the consultant? Firstly, the clause will be construed *contra proferentem* and it may well be held that the words are not sufficiently clear to cover liability where the architect has entered into a contract with another consultant. Secondly, these conditions may be subjected to the requirement of reasonableness because they are, arguably, the 'other's written standard terms of business' (see 11.3.3.4). The presumption is that an exclusion clause is unreasonable and the burden would be upon the architect to demonstrate that the clause was reasonable. In forming their view, the court might have regard to the comments of Lord Frazer in the *IBA* case where he said that he thought it was reasonable to set up a chain of responsibility (see 4.1.3). Thirdly, if the clause does provide an effective exclusion of liability, then it will only exclude liability in respect of the particular matters set out in the clause, namely, 'the competence, general inspection and performance of the work entrusted to that consultant'. In respect of any default that falls outside that description, the exclusion of liability would be ineffective. In particular, there is no doubt that to exclude liability for negligence, very clear words indeed have to be used and this probably necessitates using the word 'negligence' or some synonym for it in the wording of the clause. In considering the effectiveness of these words of exclusion and the words in clause 1.22 of the former RIBA Conditions of Engagement (1971–9) which were similar to clause 3.6 of the Appointment, it should be borne in mind that they enabled the court to say that an architect had discharged his duty of care to his employer by entrusting detailed foundation design to a consulting engineer in the case of *Investors in Industry Commercial Properties Limited* v. *The District Council of South Bedfordshire and Others*(1985). Accordingly, this clause may be effective to exclude liability in negligence, independent of contract.

Furthermore, whilst the architect is given authority to co-ordinate and integrate the consultant's design into the overall design, he will also usually have the duty so to do and he will incur liability if he is in breach of that duty irrespective of the wording of clause 3.6.

There are also clauses dealing with design by contractors, sub-contractors and suppliers:

'3.8   A specialist contractor, sub-contractor or supplier who is to be employed by the client to design any part of the works may be nominated by either the architect or the client subject to acceptance by each party. The client will hold such contractor, sub-contractor or supplier, and not the architect, responsible for the competence, proper execution and performance of the work thereby entrusted to that contractor, sub-contractor or supplier. The architect will have the authority to co-ordinate and integrate such work into the overall design.

3.9   The client will employ a contractor under a separate agreement to undertake construction or other works. The client will hold the contractor, and not the architect, responsible for the contractor's operational methods and for the proper execution of the works.'

Much the same comments apply to the purported exclusion of liability in clause 3.8 as are made above in relation to clause 3.6.

Clause 3.9 purports to exclude the architect's liability for breaches of contract by the contractor; however, as with condition 1.34 in the 1979 Conditions, the wording is almost certainly not wide enough to exclude the architect's liability for breach of duty in failing to inspect (see 6.2.1).

5.5.2   *Rules of Conduct and delegation*

The Rules of Conduct for architects may also impinge on the area of delegation. The 'Standard of Conduct for Architects' published by ARCUK in 1981, which applies to all architects on the register and not only RIBA members, requires that before an engagement is entered into, an architect will 'have defined beyond reasonable doubt the terms of the engagement including the scope of the service … the allocation of responsibilities, and any limitation of liability….'

Arguably, these words are wide enough to suggest that an architect who is a member of the RIBA should explain to a potential client the purported limitation of liability in respect of consultants and sub-contractors set out in the Appointment, including advising on the risks of nomination and the need for employer/sub-contractor warranty agreements. But as has been pointed out, the ARCUK Code of Conduct has no statutory authority and there are no sanctions which attach to breach of it. On the other hand the provisions of the Architects (Registration) Act as to 'disgraceful conduct' should be borne in mind in this context.

5.5.3   *Architects and designer sub-contractors/main contractors*

Those architects who are members of the RIBA are required to comply with Rule 1.3 of Principle 1 of the RIBA 'Code of Professional Conduct' (July 1991 Reprint) which states:

'A member shall not subcommission or sub-let work without the prior agreement of his client nor without defining the changes in responsibility of those concerned.'

This wording is wide enough to include advising a client as to the purported exclusions in the Appointment and the difficulties of nomination and the need for provision of employer/sub-contractor warranty agreements.

It follows that an architect who fails to give such advice may be liable to his client and, if he is a member of the RIBA, to disciplinary proceedings under By-law 5.1.

Architects who cause nominated sub-contractors to carry out design work should be conscious of the fact that *vis à vis* the contractor on the JCT contract, the architect remains responsible for that design. It follows that if design errors or changes in the nominated sub-contract works occur by reason of the nominated sub-contractor's changes in design, then that has the effect under the main contract as if it were a change in the architect's design. It follows that if delay is caused to the contractor and loss and expense is incurred, then the contractor will be entitled to extensions of time and to be paid the loss and expense by reason of architect's instructions and/or late instructions, and the employer will have to seek to recover lost liquidated damages and the loss and expense from the sub-contractor under the direct form of warranty NSC/W (see, for example, *Holland Hannen and Cubitts* v. *Welsh Health Technical Services Organisation* (1981)).

For the position where the contractor accepts a nomination including an element of production of drawings by the nominated sub-contractor, see *H. Fairweather & Co. Limited* v. *London Borough of Wandsworth* (1987).

Similar points should be borne in mind in relation to a requirement by an architect for the inclusion of 'Performance Specified Work' under JCT 80 (introduced by Amendment 12 in July 1993). For the first time this introduces formally into JCT 80 an element of work that involves design to be carried out by the contractor, not nominated sub-contractors or nominated suppliers. In relation to this work, the contractor will be liable to the employer for defects in the design, but the architect remains liable for co-ordination and the approval of the design.

5.5.4   Standard Form of Agreement for the Appointment of an Architect – SFA/92

SFA/92 contains the following provisions relevant to delegation:

'*Conditions Common to All Commissions*
1.3.7   The Client acknowledges that the Architect does not warrant the work or products of others...
1.4.1   Neither the Architect nor the Client shall assign the whole or any part of the benefit or in any way transfer the obligation of the Appointment without the consent in writing of the other.'

Condition 1.3.7 is unlikely to be effective in excluding the responsibility of the architect where he selects and/or approves the work and products of others. It is not clear how this provision links with conditions 3.2.3, 4.1.7 and 4.2.5 below. As drafted, condition 1.3.7 is an additional exclusion to the others. It may be that this condition is seeking to meet the argument that merely by selecting a product the architect does not give a warranty in respect of it. However, that is a different issue to liability arising from the process of selection itself.

Condition 1.4.1 contains two separate points. Firstly, there is an express prohibition on assigning the whole or any part of the benefit of the Appointment, unless the consent of the other party is obtained in writing. If this prohibition were not here, either party could freely assign the benefit without consent from the other. A purported assignment without consent will be void and of no effect: *Linden Gardens Trust Limited* v. *Lenesta Sludge Disposals Limited and Others* (1993) and *St Martin's Property Corporation Limited and Others* v. *Sir Robert McAlpine and Sons Limited* (1993).

Secondly, there is a provision that 'the obligation' shall not be transferred. If 'obligation' means 'burden' (which is a word with a particular meaning in the law), then a burden cannot be assigned in any event without the consent of the other party. Such a provision would be unnecessary. The meaning may therefore be that this provision is more to do with sub-contracting parts of the architect's duties as opposed to assignment. If that is right, then this provision is a prohibition on delegation without consent from the client *in writing*. It follows that express consent in writing is needed for any proposed sub-commissions. This is also a requirement of Rule 1.3 of the RIBA Code of Professional Conduct (see the commentary above on the Architect's Appointment, condition 3.8).

'Client's Obligations

3.2.1 The Client shall employ a contractor under a separate agreement to undertake construction or other works relating to the Project.

3.2.2 The Client shall hold the contractor and not the Architect responsible for the contractor's management and operational methods and for the proper carrying out and completion of the Works and for health and safety provisions on the site.'

See the comments above in relation to condition 3.6 of the Architect's Appointment as to the purported exclusion of liability. It is not the case that the reference here to health and safety will in any way assist the architect as to any criminal liability in relation to health and safety that he may incur arising out of the project.

'Conditions Specific to Appointment of Consultants and Specialists Where Architect is Lead Consultant

4.1.1 The Architect shall identify professional services which require the appointment of consultants. Such consultants may be nominated at any time by either the Client or the Architect subject to acceptance by each party.

4.1.2 The Client shall appoint and pay the nominated consultants.

4.1.5 The Client shall appoint and give authority to the Architect as Lead Consultant in relation to all consultants however employed. The Architect shall be the medium of all communication and instruction between the Client and the consultants, co-ordinate and integrate into the overall design the services of the consultants, and require reports from the consultants.

4.1.7 The Client shall hold each consultant however appointed and not the Architect responsible for the competence and performance of the services to be performed by the consultant and for the general inspection of the execution of the work designed by the consultant.

4.2.1 A Specialist who is to be employed directly by the Client or indirectly through the contractor to design any part of the Works may be nominated by either the Architect or the Client subject to acceptance by each party.

4.2.4 The Client shall give the authority to the Architect to co-ordinate and integrate the services of all Specialists into the overall design and the Architect shall be responsible for such co-ordination and integration.

4.4.5 The Client shall hold any Specialist and not the Architect responsible for the products and materials supplied by the Specialist and for the competence, proper execution and performance of the work with which such Specialists are entrusted.'

These provisions are different in some respects to the former Architect's Appointment. For example, the appointment of other consultants is expressly on the basis that they are to appointed and paid for by the client. There is no provision, as there was, for appointment through the agency of the architect. Further, the architect is expressly created 'Lead Consultant'. That term is defined as 'The consultant given the authority and responsibility by the Client to co-ordinate and integrate the services of other consultants'. That definition does not include co-ordination of specialists but that aspect is covered at condition 4.2.4. If a client wishes to have a lead consultant who is not the architect, this provision will need amendment

It should be noted that there are express provisions purporting to limit liability for breach of this agreement and purporting to limit the damages recoverable. These are to be found in the Memorandum of Agreement at clauses 5, 6.1, 6.2 and 6.3. These provisions are discussed further at 11.3.4.

It is not clear what is intended by the words 'require reports from consultants' in condition 4.1.5. It is probably too imprecise in law to have any effect.

As to the purported exclusions of liability, see the commentary on condition 3.6 of the Architect's Appointment above in 5.5.1.

5.6   Engineers

5.6.1   *ACE Conditions of Engagement*

The ACE Conditions of Engagement for work where an architect is not appointed by the client (Agreement 2, 1981, 1990 Version) includes the following conditions that are relevant to delegation:

'2.2   The Consulting Engineer shall not, without the consent of the client, assign the benefit or in any way transfer the obligation of this Agreement or any part thereof.

5.1   The Consulting Engineer shall exercise all reasonable skill, care and diligence in the discharge of the services agreed to be performed by him...

5.2   The Consulting Engineer may recommend that specialist suppliers and/or contractors should design and execute certain part or parts of the Works, in which circumstances the Consulting Engineer shall co-ordinate and integrate the design of such part or parts with the overall design of the Works but he shall be relieved of all responsibility for the design, manufacture, installation and performance of any such part or parts of the Works. Where any persons are engaged in accordance with Clause 7.4 the Consulting Engineer shall not be liable for acts of negligence, default or omission by such person or persons.

6.2(b)   Advising as to the appropriate conditions of contract to be incorporated in any contract to be made between the Client and a Contractor.

7.4   The Consulting Engineer shall obtain the prior agreement of the client to the arrangements which he proposes to make on the client's behalf for the provision of any of the services specified in Clause 7.3. The client shall be responsible to any person or persons providing such services for the cost thereof.'

The services specified in clause 7.3 include specialist technical advice, architectural, legal, financial and other professional services, services in connection with valuation, purchase, sale, leasing of land and wayleaves, carrying out of marine, air and land surveys, and special inspections or tests.

It will be a question of fact in any particular case whether the works that the consulting engineer has agreed to undertake (as defined in the Memorandum of Agreement) include work which the consulting engineer wishes to delegate. If it does include such work then clause 2.2 forbids delegation unless the consent of the client is obtained. The wording of that clause is such that, even if it were possible to imply authority to delegate, which it is not, the clause would prevent the implication of such a term. It follows that the consulting engineer must have express authority from his client to delegate any of the work which he has undertaken to carry out. It is clear from the ICE Conditions of Contract (clause 58(3)), that nominated sub-contractors can have a design responsibility; such delegation could also constitute a breach of clause 2.2 and again, the consulting engineer should have the express approval of his client to such delegation.

5.6.2   Engineers and designing sub-contractors/main contractors

The duties that the consulting engineer undertakes include advising on the appropriate conditions of contract (clause 6.2(b)) and exercising all reasonable skill, care and diligence in the discharge of his services (clause 5.1). It probably follows from these obligations that the consulting engineer is under a duty to explain to his client the difficulties and hazards involved in the field of nominated sub-contractors and in particular those relating to design. The consulting engineer's advice should extend to the general points set out above, right through to advising on the protective measures that are available to the client as employer under the ICE Conditions. These are twofold.

Firstly, the engineer can require that tendering sub-contractors complete a form of warranty similar to that referred to at 5.4. The ICE do not publish their own standard form but such a form could be prepared without difficulty and it should deal with other matters in addition to design. The employer would then have the benefit of a contract directly with the nominated sub-contractor which would provide a means of redress in case of defective design.

Secondly, there is an alternative method available to the engineer under the ICE Conditions of Contract, 6th Edition. Clause 58(3) provides as follows:

'If in connection with any Provisional Sum or Prime Cost Item the services to be provided include any matter of design or specification of any part of the Permanent Works or of any equipment or plant to be incorporated therein such requirement shall be expressly stated in the Contract and shall be included in any Nominated Sub-Contract. The obligation of the Contractor in respect thereof shall be only that which has been expressly stated in accordance with this sub-clause.'

It follows that where there are provisional sums or prime cost items and any of those items are to include design then, provided the contractor is told at the time that he tenders, and such design obligation is incorporated into the sub-contract, there will be a contractual chain in respect of the sub-contractor's design. The employer has redress against the contractor who in turn has redress against the nominated sub-contractor.

An engineer in advising his client should bear in mind that clause 59A(6) provides that, where a nominated sub-contractor is in breach of the sub-contract and that breach causes the contractor to be in breach of the main contract, then the employer cannot recover from the contractor in excess of any amount that the contractor has recovered from the sub-contractor (subject to clause 59B(6) which requires the contractor to take all necessary steps against the sub-contractor).

One of the disadvantages of this course of action is that the contractor at tender stage may feel obliged either to decline to tender because he does not wish to accept design responsibility or to increase his price to take account of the additional risk involved.

The engineer should consider which of the two courses that are open to him is the better in any particular case. Should the engineer find that he failed to state in the contractor's tender documents that a particular design requirement would be included in a nominated sub-contract, then the contractor may be entitled to refuse a nomination which includes a design obligation. It follows that, if the engineer has omitted to state his requirements in the contract documents, then he should obtain a collateral warranty from the sub-contractor in order to protect the employer's position.

Another matter that the engineer may wish to consider drawing to the employer's attention is the possibility of using both methods of protection. The construction industry is by its nature a risky field. It is not at all unknown for construction companies to go into liquidation and in such circumstances, the employer would lose his design protection against the sub-contractor in respect of defective design if only the clause 58(3) method had been adopted. The use of a collateral warranty in addition to the 58(3) route does give added protection to the employer.

In order to be certain that the chain of responsibility set up by the provision of clause 58(3) of the ICE Conditions is effective, the engineer must see that there are no inconsistencies in the tender documents for the main contract and the sub-contracts. It is likely for example that the engineer will want to see and approve any drawings produced by the sub-contractor and it is clearly advisable that this same obligation should be included in the main contract in order to complete the chain of responsibility.

5.7   Delegation by employer's designer

It is not at all unusual to find designers in the employment of the employer. In this capacity, they are in a position to give technically informed instructions to independent firms of designers. Insofar as contracts between the employer and the contractor are concerned, the designer to be named in that contract is sometimes chosen to be the designer in the employment of the employer, rather than the independent firm of designers. Such an appointment for the purposes of administering the JCT or ICE contracts can lead to great difficulties. The two most important difficulties are conflict of interest and the effect on tortious liability.

5.7.1   Conflict of interest

Both the ICE and the JCT contracts envisage that the architect and engineer will act fairly between the parties to the contract; there should be no interference by the employer under either contract with the architect or engineer's duties. Clearly, if the architect or engineer named in the construction contract is in the employment of the employer, he can be put in an extremely difficult position unless he is able to scrupulously maintain his independence when carrying out his functions under the contract. For example, it is not unknown for architects in private firms to come under considerable pressure not to issue certificates: how much greater will the difficulty be where the architect is in the employment of the employer.

5.7.2   *Tortious liability*

The general rule of law is that a person cannot be held liable for a tort committed by his independent contractor (see section 2.2.1.1); there are only a few narrow exceptions to this rule. In the usual relationship between employers and designers, where a firm of designers is engaged by the employer, then that firm will usually be regarded as independent contractors; the employer will not usually be liable for the torts of that firm of designers because they are independent contractors. The position can be different where the designer is in the employment of the employer because he will not usually be regarded as an independent contractor. This can be so even where he delegates the detailed design to an independent firm of designers: *AMF International Limited* v. *Magnet Bowling Limited and Another* (1968).

AMF contracted with Magnet to provide and fix timber and bowling alley equipment in a building being constructed by a contractor under a contract with Magnet. The timber, which was of very high quality, had to be kept at a low moisture content. In due course Magnet asked AMF to start work on the site with the agreement of the contractor. After delivery of the timber, the site became flooded as a result of water entering the building through an uncompleted doorway. The architect was found by the court to be in the fulltime employment of Magnet and the outside firm of architects were not independent contractors. It was held, *inter alia*, that Magnet were not entitled to rely on section 2(4)(b) of the Occupiers Liability Act 1957, which would have provided a defence, because although an occupier could be said to be acting reasonably by engaging an independent contractor to fulfil his duty and would not incur liability for the negligence of that independent contractor, the facts were that the firm of architects in this case were not independent contractors in relation to Magnet.

This case amply demonstrates the additional risk to which the employer is put by adopting the practice of having his own architect in charge of the works. The effect of the *AMF* case is to put the employer under a liability to his own subcontractor in circumstances where that sub-contractor's work was damaged as a result of the main contractor's breach of contract: in that case failing to protect materials from injury by weather and failing to prevent the accumulation of water on site.

Chapter 6

Negligent inspection

6.1 Inspection

6.1.1 General considerations

It is commonplace nowadays for an employer who finds that he has defective construction to bring proceedings against both the contractor and the designer. The reason for this is twofold. Firstly, it can be extremely difficult in practice to distinguish between damage caused by defective workmanship, for which the contractor will be liable, and damage caused by defective design, for which the designer will be liable. By bringing proceedings against both the designer and the contractor, the employer will hope to avoid falling between two stools.

Secondly, where there is defective workmanship, then there is, on the face of it, the possibility of an allegation that the designer was negligent in carrying out his duty as to inspection and superintendance of the contractor's work.

In very general terms, that duty is to see that the contractor constructs the work in accordance with the contractual obligation of the contractor to the employer. It must be emphasised that the designer's duty as to inspection is owed to the employer and not to the contractor: the designer's duty of care does not extend to how the contractor carries out his work: *Clayton* v. *Woodman & Son (Builders) Limited* (1962).

'Not only has he no duty to instruct the builder how to do the work, or what safety precautions to take, but he has no right to do so; nor is he under any duty to the builder to detect faults during the progress of the work. The architect, in that respect, may be in breach of his duty to his client, the building owner, but this does not excuse the builder for faulty work': *Oldschool and Another* v. *Gleeson (Construction) Limited and Others* (1976).

In any particular case, it is necessary to look at the conditions of engagement of the designer and the contract between the contractor and the employer as well as the general law. The reason for this is that the conditions of engagement may set out particular obligations, and the construction contract may give guidance as to the obligations that the designer undertakes in respect of the contractor's work. For example, the construction contract may provide that the works shall be executed as set out in the specification and to the reasonable satisfaction of the designer. Such a clause will impose two obligations: to execute the works in the manner set out in the specification and also to execute them to the reasonable satisfaction of the designer: *National Coal Board* v. *William Neill & Son* (1983).

The dangers to an employer in having wording which imports conclusiveness into certificates of an architect or engineer is amply demonstrated by the case of *Ata Ul Haq* v. *The City Council of Nairobi* (1962), Privy Council. Ata Ul Haq was a contractor engaged to build 17 blocks on a housing estate for the City of Nairobi. Amongst other things the contract between the parties contained the following terms:

'7.(iv) When the Works have been completely executed according to the provisions of the Contract and to the satisfaction of the Engineer, the date of such completion shall be certified by him, and such date shall be the date of commencement of such period of maintenance as may be provided by the Contract.'

It was held by the Privy Council that the whole scheme of the contract, including clause 7(iv), demonstrated that a certificate issued under that clause was intended to be conclusive; the issue by the engineer of a certificate under clause 7(iv) certifying that the work complied with the specification and that it had been completed to his satisfaction terminated the contractor's liability subject only to the maintenance period provisions. It is the case that this decision was on the particular facts and on the particular contract there involved. However, the speeches in the House of Lords are a useful indication of the court's approach to the construction of conclusivity clauses in construction contracts.

There are general points of law that apply to all designers carrying out inspection which are now examined, before looking at the particular duties of architects and engineers.

6.1.2 *Nature of duty*

There will not usually be a claim for negligent inspection unless there is also defective workmanship or materials, because in the absence of the latter, there will not usually be any damage that would make it worthwhile to pursue an allegation of negligent inspection. Where there is defective workmanship, then the contractor will be liable in damages, usually for the costs of repair. What, therefore, is the position where there is defective workmanship for which the employer has a cause of action against the contractor, and there is also negligent inspection? Does the employer have an additional cause of action against the designer for his negligent inspection?

It is quite clear that the employer has a cause of action against both the contractor and the designer. Against the contractor, there will be a claim for breach of contract at the very least, and against the designer there will be a cause of action for breach of duty in negligently failing to prevent, or detect and have corrected, the defective work. The causes of action are separate and distinct: the employer can choose which to pursue or he may pursue both causes of action. Judge Fay QC, Official Referee, in *Hutchinson* v. *Harris* (1978), which subsequently went to the Court of Appeal, but not on this point, put it this way:

'Where the duty of a contracting party is to supervise the work of another contracting party, it seems to me that there is a direct causal connection between the supervisor's negligent failure to prevent negligent work and the damage represented by their negligent work. No doubt the builder is also liable. It is a case of concurrent breaches of contract producing the same damage. In my judgment the plaintiff has an action against both, although she cannot obtain damages twice over.'

A similar point arose in *London Borough of Merton* v. *Lowe and Pickford* (1981) where it was argued by the architect defendant that he should not be held liable by reason of the fact that the self-same damage could have been recovered in tort from a solvent sub-contractor; the building owner had chosen not to do so. The Court of Appeal rejected that argument and held the architects liable.

In such a case, where there is liability for the same damage on the part of both defendants, and whether or not that liability is in tort or contract, the court has power to apportion liability between the parties who are liable under the Civil Liability (Contribution) Act 1978 (see 9.2.2). It has been held in the Court of Appeal that, where a plaintiff sues designers and contractors as co-defendants, and the action against the contractors is settled by the plaintiff accepting a sum of money paid into court by the contractors, the action can proceed against the designer where there is a separate cause of action, but that no one should recover more in damages than the loss suffered. The burden is on the wrongdoer to show that the plaintiff has already received compensation – in this case, the judge had taken the view that part of the contractor's payment-in was for losses attributable to both defendants and the judge had only awarded a further small sum against the architects; the Court of Appeal did not disagree with the judge's assessment: *Townsend and Another* v. *Stone Toms & Partners and Others* (1984). The courts, in apportioning liability between such co-defendants, have to determine what contribution is just and equitable, having due regard to the extent of each defendant's liability for damage.

The courts tend to the view 'that the blameworthiness of the policeman who fails to detect the crime is less than that of the criminal himself': *per* Judge Edgar Fay QC in *Eames London Estates Limited and Others* v. *North Hertfordshire District Council and Others* (1980). However, there are circumstances that can arise where the designer can find himself in a position where he has to meet the full amount of the employer's claim. This position could arise where the contractor is unable to meet his liabilities because of lack of funds; it is well known that construction is a risky business and there is a higher rate of company insolvency in this sphere of activity than in most others.

The designer can also find himself in the position of meeting the whole of the employer's claim in circumstances where he has deprived the employer of his right to bring an action against the contractor in respect of his defective workmanship. Under earlier versions of the 1963 Edition of the JCT Contract (subsequently altered), clause 30(7) provided that a final certificate should be 'conclusive evidence in any proceedings ... that the works have been properly carried out and completed in accordance with the terms of this contract....' Subject to some exceptions which were expressly set out in the contract, the employer would be deprived of any right of action against the contractor in respect of defective workmanship once that certificate was issued. One of the exceptions was in relation to any defect which reasonable inspection during the carrying out of the works or before the issue of the final certificate would not have disclosed. It followed that, where the architect failed to discover a defect which reasonable inspection would have disclosed, or where he knew of a defect and issued the final certificate, the employer's right of action against the contractor would be extinguished, but the employer would be likely to have a cause of action against the architect. In a case on the 1963 Edition of the JCT Contract, architects were held liable in respect of defective workmanship by a contractor's nominated sub-contractors in circumstances where they knew of the defective workmanship at the time that they issued the final certificate: *The London Borough of Merton* v. *Lowe and Pickford* (1981).

A designer will not be liable for negligent inspection if he fails to discover every single defect in a contractor's work. The question in every case is whether the designer exhibited that degree of skill that an ordinary competent designer would exhibit in the same circumstances. It follows that the duty may vary according to the circumstances and laying down rigid guidelines as to what is appropriate in general is impossible. A useful indication of the way in which a court approaches the problem was given by Lord Upjohn in the case of *East Ham Corporation* v. *Bernard Sunley & Sons Limited* (1966):

'As is well known, the architect is not permanently on the site but appears at intervals, it may be of a week or a fortnight, and he has, of course, to inspect the progress of the works. When he arrives on the site there may be many very important matters with which he has to deal: the work may be getting behind-hand through labour troubles; some of the suppliers of materials or the sub-contractors may be lagging; there may be physical trouble on the site itself, such as, for example, finding an unexpected amount of underground water. All these are matters which may call for important decisions by the architect. He may, in such circumstances, think that he knows the builders sufficiently well and can rely upon them to carry out a good job; that it is more important that he should deal with urgent matters on site than he should make a minute inspection on site to see that the builder is complying with the specifications laid down by him ... it by no means follows that, in failing to discover a defect which a reasonable examination would have disclosed, in fact the architect was necessarily thereby in breach of duty to the building owner so as to be liable in an action for negligence. It may well be that the omission of the architect to find the defect was due to no more than an error of judgment, or was a deliberately calculated risk which, in all the circumstances of the case, was reasonable and proper.'

It is evident from that speech, and other cases, that the courts do not take a rigid view of the designer's duty to supervise: the theme running through the cases is that a designer's supervision must be reasonable in all the circumstances. However, it has been held that an architect's duty as to supervision must enable him to be in a position to properly certify that the construction work has been carried out in accordance with the contract: *Jameson* v. *Simon* (1899). The liability is on the basis that the designer, having passed, by reason of his certificate, defective work, is liable in damages in respect of his lack of supervision that led to his giving an improper certificate. In the same way, if a designer discovers defective work but nonetheless certifies the payment, he will be liable in damages to the building owner: *Sutcliffe* v. *Thackrah* (1974).

6.1.3   Standard of duty

Subject to the designer being able to give a proper certificate as to the compliance of the work with the construction contract, it is clear that the standard of the supervision duty may vary with the circumstances. The terms of the construction contract may be relevant; the designer may rely on a contractor whom he knows to be competent, to produce a competent job; the designer may legitimately delegate some of his supervision duties (although he will not necessarily escape liability in this way); the standard of specification of the construction work may affect the standard of work that the designer passes as being satisfactory in much the same way as where a contractor is 'building down' to a price. In the case of *Cotton* v. *Wallis* (1955) where the building owner brought an action for professional negligence against a designer, it was alleged that the designer had failed in his duty by passing certain work. Lord Justice Morris said:

> 'It seems to me only natural that where there is a house that is being built at a very great expense, and another house that is being built at a very moderate price, one would expect different quality in the work. Of course, everything must depend upon the exact contract that is made. If someone contracts to give the very best possible price, then, of course, the contract must be carried out.'

He went on to cite the words of the trial judge:

> 'Mr Cotton [the designer] and his assistant, Mr Lofthouse, might well have been rather more hard on Mr Hillman [the contractor] than they were, but they knew that this was being done as a cheap job and could not afford any very expensive work. They applied perhaps a lower standard than another architect might have done under different circumstances, but they never passed anything "rank bad" and I cannot find them guilty of professional negligence.'

The finding in that case is a little difficult to reconcile with the contractual obligation of the contractor. Lord Denning in his dissenting judgment put it this way:

> 'The duty the architect owes to the building owner is to see that the builder does his work and does it properly. The specification required that the whole of the materials and workmanship were to be the best of their respective kind and to the full satisfaction of the architect.'

Amongst the defects complained of were paraffin stains, which could not be removed, on floor tiles. It is difficult to see how such stains could not be a breach of the workmanship obligation and consequently, the passing of that work by the designer would be a breach of duty. It may be that the judgment in this case reflects the merits of the parties in that the building owner had made no complaint of the defective supervision until the designer claimed to be paid his fees, although it should be said that the Court of Appeal emphasised that the judge had dealt with the claim of the building owner on its merits: 'that there is a bad reason for putting forward a claim does not necessarily invalidate the claim, if it can be shown to be a good one.' In any event, it is clear from the judgment that everything must depend upon the exact contract that is made between the contractor and the building owner: the designer's duties as to supervision are inextricably linked with the contractor's obligations under that contract.

Judge Bowsher QC, Official Referee, had to deal with the issue of supervision in 1992: *Corfield* v. *Grant and Others*. This case arose, as do so many others, from an architect suing for his fees. The client counterclaimed for damages for breach of contract, including damages for failure adequately to supervise. It is on this point alone that the case is reported. The judge said:

'What is adequate by way of supervision and other work is not in the end to be tested by the number of hours worked on site or elsewhere, but by asking whether it was enough. At some stages of some jobs exclusive attention may be required to the job in question (either in the office or on site): at other stages of the same jobs, or during most of the duration of other jobs, it will be quite sufficient to give attention to the job only from time to time. The proof of the pudding was in the eating. Was the attention given enough for this particular job?'

He went on to discuss the facts of this case against that statement and in particular the large amount of work facing the architect on this job in a relatively short space of time. Then, he said:

'Plainly one man could not do all these things at once. He needed at least one skilled and experienced assistant. One of the complaints, which I find justified, is that the [architect] did not have a skilled and experienced assistant. For this job, he used [an assistant] who had previously had only a few months experience in training in an architect's office . . . an expert witness on behalf of the [architect], described the job as a "controlled muddle", meaning to refer to the need to do everything at once. For my part, I would not refer to it as uncontrolled muddle, but it was inadequately controlled muddle and in that regard the [architect] was in continuous breach of contract.'

Where there is an obligation to supervise, therefore, being too busy on other aspects of the project and not having enough staff of appropriate experience for the project will not constitute any sort of defence to an allegation of negligent supervision.

The relationship between the degree of supervision to be expected of an architect and the competence of the contractor has been considered in two cases. The first in time was a case heard by Judge Stabb QC: *Sutcliffe* v. *Chippendale and Edmondson* (1971). This case subsequently went to the Court of Appeal when it became known as *Sutcliffe* v. *Thackrah* but the statements of the judge on this aspect of the dispute were not involved in the appeal.

'If and when something occurs which should indicate to [the architect] a lack of competence in the contractor, then, in the interest of the employer, the standard of his supervision should be higher. No-one suggests that the architect is required to tell a contractor how his work is to be done, nor is the architect responsible for the manner in which the contractor does the work. What his supervisory duty does require of him is to follow the progress of the work and to take steps to see that those works comply with the general requirements of the contract in specification and quality. If he should fail to exercise his professional care and skill in this respect, he would be liable to his employer for any damage attributed to that failure.'

In a more recent case, *Brown* v. *Gilbert-Scott and Payne* (1993), an Official Referee had to deal with the issue of a duty to 'supervise' an inexperienced builder. Tenders had been sought for the construction of a conservatory but they were all over budget and that was how the inexperienced builder came to be appointed. There were extensive and expensive remedial works required. The court found that an inexperienced builder required more supervision than a more experienced one would have done, and that the architect's duty was to give that supervision even though he had to travel a long distance and was working on a low profit. It was said that the architect should have been present at crucial stages such as the laying of the damp proof membrane.

Whether the designer acted reasonably in any particular case is a matter of expert evidence of other designers; the circumstances may mean that a higher duty is required. In an Australian case, *Florida Hotels Pty* v. *Mayo* (1965), where the circumstances were unusual, an architect was held liable in respect of injured workmen.

Architects were engaged to supervise the execution of construction work. The architects did not see reinforcement that had been wrongly fixed before the concrete was placed in the formwork. When the formwork was removed several workmen were injured by the collapse of the reinforced concrete. There was no contractor, the employer having employed workmen direct. It was held that:

(1)   the architects were in breach of duty in failing to supervise;
(2)   the architects must have had in their contemplation when carrying out their supervising duties that the employer would suffer loss in the event that workmen were injured; and,
(3)   the architects were liable to the employer in respect of the damages paid by the employer to injured workmen.

This case probably represents an extreme position because of its unusual facts, there being no contractor and the workmen being employed by the employer direct.

6.1.4   Delegation

It is commonplace on modern construction projects for supervision work to be carried out by clerks of works or resident engineers or inspectors. Various aspects of the supervision process may be handled by these people and their positions and authority are sometimes set out in the construction contract. The question arises as to whether the delegation to such people by a designer of his duty to supervise relieves him of part or the whole of his duties to supervise, such that he incurs no liability if there is a breach of duty by the person to whom the supervision has been delegated. In order to answer this question, it is necessary to look at the two ways in which delegation takes place because the legal consequences are different.

6.1.4.1 *Employees of the designer*

It is not unusual in civil engineering contracts for the resident engineer to be an employee of the engineer although it is very much less common for the clerk of the works to be an employee of the architect. In any event, the position where the designer delegates to his own employee some or all of his supervisory duties is reasonably straightforward. The designer will remain liable for the acts and omissions of his employee, both under the law of contract, and under the law of tort on the principle of vicarious liability. The designer cannot escape liability even in circumstances where his employee acted for his own benefit such as, for example, taking a bribe or turning a blind eye: *Lloyd* v. *Grace, Smith & Co.* (1912). Where the designer has instructed his employee as to the way in which he should carry out his supervision, he will not escape liability if the employee ignores what he has been instructed to do: *London County Council* v. *Cattermoles (Garages) Limited* (1953). However, the overriding principle still applies that the designer will not necessarily be held liable for failing to inspect every aspect of the construction process or failing to detect every minor piece of poor workmanship.

6.1.4.2 *Employees of the employer*

It is common for the clerk of the works and, sometimes, the resident engineer to be an employee of the employer rather than of the designer, although the latter may have a say in the selection of an appropriate person, and his terms and conditions of engagement. In such circumstances, it has been held that an architect cannot delegate matters of importance so as to divest himself of responsibility but he can delegate matters of minor importance.

In the case of *Leicester Guardians* v. *Trollope* (1911), architects were engaged to design and to supervise the construction of new buildings for a hospital in Leicestershire. Extensive dry rot in the floors was discovered four years after the work was completed. It was found that the cause of the dry rot was that the timber joists had been supported on pegs driven into the ground, through which moisture could pass, before laying of concrete, instead of joists being placed on previously laid concrete. The architects denied that it was their duty to supervise the laying of the concrete, saying that was the duty of the clerk of works. The court found that the duty of a clerk of works was to supervise the details of the work; the work complained of here was not such a detail and the architects were liable.

In the *Leicester Guardians* case expert evidence had been given to the court, that an architect's duty was to supervise the general scheme and that the clerk of works' duty was to see that the details of construction were properly carried out. The court adopted that evidence and the trial judge said:

> 'The defence is that this dry rot was the fault of the clerk of the works. That is so in one sense. It clearly was the duty of the clerk of the works to attend to the laying of concrete in accordance with the design, but does that relieve the defendant? To my mind there is little difficulty in deciding the point. The position of the architect and of the clerk of the works was made quite clear. The details were to be supervised by the clerk of the works. The architect could not be at the works all the time, and it was for that reason that the clerk of the works was employed to protect the building owner... If the architect had taken steps to see that the first block was all right, and had then told the clerk

of the works that the work in the others was to be carried out in the same way, I would have been inclined to hold that the architect had done his duty; but in fact he did nothing to see that the design was complied with. In my view, this was not a matter of detail which could be left to the clerk of the works. It may have been natural to leave it to him, but in my judgment it was an omission to do that which it was his duty to do': Mr Justice Channell in *Leicester Guardians* v. *Trollope* (1911)

Further support for the view that only minor matters can be delegated, so as to relieve the designer of responsibility, is to be found in *Lee* v. *Bateman* (1893). There, the architects were engaged in relation to the restoration of the kitchen wing of a mansion house after a fire. The architects left it to the clerk of works, who was employed by the employer, to decide whether new beams were required. It was held that, although the architects were not liable for the negligence of the clerk of works, the question as to whether new beams were required or not was one that the architects should have answered and not the clerk of works.

It may be that the clerk of works or resident engineer appointed by the employer is incompetent. However, such incompetence will not usually provide a defence to a claim against the designer for breach of his duty to supervise, at least in circumstances where the designer relied on the clerk of works or engineer, knowing that he was incompetent or unreliable: *Saunders* v. *Broadstairs Local Board* (1890). It follows from these cases that the designer will usually be liable for breach of duty in supervision where he has delegated if:

(1)   He purports to delegate a matter which he should not have delegated but rather should have seen to himself: *Leicester* and *Lee*.
(2)   He purports to delegate where he should give instructions as to how the supervision was to be carried out, and he failed to give such instructions: *Leicester*.
(3)   He relies on an unreliable clerk of works or resident engineer when he knows that that clerk of works or resident engineer is unreliable: *Saunders*.

A further and important point arises in relation to the effect of the negligence of a clerk of works employed by the employer on any claim that the employer may make in relation to defects against a contractor. This point was considered in *Kensington and Chelsea and Westminster Area Health Authority* v. *Wettern Composites and Adams, Holden and Pearson* (1984). In this case, the court found that the clerk of works had been negligent in his supervision and inspection duties. He was employed by the employer but was under the control and direction of the architect – a very common approach to the appointment of a clerk of the works. Judge David Smout QC, Official Referee, said that:

'The clerk of works by the very nature of his occupation carries out his duties at the premises of the building owner and for the protection and interests of the building owner. In those circumstances, it would need strong evidence indeed to displace the inference that the clerk of works was acting otherwise than as the servant of the building owner. There is no such evidence in this case. In my view the plaintiffs are vicariously liable for the negligence of the clerk of works.'

It followed from this that the burden of proof rested on the employer plaintiffs to shift the *prima facie* responsibility for the negligence of the servant employed and paid by them, and the judge applied *Mersey Docks and Harbour Board* v. *Coggins and Griffiths (Liverpool) Limited* (1947). The judge then went on to reduce the damages recoverable from the architect defendants by 20% in respect of this negligence by the plaintiffs' employee, the clerk of works. The judge put it this way:

> 'I have reached the conclusion that the clerk of works' negligence whilst more than minimal is very much less than that of the architects. If I may adapt the military terminology: it was the negligence of the chief petty officer as compared with that of the captain of the ship. I assess responsibility as to the clerk of works at 20% and as to the architects at 80% by reason of the vicarious liability of the plaintiff [employer] I make a finding of contributory negligence of 20%.'

For further discussion of contributory negligence in general and in relation to contract, see section 9.2.1.

6.2   Architects

6.2.1   *The Architect's Appointment*

The Architect's Appointment provides certain conditions as to site inspection:

> '3.10   The architect will visit the site at intervals appropriate to the state of construction to inspect the progress and quality of the works and to determine that they are being executed generally in accordance with the contract documents. The architect will not be required to make frequent or constant inspection.'

The obligation as to site visits and inspections is to see whether or not the work is proceeding in accordance with the building contract. The wording is such that the frequency of the visits that are required is what the architect considers necessary. This means that, in practice, whether or not there has been a breach of this obligation will be judged by expert evidence as to the frequency of visits that would be appropriate to the particular circumstances of the building contract in question.

It is not inconceivable that in certain circumstances the first sentence and the second sentence of the clause could be inconsistent: it may well be that, in order to comply with this obligation in the first instance, the architect will have to make frequent or constant inspections. In such circumstances, it is submitted that the second sentence would provide no defence to a charge of negligent inspection.

Furthermore, the architect must not forget that his supervision and inspection must enable him to give proper certificates both as to interim payment and final payment: *Jameson* v. *Simon* (1899). Clause 30.2 of the JCT 80 contract requires the architect to state the sum due on an interim certificate and the main ingredient of the value on that certificate is 'the total value of work *properly executed*' by the contractor: clause 30.2.1.1. Similarly, the final certificate is 'conclusive evidence that where the quality of materials or the standard of workmanship are to be to the reasonable satisfaction of the architect the same are to such satisfaction': clause 30.9.1.1. Clearly, the architect's inspections must enable those certificates to be properly given otherwise he risks an action by the employer for breach of duty in inspection and/or certification: *Sutcliffe* v. *Thackrah* (1974).

> '3.11   Where frequent or constant inspections are required a clerk or clerks of works will be employed. They may be employed either by the client or by the architect and will in either event be under the architect's direction and control.'

Clause 3.11 states that the clerk of works will be under the architect's direction and control. This wording may have the effect of putting the architect under an even stricter duty as to the matters that he can delegate to the clerk of the works so as to relieve himself of responsibility.

> '3.12   Where frequent or constant inspection by the architect is agreed to be necessary, a resident architect may be appointed by the architect on a part or full-time basis.'

Whilst the Architect's Appointment makes provision for resident architects to be appointed in appropriate circumstances, there is no status for such a person under the JCT contracts, and an architect would have to be circumspect as to precisely the function that the resident architect is to carry out. In any event, it is probably part of the architect's duty to his client to advise in respect of every project whether or not a clerk of works or resident architect should be appointed. In the event that the architect advises that a clerk of works should be appointed and the employer refuses to appoint one, then particularly in view of clauses 3.10 and 3.12 of the Architect's Appointment, it is likely that the architect's duty to inspect is unaltered. However, in those circumstances he will not be able to rely on the regular inspection by a clerk of works and this may mean that the architect's inspection should be more frequent. He will not be able to argue that his duty as to inspection was reduced because of the employer's refusal to appoint a clerk of works.

6.2.2   Standard Form of Agreement for the Appointment of an Architect (SFA/92)

SFA/92 contains rather different provisions to those in Architect's Appointment. The relevant provisions are:

> '3.1.1   The Architect shall in providing the Services specified in stages K and L of Schedule Two make such visits to the Works as the Architect at the date of the Appointment reasonably expected to be necessary. The Architect shall confirm such expectation in writing.
>
> 3.1.2   The Architect shall, on its becoming apparent that the expectation of the visits to the Works needs to be varied, inform the Client in writing of his recommendations and any consequential variation in fees.
>
> 3.1.3   The Architect shall, where the Client requires more frequent visits to the Works than those specified by the Architect in condition 3.1.1,

inform the Client of any consequential variation in fees, The Architect shall confirm in writing any agreement reached.'

The intention of these provisions is as follows: the architect specifies at the outset the visits that he expects to make to the site. His expectation is to be judged at the date of the Appointment. That date will be well before the design has progressed and well before a contractor has been appointed; the architect will therefore be making an assessment in a vacuum with very little of the relevant information available to form a view as to how much time he should allow in his fees for inspection. He has also to remember to put this expectation in writing to his client, although no time is specified. It is submitted that, in order to have contractual effect, it must be done contemporaneously, at the latest, with signing the Appointment. The effect of not so confirming in writing is not fatal to these provisions. In such a case, the architect will be deemed to have included in his fees for the inspections he could have expected at the time of the Appointment and the position will have to be judged on that basis. It is not difficult to see that such a situation could leave scope for considerable argument.

Thereafter, if the architect feels more inspections are needed (say, because an inexperienced builder has been appointed which he could not have foreseen at the time of his Appointment), he has a duty to notify that fact to the client together with his extra fee proposal. If he fails to recognise the need for extra inspections and/or fails to make a recommendation to the client, he will be in breach of contract. There is no provision as to what is to happen if the client does not accept the recommendation or the fees or point blank refuses to pay for this additional service. If extra inspections are needed but the client refuses them, difficult questions will arise as to responsibility for the failure to dis-cover defective work. If it can be shown that all the defects would have been found on additional visits that did not take place because the client refused them, then he will have no claim against the architect. If, as is more likely, such a separation cannot be demonstrated between defects, there is likely to be an allegation of contributory negligence against the client, although this may be very difficult to assess as to quantum: *Forsikringsaktieselkapet Vesta* v. *Butcher and Others* (1988).

At any time, the client can require more inspection on payment of extra fees. The effect is, in summary, to fix at the outset of the Appointment a finite quantity of inspection time for which the architect has included in his fees. Thereafter, if there is a variation to that inspection allocation, either suggested by the architect and accepted by the client or required by the client, the architect provides it and is paid extra for it.

As to the purported exclusions of liability in these provisions, see the com-mentary on the Architect's Appointment above.

6.2.3 Delegation risk management

The *Handbook of Architectural Practice and Management* (4th Revised Edition, 1980, RIBA Publications Limited) has a section dealing with inspection and super-vision, and in particular, with the appointment of clerks of works and resident architects.

The *Clerk of Works Manual* (RIBA Publications Limited) has been prepared jointly by the RIBA Management Advisory Committee and the Institute of Clerks of Works. This manual sets out, in some detail, the responsibilities and duties of clerks of works, and contains checklists based on the elements of a building so that inspection can be carried out of all the important elements. A series of standardised forms includes daily diary sheets and weekly report forms. Architects should remember that, whilst they can delegate to clerks of works and resident architects, they cannot generally delegate their responsibility for the work carried out by such people (see section 5.2). Clause 12 of the JCT 80 contract empowers the employer to appoint a clerk of works and an obligation on the contractor 'to afford every reasonable facility for the performance of that duty'. However, no instructions given by the clerk of works to the contractor are of any effect unless the architect confirms them within two working days of instructions being given: clause 12. The scheme of the JCT contract is that the architect, and not the clerk of works, has control over inspection and defects: see, for example, opening up for inspection (clause 8.3), removal of materials not in accordance with the contract (clause 8.4), practical completion, defects shrinkages and other faults, certificates of making good defects and damage by frost (clause 17), certifying of the value of work properly executed (clause 30.2), final certificates (clause 30.9 and 30.10). In respect of all these clauses, the obligations are upon the architect and not the clerk of works and whilst the architect may, in practice, delegate some of this work such as, for example, inspection prior to the certificate of making good defects, the architect cannot delegate his responsibility.

Achieving Quality on Building Sites was published by National Economic Development Office (NEDO) on behalf of the Building Economic Development Committee in 1987. This document should be compulsory reading for all those engaged in the building process who wish to achieve quality in building projects. The report is to some extent based on research carried out on real building projects; there is a very interesting analysis of quality related problems in the construction process both in relation to design and to workmanship. Furthermore, there are extensive recommendations as to what should be done in terms of management, relationships between the parties, education and training, and various other aspects. The report even contains a recommendation that the formal education of architects should include compulsory periods of site and management training.

6.3   Engineers

The ACE Conditions of Engagement also have provisions relating to supervision on site which are substantially the same in both Agreement 2 (where there is no architect) and Agreement 3 (where there is an architect appointed by the client). The conditions and comments on them are as follows:

> '8.1   If in the opinion of the Consulting Engineer the construction of the Works, including the carrying out of any geotechnical investigations pursuant to Clause 6.1 warrants full-time or part-time engineering staff to be depoloyed on site, the Client shall agree to the appointment of such

suitably qualified technical and clerical site staff as the Consulting Engineer shall consider reasonably necessary.'

The effect of this clause may be that the client has to agree to the appointment of those site staff which the consulting engineer considers to be reasonably necessary. It would follow that, if the client does not agree, he will be in breach of contract and at the same time, the engineer will not be relieved of his responsibility. In these circumstances, the engineer would probably be entitled to appoint such staff as he considers necessary and he may be entitled to recover the cost from his client under the contract. This issue would turn on whether or not the word 'agree' involves an act of agreement by the client on receipt of a proposal. If it does, this clause will be ineffective in law because agreements to agree are not binding in law.

'8.2   Persons appointed pursuant to Clause 8.1 shall be employed either by the Consulting Engineer or, if the Client and Consulting Engineer shall so agree, by the Client directly, provided that the Client shall not employ any person as a member of the site staff unless the Consulting Engineer has first approved such person as suitable for employment.'

The consulting engineer's approval of staff to be appointed by the client is more than a rubber stamp. It enables the consulting engineer to be satisfied that the person to be appointed is reliable and competent; the consulting engineer is not able to rely on a defence that the staff employed by the employer were incompetent: *Saunders* v. *Broadstairs Local Board* (1890).

'8.3   The terms of service of all site staff to be employed by the Consulting Engineer shall be subject to the approval of the Client, which approval shall not be unreasonably withheld.

8.4   The Client shall procure that the contracts of employment of site staff employed by the Client empower the Consulting Engineer to issue instructions in relation to the Works to such staff and shall stipulate that the staff so employed shall in no circumstances take or act upon instructions other than those of the Consulting Engineer.'

These conditions enable the consulting engineer to retain control of the way in which site staff carry out their duties. In other words, even though they may be employees of the client, their duties on the site are controlled by the consulting engineer. This is an important safeguard to the consulting engineer which is complemented by clause 8.5 which purports to exclude the consulting engineer's liability in circumstances where site staff employed by the client do not comply with the consulting engineer's instructions:

'8.5   Where site duties are performed by staff employed other than by the Consulting Engineer, the Consulting Engineer shall not be responsible for any failure on the part of such staff properly to comply with any instructions given by the Consulting Engineer.'

Whether or not site staff are appointed, the conditions impose duties on the consulting engineer in respect of site inspection:

'6.5   *Construction Stage*

. . .

(b)   Advising the Client and the Architect in relation to the need for special inspections or tests arising during the construction of the project.

(c)   Advising the Client and the Architect on the appointment of site staff in accordance with Clause 8.

. . .

(e)   Attending relevant site meetings and making other periodic visits to the site in order to assist the Architect to monitor that the Works are being executed generally in accordance with the contract and advising the Architect on the need for instructions to the contractor. The frequency of site visits allowed under Clause 10 [Payment] is fortnightly throughout the construction of the Works unless agreed otherwise at the appointment stage. The presence of the Consulting Engineer, his employees, agents or any site staff appointed pursuant to Clause 8, on site shall not relieve the contractor of his responsibility for the correctness of the materials and methods used by the contractor, nor for the safety of the Works or any temporary works during the course of the construction.'

It follows from 6.5 (e) that the only visits allowed for in the fees are fortnightly, unless otherwise agreed. This may well be thought by some to be inadequate even though fixed in law. It remains to be seen what view a court will take of the standard of the duty here which is fixed by timing when all the decided cases indicate that the visits should be fixed by need. Any engineer working on this form with fortnightly visits would be well advised to notify his client in writing if he feels, say because of an inexperienced contractor or some other factor on site, that more frequent visits are required.

The ICE Conditions of Contract, 6th Edition, contain provisions in relation to resident engineers who are defined in the contract as 'Engineer's Representative' but who are generally known as 'REs'. To be an effective appointment under the contract, the name of the RE has to be notified in writing to the contractor and his duties are to 'watch and supervise the construction and completion of the Works' (condition 2(3)(b)). The engineer or the RE can appoint assistants for particular purposes (condition 2(5)(a)). The RE can be authorised by the engineer to act in respect of any of the engineer's functions under the conditions of contract provided that prior notice is given in writing by the engineer to the contractor (condition 2(4)).

Chapter 7

Liability to contractor and third parties; collateral warranties

In the traditional arrangement for carrying out construction work, the designer will be in contract with the employer; he will not have a contract with any third party or the contractor. It follows that neither the contractor nor any other third party will be able to bring an action against a designer in contract and will have to rely on the law of tort. It is useful to consider the liabilities that can be incurred to contractors and other third parties separately.

7.1   Contractors

Whether or not a contractor is entitled to rely on a design as being capable of construction or lawful has been considered in a number of cases. One of the leading cases in this field, now more than 100 years old, is authority for the proposition that, by inviting tenders for specified work, an employer does not impliedly warrant to the tenderers that the design is capable of construction: *Thorn* v. *Corporation of London* (1876). The facts of the case were as follows.

A contractor contracted with an employer to take down an old bridge and build a new one. Plans and a specification had been prepared by the employer's engineer. The design involved the use of caissons which turned out to be useless and the bridge had to be built in a different manner. The contractor sought compensation for his losses caused by the failure of the caissons on the basis that the employer had warranted that the bridge could be inexpensively built according to the plans and specifications. The House of Lords held that no such warranty could be implied.

Whilst the *Thorn* case provides a general rule, the position is different where there is an express warranty that the works are capable of construction in accordance with plans and specification, or in circumstances where the designer owes a duty of care to the contractor and is in breach of that duty, or where the designer negligently makes a statement that the contractor relies upon. The designer can also incur liability in respect of his design where he exceeds the authority vested in him by the employer.

7.1.1   Claims by contractors: the historical perspective

It used to be thought that, where a third party has the role of deciding a question between two other parties in circumstances where he has to act fairly between the two parties, the third party could not be held liable in negligence for anything done while he was so acting. This was thought to apply, for example, to architects when certifying. It was said that architects, when certifying, were in the position of quasi-arbitrators and were immune from liability. The case of *Sutcliffe* v. *Thackrah and Others* (1974) considered that issue.

The employer engaged architects to act in respect of the design and erection of a house. Eventually, a JCT 63 Contract was entered into between the employer and a contractor. The contractor was slow and in due course the building contract was determined. The architect's interim certificates had been issued without deduction in respect of defective work. The employer could not recover his losses from the contractor, who was now insolvent, and sought damages from the architect. It was held that the architect, in issuing interim certificates, was not acting as a quasi-arbitrator and was not, therefore, immune from liability. An architect issuing interim certificates has a duty to act fairly between the employer and the contractor. The employer can therefore recover his loss from an architect who has negligently issued interim certificates.

In *Sutcliffe*, Lord Reid, having described many of the decisions that an architect makes which affect the amount of money a contractor will receive, said:

'... and, perhaps most important, he has to decide whether work is defective. These decisions will be reflected in the amounts contained in certificates issued by the architect. The building owner and the contractor make their contract on the understanding that in all such matters the architect will act in a fair and unbiased manner and it must, therefore, be implicit in the owner's contract with the architect that he shall not only exercise due care and skill but also reach such decisions fairly holding the balance between his client and the contractor.'

Whilst this passage did not go so far as to state unequivocally that the architect owed a duty of care in such circumstances, a later case, which concerned negligent valuation of shares by a firm of chartered accountants, made it tolerably clear that the architect did owe such a duty to the contractor: *Arenson* v. *Casson, Beckman, Rutley & Co.* (1975). In *Arenson* Lord Salmon said, in the House of Lords, having referred to *Sutcliffe*:

'The architect owed a duty to his client, the building owner, arising out of the contract between them to use reasonable care in issuing his certificates. He also, however, owed a similar duty of care to the contractor arising out of their proximity: see *Hedley Byrne Co. Limited* v. *Heller & Partners Limited*. In *Sutcliffe* v. *Thackrah* the architect negligently certified that more money was due than was in fact due, and he was successfully sued for the damage which this had caused his client. He might, however, have negligently certified that less money was payable than was in fact due and thereby starved the contractor of money. In a trade in which cash flow is especially important, this might have caused the contractor serious damage for which the architect could have been successfully sued.'

In a case in the Hong Kong Supreme Court, *Shui On Construction Co. Limited* v. *Shui Kay Co. Limited and Another* (1985), an application was made to the court by defendant architects that the claim brought against them by main contractor plaintiffs should be dismissed. The essence of the claim was that the architects owed the main contractors a duty to exercise reasonable skill and care in the performance of their functions pursuant to the contract, and to act fairly and impartially in the performance of those functions. Although of course on this preliminary point the judge did not make a final finding as to a duty or to liability, he refused to strike out the claim against the architects on the basis that there was an arguable claim against them. The report of the application, however, sets out an interesting analysis of the then relevant cases, including *Sutcliffe* and *Arenson*.

In a case on a most complex set of facts, *Lubenham Fidelities and Investment Co. Limited* v. *South Pembrokeshire District Council and Another* (1986), the Court of Appeal had to consider various matters arising out of a judgment of Judge John Newey QC, Official Referee. In order to understand this case, it is necessary to make short reference to two previous cases: *Panamena Europea Navigacion (Compania Limitada)* v. *Frederick Leyland & Co. Limited* (1943) and *Perini Corporation* v. *Commonwealth of Australia* (1969), Supreme Court of New South Wales.

In the *Panamena* case, shipowners made a contract for ship repair with a ship repairer. The shipowners' surveyor took the view that his duties were wider than provided for in the contract: the shipowners knew that he took that view and one of the issues that arose in the case was whether the shipowners owed any duty to the ship repairers in relation to the carrying out of his activities by the surveyor. In that case, Lord Justice Scott said:

> 'It seems to me plain if shipowners had known that he [the surveyor] was departing from his proper function under the contract, it would have been their [the shipowners'] duty to stop him and tell him what the function was for which the contract provided.... It obviously was not the contractual duty of the repairers to bring him to book. It is equally obvious that they would count on his carrying out his proper function. In those circumstances, I think the court ought to imply an undertaking by the owners that in the event of its becoming known to them that their surveyor was departing from the function which both parties had agreed he was to perform, they would call him to book, and tell him what his real function was. This seems to me an implication exactly on the lines of all the authorities on implied terms....'

That decision was carefully considered in the Australian case of *Perini*. This case concerned a building contract which gave to the supervising officer certain duties. Perini, the contractor, argued that the supervising officer, known in this contract as the 'Director of Works', was under a duty to act impartially and that it was an implied term of the contract that the employer, Commonwealth of Australia, should direct the Director of Works to so act. The case was put by the contractor in two ways: firstly that the employer should not interfere with the proper performance by the Director of Works of the duties imposed on him by the contract (called the negative implied term). Secondly, that the employer was bound to ensure that the Director of Works performed the various duties imposed upon him by the contract (called the positive implied term). The judge found both the negative and the positive implied terms were to be implied into the contract.

Both of these cases came to be considered in *Lubenham*. Lubenham were bondsmen who had elected to complete certain building contracts in place of the original contractors who had fallen out. The facts are particularly complicated, but in essence, interim certificates that were issued by the architects, who were a party to the proceedings, were not in accordance with the contract and in due course Lubenham determined their employment under the building contracts. The employer also served determination notices and a great many claims were made by each party against the other in the proceedings.

In particular, both Lubenham and the employer made claims against the architects on the basis that their negligence in relation to the certificates was the cause of the loss suffered; further, Lubenham sought to argue that the architects were liable in damages in that they had procured breaches of, or an interference with, the execution of the building contracts by the employer. The judge at first instance, Judge John Newey QC, Official Referee, found that although the architects had been in breach of their duties of care owed to both Lubenham and to the employer, those breaches had not been the cause of the loss, and accordingly he dismissed the claims against the architects. On appeal to the Court of Appeal, careful consideration was given to the effect of *Panamena* and *Perini* and the court rejected Lubenham's claim that the architects were liable in damages for procuring breaches of, or interfering with, the execution of the building contracts. The Court of Appeal appears to have come to this view on the basis that the architects, although entirely misguided, did not act with the express intention of interfering with the performance of the contracts. Lord Justice May put it this way:

'We would not accept the broad contention that an architect, in effecting an interim valuation under this form of building contract, could never in any circumstances expose himself to a claim under this head of tort. It seems to us, for example, quite possible that he could expose himself to an actionable claim that he had interfered with the building contractor's contractual rights if, in effecting a clause 30 valuation, he deliberately misapplied the provisions of the clause with the intention of depriving the contractor of the larger sums to which he would otherwise be entitled.'

In other words, the court regarded the deliberate misapplying of the provisions of the contract as being an essential ingredient to such a cause of action.

The Court of Appeal also considered whether the implication of the term in *Panamena* (namely an implied term that the employer would call his surveyor to book and tell him what his proper function was) was to be implied into the JCT 63 contract. Lord Justice May said:

'There is in our opinion one fundamental difference between the contract [in this case] and the one under consideration in *Panamena*. This is the presence in the contract which we have to consider of the very wide arbitration clause 35 which expressly permitted arbitration upon interim certificates during the currency of the contract and before practical completion. There was no arbitration clause at all in the contract before the courts in *Panamena*. In the light of the arbitration clause in the instant contract, we do not think there is any need or scope for the implication of any further term in it, as there was in *Panamena*. If, as is now common ground, the two challenged interim certificates in our case were not in accordance with the terms of the building contract, there was one simple remedy available to Lubenham needing no implied term, namely to go to arbitration upon them and have them corrected. For these reasons, we do not think that the appellants [the bondsman/contractor] can derive any assistance from the decision in *Panamena* and in our opinion the learned Judge below was totally right in his decision...'

Although in this case the question as to whether or not a duty is owed by an architect to a contractor was canvassed, it is probably the case, it is submitted, that the *Lubenham* decision makes no finding on that point.

7.1.2   Claims by contractors: current position

In *Michael Salliss & Co. Limited* v. *E. C. A. & F B. Calil and William F. Newman & Associates* (1987). Various issues arose between the contractor, an employer and the architects. The contractor was the plaintiff and he made allegations against the architects who were joined in as second defendants in the proceedings. The court reviewed *Thackrah, Arenson* and *Lubenham*, as well as considering the *Shui On* case referred to above. In relation to *Lubenham*, the judge decided that the Court of Appeal in *Lubenham* did not make any finding as to whether or not a duty relationship existed between the architects and the contractor. Having reviewed all the authorities, Judge Fox-Andrews QC, Official Referee, went on to find, amongst other things, that in relation to the JCT 63 contract involved in this case:

(1) The architects owed the contractor a duty to use all proper professional skill and care in authorising extensions to the contract period under clause 23.

(2) The architects had breached their duty by certifying an extension of only 12 weeks.

(3) The architects owed to the contractor a duty to act with reasonable expedition in certifying the extension of time, and that compliance with the duty at (1) above would have resulted in a 29 week extension of time for completion.

(4) The architects were in breach of duty to the contractor in failing to certify that the costs, other than the on-site establishment costs, were due from the employer to the contractor pursuant to clause 24(1) (being the clause relating to direct loss and/or expense) during the extension of 12 weeks, or alternatively that such other costs during the period of 12 weeks and/or the period of 29 weeks fell out of the scope of their certificate by clause 24(2) and were therefore recoverable from the employer subject to the general law of contract.

These findings were made in a sub-trial which had been heard on the application of the architects, as to whether the contractor could recover damages for negligence from the architects on the facts pleaded by the contractor, or whether the damages claimed were too remote. In finding that the architects did owe duties to the contractor, the court adopted the reasoning of *Thackrah* and *Arenson* and said that, to the extent that the contractor was able to establish damage resulting from the architects' unfairness in respect of matters in which, under the contract, the architects were required to act impartially, damages were recoverable and were not too remote.

Further, where the architect was acting in his capacity as the employer's agent, for example, ordering a variation, there was no such duty but, for example, once having ordered a variation, he had an obligation to act fairly in pricing the variation. It followed from these findings that the judge concluded that there was no duty owed to the contractor by the architect to use all proper professional skill and care in the preparation of the specification and drawings; there was no such duty to take all such steps as were necessary to ensure that the contractor would carry out work continuously from the commencement date; there was also no duty owed to the contractor to carry out a full and accurate survey prior to the preparation of the specification and plans and in any event before commencement of the works.

7.1.2.1   *Pacific Associates*

The decision in the *Salliss* case was delivered in the same year as the judgment of another Official Referee, Judge John Davies QC, in *Pacific Associates Inc. and RB Construction Limited* v. *Halcrow International Partnership and Others* (1987). In this case, the contractor plaintiffs were engaged on the FIDIC contract (the international form of civil engineering contract) to carry out dredging and reclamation works for the Ruler of Dubai, who was the employer. Halcrow were the engineers engaged by the Ruler to administer the contract.

In the construction contract between the contractor and the Ruler of Dubai, there had been an arbitration clause and another provision in the following form:

> 'Neither ... the Engineer nor any of his staff, nor the Engineer's Representative shall be in any way personally liable for the acts or obligations under the contract, or answerable for any default or omission on the part of the Employer in the observance or performance of any of the acts, matters or things which are herein contained.'

Disputes arose between the contractor and the Ruler which went to arbitration. Those disputes were the subject of an agreed settlement. Thereafter, the contractor started proceedings against the engineers seeking to recover money that they claimed arose from negligent certification by the engineers. The engineers applied to the court to have the claim against them struck out.

The Official Referee came to a very different conclusion from that in *Michael Saliss*: no duty of care was owed by the engineers to the contractor and the judge struck out the claim against the engineers. This case then went to the Court of Appeal which upheld the judge's decision. The basis of the decision in the Court of Appeal was twofold; firstly, they said that the arbitration clause entitled the contractor to challenge, in arbitration with the Ruler, the certification of the engineers. Secondly, the disclaimer of liability of the engineers set out above could not be ignored. These two points taken together prevented the imposition of a duty of care on the engineers.

It is, of course, the case that both the JCT family of contracts and the ICE family of contracts all contain arbitration clauses, although none of them contain any disclaimer of liability on behalf of the certifier. However, the presence of an arbitration clause in *Michael Salliss* did not prevent the judge there finding a duty of care. In *Pacific Associates*, the Court of Appeal were referred to *Michael Salliss* but they did not overrule it: Lord Justice Purchas, however, did say that he

doubted the earlier decision. It seems that the present state of the law is represented by the decision in *Pacific Associates*. Indeed, in *Leon Engineering & Construction Co. Limited* v. *Ka Duk Investment Co. Limited* (1990), *Pacific Associates* was
followed in the Hong Kong courts. Here, a contractor failed to have the architects
joined into the proceedings as defendants. They had sought to argue that the
architects owed them a duty to give timely, proper and impartial consideration
to the claims of the contractor. Mr Justice Bokhary founded his decision on there
being machinery in the contract between the contractor and the building owner
to deal with such issues.

However, there may be some very exceptional situations in which the decision
in *Pacific Associates* could be distinguished. For example:

(1) Where there is no arbitration clause in the construction contract or other
method of challenging certification by the certifier, and, no disclaimer, or

(2) Where the certifier has under-certified, the employer has become insolvent and the construction contract did not permit the challenging of
certificates in arbitration or otherwise until after practical completion.

7.1.2.2 Canadian cases after Pacific Associates

The British Columbia Court of Appeal in *Edgeworth Construction Limited* v. *N.D.
Lea & Associates Limited* and *Edgeworth Construction Limited* v. *Walji and Others*
followed *Pacific Associates* in a case on a rather different issue. Here, the engineers
had prepared designs for a road for the Ministry of Highways; the contractors
had obtained the contract at tender; the engineers were not the engineers for the
purposes of the construction contract. The contractors claimed that the design
had been negligently prepared and that the engineers were liable for negligent
mis-statements arising out of the preparation of the tender drawings, plans and
specifications which had led to the contractors incurring substantial additional
expenditure. The engineers applied to the court for summary judgment on the
grounds that they owed no duty of care: they were successful.

The British Columbia Court of Appeal emphasised the need for foreseeability,
reliance and proximity as essential ingredients in a duty of care. Here, when the
Ministry used the engineers' designs, they became representations of the Ministry to prospective bidders, and they ceased to be representations of the engineers. Any questions as to defects and the like in the design became matters for
the contract between the contractor and the Ministry. There was no direct relationship between the engineers and the contractor. The necessary proximity was
missing. (There is a useful summary of other relevant Canadian cases in the
commentary on *Edgeworth* in *Building Law Reports*.)

Edgeworth does not decide the position where the facts may be different: for
example, where the engineers are the engineers making the representations (as
opposed to the Ministry) where a *Hedley Byrne* relationship would more easily be
created. In another Canadian case, for example, engineers were held liable to the
contractor in relation to pre-tender matters: *Auto Concrete Curb Limited* v. *South
Nation River Conservation Authority* (1992, Ontario Court of Appeal). Factors
present here included the fact that the engineers knew or ought to have known of
reliance by the contractor on the tender documents; that failure to include relevant information was a negligent misrepresentation; and that the contractor
could not be expected to make enquiries in the short tender period whereas the

engineers had had many months to make those enquiries themselves, had they chosen to do so.

7.1.2.3   Defects

Many attempts have been made by contractors, when sued in respect of defective workmanship, to seek to argue that the designer, in carrying out his supervisory duties, owed the contractor a duty of care to detect or prevent the defective workmanship. Such an argument was put forward in the case of *Oldschool and Another* v. *Gleeson (Construction) Limited and Others* (1976) where a party wall collapsed during building works. The contractor, having admitted liability to the employer, claimed against the consulting engineers by alleging that they owed the contractors a duty of care in relation to the design and supervision of the works. Of this contention, Judge Stabb QC said:

> 'I take the view that the duty of care which an architect or a consulting engineer owes to a third party is limited by the assumption that the contractor who executes the works acts at all times as a competent contractor. The contractor cannot seek to pass the blame for incompetent work on to the consulting engineer on the grounds that he failed to intervene to prevent it ... the responsibility of the consulting engineer is for the design of the engineering components of the works and his supervisory responsibility is to his client to ensure that the works are carried out in accordance with that design. But if, as was suggested here, the design was so faulty that a competent contractor in the course of executing the works could not have avoided the resulting damage, then on principle it seems to me that the consulting engineer responsible for that design should bear the loss.'

It was found that the consulting engineer's design was not fundamentally unsound and the contractor's claim failed. However, the statement of the consulting engineer's duty in this case makes it clear that a consulting engineer might incur liability to the contractor in circumstances where his design was such that a competent contractor could not have avoided the resulting damage.

The designer, in certain circumstances, is under a duty not to make careless statements to the contractor and in order to establish such liability, the contractor will have to show that he relied on the special skill and judgment of the designer and that the designer knew or ought to have known of the contractor's reliance. This principle was established in *Hedley Byrne & Co. Limited* v. *Heller & Partners Limited* (1964). However, the principle established by that case appears to have been foreseen by the Court of Appeal in *Townsend (Builders) Limited* v. *Cinema News Property Management* (1959) when an architect was held liable to a contractor.

A contractor carried out work for an employer subject to an architect's directions and satisfaction. Part of the works did not comply with the building by-laws, in breach of the contractor's express obligations. The architect, who had agreed to serve the statutory notices, did not do so until after completion of the work and the local authority condemned the construction. The Court of Appeal held that the employer could recover damages from the contractor for breach of his obligation to comply with the by-laws and the contractor was entitled to recover his loss from the architect for breach of the duty he had undertaken to the contractor to serve a statutory notice.

There are two important points to note from the *Townsend* case. Firstly, the fact that the contractor relied on the architect to see that by-laws were complied with in his design did not prevent the contractor being held liable for breach of his express obligation to comply with the by-laws. There are such express obligations in both the JCT and the ICE forms of contract. Secondly, the contractor recovered a 100% contribution from the architect; this will not always be so: see also *Eames London Estates Limited and Others* v. *North Hertfordshire District Council and Others* (1981).

7.1.2.4   *Information on ground conditions*

It is very common for designers to obtain information about the nature of the subsoil on a site from firms of expert geotechnical engineers. These soil investigations often take the form of a series of bore holes across the site to enable the strata at each location to be plotted. This information is more often than not made available to tendering contractors but usually on the basis that the employer does not warrant its accuracy and that the contractor is advised to make his own investigation. Such a clause appears in condition 11(2) of the ICE Conditions of Contract, 6th Edition:

'11(2)   The Contractor shall be deemed to have inspected and examined the Site and its surroundings and information available in connection therewith and to have satisfied himself so far as is practicable and reasonable before submitting his Tender as to

(a)   the form and nature thereof including the ground and subsoil
(b)   the extent and nature of work and materials necessary for constructing and completing the Works and
(c)   the means of communications with and access to the Site and the accommodation he may require

and in general to have obtained for himself all necessary information as to risks contingencies and all other circumstances which may influence or affect his tender.'

The words 'so far as is practicable and reasonable' are new to the 6th Edition of the contract and their effect is not clear. However, it may be that these words entitle the contractor to rely on information given by or on behalf of the employer so as to bring an action for negligent mis-statement or misrepresentation in the event that the information is inaccurate. An action for misrepresentation could only be brought against the employer (i.e. the other party to the contract). However, this does not mean that the designer could not also incur liability in negligence.

In an Australian case, contractors contended that information provided to them at tender stage as to the soil conditions at the site was false, inaccurate and misleading. There were words similar to condition 11(2) of the ICE Conditions of Contract and the site information was endorsed with the words 'this document does not form part of the contract document'.

The High Court of Australia found that they could not deal with the issues before them until they had heard evidence on all the relevant facts but they did find that the documents did not, of themselves, show that the contractors had no cause of action. Chief Justice Barwick said, in *Morrison-Knudsen International Co. Inc. and Another* v. *Commonwealth of Australia* (1972), Australia:

'The basic information in the site information document appears to have been the result of much highly technical effort on the part of a department of the [employer]. It was information which the [contractors] had neither the time nor the opportunity to obtain for themselves. It might even be doubted whether they could be expected to obtain it by their own efforts as a potential or actual tenderer. But it was indispensable information if a judgment were to be formed as to the extent of the work to be done in making the landing strip of the proposed airport.'

It is likely that, to succeed in such a claim, the contractor would have to show that he relied on the special skill or knowledge of the employer or designer and that the employer or designer knew or ought to have known of the reliance when they were making their statements.

Another Australian case illustrates how a contractor's claim can fail by not satisfying these basic criteria. In *Dillingham Construction Pty Limited and Others* v. *Downs* (1972), Australia, a contractor agreed to execute work for the deepening of a harbour. Progress in blasting was slower than expected because it appeared that there were underground mine workings which might be dissipating the effect of blasting. The contractor sued the employer for negligent mis-statement on the basis that the employer had known of the underground mine workings at the time of tender, but had not told the contractor. The court held that in such circumstances there could be a duty of care, but that in this particular case the government had not accepted the task of providing full and accurate information as to the site, and in any event the contractor had not relied upon that information, and the claim failed.

The essential element of 'reliance' was in the mind of the court in the *Dillingham* case. In order to satisfy this criterion, it is not essential that the party making the statement should *know* that reliance is being placed on the statement provided that he *ought to have known* there was such reliance. For example, in *Yianni* v. *Edwin Evans & Son* (1981) a surveyor who was reporting to a building society in respect of a building society valuation was held liable to a house purchaser: the surveyor should have known that the purchaser would not have proceeded if the building society had not proceeded with the loan.

There is well established authority for such claims in the United States of America. The most commonly cited case is *Helene Curtis Industries Inc.* v. *The United States* (1963), United States Court of Claims. The issue concerned the failure of the government to tell a contractor what it should about an active ingredient to be utilised in the preparation of novel disinfectant powder but the findings are applied on a regular basis to construction disputes where there was a lack of soils information given to the contractor but the employer had such information available to him. Mr Justice Davis in that case said:

'In this situation, the government, possessing vital information which it was aware the bidders needed but would not have, could not properly let them flounder on their own. Although it is not a fiduciary towards its contractors, the government where the balance of knowledge is so clearly on its side ... can no more betray a contractor into a ruinous course of action by silence than by the written or spoken word.'

That case is not, of course, binding on the English courts. There is an interesting discussion on similar cases from Canada to be found in Volumes 21 and 54 of *Building Law Reports*, and see *Edgeworth* above.

7.2 Third parties other than contractors

Designers can incur liability to parties who were not parties to the original principal contracts. These possible plaintiffs include subsequent owners and purchasers, occupiers/users of the building, and workmen during construction. Liability can arise under statute, in tort and under contracts with the third parties, known as collateral warranties. All of these points are now considered separately.

7.2.1 Statutes

For a discussion of liability that may arise under the Building Regulations and for breach of statutory duty, see section 4.3.

The Defective Premises Act 1972 imposes a duty on 'a person taking on work for or in connection with the provision of the dwelling (whether the dwelling is provided by the erection or by the conversion or enlargement of the building) ... to see that the work which he takes on is done in a ... professional manner ... so that as regards that work the dwelling will be fit for habitation when completed': section 1(1).

This duty is owed both to the person for whom the dwelling is provided and to every person who acquires an interest in the dwelling. That interest can be either a freehold interest or a tenancy. The duty is clearly owed to subsequent purchasers (section 1(1)(b)). The Act is discussed at section 2.3.4.

7.2.2 Liability to subsequent owners and tenants

Liability to subsequent owners and tenants has to be discussed by reference to three categories of possible claim: tort, the possibilities discussed in *St Martin's*, and under collateral warranties (contracts with the third party direct). These are now taken separately.

7.2.3 Tort

Since *D & F* and *Murphy*, subsequent owners and tenants have had an avenue of claim largely cut off from them. Where defects are discovered before they cause either or both personal injury or damage to property other than the 'thing itself', damages are not recoverable. Those damages are categorised in law as irrecoverable economic loss. It is not now possible to recover economic loss in building cases except where the 'complex structure' argument can be used or there is negligent advice under the principle established in *Hedley Byrne*. These matters are discussed in detail at section 2.2.

7.2.4   *Linden Gardens Trust Limited v. Lenesta Sludge Disposals Limited; St Martin's Property Corporation Limited and Another v. Sir Robert McAlpine Limited*

Linden Gardens (1993) and *St Martin's* (1993) were both heard at the same time in the House of Lords. They are cases that have a profound series of consequences. Before turning to those consequences it is necessary to look at the facts.

7.2.4.1   *The facts of Linden Gardens*

Linden Gardens concerned the removal of blue asbestos from a building in London then owned by Stock Conversion and Investment Trust Limited, who entered into a contract with McLaughlin and Harvey plc for that purpose. The contract, which was let in 1979, was a JCT 63 contract and clause 17 provided:

'17(1)   The Employer shall not without the written consent of the Contractor assign this Contract.

(2)   The Contractor shall not without the written consent of the Employer assign this Contract, and shall not without the written consent of the Architect (which consent shall not be unreasonably withheld to the prejudice of the Contractor) sub-let any portion of the Works.

Provided that it shall be a condition in any sub-letting which may occur that the employment of the sub-contractor under the sub-contract shall determine immediately upon the determination (for any reason) of the Contractor's employment under this Contract.'

In 1987, Stock Conversion transferred its rights in the building to Linden Gardens. The contractor's consent was not obtained under Clause 17 or at all. Subsequently, more blue asbestos was found in the building which cost £236,000 to remove.

7.2.4.2   *The facts of St Martin's*

The facts of *St Martin's* were similar. St Martin's Property Corporation Limited ('Corporation') developed a site in Hammersmith and Sir Robert McAlpine Limited were the contractors on a JCT 63 contract which contained a prohibition on assignment. That prohibition was for all practical purposes in terms identical to those in *Linden Gardens*.

During the work on site, at a time before any defects were discovered, Corporation assigned its rights in the development to St Martin's Property Investments Limited ('Investments'). The contractor's consent was not obtained under clause 17 or at all. In 1980 the project was finished but in 1981 leaks developed in part of the building. Part of the remedial works cost approximately £800,000 and was paid for by Corporation but recovered from Investments. Corporation and Investments claimed against McAlpine.

7.2.4.3   *The House of Lords decision*

In *Linden Gardens*, the House of Lords decided that the purported assignment of the benefit of the building contract was ineffective because the contractor's consent was required under the contract and had not been obtained. They referred to the 'unhappily drafted' and 'inelegant phraseology' of clause 17 which referred to the assignment of the 'contract' rather than the 'benefit of the contract' but they had little difficulty coming to the conclusion that the words were not limited to sub-contracting. Linden Gardens' further argument that the clause only prohibited the right to have the contractual obligations carried out and not the right to damages was also rejected by the House. Lord Browne-Wilkinson said:

> 'The reason for including the contractual prohibition viewed from the contractor's point of view must be that the contractor wishes to ensure that he deals, and deals only, with the particular employer with whom he has chosen to enter into a contract. Building contracts are pregnant with disputes: some employers are much more reasonable than others in dealing with such disputes. The disputes frequently arise in the context of the contractor suing for the price and being met by a claim for abatement of the price or cross-claims founded on an allegation that the performance of the contract has been defective. Say that, before the final instalment of the price has been paid, the employer has assigned the benefits under the contract to a third party, there being at the time existing rights of action for defective work. On the Court of Appeal's view, those rights would have vested in the assignee. Would the original employer be entitled to an abatement of the price, even though the cross-claims would be vested in the assignee? If so, would the assignee be a necessary party to any settlement or litigation of the claims for defective work, thereby requiring the contractor to deal with two parties (one not of his own choice) in order to recover the price for the works from the employer? I cannot believe that the parties ever intended to permit such a confused position to arise.'

Linden Gardens' final argument was that the prohibition on assignment was contrary to public policy also failed and Linden Gardens failed to recover any damages.

In consequence of all of that, Investments in *St Martin's* could not succeed but this left to be decided the arguments put forward by Corporation. McAlpine had an apparently formidable argument in law: Investments had suffered the loss but had no cause of action, whereas Corporation had a cause of action but had suffered no loss – either way, they argued, they should have no liability. This powerful, but perhaps unmeritorious, argument was rejected by the House with Lord Browne-Wilkinson borrowing the words of Lord Keith in *G.U.S Property Management Limited* v. *Littlewood Mail Order Stores Limited* (1982):

> '... the claim for damages would disappear ... into some legal black hole, so that the wrongdoer escaped scot-free.'

The decision of the House on this point is that Corporation were entitled to recover under their contract with McAlpine the loss suffered by Investments. This was said to be a new exception to the general rule that a party can only sue in respect of a loss that it has suffered. In this respect, it is a surprising result to lawyers who hold more traditional views. Lord Browne-Wilkinson put it this way:

'The present case falls within the rationale of the exceptions to the general rule that a plaintiff can only recover damages for his own loss. The contract was for a large development of property which, in the knowledge of both Corporation and McAlpine, was going to be occupied, and possibly purchased, by third parties and not by Corporation itself. Therefore it could be foreseen that damage caused by a breach would cause loss to a later owner and not merely to the original contracting party, Corporation. As in contracts for the carriage of goods by land, there would be no automatic vesting in the occupier or owners of the property for the time being who sustained the loss of any right of suit against McAlpine. On the contrary, McAlpine had specifically contracted that the rights of action under the building contract *could* not without McAlpine's consent be transferred to third parties who became owners or occupiers and might suffer loss. In such a case, it seems to me proper, as in the case of carriage of goods by land, to treat the parties as having entered into the contract on the footing that Corporation would be entitled to enforce contractual rights for the benefit of those who suffered from defective performance but who, under the terms of the contract, could not acquire any right to hold McAlpine liable for breach. It is truly a case in which the rule provides "a remedy where no other would be available to a person sustaining loss which under a rational legal system ought to be compensated by the person who has caused it".'

In coming to this view, the House expressly rejected argument put by counsel for McAlpine that this was an exceptional case and that it would be wrong to distort the law in this way just for such an exceptional case. The difficulties consequent on this case will therefore have to be worked out in future cases. For example, what is the position where a subsequent purchaser has a collateral warranty – is the original owner precluded from bringing this kind of action where a collateral warranty exists? Can a subsequent owner force the original developer to take action on his behalf where the original owner refuses to do so? Will there be a movement to granting such obligations to tenants in commercial leases? Will there be a trend to amend the assignment provisions in standard form contracts, bearing in mind that JCT 80, for example, contains a similar provision to that in these cases? Will lawyers dealing with the sale of property obtain approval in writing to assignments where approval is required (the issue that really led to these cases)?

The House of Lords, having effectively killed actions in tort by subsequent owners and occupiers in respect of defects by their decisions in *D & F* and *Murphy*, have now given back some rights by changing the law of contract in a fairly radical and fundamental way, the implications of which may take some time to work through.

7.2.4.4   *Linden Gardens/St Martin's – summary of present position*
However, in the meantime, the following might be said to represent the position created by this case and its possible consequences:

(1)   Where there has been a valid assignment:

(a)   and transfer of the property before the breach of contract, such as a sale of a building during construction, there should be no problem in the assignee being able to sue (although this point did not arise expressly for decision in the House of Lords).

(b) and transfer of the property after the breach of contract, the position is more difficult. The Court of Appeal in *Linden Gardens* regarded the situation of a *simultaneous transfer of property and the assignment* as being decided by *Dawson* v. *Great Northern and City Railway Co.* (1905, Court of Appeal) in which it was decided that the assignee could recover in respect of the assignor's rights. The point was that the purpose of the arrangements was to put the assignee in as nearly the precise position as the assignor was in relation to his pre-existing rights. Is the position the same if the assignment is at a later date than the transfer of the property?

Here, the no-loss argument comes into its own: the assignor receives the value of the building and, it may be said, the accrued rights sought to be transferred by the assignment are therefore valueless. This is what happened in *Linden Gardens*. Although the Court of Appeal decided that the assignee could recover the assignor's claim to substantial damages, the House of Lords did not deal with the point. It seems, therefore, that the Court of Appeal remains good authority on this point.

(c) before the breach of contract but that breach took place after the transfer of the property, there could be difficulties for the assignee. Here, the right to sue under the contract remained with the assignor after transfer of the property and it is apparently easy to argue that he does not suffer a loss because he does not own the building; therefore the assignment passed no rights to the assignee. This point remains arguable after *St Martin's* in cases where there is a valid assignment but in that case the difficulty was overcome by the device at (2) below.

(2) Where there is no assignment, or an invalid assignment, and the purchaser bears the loss (defects made good, for example), the vendor can recover the loss, even though he has not suffered any loss himself. The vendor must account to the purchaser for the proceeds. It seems this position may not apply where there exists, for example, a valid collateral warranty for the benefit of the purchaser:

'The original building owner will not be able to recover damage for loss suffered by others who can themselves sue for such loss': Lord Browne-Wilkinson in *St Martin's*.

That statement is probably *obiter dicta* (not binding) and this issue therefore will remain an open question until it is decided in some future case.

(3) There is however no machinery or other means, in the absence of relevant contract provisions, that enables the purchaser to force the vendor to take the proceedings envisaged at (2) above. In other words, in the absence of willing co-operation from the vendor, the rights created for the benefit of the purchaser in *St Martin's* are worthless. It may be that conveyancers acting for purchasers will be looking to create contractual obligations on vendors in this respect in the contract for sale, in provisions that survive completion and are capable of being assigned to future purchasers. Indeed, this will be essential where valid and effective collateral warranties cannot be obtained from the design and construction team.

However, where there are such warranties, the remedy at (2) may be ineffective. Purchasers may therefore seek to secure every possible right (i.e. collateral warranties and the remedies at (2) and (3)) in case some later prove to be ineffective when needed through invalid assignment, the no-loss argument, insolvency or the like. If this occurs, as seems likely, then there will be multi-party litigation that simply cannot be in the public interest.

(4) The House of Lords probably did not affect the result of an earlier case heard by Judge John Newey QC, Official Referee: *IMI Cornelius (UK) Limited* v. *Alan J. Bloor and Others* (1991). In that case, building work had been done for IMI on a factory occupied and leased to them. Subsequently, IMI assigned their interest in the property, for group administrative purposes, to another company in the group. Thereafter, IMI began proceedings against Bloor, the contractor, in respect of the cost of making good defects or, alternatively, the diminution in value, or the return of sums overpaid. It was held that IMI could not recover the cost of repairs as IMI no longer had the proprietary interest in the property and no longer had the right to repair it. However, they had not lost the right to recover damages for the diminution in value of the building.

(5) The House of Lords did not grapple with the question as to what kind or quantum of damages an assignee can recover. The Court of Appeal allowed that the assignee could recover the cost of remedying defects. It may be that the position is still best covered by *Dawson*, in the Court of Appeal, in which the approach was to allow categories or types of loss to be recovered by the assignee provided they were the categories or types of loss that could have been recovered by the assignor. In other words, the party being sued cannot be put in any worse position as regards damages for breach of contract than he was prior to the assignment.

(6) The JCT are likely to amend their assignment provisions in the standard forms. There will be pressure from developers for contracts (building contracts, conditions of engagement and collateral warranties) to be drafted so as to permit assignment without the consent of the other party. This will be potentially in conflict with the usual professional indemnity policy terms (see section 10.3.2) at least in respect of collateral warranties.

(7) It is more than a little unfortunate that property development and construction generally should be in the position of having such complication surrounding issues that ought perhaps to be addressed by legislation rather than the system of judicial precedent, with its almost inevitable fluctuations over time. Property is a long term investment: certainty in this area of the law should be an essential ingredient of its success. Statutory intervention is probably now desirable.

7.2.4.5   *Cases following Linden Gardens and St Martin's*
The two House of Lords decisions fell to be considered in *Darlington Borough Council* v. *Wiltshier Northern Limited and Others* (1993). Those who thought the House of Lords had created in *St Martin's* a panacea for all ills found that this Official Referee's case meant that that was not so.

Darlington decided to redevelop its town centre in the 1970s and borrowed from Morgan Grenfell for that purpose. The arrangements were that Morgan Grenfell would carry out the developments on Darlington's land; Darlington would enter into finance agreements with Morgan Grenfell who also appointed Darlington as their agents to exercise their rights and duties under the contracts, so that Morgan Grenfell were the employers under the building contract. Morgan Grenfell were to pay the contractor direct but gave no warranties to Darlington as to the contractor's performance. The building contracts contained no prohibition on assignment and Morgan Grenfell agreed to assign the benefit to Darlington. They also assigned to Darlington warranties, terms and conditions in relation to the construction and to assist with their enforcement. If liquidated damages became payable then they were payable to Darlington, not Morgan Grenfell.

After construction was finished, defects appeared. Darlington received the promised assignment of Morgan Grenfell's rights and causes of action and issued proceedings against the contractor.

In *Linden Gardens* it had been held that an assignee cannot recover greater damages than the assignor could have recovered. To recover its loss, therefore, Darlington had to show that Morgan Grenfell could have recovered. It was argued by Darlington that Morgan Grenfell had entered into the contract for the benefit of Darlington in the same way that St Martin's Property Corporation Limited had entered into the contract for the benefit of St Martin's Property Investments Limited. The Official Referee, Judge John Newey QC said:

'The question posed ... is whether Darlington as assignee of Grenfell has a valid claim against Wiltshier for damages other than nominal for breach of each building contract.

It is, I think, clearly established, most recently by judgments in the Court of Appeal in *Linden Gardens Trust Limited* v. *Lenesta Sludge Disposals Limited and Others* and *St Martin's Corporation Limited and Another* v. *Sir Robert McAlpine & Sons Limited* (1992) of Lord Justice Staughton at p.80 and of Sir Michael Kerr at p.97, that an assignee can only enforce claims against the debtor which his assignor could have done and cannot recover greater damages than the assignor could have done. If, therefore, Darlington is to recover more than nominal damages from Wiltshier, it must be because Grenfell could have done so.

If at material times Grenfell had owned or been lessees of the Dolphin Centre site and had been developing it on their own account they would undoubtedly have recovered substantial damages from Wiltshier for breaches of contract. The measure of damages would have been the difference in value of the Centre with and without the defects, which would almost certainly have been the cost of repairs.

If after the breaches of contract had occurred Grenfell had parted with its freehold or leasehold interest in the property, so that it could no longer carry out repairs, it could still I think have recovered the difference in value – as I held that the plaintiff could in *IMI Cornelius (UK) Limited* v. *Alan J Bloor* (1991). If after the breach had occurred and Grenfell had both conveyed its interest in the Centre and assigned its rights under the building contracts to the same person, the assignee could have recovered the difference in value, being the cost of repairs.

In fact in this case Grenfell had neither a freehold nor a leasehold interest in the site, but only a licence for the period which it took to complete the works. Grenfell were not carrying out development on their own account. Under the financing agreements what it had to do was to enter into the building contracts and to make payments under them on certificates issued by Darlington's architect. Pursuant to clause 3(5) it assigned immediately any warranties and the like which it would receive from Wiltshier. On completion of the works Grenfell's licence came to an end and so did its connection with the site.

That Grenfell would not suffer any loss in the event of Wiltshier being in delay was realised by the parties before Grenfell and Wiltshier entered into the building contracts and was the reason for the deeds, which sought to provide for liquidated damages to be paid to Darlington. Similarly the creation of the novation letters arose out of concern that an assignment from Grenfell would not confer any worthwhile rights upon Darlington.

In [St Martin's] in the House of Lords, . . . the House held that the St Martin's Corporation, which had entered into a contract with McAlpine for a large property development, which it was known would be occupied by others, and then parted with its interest in the property before breaches of contract occurred, could, as an exception to the general rule that a party could only recover damages for his own loss, recover damages for the benefit of the occupiers, who had incurred expenditure in putting right defects – see Lord Browne-Wilkinson at p.23.

Lord Griffiths would have decided the case on broader grounds: he considered that a person who placed a contract in respect of property which he did not own, but would incur expense in the event of a breach, could recover damages from the contract-breaker – see pp.2 and 3. Lord Keith of Kinkel expressed sympathy with Lord Griffiths' view and Lord Bridge of Harwich was attracted by it, but both preferred to adopt Lord Browne-Wilkinson's narrow grounds for deciding the case.

In the present case the Dolphin Centre was, as all were aware, built for occupation by Darlington. Grenfell entered into the building contracts but their function was simply that of financiers and there were elaborate provisions in the financing agreements aimed at ensuring that Grenfell would not become involved in bringing any claim against Wiltshier. It would, I think, be turning the arrangements made by Grenfell and Darlington upside-down to decide that it was ever intended that Grenfell should be able to recover damages for Darlington's benefit. I do not think that Grenfell's position resembles that of the Corporation in Linden Gardens. Grenfell is not a party to the action and I do not think that it had any rights to sue for the benefit of Darlington, which could have passed to Darlington on the assignment.

This case could not, I think, fall within Lord Griffiths' broader principle, since, although Grenfell entered into contracts relating to Darlington's property, Grenfell has not paid and there is no question of Grenfell being liable to pay for the repairs or paying for them voluntarily.

My conclusion with regard to [this issue] is that Darlington as assignee of Grenfell may recover only nominal damages from Wiltshier'.

The judge also held that Morgan Grenfell were not agents for Darlington and, therefore, Darlington could not recover as principals.

A collateral warranty given by the contractor to Darlington at the outset would probably have avoided the inability of Darlington to recover. It is clear that, notwithstanding *Linden Gardens* and *St Martin's*, collateral warranties continue to be an essential requirement of developers, purchasers and their tenants.

7.2.5   *Other third party claims*

Whether a landlord parent company could recover the losses of its tenant subsidiary was considered in *Richard Roberts Holdings Limited* v. *Douglas Smith Stimson Partnership and Others* (1988). RRH had entered into the contracts with the architect and contractors. They were also the freehold owners. Their subsidiary, Dyers, was the tenant of a dyeworks. If repairs were not completed within Dyers' next two week holiday period, Dyers would sustain abortive expenditure, large losses of profit and some loss of goodwill. RRH claimed to be entitled to recover those sums either on their own behalf or as agents for Dyers. Judge Newey had to try to decide by reference to two irreconcilable Court of Appeal decisions and he said:

> 'It is, I think, impossible to reconcile the decision in [*Lee* v. *Sheard* (1956)] with the statements of principle in [*Prudential Assurance Co. Limited* v. *Newman Industries Limited (No. 2)*]. I think it is possible today that the Court of Appeal would regard *Lee's* case as decided on its particular facts. I have no doubt that it is the *Prudential* case which I should follow.'

He went on to hold that RRH themselves could not recover Dyers' losses. He also held they could not recover Dyers' losses as agents.

A different view was arrived at in *George Fischer (Great Britain) Limited* v. *Multi-Construction Limited and Dexion Limited* (1992); Judge John Hicks QC, Official Referee, had to consider whether a parent company could recover losses sustained by its subsidiaries. He was referred to *Lee*, *Prudential* and *Richard Roberts Holdings* and felt himself bound by *Lee*, unlike Judge Newey in *Richard Roberts Holdings*. He said:

> 'Restrictions arising from the need to protect a specific rule primarily concerned with entitlement to sue rather than measure of damages, such as the rule in *Foss* v. *Harbottle*, should not be applied more widely than their reason for existence requires. The rule in *Foss* v. *Harbottle* has nothing to say about the situation where the company has no cause of action, and there is no occasion for it to influence the measure of damages in such a case. There may be intermediate situations raising more difficult questions about where to draw the line between *Lee* side of any defensible line, and I so hold.'

It is clear that the decisions in *Richard Roberts Holdings* and *George Fischer* are impossible to reconcile and it is open to the Court of Appeal to decide this issue.

7.3   Collateral warranties

It is the case that remedies in tort, in the case of defective design and construction, are not now widely available. This is particularly so since *D & F* and

Murphy. There has thus been created an impetus to have contractual relationships to fill this gap. This is the reason for the emergence and growth of collateral warranties. This book is not the place for a detailed treatise on collateral warranties but it would, on the other hand, be incomplete without some discussion. For those who require a fuller discussion, regard should be had to *Collateral Warranties – A Practical Guide for the Construction Industry*, Winward Fearon, published by Blackwell Scientific Publications.

Collateral warranties can create extremely onerous burdens on those who give them, sometimes resulting in greater and longer lasting burdens than those which exist under the principal contract to which they relate, and which can in turn cause serious problems to the professional indemnity insurance position. In order to understand the reasons for the common issues that arise, it is necessary first to consider what drives those who wish to have the benefit of warranties: tenants, purchasers and funding institutions.

7.3.1   The tenant's problems

The law relating to landlord and tenant is a very complex area. It is therefore not surprising that there has been a great deal of litigation in relation to the meaning and effect of leases. In looking at collateral warranties, the repairing covenant in the lease is likely to be the most important provision. Some repairing covenants can require the rebuilding of the premises irrespective of the cost or the reason for the works. At the other end of the scale, there can be a proviso in the repairing covenant excluding from the tenant's repairing obligations a liability to remedy latent defects in the building. However, a more usual simple form of repairing covenant is in the form:

'to repair the Premises and keep them in repair.'

It has to be doubted whether such a covenant is sufficient to require a tenant to completely rebuild. However, what is clear is that, if there is a lack of repair caused by a latent defect, then that lack of repair falls to be dealt with under the repairing covenant by the tenant. The more difficult question is whether the latent defect itself falls to be rectified by the tenant. If the only realistic way of effecting the relevant repairs is also to rectify the latent defect, then that is likely to fall within the repairing covenant: *Quick* v. *Taff-Ely Borough Council* (1985). In *Ravenseft Properties Limited* v. *Davstone (Holdings Limited* (1979) a tenant was required to lay out substantial sums to remedy a latent defect, but the court did so without stating a principle that latent defects would always fall within the repairing covenant.

On the other hand, where the work required to make the premises safe is more than repair, it may be held that it is not within the repairing covenant: *Brew Bros Limited* v. *Snax (Ross) Limited* (1970). In *Post Office* v. *Aquarius Properties Limited* (1987), unusually, there was an inherent defect in the building that did not cause disrepair; defective retaining walls permitted flooding of a basement, ankle deep. No damage had been caused to the building by the flooding and as the building was in the same condition as when it was completed and let, the Court of Appeal held that the tenants were under no obligation to the landlord to remedy the defect.

What is clear is that a tenant on a repairing covenant under a commercial lease is taking on a risk, the full extent of which may, of itself, be the subject of some uncertainty. It is not a surprise, therefore, that tenants look for means of re-allocating that risk to any member of the team who designed and constructed the development: that is why tenants feel the need to have collateral warranties.

The tenant is looking for designers to undertake an obligation to him in respect of design; that certain materials have not been specified for use in the building; that the designers have professional indemnity insurance and will maintain it; and that the tenant can assign the benefit of the collateral warranty to third parties when he comes to dispose of the lease. From a design and build contractor, the tenant will want, amongst other things, a warranty in relation to design and that the contractor has and will maintain professional indemnity insurance. From sub-contractors and trade contractors, the tenant may look for similar warranties; a tenant should be careful to look at the issue of design where a sub/trade contractor is designing.

7.3.2 The purchaser's problems

The fundamental problem faced by a purchaser of freehold property is the principle of *caveat emptor*: buyer beware. Put more simply, on a sale of freehold land and premises, it is up to the purchaser to find out whether or not it contains any latent or patent defects. It simply is not possible to imply a term into the contract for sale of property to the effect that the property is free from defects.

Different considerations are likely to arise depending on whether the purchaser is completing his purchase before or after completion of the building project. It is not at all uncommon for a freehold commercial property development to be sold during construction by one party to another (for example, between pension funds). Depending on the particular circumstances, the transfer of a project in progress is probably best dealt with by way of novation agreements with all the members of the professional team and the contractor, whereby the purchaser stands in the shoes of the vendor, the project otherwise continuing without interruption. It may well be necessary in these circumstances for there to be no collateral warranties for the simple reason that the purchaser will take over the benefits of all the contracts of the professional team and the contractor.

Purchasers after completion of the building project will be looking for all the same things as were discussed above in relation to tenants. Additionally, they are likely to be looking for a right to obtain copies of plans, drawings, specifications, calculations and similar documents and this will involve considering issues of copyright.

7.3.3 The funding institution's problems

The funding institutions behind property developments come in many forms: banks, merchant banks, insurance companies and the pension funds of large corporations. Before entering into a funding arrangement, funding institutions will naturally satisfy themselves that their involvement will be satisfactory from a financial point of view but also that, if things do not go according to plan, they are as well safeguarded as can be reasonably achieved. The funding agreement between the fund and the developer will allocate risk between those two parties and set out each party's rights, duties and obligations. If the developer gets into serious difficulties, for example a serious breach of the finance agreement in not meeting interest payments on the due date, then the funding institution wishes to protect its investment. In order to do so, it will wish to have the right in collateral warranties with the professional team and the contractor to take over those contracts itself so that it can secure completion of the project with the minimum of extra expense, disruption and delay.

Generally funds will be looking for similar matters to those set out above in relation to tenants; however, they may well seek wider duties than just design, workmanship and materials. Sometimes they seek to have the same duties owed to them as are owed under the principal contract – the extent of that sort of obligation can give rise to unintended results in a warranty. In addition, they will wish to have the right to take over and complete the project themselves, but only if they wish to do so, in the event of default by the developer under the funding agreement. This will sometimes take the form in law of a novation agreement but there are other methods.

7.3.4   Obligation to enter into collateral warranties

Save for commercial pressure, there is no obligation on anyone to enter into a collateral warranty unless there is a binding obligation contained in another contract: for example, the architect's conditions of engagement could contain a clause requiring that architect to give collateral warranties to certain parties 'in accordance with a draft attached'. Provided the obligation and the draft are certain, this is likely to be a binding obligation. Such a well drafted clause is likely to be effective in law even though the name of the tenant/purchaser is not known at the outset, provided the clause is drafted on the basis that the name of the tenant/purchaser can be fixed by a determination by one party and which determination does not depend upon agreement between the parties: (*May and Butcher Limited* v. *The King*) (1934).

7.3.5   Insurance implications

The insurance problems created by warranties are discussed in Chapter 10 (at 10.3.2).

7.3.6   Typical terms

7.3.6.1   General considerations

A draughtsman should always bear in mind that the intention of the collateral warranty is to create a contractual relationship that is collateral to the obligations created by the principal contract. That principal contract can take a great many different forms: Architect's Appointment or SFA/92, one of the several ACE forms, the RICS Conditions of Engagement, the main construction contract and all the various forms of sub and trade contracts. The draughtsman's guideline principles should be that the collateral warranty should not properly seek to impose any greater or more extensive obligations than those which are created under the principal contract; one exception to this principle is where a sub-contract between a contractor and a sub-contractor contains no obligations as to design, whereas the sub-contractor is in fact designing. Clearly that design obligation should be the subject of a clause in a collateral warranty so as to create a contractual cause of action in the event of default in the design obligation.

In the drafting, the language of tort is inappropriate. For example, some draughtsmen seek to try to create a tortious obligation by means of a contract term: 'The architect hereby agrees that it owes to the tenant a duty of care in tort.' It is highly unlikely that such a clause has the effect of creating any tortious duties whatsoever.

7.3.6.2   Terms

There are no *universally accepted* standard forms of collateral warranty although there are standard forms: the BPF Forms for a fund and tenants, the RIAS Form in Scotland, and the standard forms now produced by the JCT (MCWa/P&T for purchasers and tenants and MCWa/F for funders) for main contractors. Most of the problems in the agreement of warranties arise because there are a great number of purpose drafted forms. It is therefore unproductive to look in detail at the precise wording of many of the clauses that appear in practice. However, it is possible to put into categories the types of terms that are commonly found.

7.3.6.3   Design

An approach sometimes adopted is that the designer gives a warranty to the third party that he has and will perform his design agreement with his client in all respects in accordance with that design agreement. Although this has the benefit of being truly collateral to the principal contract, it may well have the effect that the designer owes all the duties under his design agreement to the third party, in addition to the client. This could result, for example, in a design and build contractor owing all the duties that he owes to the employer under the contract to a tenant including, by way of further example, an obligation to complete on or before the completion date and an obligation to pay liquidated and ascertained damages. The effect of such wholesale incorporation of the principal contract is likely to lead to wholly unintended results. It has to be said, however, that some funds may well want more than just a design warranty.

The better way to proceed in relation to design is to repeat in the warranty the clause, or part of the clause, that appears in the principal contract in relation to design. For example, condition 3.1 of the Architect's Appointment provides:

'The Architect will exercise reasonable skill and care in conformity with the normal standards of the Architect's profession.'

Such a clause can easily be transposed into a collateral warranty.

A similar approach can be taken to an engineer, a designing main contractor and designing sub-contractors (see for example ACE Conditions of Engagement, NSC/W, ESA/1, Works Contract/3, DOM/2 and JCT with Contractor's Design 1981).

Difficulties are sometimes perceived where architects and engineers are engaged by contractors in relation to a design and build project of the contractor. In relation to design, a contractor on such a project is in a position to give warranties in relation to the design to the fund, purchasers and tenants. Should the architect and engineer therefore be asked to give warranties as well? Such warranties will usually be needed in relation to a fund and a purchaser where they might wish to protect their position by taking over the project if the contractor/developer fall out of the equation. Usually there will be a chain of contracts, providing a route for a claim but, of course, a chain is only as strong as its weakest link and if a contractor, for example, becomes insolvent, then this chain of contracts will be broken and a tenant would have no right in tort against the contractor's architect. It is for this reason that warranties are often sought from the design team on a design and build project.

Architects and engineers should beware of the supervision issue in relation to warranties; their conditions of engagement will usually provide for certain inspection functions. If collateral warranties are drafted so as to incorporate all the principal contract obligations, then the architect and the engineer will owe duties of inspection to the parties to whom they give such warranties. This issue often arises on design and build projects where it is never intended that architects and engineers have inspection functions but they can inadvertently take on such obligations to third parties by the incorporation of standard form condition of engagement obligations into warranties.

7.3.6.4   Fitness for purpose

Provisions as to fitness for purpose in design are not usually sensible provisions to be incorporated into collateral warranties for the following reasons:

(1)   Professional indemnity insurance policies, including those of design and build contractors, are written on the basis of reasonable skill and care. Furthermore, professional indemnity policies usually exclude any liability assumed under a contract which increases the standard of care or measure of liability above that which normally applies under the usual conditions of engagement. It is to the benefit of every party to a collateral warranty that its provisions do not prevent the designer from having recourse to the policy should a claim arise. To put it another way, there is no commercial benefit in drafting and securing harsh provisions if, when liability is established, there is no money available to meet the liability.

(2)   The basis of the appointment under the principal contract of designers is that of reasonable skill and care – designers do not guarantee that they will produce a particular result. There is a distinction to be drawn between a term as to fitness for purpose that could be implied as a matter of fact to give effect to the actual intentions of the parties and a term to be implied in law (to give effect to the presumed intention of the parties). An express obligation as to reasonable skill and care does not exclude the former.

Sometimes there is an obligation that a contractor or sub-contractor warrants that materials will be fit for their purpose insofar as they have been or will be selected by the contractor/sub-contractor. Such a clause creates no particular difficulties where it is in relation to a contract for the supply of work and material and the contract includes no design obligations: it is nothing more nor less than the position at common law (see for example *Young and Marten* v. *McManus Childs* (1968)) and under statute (see Supply of Goods and Services Act 1982). Where the term is to be included in a contract where there is design in addition to work and materials, then consideration must be given as to whether or not such an obligation seeks to impose a fitness for purpose obligation in relation to design; where design stops and construction takes over is a vexed issue. Where there is any doubt, it is likely to be commercially sensible for all the parties to make such a fitness for purpose obligation in relation to materials subject to a duty to use reasonable skill and care in the selection – that is the formula adopted in the standard forms NSC/2, ESA/1 and Works Contract/3.

7.3.6.5   *Workmanship*

Main contractors are often asked to warrant to third parties that they will carry out and complete the project in accordance with the building contract. However, the words used often seek to impose much greater obligations than are created by the building contract itself. A contractor should not reasonably be asked to give warranties to third parties that go beyond his obligations as to quality contained in the building contract. As with design, this warranty can often be drafted by reference to the wording of the building contract itself in respect of quality. For example, where the main contract is JCT 80, the warranty might take the following form (substantially based on clause 2.1 of JCT 80):

> 'The Contractor warrants to the tenant that he has and will use in the construction of the Works (as defined in the Building Contract) materials and workmanship of the quality and standard specified in and/or required under the Building Contract.'

Warranties that seek to oblige the contractor to warrant to the tenant that he will carry out and complete the works in accordance with the building contract should be avoided by contractors. Which of the contractor's duties in the building contract are intended to be owed under such a warranty to the tenant?

7.3.6.6   *Deleterious materials*

Every warranty contains a provision that certain materials will not be specified for use and/or used in the construction of the project. It is doubtful whether this is a sensible and logical way to specify what materials are to be used. The most usual place to specify the quality of the project is in the main contract specification. If certain materials are not to be used, then those materials can easily be incorporated into the specification by way of prohibition. If that were done, then there would be no need for a deleterious materials provision in collateral warranties.

There are other reasons for not having a list of particular deleterious materials in the warranty. Firstly, such a list cannot, by definition, ever be a complete list. Secondly there is the danger that on a particular wording, anything that is not specified as deleterious can be used. Thirdly, and most importantly, there is no reason why the third party should not rely on the general and positive obligations created by warranties as to design and quality of materials and workmanship. For example, could it really be seriously suggested that an engineer would not be in breach of a duty to use reasonable skill and care in circumstances where he had specified the use of high alumina cement concrete for the structural beams in the roof of a swimming pool? The same point can be made in relation to all of the seven or eight most commonly stated deleterious materials.

There does seem little point in having a definitive list of specific negatives when there is available an overriding positive general duty to exercise reasonable skill and care.

That said, the current convention or perceived wisdom (probably coupled with pressure from tenants and commercial conveyancing solicitors) is to have a deleterious materials provision. A common list of materials is high alumina cement concrete in loadbearing structures; calcium chloride used as an additive in the mixing of concrete for use in reinforced concrete; crocidolite (blue asbestos); asbestos; woodwool slabs used as permanent shuttering; high alkali cement not conforming with certain British Standards when used with aggregates containing reactive silica; urea formaldehyde foam; sea-washed or sea-dredged aggregates for use in reinforced concrete (except where they comply with a strict specification).

The list varies dramatically from project to project; many of these lists are now extremely lengthy and many items so lack definition that they are unhelpful and pointless in a practical building sense, let alone from the point of view of a lawyer trying to construe a meaning.

There is often a sweep-up provision at the end of the deleterious materials clause – again from a drafting point of view, it is almost certainly more satisfactory to rely on the positive duty to exercise reasonable skill and care than to have a sweep-up clause as a negative obligation. Some sweep-up clauses are so wide and general that they should not be included in any warranty.

It is important to check that deleterious materials provisions in collateral warranties are not in conflict with the provisions of the contracts to which the warranties are collateral; what is to happen if a material banned in the collateral warranty is specified by the architect to be used in circumstances where the contractor under his building contract has an obligation to comply with architect's instructions?

A designer, who is not also building, can warrant that he will not specify particular materials but he cannot properly warrant that he will see that the contractor does not incorporate such materials into construction (even where the designer has not specified them). A similar point arises on the wording of the JCT Contract with Contractor's Design where the employer can require a change.

7.3.6.7   *Copyright*

Occasionally, a fund or tenant will seek to have the copyright in drawings and the design assigned. Such a provision is in direct conflict with the provisions of standard forms of engagement including, for example, the Architect's Appointment, SFA/92 and the ACE Conditions of Engagement. The simplest way to avoid this problem is for the copyright to remain with the designer but for the designer to grant a licence in the warranty in respect of the copyright but limited to the purposes of the development – it would not be sensible for a designer to give a licence in his intellectual property in the absence of such a limitation. A further point is that the Architect's Appointment reserves copyright, not only in documents and drawings, but also 'in any works executed from those documents and drawings'. It is again important that the warranty should reflect the principal contract.

Professional designers may want to see that the granting of the licence in the warranty is conditional upon them having been paid in respect of the work that they have done – this is the position in the Architect's Appointment but that restriction is not reflected, for example, in the BPF Form. (See also 'Copyright' in section 2.4).

7.3.6.8 Insurance

In warranties given by a party who is carrying out design, there is often a requirement as to the provision of professional indemnity insurance. These provisions vary enormously in their content and effect. A typical term may require the insurance to be in force at the date of the warranty, that the premiums have and will be paid and that the insurance will be maintained into the future, sometimes without limit in time and sometimes with a limit.

These provisions give rise to real practical and legal issues. The professional indemnity market changes from time to time both in the average levels of premium available and in terms of the capacity and, consequently, the amount of the insurance. Professional indemnity insurance is renewable annually and is made on the basis that it covers claims made during the period of insurance. Given the vagaries of the professional indemnity insurance market and the annual basis of this type of insurance, it is very difficult for a designer to give warranties in relation to future insurance, even one or two years ahead, let alone six or 12 years.

This type of provision assumes that the designer's firm or company will continue in business into the future in the same legal form. Where it is a firm, the partners who entered into the warranty (and who are liable for breaches) may cease to be partners and/or may retire or die. Where the designer is a company, it may cease to trade with or without going into liquidation or receivership. These points should be borne in mind by parties seeking onerous insurance provisions in warranties.

There is sometimes a prohibition in policies preventing disclosure of the existence of the insurance to third parties – in such circumstances insurer's express permission should be obtained on this point prior to discussing the terms of such a warranty with the third party.

Finally, what is to happen if the designer is in breach of his obligation under such a clause? Clearly the designer would be in breach of contract under the warranty and that would give rise to a claim on the part of the other party for damages. Those damages are the sum of money that would put the receiver of the warranty in the position he would have been but for the breach. That sum of money might be the whole or part of the premium for the professional indemnity insurance – however, it is highly unlikely that a third party would be able to take out professional indemnity insurance on behalf of the designer in any event. It follows that the consequences of breach of a provision of this kind are not terribly helpful to the party in receipt of the benefit.

A fairly unobjectionable provision might be for the designer to warrant that there is insurance in existence at the date of the warranty and that the premium has been paid; the designer could further warrant that he will use his best endeavours to obtain professional indemnity insurance in succeeding years provided that such insurance is available in the market place at commercially reasonable rates; the designer could undertake to notify the other party or parties in the event that he cannot obtain insurance at commercially reasonable rates. This kind of provision is to be found in the BPF Warranty to a Fund.

7.3.6.9   Novation

This kind of provision is not appropriate for tenants; purchasers and funds may wish to have the right to continue with the project, if they so elect but not otherwise, if the employer/developer is unable to continue, perhaps through receivership or liquidation or a serious breach of the funding agreement.

One method is a novation agreement proper whereby, for example, in the building contract the contractor continues as before and the fund/purchaser, as the case may be, is substituted for the employer/developer in the building contract on the basis that the fund/purchaser takes on all the rights and obligations of the employer/developer. That would mean all the rights and obligations both existing and future. It is not unusual for funds and purchasers to try to avoid a commitment as to past liabilities by providing that they shall only be liable on the agreement from the date of the novation.

The consequences for, say, the contractor as in the example above of entering into a fresh agreement with a third party is that such a step is likely to be a repudiatory breach of the principal contract. There must, therefore, be a provision to the effect that the contractor will not be in breach of his principal contract if the fund/purchaser exercises its right to step into the shoes of the developer/employer. The most usual way of dealing with these issues is to have a provision that such novation type arrangements are contained in a tripartite agreement, that is to say in the case of a contractor, the contractor, the developer/employer and the fund/purchaser should all be parties to the agreement.

The most satisfactory method of dealing with these issues is to provide in the warranty that the contractor and the employer/developer will enter into a novation agreement in the form of a draft attached if the fund so requires; there is much confused drafting around on these issues. Sometimes, draughtsmen seek to amend, in the warranty, the principal contract – this is not sensible. Nor is it sensible to provide in the warranty that the contactor will not exercise his rights to determine under the building contract without giving 28 days prior notice to the fund. Such provisions should be carefully checked to see that they are not in conflict with the provisions of the principal contract. For example, liquidation of the employer in the JCT forms creates an automatic determination of the employment of the contractor. How is the contractor to give 28 days clear notice to the fund? Convoluted provisions to deal with these kinds of issues are only likely to lead to a lack of clarity and uncertainty. The simplest provision is to provide that, where there is any notice of termination or determination, a copy of that notice is to be given at the same time to the fund.

7.3.6.10   Assignment

This is one of the most difficult areas of collateral warranties.

If there is no provision for assignment in the warranty, then the benefit of a warranty is freely assignable without the consent of the other party. Such an assignment can be either legal or equitable.

Where there is in a contract an express prohibition on assignment, then such prohibition is likely to be effective in law. It follows that, if there is a purported assignment in such cases, it is likely that the assignment will be void: *Linden Gardens Trust Limited* v. *Lenesta Sludge Disposals Limited and Others* (1993) and *St Martin's Property Corporation Limited and Another* v. *Sir Robert McAlpine and Sons Limited* (1993) – see the discussion in section 7.2.4.

The most difficult issues arise where there is a purported restriction on assignment in the warranty. It is common to see warranty provisions which seek to impose a limit on the number of assignments that can be made. This can arise where the draughtsman is attempting to make the provision on assignment and the warranty consistent with the provisions of the professional indemnity insurance policy (where there are restrictions on assignment in the policy). For example, the policy wording might restrict cover to two assignments. If that provision is simply incorporated into the warranty, then every time there is an assignment, the assignee steps into the shoes of the assignor and he has the right to make two assignments – in other words the counting never starts and assignments can continue *ad infinitum*. The simplest legal solution to this conundrum is to provide in the warranty that assignment is prohibited save where the express consent in writing of the original giver of the warranty has been obtained. The provision could continue to recite that the giver of the warranty shall not withhold his consent where the assignment is a first or second assignment. Such a provision puts the control in the hands of the original contracting party who needs to have that control, namely, the insured in this example.

Sometimes a provision is inserted into a warranty that the agreement is personal to the parties. This is an attempt to take advantage of the rule of law that the benefits of a personal contract cannot be assigned either by a legal or equitable assignment. However, there is real doubt as to whether a personal contract can be created in law by a provision in the contract that says a contract is personal. The test, which is an objective test, is whether 'it can make no difference to the person on whom the obligation lies to which of two persons he is to discharge it': *Tolhurst* v. *Association Portland Cement Manufacturers Ltd* (1902). It is to be noted that that test is not concerned with the personal skill of the debtor so that, for example, if an architect gives a collateral warranty relating to his design work, whilst the design work will involve personal skill on his part and will not be assignable by the architect to a third party, the benefits of the undertakings arising under the warranty given to a tenant will be assignable to a future tenant because, applying the objective test, it can make no difference to the architect whether its obligations lie to the first tenant or to a future tenant. In relation to assignment there are questions that arise in relation to damages recoverable under collateral warranties. This is dealt with in outline in section 7.2.4.4.

7.3.6.11 *Other Parties Clause*

The Civil Liability (Contribution) Act 1978 deals with contribution between people liable in respect of any damage whether tort, breach of contract or otherwise. Under the provisions of the Act where two or more people are in breach of separate contracts with the same third person producing the same damage, those two or more persons can claim contribution against each other.

Concern has arisen, particularly in the construction professions, that if they give written warranties and other people do not, they will be liable to the third party for the full amount of the loss and unable to claim contribution from those other parties who did not sign collateral warranties – those other parties cannot be liable in respect of the same damage, there being no remedy in tort following the recent changes in the law. The givers of warranties have therefore sought methods to try to make sure they are not liable for the full amount of the loss in circumstances where other parties ought properly to be liable at the same time. The creation of enforceable provisions to this effect is not easy.

The most effective provision (which is not likely to be acceptable to the third parties) is that a warranty does not come into force and effect at all (a condition precedent) unless certain named other parties have entered into collateral warranties with the same third party to the same effect. This is sometimes called the 'three musketeers' clause – all for one, and one for all.

Another method is for the developer to give an undertaking in the warranty that he will obtain warranties in the same or very similar form from certain other named parties. This is the method used in the BPF warranty. What is the effect of this clause in relation to, say, an architect's liability where the developer has failed to obtain those other warranties? Clearly there will be a breach by the developer but does that breach give rise to only nominal damages or something more useful to the architect? This issue will be determined by the rules on remoteness and whether or not those damages are simply too uncertain to be ascertained.

If the client had entered into the other warranty agreements, then the firm would be entitled to bring contribution proceedings under the Civil Liability (Contribution) Act 1978 against any other firm who had given a warranty, provided, of course, that the other firm was liable in respect of the same damage. The absence of the warranty would prevent such a claim being brought, there being no liability in tort. It follows that the failure by the developer to obtain the other warranty agreements will have prevented the architect from seeking contribution from the other firm or firms that would otherwise have been liable in respect of the same damage. Assuming that the architect could satisfy a court that the other firms would have been liable in respect of the same damage had a collateral warranty been entered into, the next issue would be whether the amount of that contribution could be ascertained with any certainty by a court. Courts have entertained such relatively speculative calculations, namely, where assessment is dependent on a contingency (see, e.g. *Chaplin* v. *Hicks* (1911) and *Cook* v. *Swinfen* (1967)). If the court did entertain that calculation, then the architect would recover the amount of the calculated contribution, not from the other firm liable in respect of the same damage, but from the developer as damages for breach of his obligation to obtain collateral warranty agreements from the other firms.

The other type of provision that is being used is the so called 'net contribution clause.' Such a clause appears in the Memorandum of Agreement in SFA/92 at clause 6.1 and is set out in section 11.3.4. That agreement is not a collateral warranty but the principles are the same. An attempt is made to limit the designer's liability to the other party to such sum as he ought reasonably to have to pay, having regard to his responsibility for it and also on the basis that the contractor, engineer and so on shall be deemed to have paid their liability in respect of their contribution to the other party. It is an attempt to achieve by contract that which would take place in the courts under the Civil Liability (Contribution) Act 1978 if all the parties were liable in respect of the same damage, namely an apportionment of liability between the defendants. It also has the effect of limiting the designer's liability to his share even though the other party may not, in fact, have received any contributions from the contractor, engineer and so on. It has yet to be seen how the courts will deal with such provisions. There is also the possibility of such clauses being subjected to the test of reasonableness under the Unfair Contract Terms Act 1977 (see section 11.3.3).

7.3.6.12 *Limiting liability*
The parties to a contract can in English law agree a term excluding liability or limiting the consequences of liability subject only to some statutory regulation, including the Unfair Contract Terms Act 1977 (see section 11.3.3). The whole question of consequential loss is a matter that gives rise to great concern amongst the givers of warranties and their professional indemnity insurers. It is one thing, they say, to be liable for the direct costs of remedial works following defective design or workmanship; it is another to have to pay all the other economic consequences that may flow from such a breach of contract. These can include loss of rent, the costs of the tenant moving out of the building whilst repairs are carried out, the costs of disruption/loss of profit and business and the costs of returning after the remedial works. Often, the indirect costs exceed the cost of the remedial works. Various attempts have been made in warranties to try to restrict that potentially wide liability.

One method is to exclude economic and consequential loss. However, those words do not have a precise legal meaning for this purpose and could give rise to difficulty of interpretation on particular facts. There is now a tendency for draughtsmen to provide expressly for what is covered, rather than seeking to limit the scope of general damages. For example, an architect might seek to limit his liability under the warranty to the direct cost of remedying the defective work, all other costs, losses, damages and expenses being excluded. It goes without saying that developers, funds, purchasers and tenants are not keen on such provisions.

7.3.7 *Other solutions: present and future*

A great many people are saying there must be a better way. However, there is no magic answer.

7.3.7.1 *Possible solutions – the present*
The terms of commercial leases which usually include full repairing covenants on the part of tenants are not necessarily fixed in stone. There is no reason why there could not be a provision, for example, for the landlord to remedy latent defects, or for the landlord to pay to the tenant the cost of repairs in respect of latent defects.

In respect of purchasers, where the obligations under the principal contracts have all been fulfilled, then the benefits of those principal contracts can be assigned to the purchaser.

The insurance industry is beginning to respond in this area. In 1988, the construction industry sector group of the National Economic Development Council produce a report called 'Building Users' Insurance against Latent Defects' known by the acronym BUILD. This is discussed in section 10.6.

7.3.7.2 *Possible solutions – the future*
Clearly more widely accepted standard forms of collateral warranty would be of

great benefit but the drafting and agreement of standard forms is fraught with difficulty.

The Defective Premises Act 1972 only applies to the provision of dwellings. It creates a statutory duty that anyone taking on work for the provision of a dwelling will owe a duty to any person who ordered the construction work and who acquires an interest, legal or equitable, in the property that the work will be fit for habitation on completion. If the government had the necessary will, the Law Commission could be asked to produce either a new draft statute along the lines of the Defective Premises Act or indeed draft amendments to the Defective Premises Act, to extend the scope of the Act to construction work in general. This drafting would not be an easy task but it is an anomaly in our present law that certain types of duty are created by statute in respect of the provision of dwellings but not in respect of any other kind of construction. That anomaly is even more profound since the restriction of tortious duties. It cannot be in the public interest for there to be a continuation of the present explosion in the use of collateral warranties which can only, in the long term, create difficulties of legal interpretation, uncertainty and extensive legal costs for those involved in the consequential litigation on the warranties that have been and will be signed.

7.4   Users of construction works after completion

On the usual rules of negligence, a person who is injured when using a building can pursue a claim against the designer provided his injuries were directly attributable to the design. The following two cases illustrate this principle.

In *Voli* v. *Inglewood Shire Council* (1963), the plaintiff, a member of the public, was injured when the stage in a public hall collapsed. He sued the owners of the hall and the architect. The court held that nothing in the architect's contract with the owner could affect his liability to the public and that the architect was liable to the plaintiff. Furthermore, the owners were liable for their architect's negligence on the principle of vicarious liability.

In the case of *Kelly* v. *Frank Mears & Partners* (1981), Scotland, a plaintiff was helping his friend, who was drunk, home to his flat in a block of flats. The two men fell through a glazed panel in balustrading and then some 80 feet on to a roof below. The plaintiff was seriously injured and his friend died. The plaintiff sued the designers of the balustrading in negligence. He succeeded on the basis that the designers should have foreseen the possibility of such an accident and guarded against it in their design. However, his damages were reduced by 15% on the basis of contributory negligence.

Local authorities, not as landlords but through their architects and building departments, can render themselves liable for defective *design* many years after the design took place. An example of this kind of liability is to be found in *Rimmer* v. *Liverpool City Council* (1984), and *Targett* v. *Torfaen Borough Council* (1991).

It is possible for plaintiffs with personal injuries to succeed against negligent designers whereas subsequent owners and occupiers of premises are now in difficulties in tort in respect of defects. A further example of this is the Abbeystead explosion: *T. E. Eckersley and Others* v. *Binnie & Partners and Others* (1988). Visitors to civil engineering works after completion of those works were injured and killed, and the survivors and personal representatives succeeded in an action in negligence against the consulting engineer responsible for the design.

7.5 Workmen on the construction site

Designers may be surprised to find that they can incur liability to contractor's workmen who are injured on a site during construction of the works. There is, of course, no contract between the designer and the contractor's workmen so that any liability is in tort.

The liability can arise in two ways; firstly, where 'the design was so faulty that a competent contractor in the course of executing the works could not have avoided the resulting damage, then on principle it seems to me that the consulting engineer responsible for that design should bear the loss': Judge Stabb QC in *Oldschool and Another* v. *Gleeson Construction and Others* (1976). Secondly, the liability can arise where the designer has actual control of the contractor's work. In the normal arrangement for construction work, the designer does not control the manner, method or sequence by which the contractor carries out his work. Where the designer does not control the work, then he will usually escape liability.

In the case of *Clayton* v. *Woodman and Sons (Builders) Limited and Others* (1962), a bricklayer was injured when a wall collapsed while the bricklayer was cutting a chase in the side of the wall. Prior to the collapse the architect had visited the site to look at the wall; he decided not to order that the wall be demolished and rebuilt as had been suggested by the bricklayer. The contractor did not provide any support for the wall during the cutting of the chase, as he was required to do by the specification. The Court of Appeal held that the architect had merely refused to vary the work and that he did not owe a duty of care to the bricklayer.

In the *Clayton* case, the designer had refused to sanction a variation in the design of the work that had been requested by the contractor. However, the position will be different where the designer does order a variation which is inherently dangerous.

In *Clay* v. *A.J. Crump & Sons Limited and Others* (1963), a labourer employed by building contractors was injured and other workmen killed when an existing wall fell on to the site hut. The history was that the wall that collapsed should have been demolished by a demolition contractor employed directly by the building owner. However, he did not demolish it. The wall was shown as being demolished on the drawing supplied to the building contractor by the architect so that when he came on the site and saw the wall, he sought the architect's instructions. The architect was advised by the demolition contractor that the wall was safe but did not inspect it himself; the architect informed the building contractor that it was safe to leave the wall standing. The labourer sued the building contractors, the demolition contractors and the architect. The Court of Appeal held all three liable. The Court of Appeal did not alter the apportionment of liability of the judge: the architect 42%; the demolition contractors 38% and the building contractors 20%.

The designer's duty to foresee such problems may be more readily found in cases where the designer is supervising work being carried out by the employer directly in the absence of a building contractor: *Florida Hotels Pty* v. *Mayo* (1965), Australia.

The JCT 80 contract gives the architect power to vary by addition, alteration or omission any obligations or restrictions contained in the bills of quantities in relation to access, limitations of working space and working hours, and the execution of the work in any specific order. Similar powers are given to the employer under the JCT with Contractor's Design 1981 Contract. The architect should beware of the possible liabilities he may incur in operating these provisions, which are discussed in the next chapter.

See also section 4.3.5 on health and safety.

Chapter 8

Design and build contracts

8.1 Generally

In the traditional method of contracting, where a designer is engaged by the employer to carry out the design and a contractor is engaged to carry out the construction of the work, there is a sharp distinction drawn between design on the one hand and workmanship and materials on the other hand. The design is firmly in the hands of the designer and the construction work firmly in the hands of the contractor.

The JCT Standard Form of Building Contract in particular, and the ICE Contract to a lesser extent, perpetuate this distinction. An employer faced with a defective building may have to bring claims against both the designer and the contractor because many defects fail to fall clearly into either the design or the workmanship category. In a design and build contract or turnkey project, the philosophy is different; the contractor not only takes on the job of constructing the works but also designing them. This has the effect of fundamentally altering the contractor's obligations in respect of design.

There are several terms that are to be implied into building contracts, whether they are design and build contracts or the traditional building contract:

(1) To carry out the work in a workmanlike manner.
(2) To use materials of good quality.
(3) The materials and the work will be reasonably fit for their respective purposes.

See The Supply of Goods and Services Act 1982, *Young and Marten* v. *McManus Childs* (1969); *Cammell Laird* v. *Manganese Bronze and Brass Co. Limited* (1934); *Hancock and Others* v. *B.W. Brazier (Anerley) Limited* (1966); *Miller* v. *Cannon Hill Estates Limited* (1931); *IBA* v. *EMI and BICC* (1981).

The implied warranty to carry out the work in a workmanlike manner will not readily be excluded. Likewise, the warranty to use materials of good quality will not be displaced, even in circumstances where the particular materials have been specified by the employer or the designer (save, perhaps, in circumstances such as those in *Gloucestershire County Council* v. *Richardson* (1968)).

However, the fitness for purpose warranty is readily excluded in traditional building contracts (other than design and build contracts) where the employer does not rely on the skill and care of the contractor in selection of the materials. The position is, of course, different in design and build contracts, where usually the employer will be relying on the contractor in the selection of the materials.

The warranty as to fitness for purpose almost certainly extends to the design in design and build contracts where there is room for such an implied term.

In the case of houses, there is an implied warranty that the house will be reasonably fit for human habitation, which is a species of fitness for purpose.

In relation to a design and build contract, it was said by Lord Denning MR in *Greaves (Contractors) Limited* v. *Baynham Meikle & Partners* (1975):

> 'Now, as between the building owners and the contractors, it is plain that the owners made known to the contractors the purpose for which the building was required, so as to show that they relied on the contractors' skill and judgment. It was, therefore, the duty of the contractors to see that the finished work was reasonably fit for the purpose for which they knew it was required. It was not merely an obligation to use reasonable care, the contractors were obliged to ensure that the finished work was reasonably fit for the purpose. That appears from the recent cases in which a man employs a contractor to build a house *Miller* v. *Cannon Hill Estates Limited* (1931); *Hancock* v. *B. W. Brazier (Anerley) Limited* (1966). It is a term implied by law that the builder will do his work in a good and workmanlike manner; that he will supply good and proper materials; and that it will be reasonably fit for human habitation.'

That statement was made in a case where the liability of the package deal contractor to the building owner had been admitted and it is not, therefore, binding, although it is of great persuasive authority. The same applied to statements made in the House of Lords in *IBA v. EMI and BICC* (1981) where Lord Scarman said:

> 'In the absence of any term (express or to be implied) negativing the obligation, one who contracts to design an article for a purpose made known to him undertakes that the design is reasonably fit for the purpose.'

Lord Scarman had likened the position to that of a dentist making a set of false teeth where it has been held that there is an implied term that the false teeth will be reasonably fit for their intended purpose: *Samuels* v. *Davis* (1943). In *Samuels*, Lord Justice Du Parcq said:

> 'If someone goes to a professional man ... and says: "Will you make me something which will fit a particular part of my body?" and the professional gentleman says "Yes", without qualification, he is then warranting that when he has made the article, it will fit the part of the body in question ... If a dentist takes out a tooth or a surgeon removes an appendix, he is bound to take reasonable care and to show such skill as may be expected from a qualified practitioner. The case is entirely different where a chattel is ultimately to be delivered.'

Those words were approved by Lord Scarman in *IBA*.

Since the case of *Viking Grain Storage Limited* v. *T. H. White Installations Limited and Another* (1985), there is now little doubt on the issue of fitness for purpose on design and build projects. This case concerned a preliminary issue before the court as to whether terms were to be implied:

(1)   that the design and build contractor would use materials of good quality and reasonably fit for their purpose, and
(2)   that the completed works would be reasonably fit for their purpose.

The works in this case were a grain drying and storage installation. The Official Referee had little difficulty in concluding that there was reliance by the plaintiff owners on the skill and judgment of the defendant contractors and it followed that those two implied terms contended for were implied.

The effect of this is that a design and build contractor's obligation, in the absence of a contrary intention in the contract, in respect of design is that it shall be fit for its purpose. This is an absolute obligation independent of negligence, and it is therefore to be contrasted with the obligation of a designer as to design, under the traditional arrangements, where his duty is only to use reasonable skill and care. In other words, if a design and build contractor uses the reasonable skill and care of a designer, he will nevertheless be liable if his design is not fit for its purpose; the employer will not have to enquire into the distinction between defects arising from design or workmanship and neither will he have to show that there was negligence on the part of the contractor.

It is very important for both parties to a design and build contract to have a contract that is suitable and appropriate. For example, the JCT Standard Form of Building Contract, Local Authorities Edition, is wholly inappropriate for use where the contractor is to design and build. The philosophy of that contract is that the architect will design and carry out many administrative functions; there is no provision expressly setting out the contractor's liability and the extent of his liability should he design the works. Similarly, the ICE Conditions of Contract, 6th Edition, are also inappropriate: clause 8(2) of those Conditions provides that the contractor shall not be responsible for the design or specification of the permanent works 'except as may be expressly provided in the Contract'. This exclusion was probably included so as to be consistent with condition 58(3), which provides for the contractor to be responsible for the nominated sub-contractor's design provided certain conditions are fulfilled.

However, if this contract were used for design and build works without further amendment, the wording of condition 8(2) would be likely to operate to exclude the contractor's liability for design. Notwithstanding these difficulties, it is now less common, but not unknown, to find parties using standard forms of contract not drafted for design and build works when those contracts do not set out and define the responsibilities of the parties. Because the wording of such contracts is so inappropriate, the job of trying to attribute meaning to the words can be so difficult that it is a recipe for litigation. An Australian case *Cable (1956) Limited* v. *Hutcherson Limited* (1969), Australia, illustrates the problem.

A contractor tendered on a design and build basis for the construction of a storage hopper. The employer's engineer had prepared a specification and drawings. The specification required the contractor to construct foundations and he designed them, although the engineer required amendments to the design. The parties then entered into what was substantially a standard form of contract under which the contractor agreed to carry out the work shown in the drawings and specification. The foundations turned out to be inadequate but the court held that the contractor had only agreed to carry out the work that had been specified in a workmanlike manner. The moral is to use a form of contract that sets out the duties and liabilities of the parties in such a way as to reflect what the parties actually intend.

A similar point was decided in the Saskatchewan Court of Queen's Bench, Canada, in *Sunnyside Nursing Home* v. *Builders Contract Management Limited and Others* (1985). The facts in this case were that the employer invited tenders from contractors and the tenderers were invited to suggest a proposed structural system. The employer had engaged architects and engineers to prepare tender documents and after the acceptance of the tender to complete the plans and specifications based on the system for the structure designated by the successful tenderer. Builders Contract Management Limited were the successful tenderers and the work proceeded in the way envisaged save that there were design (and workmanship) defects in the work and an issue inevitably arose as to whether or not Builders Contract Management had a design responsibility. It was held in this case that the employer did not rely entirely, or at all, on the experience, judgment or skill of Builders Contract Management in the design, and that in general, a contractor is unlikely to have a design obligation where the employer engages an architect and/or an engineer, at least in the way in which this matter proceeded.

8.2   Standard Form of Building Contract with Contractor's Design, 1981 Edition (July 1987 Revision)

Although considerable doubts were expressed by the RIBA at the time as to whether it was sensible to produce a design and build contract, the Joint Contracts Tribunal published in 1981 a new form of contract for design and build known as the Standard Form of Building Contract with Contractor's Design (1981 Edition). At the same time, the JCT have published two practice notes; Practice Note CD/1A has a general description of the new form of contract and Practice Note CD/1B has detailed notes on the new form of contract. The contract is intended for use where the employer has told a contractor in writing what he requires and the contractor has prepared the design and tendered for the work. The wording of the contract generally follows that of the JCT Standard Form of Contract 1980 but with many alterations.

The most important conditions of that contract (incorporating Amendments 1–6 inclusive) that relate to design are now set out together with a commentary. It should be noted that the Conditions are not set out in full.

8.2.1   The Articles of Agreement – generally

'ARTICLES OF AGREEMENT

made the   day of _____ 19

between _____

of (or whose registered office is situated at) _____

(hereinafter called 'the Employer') of the one part and _____

of (or whose registered office is situated at) _____

(hereinafter called 'the Contractor') of the other part

WHEREAS

First Recital	the Employer is desirous of obtaining the construction of the following works _____ for which works he has issued to the Contractor his requirements (hereinafter referred to as "the Employer's Requirements");
Second Recital	the Contractor has submitted proposals for carrying out the works referred to in the First recital (hereinafter referred to as "the Contractor's Proposals") which include the statement of the sum which he will require for carrying out that which is necessary for completing all such works in accordance with the Conditions (which is the Contract Sum stated in Article 2), and has also submitted an analysis of that sum (hereinafter referred to as "the Contract Sum Analysis") which is annexed to the "Contractor's Proposals";
Third Recital	the Employer has examined the Contractor's Proposals and the Contract Sum Analysis and, subject to the Conditions and, where applicable, the Supplementary Provisions hereinafter contained is satisfied that they appear to meet the Employer's Requirements;
Fourth Recital	the status of the Employer, for the purposes of the statutory tax deduction scheme under the Finance (No. 2) Act 1975, is as stated in Appendix 1 to the Conditions.'

There is no provision for an architect or a quantity surveyor. Accordingly, many of the functions given to the architect under the JCT 80 Contract are given to the employer under this contract, including opening up for inspection any work covered up (condition 8.3), requiring the removal of work, materials or goods not in accordance with the contract (condition 8.4), stating that the works are practically complete (condition 16.1), preparing a schedule of defects (condition 16.2), requiring defect shrinkages or other faults to be made good (condition 16.3), issuing a notice of completion of making good defects (condition 16.4), handling the machinery for liquidated damages (condition 24) including granting extensions of time (condition 25) and so on. It is extremely difficult to conceive of an employer coping with the contractual machinery of this contract unless he has in his employment people who are used to dealing with such matters. Alternatively, there is nothing to prevent the employer from engaging firms of architects and quantity surveyors to advise him how to deal with the more difficult matters. This must, of course, be a matter for the judgment of the employer in any particular case.

8.2.2   *First Recital and the Employer's Requirements*

The 'Employer's Requirements' are, in essence, the work that the employer wishes to be carried out by the contractor. The meaning of this phrase for the purposes of the contract is what is contained within the documents identified in Appendix 3 (see Article 4) but there is within the contract no practical definition as to what the Employer's Requirements should contain. Some guidance is given in the Practice Note CD/1A. The Practice Note suggests that the Employer's Requirements may vary from a 'description of accommodation' right through to a 'scheme design'. The whole spectrum is therefore envisaged from a simple request to 'provide a six-bedroomed house' right through to a scheme that is in an advanced state of preparation with drawings showing layouts and a specification detailing the materials and standard of workmanship.

There are two advantages in keeping the Employer's Requirements simple; firstly, this would lessen the possibility of there being a divergence between the Employer's Requirements and the Contractor's Proposals (see section 8.2.6). Secondly, where the employer chooses materials or methods to be used in workmanship, then it is likely that the contractor will not be liable should those materials or workmanship not be fit for their purpose (see 8.2.6: commentary on condition 2.1).

A point of importance is that there is no provision in the conditions for the Employer's Requirements to be altered after the date of contract unless there is a 'change' under condition 12 which carries certain consequences (see 8.2.9: commentary on condition 12).

Whether or not the contractor has an obligation to obtain planning permission, known in this contract as 'Development Control Requirements', is not expressly defined in the conditions. Clearly, this is a matter of fundamental importance. Practice Note CD/1A suggests that the position should be clearly defined in the Employer's Requirements. The need to deal with the responsibility in this area cannot be over-emphasised; starting work under a contract where no planning permission has been given may result in the contract being void for illegality which would prevent the contractor recovering any payment for work done. Furthermore, the employer could be required by the planning authority to demolish the work that had been carried out. Alternatively, where the contract is signed and planning permission, sufficient to enable the contractor to proceed with the work, has not been obtained by the date for possession, the contractor will probably be entitled to an extension of time for completion (condition 25.4.13) and loss and expense (condition 26.2.2) even though he may not have put one foot on the site. Furthermore, there is provision for the contractor to determine his employment under the contract if the whole or substantially the whole of the work is suspended for a particular period by reason of the lack of planning permission (condition 28.1.2.8).

The consequences of failing to deal properly with this aspect of the contract can therefore be very serious. Whilst there is a footnote to condition 6, referring to Practice Note CD/IA, it may be that the omission to deal with this matter expressly in the conditions (by alternative clauses) may result in disputes that could otherwise have been avoided.

Amongst the matters that the Practice Note CD/1A suggests should be dealt with in the Employer's Requirements is 'the extent the Contractor is to base his Proposals on information supplied by the employer concerning the topography of the site and the subsoil and the availability of public utility services'. There could be difficulties in this sphere where the contractor bases his design on such information. For example, where the Employer's Requirements provides the contractor with a site investigation report giving the loadbearing capacity of the ground for foundations, it is likely that the contractor will base his design on that information. What happens subsequently if the bearing capacity of the ground turns out to be lower than the Employer's Requirements? Who pays for the extra cost involved in the redesign and the more expensive foundations? There is no doubt that the contractor would have to redesign and put in appropriate foundations because of his obligation to complete the works (Article 1 and condition 2.1).

There is probably not a divergence between the 'Statutory Requirements' and the Employer's Requirements or the Contractor's Proposals under condition 6.1.2 because the requirements and proposals were based on a hypothesis and there would be no divergence between that hypothesis and the Contractor's Proposals. Accordingly, it would not follow from condition 6.1.2 that the contractor should meet the extra cost. Condition 12 does not provide that the employer *shall* issue an instruction effecting a change in such circumstances. It may be that the contractors would be able to contend that there was an implied term or an implied warranty on the part of the employer that the ground conditions would accord with the hypothesis upon which they were instructed to design the foundations, and that the contractors could recover the extra cost as damages for breach of that term: see for some assistance *Bacal Construction (Midlands) Limited* v. *Northampton Development Corporation* (1975). This is, perhaps, another reason for keeping the Employer's Requirements simple and not too detailed.

8.2.3 *Second Recital, the Contractor's Proposals and the Contract Sum Analysis*

It is suggested in Practice Note CD/1A that the Contractor's Proposals should incorporate the following documents:

(1) plans, elevations, sections or typical details and the scales to which they should be drawn
(2) information about the structural design
(3) layout drawings which indicate the services being incorporated
(4) specifications for materials and workmanship.

However, as with the Employer's Requirements, there is no definition that is of any practical help in the conditions; nevertheless, it is essential that the Employer's Requirements and the Contractor's Proposals taken together should properly and adequately define the works that are to be carried out.

The Contract Sum Analysis is an analysis of the sum the contractor requires for carrying out the works. However, the conditions again give no guidance as to the contents of this analysis. Practice Note CD/1B suggests that the Employer's Requirements should stipulate the 'form and degree' of the analysis and the note contains a suggested list of sections of work that might form the basis of the Contract Sum Analysis. In any event, the Contract Sum Analysis should be adequate to enable it to be used for the following purposes:

(1) valuation of changes in the Employer's Requirements (condition 12.5)
(2) to facilitate the use of the Formula Rules (condition 38)
(3) to assist in the preparation and checking of applications for interim payment (Alternative B, Appendix 2)

(4)   to set out the value of design work:
    (a)   completed before the date of contract
    (b)   during construction, and
    (c)   for the purposes of valuing the design element in a change in the Employer's Requirements (see commentary on condition 12.4).

By stating in the Contract Sum Analysis the value of design work completed before contract, the contractor would be able to include the value in the first application for interim payment. As to VAT on the design value, the JCT have been advised by the Commissioners of Customs and Excise that 'the liability to VAT of the design element will ... follow the VAT liability of the main works as in the case of other lump sum contracts where the design sum is not separately identified. In a mixed-work package of course, the design sum element will have to be apportioned between the standard rated and zero rated work in an appropriate manner' (Practice Note CD/1A page 12). This presumably implies that in the case of work which is zero rated, the whole design element charge will be free of VAT. If so, there may be a substantial saving for the employer in using a design and build contract instead of the usual form, in that VAT will not be payable on the design fee.

8.2.4   Third Recital

The Third Recital is not a warranty on the part of the employer that the Contractor's Proposals meet the Employer's Requirements. The wording falls far short of that for two reasons. Firstly, the words 'they appear to meet' are not unequivocal. Secondly, the whole recital is 'subject to the Conditions hereinafter contained' and those conditions provide expressly for matters that are inconsistent with the recital being a warranty, such as discrepancies (condition 2.4) and the contractor's design warranty (condition 2.5).

The Works are the work described in the First Recital, the Employer's Requirements and in the Contractor's Proposals. There is no machinery in the contract for resolving any discrepancy between the Employer's Requirements and the Contractor's Proposals. There is a footnote to the third recital pointing out that, where the Contractor's Proposals diverge from the Employer's Requirements, and the employer accepts that change, the Employer's Requirements should be amended before the contract is signed. The Practice Note CD/1B says: 'It was considered more appropriate to emphasise the need to follow the advice in the footnote than to include any specific provision on such divergence'. This is a surprising omission because it is these two documents that determine the extent of the 'Works'. Until the extent of the works is known, it is not possible to determine whether an employer's instruction is a change in the Employer's Requirements. The provision as to divergences in the conditions is often amended in this respect.

Further difficulties may arise if the employer issues instructions requiring removal from the site of work, materials or goods which are not in accordance with the contract in circumstances where there is a divergence. It may well be that problems will arise in relation to the quality rather than the quantity of the work. Suffice it to say, it is essential that both parties to the contract should check that there are no such divergencies before they sign the contract.

8.2.5   *The agreement*

'NOW IT IS HEREBY AGREED AS FOLLOWS

Article 1
Upon and subject to the Conditions, and where stated in Appendix 1, upon and subject to the Supplementary Provisions issued February 1988 which modify the aforesaid conditions, the Contractor will, for the consideration mentioned in Article 2, both complete the design for the Works and carry out and complete the construction of the Works.

Article 2
The   Employer   will   pay   to   the   Contractor   the   sum   of
_____ (£   )
(hereinafter referred to as 'the Contract Sum') or such other sum as shall become payable hereunder at the times and in the manner specified in the Conditions.

Article 3
_____

or such other person as the Employer shall nominate in his place for the purpose shall be the Employer's Agent referred to in clauses 5.4 and 11 and, save to the extent which the Employer may otherwise specify by written notice to the Contractor, for the receiving or issuing of such applications, consents, instructions, notices, requests or statements or for otherwise acting for the Employer under any other of the Conditions.

Article 4
The Employer's Requirements, the Contractor's Proposals and the Contract Sum Analysis have been signed by the Parties and are identified in Appendix 3 to the conditions.

Article 5
If any dispute or difference as to the construction of this contract or any matter or thing of whatsoever nature arising hereunder or in connection therewith shall arise between the Employer and the Contractor either during the progress or after the completion or abandonment of the Works except under Clause 31 (Statutory Tax Deduction Scheme) to the extent provided in Clause 31.9 or under Clause 3 of the VAT Agreement it shall be and is hereby referred to arbitration in accordance with Clause 39.'

Article 3 provides for the employer to name an agent in the contract and provides that, unless the employer limits his authority by a written notice to the contractor, the agent can perform all the duties and obligations of the employer in the contract. By Article 3, the employer is warranting the authority of the agent and the contractor should be careful to note the contents of any written notice limiting that authority because if the contractor has such written notice, the agent will not have authority to act in respect of the matters set out in the notice and the contractor must deal with the employer on those matters. There is also provision for the employer to nominate another person so that, for example, should the agent named in the contract die, the employer can appoint someone else in his place.

Clause 39 sets out the detailed machinery for arbitration. It used to be the case that, if the parties did not specify in the Appendix who is to appoint the arbitrator, if they could not agree as to an arbitrator, the machinery of the arbitration clause would be unworkable and an application would have had to be made to the court for the appointment of an arbitrator under section 10 of the Arbitration Act 1950. However, by Amendment 2 to this form of contract, issued in July 1987, the Appendix now provides that, in the absence of a particular appointor being selected, the appointor shall be the President or a Vice-President of the Chartered Institute of Arbitrators. Rules have been published by the Joint Contracts Tribunal (1988) which will apply to arbitrations under this form of contract (see section 13.3.4.2).

Secondly, the contract envisages, and it is likely that, both design and construction work will be sub-let (although there is no provision for nominated sub-contractors). In the event that there is a dispute in the sub-let work, the contractor will have two disputes, one with the employer and one with the sub-contractor or designer. It would be usual to try to have such disputes heard in one arbitration and it is for this reason that the JCT 80 Contract has procedure for both disputes to be heard together by the same arbitrator. There is no such comparable procedure in this contract. This is likely to produce the result that where the contractor finds himself in such a position, he will prefer to have his dispute heard in the High Court where both the employer and the sub-contractor or designer can all be joined in the same proceedings. It is unlikely in such circumstances that the court would order a stay of the High Court proceedings to arbitration, but see the comments on *Northern Regional Health Authority* v. *Crouch* (1984) and developments in the law relating to stays to arbitration in section 13.4.

Thirdly, an arbitration cannot be opened before practical completion except in certain circumstances and where either party has withheld or delayed a consent or statement where the contract provides that they shall not be unreasonably witheld or delayed. Such matters that are relevant to design include divergencies between the Statutory Requirements and either the Employer's Requirements or the Contractor's Proposals (condition 6.1.2), the consent of the contractor to a change in the Employer's Requirements (condition 12.2) and the consent of the employer to the sub-letting by the contractor of design or work (condition 18.2).

8.2.6   Conditions – standards, divergencies and discrepancies

'2.1   The Contractor shall upon and subject to the Conditions carry out and complete the Works referred to in the Employer's Requirements, the Contractor's Proposals (to which the Contract Sum Analysis is annexed), the Articles of Agreement, these Conditions and the Appendices in accordance with the aforementioned documents and for that purpose shall complete the design for the Works including the selection of any specifications for any kinds and standards of the materials and goods and workmanship to be used in the construction of the Works so far as not described or stated in the Employer's Requirements or Contractor's Proposals.

2.2   Nothing contained in the Employer's Requirements or the Contractor's Proposals or the Contract Sum Analysis shall override or modify the application or interpretation of that which is contained in the Articles of Agreement, the Conditions and where applicable, the Supplementary Provisions, or the Appendices.'

Condition 2.1 clearly envisages that the Employer's Requirements may specify the 'kinds and standards of materials and goods and workmanship to be used'. The effect of such specification, therefore, is likely to be to displace the contractor's implied warranty of fitness for purpose; the contractor's continuing obligation to supply materials of good quality will not necessarily avail the employer where those materials are good of their kind; for example, where a particular type of brick is specified to be used in manholes, and those bricks, which were equal in quality to an approved sample, were used but failed, it is likely that the employer would have no remedy against the contractor: *Adcocks Trustee* v. *Bridge RDC* (1911); *Young and Marten* v. *MacManus Childs* (1969); *Gloucester County Council* v. *Richardson* (1968).

Condition 2.2 is important because its effect is to prevent any obligation contained in the Employer's Requirements or the Contractor's Proposals or the Contract Sum Analysis overriding or modifying anything contained in the conditions and Articles. For example, if there were an obligation for phased completion in the Employer's Requirements, and the conditions and the Appendices (including the date for completion) were unamended, then the contractor would probably be under no obligation to complete in phases: *M.J. Gleeson (Construction) Limited* v. *Hillingdon Borough Council* (1970).

Particularly difficult problems may arise where the Employer's Requirements and the Contractor's Proposals make it clear that the contractor was accepting an obligation to provide a building that was fit for its purpose because on the face of it, this will be seeking to override or modify the obligations in condition 2.5.1 which provides that the contractor will only be liable in respect of his design as if he were in the position of an independent architect (see commentary on that clause). In any event, if the parties wish to provide for a matter which will override or modify the application or interpretation of the conditions, then they must amend the conditions, the Articles or the Appendix appropriately.

'2.3.1   Any divergence between the Employer's Requirements and the definition of the site boundary to be given by the Employer as provided in clause 7 shall be corrected by an instruction issued by the Employer which instruction shall be deemed to be a Change to which the provisions of clauses 12.4, 12.5 and 12.6 apply.

2.3.2   If the Employer or the Contractor finds any such divergence as is referred to in clause 2.3.1 he shall immediately give the other written notice specifying the divergence.'

These conditions are designed to deal with the position where the employer's definition of the boundaries of the site (condition 7) conflicts with the Employer's Requirements. The procedure is that the employer is required to issue an instruction and that instruction is deemed to be a 'change'. This, in turn, means that the contractor is entitled to be paid for any modification in the design, quality or quantity of the work (condition 12.1) and where a delay is caused, the contractor will also be entitled to an extension of time for completion (condition 25.4.5.1).

> '2.4.1   Where there is a discrepancy within the Employer's Requirements (including any Change issued in accordance with clause 12.2) the Contractor's Proposals shall prevail (subject always to compliance with the Statutory Requirements) without any adjustment of the Contract Sum. Where the Contractor's Proposals do not deal with any discrepancy within the Employer's Requirements (including any Change issued in accordance with Clause 12.2) the Contractor shall inform the Employer in writing of his proposed amendment to deal with the discrepancy and the Employer shall either agree the proposed amendment or himself decide how the discrepancy shall be dealt with. Such agreement or decision shall be notified in writing to the Contractor and such notification shall be treated as a Change in the Employer's Requirements.
>
> 2.4.2   Where there is a discrepancy within the Contractor's Proposals the Contractor shall inform the Employer in writing of his proposed amendment to remove the discrepancy; and (subject always to compliance with Statutory Requirements) the Employer shall decide between the discrepant items or otherwise may accept the Contractor's proposed amendment and the Contractor shall be obliged to comply with the decision or acceptance by the Employer without cost to the Employer.
>
> 2.4.3   If the Contractor or the Employer find any such discrepancy as is referred to in clause 2.4.1 or 2.4.2 he shall immediately give the other written notice specifying the discrepancy.'

These conditions deal with discrepancies. However, they do not deal with discrepancies between the Employer's Requirements and the Contractor's Proposals; condition 2.4.1 deals with discrepancies *within* the Employer's Requirements and condition 2.4.2 deals with discrepancies *within* the Contractor's Proposals. There is no machinery here for resolving discrepancies between those two sets of documents. A discrepancy in the Employer's Requirements is resolved by providing that the Contractor's Proposals shall prevail. If the employer does not wish that to happen, then he has no alternative under the contract but to issue an instruction requiring a 'change'. Where the discrepancy is within the Contractor's Proposals, the employer has the option of deciding which item he wishes to prevail or accepting the contractor's proposed amendments. Either way, the contractor has to comply and the cost of any change is borne by him.

8.2.7   Conditions – design obligation

> '2.5.1   Insofar as the design of the Works is comprised in the Contractor's Proposals and in what the Contractor is to complete under clause 2 and in accordance with the Employer's Requirements and the Conditions (including any further design which the Contractor is to carry out as a

result of a change in the Employer's Requirements), the Contractor shall have in respect of any defect or insufficiency in such design the like liability to the Employer, whether under statute or otherwise, as would an architect or, as the case may be, other appropriate professional designer holding himself out as competent to take on work for such design who, acting independently under a separate contract with the Employer, had supplied such design for or in connection with works to be carried out and completed by a building contractor not being the supplier of the design.

2.5.2   Where and to the extent that this Contract involves the Contractor in taking on work for or in connection with the provision of a dwelling or dwellings, the reference in clause 2.5.1 to the Contractor's liability includes liability under the Defective Premises Act 1972 and where the application of section 2(1) of the Act is included in the Employer's Requirements the Contractor and the Employer respectively shall do all such things as are necessary for a document or documents to be duly issued for the purpose of that section and the scheme approved thereunder which is referred to in Appendix 1.

2.5.3   Where and to the extent that this Contract does not involve the Contractor in taking on work for or in connection with the provision of a dwelling or dwellings to which the Defective Premises Act 1972 applies, the Contractor's liability for loss of use, loss of profit or other consequential loss arising in respect of the liability of the Contractor referred to in clause 2.5.1 shall be limited to the amount, if any, named in Appendix 1: provided that such limitation of amount shall not apply to or be affected by any damages which under clause 24.2 the Contractor could be required to pay or allow at the rate stated in Appendix 1 as liquidated and ascertained damages in the event of failure to complete the construction of the Works by the Completion Date.

2.5.4   Any references to the design which the Contractor has prepared or shall prepare or issue for the Works include a reference to any design which the Contractor has caused or shall cause to be prepared or issued by others.'

Condition 2.5.1 states in essence that a contractor's liability in respect of design is to be the same as that of an architect or other appropriate professional designer. That liability is, of course, to use reasonable skill and care. There is not usually to be implied, as a matter of law, an obligation on a professional designer that his design will produce finished works that are fit for their purpose. However, such an obligation for fitness for purpose is usually implied into design and build contracts; in this contract, the parties have decided that the obligation will be reasonable skill and care and there is, therefore, no requirement to imply any term as to the duties that are owed by the designing contractor because the parties have provided for it expressly.

It follows that condition 2.5.1, which appears at first sight to operate for the benefit of the employer, is, in fact, an exclusion clause seeking to limit the contractor's liability to less than that normally implied by operation of law.

Employers who find that this condition is an obstacle to their recovering damages from a negligent designing contractor will seek to defeat the effect of this condition and they may use one or more of the following weapons that remain in their armoury.

8.2.7.1   Reasonable skill and care

Although there will be no implied term that the design should be fit for its purpose, the contractor, in order to discharge his obligation to use reasonable skill and care, has to design in such a way that the design is fit for any purpose that is made known to him by the employer: *IBA* v. *EMI and BICC* (1980). Where a designer knows that a building is to be used by fork lift trucks then he will be in breach of his duty to use reasonable skill and care if he fails to design in such a way that the floors will safely carry laden fork lift trucks without damaging vibrations: *Greaves (Contractors) Limited* v. *Baynham Meikle & Partners* (1975). Where the employer seeks to set up this argument to ground his claim, it would be a claim for breach of condition 2.5.1 of the contract.

8.2.7.2   Negligent mis-statement

Where there is a special relationship between the parties, a party making a statement to the other party has a duty not to make a negligent mis-statement: *Hedley Byrne & Co. Limited* v. *Heller & Partners Limited* (1963). This subject is discussed in sections 2.2.2.1 and 4.2.

8.2.7.3   Defective Premises Act 1972

Where the contractor's design relates to dwellings, the designing contractor owes a duty to see that the work he takes on is done in a workmanlike and professional manner and that the dwelling will be fit for habitation when completed (section 1(1) of the Act and see section 2.3.4). The Act provides that neither the duty nor the liability arising from the duty can be excluded or restricted by agreement. Section 6(3) states:

> 'Any term of an agreement which purports to exclude or restrict, or has the effect of excluding or restricting, the operation of any of the provisions of this Act, or any liability arising by virtue of any such provision, shall be void.'

It follows from this that even if the intention of conditions 2.5.1 and 2.5.2 is purporting to limit the designer's liability in the case of dwellings to reasonable skill and care, then those provisions are void and will be replaced by the duty under the Act. It sometimes happens that a dwelling is provided ancillary to the main work to be executed under the contract, for example, a caretaker's house with a school. In such circumstances, the obligation under section 6(3) of the Act would apply to the design and construction of the dwelling.

No action can be brought under the Act where the dwelling is being built under an 'approved scheme'. The NHBC Schemes dated 1973, 1975 and 1977 were approved schemes under the Act. The more recent schemes have not been subjected to the approval process (see section 2.3.4).

8.2.7.4   Misrepresentation

Whilst the principle of negligent mis-statement arises independently of contract, misrepresentation is a principle that applies only as between the parties to a contract. A misrepresentation is a statement which is false, made by one party to the other before or at the time that the contract is entered into and which is one of the reasons for which the innocent party enters into the contract. The statement must be a statement of fact; for example it will not be sufficient if the representation was merely 'puffing'. Generally, silence will not be a misrepresentation but it can be where it has the effect, taken with other statements, of producing a half truth. A misrepresentation can result in the contract being voidable, that is to say, the innocent party can either insist on the other party performing his obligations or rescind the contract. However, it would be more usual in building contracts for the innocent party to sue for damages. He can do so where he has suffered a loss under the Misrepresentation Act 1967, section 2(1), unless the maker of the statement can show that he had reasonable grounds for believing, and did believe up to the time the contract was made, that the statements he had made were true.

Where a dredging company hired barges on the basis of the barge company's manager stating that their payload was 1600 tonnes, whereas the correct payload was 1052 tonnes, the dredging company recovered damages under section 2(1) of the Misrepresentation Act: *Howard Marine and Dredging Co. Limited* v. *A. Ogden & Sons (Excavations) Limited* (1977). It follows that where the employer can show that there was a representation by the contractor that his design would be fit for the employer's requirements, and that representation was one of the matters that induced the making of the contract, the employer will be able to bring an action for damages for misrepresentation.

8.2.7.5 *Unfair Contract Terms Act 1977*
This Act imposes limits on the extent to which liability for breach of contract or negligence can be avoided by means of contract terms. For example, it is not now possible to exclude or restrict liability for death or personal injury resulting from negligence by a contract term (section 2(1)). In the case of other loss and damage, liability for negligence can only be excluded or restricted insofar as the term satisfies the requirement of reasonableness (section 2(2)). Insofar as liability arising in contract is concerned, then where one party contracts on the basis of the other party's written standard terms of business, liability in respect of breach of contract can only be excluded or restricted in the contract to the extent that the term satisfies the requirement of reasonableness (section 3).

If condition 2.5.1 is a clause restricting the contractor's liability, the question arises whether it is successful in its intention. The first question that needs to be answered is whether or not the JCT Design and Build Contract is 'the other's written standard terms of business'.

It seems likely that in cases where the employer is a member of one of the constituent bodies of the JCT that the contract will not be considered to be the other's written standard terms of business. For example, local authorities are probably in this category by reason of their representation on the JCT by the Association of County Councils, the Association of Metropolitan Authorities and the Association of District Councils.

Is it possible that were the employer, for example, a manufacturing company, the contract could be held to be the written standard terms of business of the contractor? If so, then any contract clause purporting to exclude or restrict liability has to satisfy the requirements of reasonableness. In such circumstances, in addition to the contractor's design warranty at condition 2.5.1 the limitation of liability in condition 2.5.3 would fall to be considered by the court. This clause provides that the contractor's liability for loss of use, loss of profit or other consequential loss arising from a defect or insufficiency in design is to be limited to the amount stated in Appendix 1. In *Walker* v. *Boyle* (1982) and the cases of *McCrone* v. *Boots Farm Sales Limited* (1981), *The Chester Grosvenor Hotel Limited* v. *Alfred McAlpine Management Limited* (1992) and *Tersons Limited* v. *Stevenage Development Corporation* (1963), there is support for the view that some forms of contract are 'industry' forms derived from negotiation by representative bodies of both parties. If that is right, then this clause would not be the other's standard terms of trading for the purposes of the Act. It seems likely, therefore, that this form would escape scrutiny under the Act (see section 11.3.3.4).

Condition 2.5.4 provides that the contractor shall have the same liability in respect of design work that he sub-lets to other people as he would have, had he carried out the design himself. This provision is reflected in condition 18.2.2 which provides for the employer to give his consent to the contractor but such consent is expressly stated to be subject to condition 2.5.

8.2.8   Conditions – statutory obligations

'6.   *Statutory obligations, notices, fees and charges*

6.1.1.1   Clause 6.1.1.2 shall apply except to the extent that the relevant part or parts of the Employer's Requirements state specifically that the Employer's Requirements comply with Statutory Requirements.

6.1.1.2   The Contractor shall comply with, and give all notices required by, any Act of Parliament, any instrument, rule or order made under any Act of Parliament, or any regulation or byelaw of any local authority or of any statutory undertaker which has any jurisdiction with regard to the Works or with whose systems the same are or will be connected including Development Control Requirements (all requirements to be so complied with being referred to in these Conditions as "the Statutory Requirements") and the Contractor shall pass to the Employer all approvals received by the Contractor in connection therewith.

6.1.2   If the Contractor or the Employer finds any divergence between the Statutory Requirements and either the Employer's Requirements (including any Change) or the Contractor's Proposals he shall immediately give to the other written notice specifying the divergence; the Contractor shall inform the Employer in writing of his proposed amendment for removing the divergence, and with the Employer's consent (which shall not be unreasonably delayed or withheld) the Contractor shall entirely at his own cost save as provided in clause 6.3 complete the design and construction of the Works in accordance with the amendment and the Employer shall note the amendment on the documents referred to in clause 5.1

6.1.3.1   If in any emergency compliance with clause 6.1.1 requires the Contractor to supply materials or execute work before receiving the Employer's consent under clause 6.1.2 the Contractor shall supply such limited materials and execute such limited work as are reasonably necessary to secure immediate compliance with the Statutory Requirements.

6.1.3.2   The Contractor shall forthwith inform the Employer of the emergency and of the steps that he is taking under clause 6.1.3.1.

6.2   The Contractor shall pay, and indemnify the Employer against liability in respect of, any fees or charges (including any rates or taxes) legally demandable under any Act of Parliament, any instrument, rule or order made under any Authority or of any statutory undertaker in respect of the Works. No adjustment shall be made to the Contract Sum in respect of the amount of any such fees or charges (including any rates or taxes other than value added tax) unless they are stated by way of a provisional sum in the Employer's Requirements, in which case clause 30.5.3 shall apply.

6.3.1   If after the Base Date there is a change in the Statutory Requirements affecting the Works which necessitates some amendment to the Contractor's Proposals, such amendment shall be treated as if it were an instruction of the Employer under clause 12.2 effecting a Change in the Employer's Requirements.

6.3.2   If any amendment to the Contractor's Proposals becomes necessary for conformity with the terms of any permission or approval made by a decision of the relevant authority after the Base Date for the purpose of Development Control Requirements such amendment shall be treated as if it were an instruction of the Employer under clause 12.2 effecting a Change in the Employer's Requirements provided that such treatment is not precluded in the Employer's Requirements.

6.3.3   If any amendment to that part or parts of the Employer's Requirements to which clause 6.1.1 refers becomes necessary for conformity with Statutory Requirements, the Employer shall issue an instruction effecting a Change in the Employer's Requirements.'

Under these provisions, the responsibility for complying with statutory requirements is put fairly and squarely on the contractor. The Statutory Requirements include Development Control Requirements which are defined as 'any Statutory provisions and any decision of a relevant authority thereunder which control the right to develop the site' (condition 1). Condition 6.1.1, therefore, puts the onus on the contractor to comply with all the statutory requirements including planning permission. There is no provision here as to who is to obtain planning permission, hence the fundamental need to deal with that aspect in either the Employer's Requirements or the Contractor's Proposals (see 8.2.2). Where planning permission for the contract works has not been granted at the date of contract, the wording is sufficiently wide to impose liability on a contractor for breach of contract should he proceed with the works in the absence of such permission, in addition to the other problems set out at 8.2.2.

Condition 6.1.1.2 requires the contractor to comply with Building Regulations. Non-compliance will, therefore, be a breach of contract, as well as possibly being a breach of statutory duty, subject to condition 6.1.1.1 (see 4.3.2 and 4.3.3 for a discussion).

Where there is a divergence between the Statutory Requirements (e.g. planning permission or Building Regulations) and the Employer's Requirements or the Contractor's Proposals, then the contractor has to overcome the divergence entirely at his own cost except where the Statutory Requirements have changed since the Base Date (condition 6.3.1) or where a local authority changes the terms of the development control approval after the Base Date (condition 6.3.2). In the case of either of these exceptions, the change is to be treated as if it were a 'change' in the Employer's Requirements under Condition 12.2. Such a 'change' also entitles the contractor, where there is delay, to an extension of time for completion (condition 25.4.5.1) and to loss and expense where the regular process of the work is affected (condition 26.2.6). Provided conditions 25 and 26 are complied with, this will be so even where a 'change' occurred before the contractor started work on the site.

The definition of divergence in condition 6.1.2 includes any change. It follows that where the employer instructs a 'change' that does not comply with the Statutory Requirements, the contractor should draw this to the employer's attention and where appropriate, the contractor would probably be entitled to withhold his consent to the 'change' under condition 12.2.

The contractor is liable to pay and indemnify the employer in respect of all legally demandable fees; those fees will include the charges that are now made in respect of the local authority's costs in administering the building control system. However, where it is expressly provided in the Employer's Requirements, by way of a provisional sum, then the contractor will be entitled to be paid. It follows that where there is no such provisional sum in the Employer's Requirements, the contractor should allow for paying such fees in his tender.

Condition 6.3.2, which provides one of the exceptions to the contractor bearing the cost in the case of a discrepancy, is subject to the words 'provided that such treatment is not precluded in the Employer's Requirements'. These words are included so that the employer can exclude the operation of condition 6.3.2, so that the contractor bears the cost, provided the employer says so in the Employer's Requirements. It may be that this proviso is inconsistent with condition 2.2 which provides that nothing in the Employer's Requirements shall override or modify the application or interpretation of the conditions; it may be preferable, if the employer wishes to put such costs on the contractor, simply to delete condition 6.3.2.

8.2.9   Conditions – changes

'12   *Changes in the Employer's Requirements and provisional sums*
12.1   The term "Change in the Employer's Requirements" or "Change" means:

12.1.1   a change in the Employer's Requirements which makes necessary the alteration or modification of the design, quality or quantity of the Works otherwise than such as may be reasonably necessary for the purposes of rectification pursuant to clause 8.4, including

1.1   the addition, omission or substitution of any work,
1.2   the alteration of the kind or standard of any of the materials or goods to be used in the Works,
1.3   the removal from the site of any work or materials or goods brought thereon by the Contractor for the purposes of the Works other than

work materials or goods which are not in accordance with this Contract;

12.1.2 the imposition by the Employer of any obligations or restrictions in regard to the matters set out in clause 12.1.2.1 to 12.1.2.4 or the addition to, or alteration or omission of any such obligations or restrictions, so imposed or imposed by the Employer in the Employer's Requirements in regard to:

.2.1 access to the site or use of any specific parts of the site,
.2.2 limitations of working space,
.2.3 limitations of working hours,
.2.4 the execution or completion of the work in any specific order.

12.2 The Employer may subject to the proviso hereto and to the Contractor's right of reasonable objection set out in clause 4.1.1 issue instructions effecting a Change in the Employer's Requirements. No Change effected by the Employer shall vitiate this Contract, provided that the Employer may not effect a Change which is, or which makes necessary, an alteration or modification in the design of the Works without the consent of the Contractor which consent shall not be unreasonably delayed or withheld.

12.3 The Employer shall issue instructions to the Contractor in regard to the expenditure of provisional sums (if any) included in the Employer's Requirements.

12.4 The valuation of Changes and of the work executed by the Contractor for which a provisional sum is included in the Employer's Requirements shall, unless otherwise agreed, be made in accordance with the provisions of clause 12.5. Such valuation shall include allowance for the addition or omission of the relevant design work.'

It should be noted that a 'change' includes the alteration or modification of the design (condition 12.1.1). This has two important consequences. Firstly, the employer is not permitted to instruct a 'change' which has the consequence of altering or modifying the design without the consent of the contractor (condition 12.2). This important provision enables the contractor to consider and check the consequences of any 'change' in relation to the rest of the design of the works. Secondly, in valuing 'changes' an allowance is to be made for any additional or omitted design work (condition 12.4). The valuation of that design work is to be consistent with the values of work of similar character set out in the Contract Sum Analysis. It may therefore be advisable for the contractor in the Contract Sum Analysis not only to state design work pre-tender and post-tender but also to set out the basis on which that design work has been calculated so as to facilitate valuation of 'changes'.

8.2.10 Conditions – extension of time and loss and/or expense

The provisions of conditions 25 and 26 relating to extensions of time for completion and loss and expense broadly follow those of JCT 80. However, there are differences, which are found in condition 25. There are additional relevant events for the purposes of extension of time:

- 25.4.4   is extended to include the effect of civil commotion, local combination of workmen, strike or lockout affecting any persons engaged in the preparation of the design.
- 25.4.6   provides that a relevant event includes the employer not having given to the contractor in due time necessary instructions, decisions, information or consents.
- 25.4.7   provides that the delay in receipt of any necessary permission or approval of any statutory body, which the contractor has taken all practicable steps to avoid or reduce, will be a relevant event.
- 25.4.13   provides for the position that will arise where there is a change in the Statutory Requirements after the Base Date or a change in the terms of permission or approval for development control purposes.

The list of matters entitling the contractor to recover direct loss and/or expense follows those set out in clause 26.2 of the JCT 80 Form except for condition 26.2.2 which provides for delay in the receipt of any permission or approval for development control requirements giving rise to loss and/or expense.

8.2.11   *Insurance of design obligation*

The JCT Design and Build Contract does not require the contractor to insure in respect of the obligation he takes on as to design. Most professional designers, architects and engineers do have professional indemnity insurance (although the RIBA does not presently require it). It follows that, by adopting the JCT Design and Build Contract, the employer may be more at risk in respect of a design failure than he is under the traditional method unless the contractor carries a professional indemnity policy, or is sufficiently robust to meet any design claim that succeeds against him. The fact that professional indemnity insurance is not required under the contract is a strange omission, all the more so by reason of the fact that the construction industry is a high risk operation. A detailed discussion of insurance for design and build projects is to be found in section 10.5.

8.3   JCT Contractor's Design Portion Supplement 1981

The JCT have prepared a supplement for use with the Standard form of Building Contract with Quantities, both local authorities and private, 1980 Editions, to provide for the contractor to have responsibility for the design, as well as the construction, of *part* of the works. The Supplement was produced in 1981 together with a Practice Note CD/2. The Contractor's Design Portion Supplement consists of Articles of Agreement, new conditions, amendments to the JCT 80 Conditions and a Supplementary Appendix. It is not proposed to comment on the individual amendments or additional conditions because, in the main, they follow the JCT Design and Build Form. Accordingly, most of the comments set out above in relation to that form also apply to the Contractor's Design Portion Supplement. In any event, neither the contractor nor the architect/employer should enter into the Contractor's Design Portion Supplement without carefully reading and considering the comments in Practice Note CD/2.

8.4   Performance specified work: JCT 80

By Amendment 12 to JCT 80 issued in July 1993, the Joint Contracts Tribunal have, for the first time, incorporated into JCT 80 an obligation as to design. It is a concept described in the contract as 'Performance Specified Work.' It is brought in by a new clause 42.

Performance Specified Work is work that is identified in the Appendix to the contract, to be provided by the contractor, 'for which certain requirements have been pre-determined and are shown on the Contract Drawings'; and the performance required is set out in the contract bills, which themselves have to contain either sufficient detail to permit pricing at tender stage or a provisional sum (clause 42.1). Where a provisional sum is used, sufficient information must be given in the contract bills to enable the contractor to understand the performance required of such work, its location in the building and to enable due allowance for it in programming and in pricing preliminaries (clause 42.7). It follows that any requirements for such work have to be thought through early and incorporated in the contract; they cannot be added later by, say, an architect's instruction.

The contractor has to produce a 'Contractor's Statement' before carrying out any Performance Specified Work; it has to be 'in sufficient form and detail adequately to explain [his] proposals ... include any information which is required to be included ... by the Contract Bills or ... by the instruction of the Architect...' on the expenditure of a provisional sum (clauses 42.2 and 42.3).There are provisions for the timing and approval of the Contractor's Statement (clauses 42.4 to 42.6).

The architect is expressly forbidden from issuing instructions to expend provisional sums as Performance Specified Work unless it has been incorporated in the contract bills as such (clause 42.8). It follows that Performance Specified Work cannot be carried out by nominated suppliers or nominated sub-contractors (clause 42.18).

There are further, mostly consequential, amendments to JCT 80 to deal with the Standard Method of Measurement; variations; provision of an 'Analysis' of the price; integration; conflicts between Performance Specified Work and architect's instructions; and extensions of time (clauses 42.9 to 42.16)

The standard of care to be exercised by the contractor is also set out:

'42.17.1   The Contractor shall exercise reasonable skill and care in the provision of Performance Specified Work provided that:
.1.1   clause 42.17 shall not be construed so as to affect the obligations of the Contractor under this Contract in regard to the supply of workmanship, materials and goods and
.1.2   nothing in this Contract shall operate as a guarantee of fitness for purpose of the Performance Specified Work.
42.17.2   The Contractor's obligation under clause 42.17.1 shall in no way be modified by any service in respect of any Performance Specified Work which he has obtained from others and, in particular, the

Contractor shall be responsible for any such service as if such service had been undertaken by the Contractor himself.'

Clearly, the contractor does not escape any liability if he sub-lets to a negligent designer but is the obligation on the contractor reasonable skill and care or fitness for purpose? Practice Note 25, issued with Amendment 12, states:

'. . . clause 42.17.1 defines the Contractor's liability for [work not producing the required performance] . . . as his failure to meet the normal standards of skill and care of a professional consultant (i.e. to use reasonable skill and care) and does not call for a guarantee of that performance.'

With respect to the draughtsmen, the position may well not be so simple. The question arises whether there is room here for the implication of a term for fitness for purpose of the Performance Specified Work. As was seen in section 4.1, a term as to fitness for purpose will readily be implied into contracts for the supply of goods and services. Normally, a term will not be implied where the contract already has relevant provisions dealing with the subject matter of a term that might otherwise be implied. Clause 42.17.1.2 excludes a '*guarantee* of fitness for purpose' but a guarantee is a different species of legal obligation to a straightforward primary obligation. For example, different rules apply to limitation of action in respect of guarantees. It is perhaps significant that the draughtsmen have not adopted the wording used in JCT with Contractor's Design at clause 2.5.1. It does therefore seem possible that a term as to fitness for purpose of the Performance Specified Work may be capable of being implied here, notwithstanding what is said in Practice Note 25 (which does not form part of the contract).

8.5   ACA Form of Building Agreement 1982 (1984 Edition, 1990 Revision)

This building contract was produced by the Association of Consultant Architects in 1982 and in 1984 went into its second edition. The contract is structured so that, by deleting alternative clauses, it can be used for a construction project where the architect is to carry out all the design or a project where the architect carries out only certain parts of the design and the contractor completes that design. In either case, it is necessary for the employer to have an architect and the architect is named in the contract. It follows that where the option is chosen for the contractor to complete the design, the employer's own architect will still be retained.

The choice between architect design and part contractor's design is to be found in the alternatives to recital F of the agreement; alternative 2 reads:

'The Architect shall prepare only further drawings and details as are specified in the Contract Documents in accordance with the provisions of Clause 2.1 and the Contractor shall provide all further drawings, details, documents and information for the execution of the Works in accordance with the provisions of Clause 2.2.'

It can be seen that it is necessary for the contract documents to make clear what it is that the architect is to do and what it is that the contractor is to do: that dividing line determines the responsibility and liability if things do not go according to plan.

Going hand in hand with the contractor design alternative in the recitals is an alternative clause 2 which has several sub-clauses. The architect is required to provide the contractor with two copies, not only of the contract documents but also of any other drawings or details which the architect is to produce, and he must provide such drawings and details on the dates shown in the contract (clause 2.1).

Thereafter it is up to the contractor and detailed provisions are set out to deal with aspects of the mechanics of the contractor's design. He is required to produce to the architect two copies of any drawings, details, documents or information which are reasonably necessary to explain and amplify the contract drawings, or reasonably necessary to enable the contractor to execute and complete the works or to comply with architect's instructions or any other documents which are stated in the contract documents to be provided by the contractor (clause 2.2). Within ten days thereafter, or any other time agreed in the contract, the architect has to either approve that document or return it to the contractor endorsed with his comments; if he does the latter, then the contractor has to re-submit for approval and the process repeats until approval is obtained (clauses 2.3 and 2.4). Once the architect has returned any document with no comment to the contractor, then that work becomes part of the works to be executed under the contract (clause 2.5). The contractor has an express obligation to comply with statutory requirements in the provision of his design (clause 2.5).

If the contractor comes across adverse ground conditions or artificial obstructions on the site, then that is a matter upon which the architect must make decisions and issue an instruction. The contractor is entitled to be paid for any extra work that results unless the particular problem that has arisen could reasonably have been foreseen at the date of the contract by a contractor exercising all the skill, care and diligence to be expected of a properly qualified and competent contractor experienced in carrying out work of similar scope, nature and size to this particular project (clause 1.2 and 2.6).

The contract sets out other obligations in relation to design which apply *whether or not* the architect or the contractor are designing (clauses 3.1, 9.8 and 9.9).

The contractor is expressly made responsible for mistakes, inaccuracies, discrepancies and omissions in any design provided by him and, more importantly, the contractor gives two express warranties. The first is that the works, and that includes his design, will comply with the requirements of the contract. The second is that those parts of the works which the contractor designs will be fit for the purposes for which they are required (clause 3.1). If the contract were silent on this point, then the common law would imply a term as to fitness for purpose in any event. However, it should be noted that that obligation does not and will not apply to any design carried out by the architect and the contractor will have no obligation as to fitness for purpose for such design.

If any sub-contractor or supplier carries out design, then the contract makes the contractor responsible for that design and for the co-ordination of that design into the overall works (clause 9.8). There is express provision that sub-letting by the contractor will not in any way relieve the contractor from his responsibility for the due execution and completion of the works (clause 9.9). Reading this together with the provisions of clause 3.1 means that there is a chain of contracts set up in respect of design such that the sub-contractor will be liable to the contractor and the contractor will be liable to the employer.

It is clear from the wording of the remainder of the contract that delay in design for which the contractor, or through him the sub-contractor or supplier, is responsible, will not entitle the contractor to an extension of time or a claim for loss and/or expense or disruption; the only exceptions will be where such delay arises from, for example, an architect's instruction. If the delayed design works were such that they were the contractor's obligation in the contract documents, then he will have to bear the loss of the delay and the disruption.

8.6 ICE Design and Construct Conditions of Contract

These conditions were published in 1992 by the ICE, the ACE and the FCEC (Federation of Civil Engineering Contractors). The design obligation is to be found at condition 8:

'8(1) The Contractor shall subject to the provisions of the Contract and save in so far as it is legally or physically impossible
  (a) design the Works and
  (b) provide all design services labour materials Contractor's Equipment Temporary Works transport to and from and in or about the site and everything whether of a temporary or permanent nature required in and for such design construction and completion so far as the necessity for providing the same is specified in or reasonably to be inferred from the Contract.

(2) (a) In carrying out all his design obligations under the Contract including those arising under sub-clause (2)(b) of this Clause (and including the selection of materials and plant to the extent that these are not specified in the Employer's Requirements) the Contractor shall exercise all reasonable skill care and diligence.
  (b) Where any part of the Works has been designed by or on behalf of the Employer and that design has been included in the Employer's Requirements the Contractor shall check the design and accept responsibility therefor having first obtained the approval of the Employer's Representative for any modifications thereto which the Contractor considers to be necessary.'

There are several points to note about these provisions.

Firstly, although the obligation is reasonable skill and care, there is the possibility that there may be an implied term as to fitness for purpose. The question would be whether this express term of reasonable care would prevent the implication of a term as to fitness; such a term is usually to be implied into design and build contracts. It is submitted that the term should be implied here.

Secondly, the contractor has to accept 'responsibility' for the employer's design after he has checked it. This requires pricing at tender stage and could be a burdensome requirement of uncertain scope. Does it, for example, involve the contractor in reconsidering the line and elevation of a road and the provision of bridges? It is submitted that that is design and therefore falls under this requirement. Its only limit is design included in the Employer's Requirements.

Thirdly, what does 'responsibility' mean? It is submitted that it means fitness for purpose under the implied term referred to above.

8.7   The IChemE Model Form of Conditions of Contract for Process Plant

This contract comes in two forms: lump-sum contracts (1993) and reimbursable contracts (1992). Although neither contract is drafted for use as a design and build contract, both forms are being so used, sometimes with inappropriate amendments. However, two points are important. Firstly, both contracts contain fitness for purpose obligations at least in respect of the work:

Lump Sum
'3.3   ... the Plant as completed by the Contractor shall be in every respect suitable for the purposes for which it is intended.'

Reimbursable
'3.4   ... the Plant as completed by the contractor shall be in accordance with the Contract and shall be in every respect fit for the purposes for which it was intended as defined in the Specification or in any other contractual provision.'

Arguably, the restriction of the definition of 'purposes' in the reimbursable form makes that provision slightly narrower and less open to interpretation than the lump sum form.

Secondly, the reimbursable form contains a further provision:

'3.2   If at any time during the performance of the Contract the Contractor is of the opinion that a change in the design, execution or operation of the Works

(a)   is necessary to correct any defect which has occurred or would otherwise occur, or
(b)   would be beneficial to the Purchaser

then the Contractor shall submit for the Project Manager's approval a written proposal for such change. The written proposal shall state the reasons for the Contractor's opinion.'

Contractors may find themselves, under this clause, acquiring a design responsibility they would otherwise not have, and on the basis of fitness for purpose. Contractors may be well advised to couch their proposals in the form of outline suggestions (with no detailed design) for the project manager's consideration and instructions if he thinks fit.

8.8   Model Form of General Conditions of Contract for use in connection with home or overseas contracts – with erection (Institution of Mechanical Engineers, Institution of Electrical Engineers and the Association of Consulting Engineers)

This contract is known as MF/1 (1988) and contains the following provision, which was added for the first time in this edition of the contract:

> 'The Contractor shall be responsible for the detailed design of the Plant and the Works in accordance with the requirements of the Specification. Insofar as the Contractor is required by the contract or is instructed by the Engineer to comply with any detailed design provided by the Purchaser or the Engineer the Contractor shall be responsible for such design unless within a reasonable time after receipt thereof he shall have given notice to the Engineer disclaiming such responsibility.
>
> Unless otherwise provided for in the Contract the Contractor does not warrant that the Works described in the Specification or the incorporation thereof within some larger project will satisfy the Purchaser's requirements.'

This may well create the possibility of an implied term as to fitness for purpose in design save that the last paragraph may have the effect of cutting it down; in deciding whether the last paragraph prevents that implication, it should be borne in mind that a warranty is not necessarily the same thing as an implied term as to fitness for purpose. Clearly this would not apply where the disclaimer proviso has been operated. That disclaimer proviso represents the standard practice within the electrical and mechanical plant industry (see the *Commentary* on this form published by the same bodies as publish the form).

8.9   GC/Works/1 (Edition 3), General Conditions of Contract for Building and Civil Engineering, Standard Form of Contract – Single Stage Design and Build Version

This form, first published in 1993, is for government contracts, that is to say where the employer is the government.

8.9.1   Definitions

There are definitions in the contract in relation to design:

- 'the Authority's Requirements' means the statement, drawings, and other documents which define the Authority's requirements and are attached to the invitation to tender.
- 'the Contractor's Proposals' means the drawings and documents in accordance with which the contractor has proposed to implement the 'Authority's Requirements' and any changes agreed prior to the award of the contract.
- 'the Design' means the complete design in accordance with the 'Authority's Requirements' and shall include the 'Contractor's Proposals' and all design documents which are necessary for the construction of the works in accordance with the contract.

● 'Design Document' means any plan, sketch, drawing (including setting out drawings), calculations, specification or any other document whatsoever prepared by the contractor in the performance of the contract for or in connection with the design.

8.9.2 The design obligation

It contains a design provision:

'10(1) The Contractor shall undertake and be responsible for the Design. He shall prepare all the Design Documents required for the complete and efficient execution of the Works in accordance with the Contract.

(2) The Contractor shall exercise, and warrants that he has exercised, all reasonable skill, care and diligence in the preparation of the Design Documents and the Contractor's Proposals. He further accepts that his liability to the Authority in respect of any defect or insufficiency in the Design, whether in the relevant Contractor's Proposals or Design Documents prepared by the Contractor himself or by any servant, agent, sub-contractor or supplier, shall be the same as would have applied in the same circumstances to an architect or other suitably qualified professional designer who, having held himself out as competent to undertake the Design in accordance with the Authority's Requirements, had been appointed by the Authority to prepare the Design in accordance with the intent that the Works would be executed by a works contractor.'

The effect of this provision is likely to be the same as that arising under JCT 1981, namely, that there cannot be an implied term as to fitness for purpose: the clause provides for the contractor to be judged as to his liability by reference to that applying to a designer, not also building, engaged by the Authority direct. That is by reference to reasonable skill and care.

'10(3) The Contractor shall ensure the Design meets the requirements of any relevant planning consent and the Building Regulations, and complies with all other statutory requirements.

(4) The Contractor shall ensure that all Things for incorporation conform with the standards specified in the Authority's Requirements or where no such standards are specified, with the appropriate standards and/or standard codes of practice. The Contractor shall also ensure that all Things for incorporation are of an appropriate quality for their intended use.'

It is important to note that the effect of the last sentence of sub-clause (4) is to reverse the usual rule. Where an employer does not rely on the skill of the contractor in selecting goods, there will be an implied term of good quality but there will be no implied term as to fitness for purpose. Here, there is an express term as to fitness for purpose not only in respect the materials selected by the contractor, but also in relation to materials selected by the Authority. This is an area where careful assessment of the Authority's Requirements at tender stage in the context of fitness is appropriate.

8.9.3   Discrepancies

Discrepancies are dealt with in condition 2 and in summary this provides:

(1)   The conditions take priority over the other documents forming part of the contract.
(2)   The Authority's Requirements take priority over the Contractor's Proposals.
(3)   If there is a discrepancy in the Authority's Requirements, or between them and any statutory requirement (including Building Regulations or planning consents), the project manager (PM) resolves the discrepancy and it is treated as a change.
(4)   Discrepancies in the Contractor's Proposals have to be resolved by the Contractor, subject to the PM's approval, at the contractor's own expense.
(5)   There is an obligation on the contractor to notify the PM immediately if he discovers any of the above discrepancies (but this obligation does not apply to (1) above).

8.9.4   Insurance

Condition 8(a) requires professional indemnity insurance for the amount of cover set out in the Abstract of Particulars to be maintained by the contractor for the duration of the contract and six years from certified completion.

There is an obligation to provide proof that the insurance premiums have been paid.

8.9.5   As-built drawings

Condition 9 contains an obligation to supply, free of change, to the Authority a full set of drawings and other documents to show the works as built. In addition, the contractor has to supply '... such other information necessary to explain the operation and maintenance of the Works'. All of this has to be done not later than 14 days after the PM has certified under condition 39 that the works are in a satisfactory state – that certificate cannot be given until after the end of the longest relevant maintenance period, if there are sections or early possession of parts of the works.

8.9.6   Design documents

Condition 10(a) has fairly extensive provisions in relation to the design documents. In sub-clause (1), the contractor has to demonstrate compliance with the Authority's Requirements by a 'Design Document'.

A design document has to be produced when the production of a properly documented design is to be regarded as good construction practice. Copies of all design documents have to be given to the PM before commencing the work to which they relate. The PM has the right to raise questions and the contractor has to respond 'promptly'.

Sub-clause (2) requires the contractor not to commence work in relation to any design document until he is sure:

(1) the the PM has confirmed in writing that he does not intend to raise any questions, or,
(2) the PM confirms in writing that his questions have been answered to his satisfaction.

Usually in design and build contracts and in the appointments of architects and engineers, copyright vests in the person producing the design – the employer is given a licence to use the design; sometimes that licence is subject to conditions. The condition that is most often encountered is that the employer's licence to use the design can be terminated by the designer in the event of certain breaches of contract by the employer, such as a failure to pay the designer. Such a provision gives the designer some measure of security for his fees. In this contract, copyright in all design documents is the property of and vests in the Crown (condition 10(3)). The contractor has to keep design documents on the site to which the PM can have access at all times.

The fact that the PM may have seen parts of the design, raised questions on them, and subsequently said that he is satisifed with the answers, does not relieve the contractor of any liability under the contract for defects in design, or for inconsistences or lack of co-ordination in the design documents (condition 10(5)). Further, the submission by the contractor of design documents for examination by the PM must be done in such a timescale as reasonably allows the PM time to raise queries and for the contractor to respond – all before the date on which the contractor intends to commence work (condition 10(6)).

There is a further provision in relation to discrepancies set out here, over and above those that appear in condition 2. The Authority's Requirements prevail over any design document in the case of discrepancies between them (condition 10(7)).

8.9.7 Statutory notices

Not only does the contractor have to give all the statutory notices, he also has to pay the fees and charges and supply all drawings and plans required in connection with those notices (condition 11(1)).

It is also the contractor's duty to obtain the consent (including licences) of any statutory undertakers, adjoining owners and so on – all, again, at the expense of the contractor (condition 11(2)).

Clearly these provisions are matters that contractors need to consider carefully and price at tender stage.

8.9.8 Sub-letting

There are detailed provisions in condition 62 as to sub-letting. Contractors should carefully note these provisions which not only apply to sub-contractors, in the usually accepted sense of that expression, but also sub-letting of design work to architects, engineers and mechanical services engineers, and mechanical and electrical services engineers. Firstly, the consent of the PM must be obtained. Secondly, the sub-contracts are required to contain certain provisions (which are set out in condition 62(2)). Generally, the sub-contract conditions must be such that the sub-contractor assumes to the contractor the obligations and responsibilities which the contractor owes to the Authority. Further, the sub-contract has to give to the sub-contractor rights, remedies and redress against the contractor equivalent to those given to the contractor against the Authority.

8.10   Consultant's agreements for design and build contracts

It is the case that different agreements from the norm are required in two separate and distinct areas of design and build contracts:

(1)   where the employer retains professionals to act directly for him during a design and build contract – for example, as the Employer's Agent under the JCT with Contractor's Design form of building contract, and
(2)   where the contractor sub-lets design to professionals.

It is now becoming commonplace, with the increasing use of design and build forms of contract, for the architect and the engineer to be engaged by the contractor, rather than the employer. Some aspects of that relationship were considered in *Consultants Group International* v. *John Worman Limited* (1985), a decision of Judge John Davies QC, Official Referee. There were preliminary issues before the court in this case and it was held that there was an express term in the contract between the contractor (Worman) and the employer, that the building would be fit for its intended purpose (an abbatoir) and comply with EEC standards so as to be qualified for the appropriate grant aid, and further that the design obligations of the consultants were co-extensive with those of the contractors and, on its true construction, it was a term of the agreement between the contractor and the consultant that the works would be so designed by the consultant that the completed project would be fit for the purpose defined in the contract between the contractor and the employer. This decision is entirely consistent with the present policy of the courts to enforce liability through chains of contracts. A further interesting point decided in this case is that the consultants were held liable to indemnify the contractors in respect of the design of specialist equipment to be supplied by nominated suppliers and in respect of which there were defects.

In order to try to deal with these different relationships, a considerable number of 'home grown' contracts have been drafted. In even more cases, no proper arrangements are made at all for these new relationships. The standard unamended forms of the RIBA and the ACE are not appropriate.

However, the RIBA (with the Royal Incorporation of Architects in Scotland, the Royal Society of Ulster Architects and the Association of Consultant Architects) have responded to this need by producing two forms:

(1)   Standard Form of Appointment of an Architect: Design and Build: *Employer* Client Version, and
(2)   Standard Form of Appointment of an Architect: Design and Build: *Contractor* Client Version.

Both forms are based on SFA/92 but with considerable amendments to suit the new relationships. In both cases the drafting assumes that the JCT with Contractor's Design form of building contract will be used.

Contractors who are retained on the basis of fitness for purpose (e.g. the ACA Form or the IChemE Form or, possibly, JCT 80 with Performance Specified Work) may wish to note that the architect's obligation under the Contractor Client Version is that of reasonable skill and care. It is perhaps ironical that the ACA have included fitness for purpose in their building contract but in the Contractor Client Version of SFA/92, to which they are a party, they have chosen reasonable skill and care.

Chapter 9

Damages and contribution

A person who has suffered loss as a result of a breach of contract or a tort committed by another person will usually be entitled to recover from that other person damages; the object is to provide recompense by money for the wrong that has been done. It is necessary to look at the general principles relating to damages before applying those principles to the particular categories of damage that are recoverable from a negligent designer.

9.1 Damages

9.1.1 General principles

9.1.1.1 Compensatory

The most important fundamental principle of damages is that, so far as money is able to do it, the innocent party should be put in the same position that he would have been in had the party at fault not committed the breach of contract or the tort. This is the principle known to lawyers as *restitutio in integrum*. This general principle is subject to particular rules in both contract and tort which may have the effect of limiting the damages that would otherwise be recoverable. Some damage, for example, may be so far removed from the breach of contract or the negligent act that it will not be recoverable. In such cases, the damage is said to be too remote. Another general principle of great importance is that the innocent party must bring his claims in one action for all the damages that result from the same cause of action; he cannot have successive bites at the same cherry: *Darley Main Colliery Co* v. *Mitchell* (1886). For example, if an employer brings an action for breach of contract against a designer, he must sue in that action for all the breaches of contract: *Conquer* v. *Boot* (1928).

Claims must flow from the breach of contract or breach of duty and if there is a new intervening act (known in law as a *novus actus interveniens*), then the damage will not be recoverable. An example of this arose in *Lubenham Fidelities and Investment Co Limited* v. *South Pembrokeshire District Council and Another* (1986). In this case, the architects had negligently calculated the amount due on interim certificates and it was alleged against them that this caused the loss suffered by the bondsman, who stepped into the shoes of the contractor, in circumstances where the bondsman suspended execution of the works, and there were cross allegations from the employer and the contractor in relation to determination. The Court of Appeal found that the claims of the employer and the bondsman to recover from the architects the amount of the losses suffered as a result of the determination of the contracts both failed because the architects' breach of duty in issuing the incorrectly calculated interim certificates was not the cause of the losses. The losses were in fact caused by Lubenham's breach of contract in suspending the works without reasonable cause and persisting with the suspension, notwithstanding the service of a preliminary notice of determination. In other words, the loss did not flow from the breach complained of.

In *Alfred John Jones* v. *Stroud District Council* (1986), Mr Jones received a benefit in relation to the execution of work to correct defects in his house but he did not receive an invoice and, it seems, did not pay for the works. In these circumstances, he was not able to prove any actual loss; furthermore, he had sold the property. These facts did not prevent him recovering damages. Similarly, the fact that a housing association has the right to be indemnified by the Department of the Environment in respect of actual cost does not prevent a housing association claiming and recovering damages for negligence and breach of contract against designers: *Design 5* v. *Keniston Housing Association Limited* (1986).

9.1.1.2 Contract

The kind of damage that can be recovered in respect of a breach of contract is governed by the rule set out in the case of *Hadley* v. *Baxendale* (1854). It has been said that the damage would not be too remote to be recovered if it:

(1) is such as may fairly and reasonably be considered either arising naturally, that is to say according to the usual course of things, from such breach of contract itself, or

(2) arises out of a breach of contract where the parties knew of special circumstances by reason of which that breach might cause a greater loss than might arise in the ordinary course of events: *Victoria Laundry (Windsor) Limited* v. *Newman Industries Limited* (1949) and *Koufos* v. *Czarnikow Limited* (1969).

These principles are known as the two branches of the rule. When considering the first branch the test is based on what is presumed to have been in the contemplation of the parties, whereas in the second branch of the rule, the test is based on the actual knowledge of the parties. This test differs from the test in tort which is based on foreseeability.

9.1.1.3 Tort

The question as to whether damage is too remote to be recoverable in claims made in tort is determined by the test of foreseeability. Was the sort of damage that occurred the reasonably foreseeable result of the tortious act: *The Wagon Mound* (1961)? If the damage is in that category, it does not matter whether the damage was most unlikely to occur or even that the risk was very small; the wrongdoer will be liable for the whole loss. It is for this reason that it is often said a person who commits a tort may have to bear a greater degree of damage than a person who is in breach of contract. However, in many cases the distinction is academic. For example, where a designer is sued by his client in both contract and tort and is found to be liable, the court will not usually be concerned to look at the distinction in the test for remoteness in contract and tort.

Loss which is purely financial, known as economic loss, and which is not caused by some injury to person or property is an area of damages which causes some difficulty. In cases of negligent mis-statement, there is no doubt that economic loss is recoverable: *Hedley Byrne & Co. Limited* v. *Heller & Partners Limited* (1964). The recovery of economic loss in cases of negligence can cause difficulty. The orthodox view is that economic loss which is not due to damage to persons or property is not recoverable. This view was based on two cases. In *SCM (United Kingdom) Limited* v. *W.J. Whittall & Son Limited* (1970), Whittall, contractors, cut off the power to SCM's factory by negligently cutting into an underground cable. SCM were typewriter manufacturers and molten metal solidified in their machines, which amounted to physical damage. SCM were successful in their claim for damages limited to the physical damage to the machinery and the loss of profit during the period in which the machinery was being repaired. The court also considered the position as it would have been had there been no damaged machines and just a loss of production. Lord Denning MR said:

> 'In actions of negligence, when the plaintiff has suffered no damage to his person or property, but has only sustained economic loss, the law does not usually permit him to recover that loss. Although the defendants owed the plaintiffs a duty of care, that did not mean that additional economic loss which was not consequent on the material damage suffered by the plaintiffs would also be recoverable.'

The Court of Appeal adopted the same approach in a subsequent case on similar facts: *Spartan Steel and Alloys Limited* v. *Martin & Co. (Contractors) Limited* (1973).

In a case involving solicitors' negligence, though, it has been held that a beneficiary under a will, who did not benefit because of the negligence of the solicitors who prepared the will, can recover the loss from the solicitors: *Ross* v. *Caunters* (1979). Clearly, this is pure economic loss.

A further consideration of economic loss took place in a building dispute in the House of Lords in *Junior Books Limited* v. *Veitchi Co. Limited* (1982). This case received further consideration in 1988 in *D & F Estates Limited and Others* v. *Church Commissioners for England and Others* which will be considered below. In *Junior Books* a builder owner sued a sub-contractor of his contractor in the tort of negligence; the contractor was not in the proceedings and there was, of course, no contractual relationship between the sub-contractor and the employer. The cost of replacement of the allegedly defective floor was said to be £50,000. The employer also alleged that, while the floor was being repaired, he would suffer further costs: books would have to be stored at a cost of £1000; moving machinery would cost £2000; the business would have to be temporarily closed with a loss of profit of £45,000; wages would have to be paid to employees who could not work amounting to £90,000, together with fixed overheads of £16,000 which would produce no return; it was also said that there would be a £3000 payment in respect of investigations into the treatment required. Those items totalled £206,000 and with the possible ('possible' is used advisedly in the light of the *D & F* decision see below) exception of the replacement of the floor and the investigation, all the items are properly to be described as economic loss. The House of Lords found that such losses were recoverable, but although it was hinted that the *Spartan Steel* case and others may not longer be good law, they were not expressly overruled; it was merely said that they required consideration afresh. As to the allowance of the claim for economic loss, Lord Roskill said:

'The only suggested reason for limiting the damage ... is that hitherto the law has not allowed such recovery and therefore ought not in the future to do so. My Lords, with all respect to those who find this a sufficient answer, I do not. I think this is the next logical step forward in the development of this branch of the law. I see no reason why what was called during the arguments "damage to the pocket" simpliciter should be disallowed when "damage to the pocket" coupled with physical damage has hitherto always been allowed. I do not think that this development, if development it be, will lead to untoward consequences.'

However, as was seen in Chapter 2, the *Junior Books* decision is now treated as being suspect in the more recent cases on duties of care and economic loss. Indeed, in *Simaan General Contracting Co.* v. *Pilkington Glass* (1988), Lord Justice Dillon said of *Junior Books* that it was a:

'... controversial decision ... [which] cannot now be regarded as a useful pointer to any development of the law. ... Indeed I find it difficult to see that future citation from *Junior Books* can ever serve any useful purpose.'

Economic loss was again considered by the House of Lords in *D & F Estates Limited and Others* v. *Church Commissioners for England and Others* (1988). In this case, a non-resident leaseholder sought to recover damages in negligence from a building contractor arising out of the need to repair defective plaster, the plastering having been carried out by a sub-contractor of the main contractor. Although the damages claimed comprised in part the cost of repair and estimated cost of further repairs to physical damage to part of the building, the House of Lords came to the view that, in the context of this case, that loss was economic loss and irrecoverable. Lord Bridge said:

'If the hidden defect in the chattel is the cause of personal injury or of damage to property other than the chattel itself, the manufacturer is liable. But if the hidden defect is discovered before any such damage is caused, there is no longer any room for the application of the *Donoghue* v. *Stevenson* principle. The chattel is now defective in quality, but is no longer dangerous. It may be valueless or it may be capable of economic repair. In either case the economic loss is recoverable in contract by a buyer or hirer of the chattel entitled to the benefit of a relevant warranty of quality, but is not recoverable in tort by a remote buyer or hirer of the chattel. If the same principle applies in the field of real property to the liability of the builder of a permanent structure which is dangerously defective, that liability can only arise if the defect remains hidden until the defective structure causes personal injury or damage to property other than the structure itself. If the defect is discovered before any damage is done, the loss sustained by the owner of the structure, who has to repair or demolish it to avoid a potential source of danger to third parties, would seem to be purely economic. Thus, if I acquire a property with a dangerously defective garden wall which is attributable to the bad workmanship of the original builder, it is difficult to see any basis in principle on which I can sustain an action in tort against the builder for the cost of either repairing or demolishing the wall. No physical damage has been caused. All that has happened is that the defect in the wall has been discovered in time to prevent the damage occurring.'

In agreeing with that view Lord Oliver, in the same case, said that it might be possible in a complicated structure to treat the constituent parts as separate items of property distinct from that portion of the whole which has given rise to the damage. He took as an example the foundations in *Anns* being treated as distinct from the remainder of the building. So regarded, he said:

'... this would be no more than the ordinary application of the *Donoghue* v. *Stevenson* principle. It is true that in such a case the damages would include, and in some cases might be restricted to, the costs of replacing or making good the defective part, but that would be because such remedial work would be essential to the repair of the property which had been damaged by it.'

That passage raises another vexed question. The decision in *D & F* was on the basis that, as a matter of principle, it is not possible to recover damages in the tort of negligence from a manufacturer in respect of the damaged thing itself, but only in respect of personal injury or physical damage consequent upon the defects in the manufactured article. On that basis, it seems difficult to argue (as was done in *D & F*) that, if a complicated building is regarded as being its constitutent parts, it should be possible to recover damages, for example, in respect of the cost of repair to the thing itself (e.g. the foundations) as well as to the other parts of the building damaged by the thing itself. However, that is what the decision appears to say in *D & F* although Lord Bridge, in that case, expressly left open for future decision that issue and how far the New Zealand Court of Appeal case of *Bowen* v. *Paramount Builders (Hamilton) Ltd* (1977) should be followed in English law. It was these difficulties that led to the decision in *Portsea Island Mutual Co-Operative Society Limited* v. *Michael Brashier Associates* in 1989. The case concerned brick slips, some of which fell from external walls and some of which were removed to prevent them falling. They did not cause damage to other property or to persons. The judge allowed recovery of the cost of removing the dangerous brick slips, but not the cost of replacing them.

Since *D & F* and *Murphy*, economic loss is not recoverable in building cases where the defects are discovered before they cause personal injury or unless they damage property other than 'the thing itself.' The only exceptions appear to be where the complex structure principle can be applied or where the case can be brought within *Hedley Byrne*. A recent example of this is *Preston* v. *Torfaen Borough Council and Another* (1993)

In cases of negligence, where the plaintiff has contributed to the damage that he has suffered, the position used to be that he could recover nothing from the defendants. The Law Reform (Contributory Negligence) Act 1945 now enables liability for the damage to be apportioned between the plaintiff and the defendant. This Act does not permit the court to apportion liability between two or more defendants who are liable for the same damage. An example of the reduction of the plaintiff's damages by reason of his own negligence is where a person fell through the glass panel of balustrading on a block of flats whilst helping his drunken friend home; in the action that he subsequently brought against the designer of the flats, his damages were reduced by 15% on account of his contributory negligence: *Kelly* v. *Frank Mears & Partners* (1981), Scotland.

It is now tolerably clear that, in cases where an innocent party has obtained judgment in both contract and tort, he should elect as to which measure of damages he chooses: *Archer v. Brown* (1984).

9.1.1.4 *Mitigation/reasonable cost*

A person who suffers damage cannot necessarily assume that he will recover all the loss from the wrongdoer. As soon as there is a breach of contract or the commission of a tort, the injured party has a duty to mitigate the loss that he suffers. If he does not act reasonably so as to mitigate the loss, the wrongdoer will be able to point to that failure in proceedings and the injured party will not be able to recover damages insofar as he could reasonably and properly have avoided the loss. It may be that the phrase 'duty to mitigate' is a misnomer; Sir John Donaldson MR, in *Sotiros Shipping Inc. and Another* v. *Sameiet Solholt* (1983), said:

> 'A plaintiff was under no duty to mitigate his loss, despite the habitual use by lawyers of the phrase "duty to mitigate". He was completely free to act as he judged to be in his best interests.
>
> On the other hand, a defendant was not liable for all the loss suffered by the plaintiff in consequence of his so acting. A defendant was only liable for such part of the plaintiff's loss as was properly to be regarded as caused by the defendant's breach of duty.'

When the appropriate remedial works have been decided on, the damages recoverable are the reasonable cost of carrying them out. The meaning of that general statement was considered in *Richard Roberts Holdings Limited* v. *Douglas Smith Stimson Partnership and Others* (1988) by Judge John Newey QC, Official Referee. He said that the reasonable cost was not necessarily that of the lowest tender which could be obtained. The tenderer's reputation and his willingness to enter into appropriate terms and conditions were relevant. Special circumstances might affect what was reasonable, such as paying what appeared an excessive amount in order to have the work done quickly and thereby prevent loss of profit or goodwill. If, however, tenders are received from parties who are otherwise acceptable, then usually the lowest price should be accepted.

Negligent defendants who seek to argue that the plaintiff has carried out over-elaborate or unnecessary repairs do not usually receive much sympathy in court. This will be particularly so where the employer is usually incapable of deciding for himself what repairs need to be done and he relies on the advice of experts. In circumstances where there was such reliance on one expert, and following representations from experts for the other parties, the employer sought further opinion of experts, he was successful in his claim, notwithstanding strong arguments put to the court that the remedial works carried out were not in fact justified: *Governors of the Hospital for Sick Children and Another* v. *McLaughlin and Harvey plc and Others* (1987). In this case, Judge John Newey QC, Official Referee, was confronted with difficult issues because the experts for the defendants took the view strongly that the remedial works scheme of the plaintiff was excessive and very expensive, when compared with their own very much cheaper alternative. The judge said:

'The plaintiff who carries out either repair or reinstatement of his property must act reasonably. He can only recover as damages the costs which the defendant ought reasonably have foreseen that he would incur and the defendant would not have foreseen unreasonable expenditure. Reasonable costs do not, however, mean the minimum amount which, with hindsight, it could be held would have sufficed. When the nature of the repairs is such that the plaintiff can only make them with the assistance of expert advice, the defendant should have foreseen that he would take such advice and be influenced by it.'

The judge then considered the effect that negligence might have in the independent advice received by a plaintiff and the difference between the position where remedial works have been carried out before trial and where they have not. He went on:

'However reasonably the plaintiff acts, he can only recover in respect of loss actually caused by the defendant. If, therefore, part of a plaintiff's claim does not arise out of the defendant's wrongdoing, but is due to some independent cause, the plaintiff cannot recover in respect of that part: *The Liesbosch Dredger* v. *Edison SS* (1933) and *Compania Financiera Soleada SA* v. *Hamoor Tanker Corporation Inc., The Borag* (1981). The independent cause may take the form of an event which breaks, that is to say, brings to an end, a chain of causation from the defendant's breach of duty, so that the plaintiff cannot recover damages for any loss which he sustains after the event. The event may take the form of negligent advice upon which the plaintiff has acted. Another way of expressing the matter might be that the defendant could not reasonably have foreseen that the plaintiff would act on negligent advice. Advice which is not negligent will not by itself break the chain. . . . If at the date of trial no remedial works have been carried out by the plaintiff, then the court has, in order to assess damages, to decide what works should be done. The parties are entitled to put forward rival schemes and the court has to choose between them or variants of them. . . . Where works have been carried out, it is not for the court to consider *de novo* what should have been done and what costs should have been incurred either as a check upon the reasonableness of the plaintiff's actions or otherwise.'

In *Chancellor, Masters and Scholars of the University of Oxford (Trading as Oxford University Press)* v. *John Stedman Design Group (A Firm)* (1990), the court had to consider the reasonableness of the cost of remedying defective work against the background of a partial settlement of proceedings. Problems had arisen with a grano floor, laid by sub-contractors to Norwest Holst Western Limited, which had developed numerous cracks and extensive surface crazing. After the start of the trial, a settlement took place which left only two parties in the action for the purpose of contribution between Norwest Holst and their sub-contractor. It was argued by the sub-contractor that Norwest Holst's settlement with OUP was unreasonable. The judge reviewed the authorities on this issue (*Biggin* v. *Permanite* (1951), *Karpenko* v. *Paroian Courey Cohen and Houston* (1980, Ontario, Canada), *Radford* v. *De Froberville* (1977) and others) and decided that the settlement, made on legal advice, was reasonable. The judgment is a useful resumé of the matters to be considered in such a situation.

The alleged unreasonable behaviour of a plaintiff had to be considered by Judge Bowsher QC, Official Referee, in *Philip Derek Kremin* v. *Duke Street Investments Limited and Others* (1993). Here, it was said that if liability were established, 'the wrongdoer must take the victim as he finds him' (*Bourhill* v. *Young* (1943)). The judge found that the plaintiff and his wife had

> 'inflicted their perfectionism on other people to such an extent that dealings with them were difficult and their behaviour described in evidence was found in many respects to have been unreasonable. Their behaviour in relation to the defendants with regard to the subject matter of this action was also in some respects unreasonable. For the plaintiff, it was submitted that that behaviour is not out of character with their behaviour in relation to other people.'

The judge held that if a plaintiff suffers from a mental condition which makes it impossible or difficult for that person to behave in the manner to be expected from the man on top of the Clapham omnibus, the defendant must take him as he finds him in that condition. But if the plaintiff of his own freewill chooses to be a difficult and unreasonable person, that should not be allowed to add to the defendant's burden in damages.

9.1.2   Damages and designers

Having looked at the basic principles that govern awards of damages, it is necessary to look at the application of those principles to the damages that are likely to be awarded against designers for breach of duty and to set out some further principles which are of importance in that field.

It will not usually be possible for a building owner to obtain an order of the court requiring defective construction or design to be put right by the parties responsible – such an order would be in the form of a mandatory injunction and was refused by the Court of Appeal in relation to defects which had appeared in precast concrete cladding panels and tiles used in the construction of the Arndale Centre in Manchester: *Taylor Woodrow Construction (Midlands) Limited* v. *Charcon Structures Limited and Others* (1982) applying the principles in *American Cyanamid Co.* v. *Ethicon Limited* (1975) in which case it was held, amongst other things, that an injunction will not be granted where a claim for damages is an adequate remedy. It was argued for the employer in *Taylor Woodrow* that there was a breach of a statutory obligation in relation to the Building Regulations and that this therefore obliged the contractor to take action to remedy the problem. This argument was also rejected by the Court of Appeal.

In *Lubenham Fidelities and Investment Co. Limited* v. *South Pembrokeshire District Council and Others* (1985), Judge James Fox-Andrews QC, Official Referee, decided that a *Mareva* injunction was not appropriate to be ordered in circumstances where architects' professional indemnity insurance underwriters were just about to, or had withdrawn their previous written consent for incurring the costs of the defence of the third party proceedings in which the architects were involved. The underwriters proposed to pay to the architects a sum equal to the limit to indemnity under the policy. The court refused an injunction seeking to have the insurance monies frozen. In *Normid Housing Association Limited* v. *Ralphs and Others* (1988), the plaintiff housing association sought an injunction to restrain a settlement between the three defendant architects and their professional indemnity insurer, the fourth defendant. It was held by the Court of Appeal that, even on the assumption that the architects in entering into the proposed settlement with the insurers were giving up their rights under the policy for substantially less than their true value, the housing association would have no rights under the Third Parties (Rights against Insurers) Act 1930 to restrain such a settlement since that Act confers no rights on third parties until the insured becomes insolvent. They said the position might have been different if the architects had been under a contractual duty to insure or under a professional duty to do so. The injunction that had been previously granted by the judge at first instance was discharged.

9.1.3   Defects in construction

Where there are defects in the design or the supervision is negligent, then this is likely to manifest itself by defects in the construction. It is because of this chain leading to the designer that damages will only be recoverable where the damages that are claimed arise from the designer's breach of duty; it does not necessarily follow that because there is a defect in the construction that there is a defect also in the design. The usual measure of damages is the cost of the remedial work that is reasonably necessary. That cost will include the professional fees that were necessarily expended in arranging for and supervising that remedial work. All the figures put forward by the injured party can be disputed; however, unless any particular aspect of the amount of the claim for damages is disputed on some matter of substance, a defendant is not likely to succeed in reducing the amount of the damages, by nit picking at every item. On the other hand, the plaintiff has to prove his loss.

In some cases, it has been argued that the proper measure of damages is not the cost of repair but rather the difference in the value of the property with the defects and the value of the property without the defects, known as the diminution in value. This will usually be the measure of damages in cases where a negligent survey has been carried out for a prospective purchaser of a property: *Phillips* v. *Ward* (1956), *Perry* v. *Sidney Phillips & Son* (1982).

In *Treml* v. *Ernest W. Gibson & Partners* (1984), an issue arose where the plaintiff had received a grant towards the cost of repairs under Schedule 12 of the Housing Act 1980, and the defendant argued that that reduced pro rata the claim against him. However, the judge took the view that that argument did not affect the proper measure of damages in this case which was assessed on the basis of difference in value. In other words, the grant reduced the cost of repairs but did not reduce the diminution in value.

The approach of the courts in assessing the calculation of diminution in value is usefully examined in the case of *Wilson* v. *Baxter Payne and Lepper* (1985). The judge in this case, in assessing the diminution in value, had regard to the appropriate cost of rectification and the risk of additional expenditure in the future and formed views as to how those costs would be reflected in the market value. In circumstances where there had been negligence in a survey such that there ought to have been repairs to a wall which had not been taken into account at the time of purchase, the courts have held that diminution in value was the correct measure of damages and that the difference was not necessarily equal to the cost of repairs but in this case the purchaser would probably have taken upon himself a risk as to 25% of the cost so that the correct measure of damages was 75%: *Bolton* v. *Puley* (1983).

However, it will not necessarily be the proper measure in cases of negligent design or supervision. Whether diminution in value or cost of remedial work is the appropriate measure of damages in any particular case will depend on the facts of the case and, it may be, that the choice is an aspect of mitigation. For example, where a car is involved in an accident, it would not be reasonable to spend more on repairs than the value of the car before the accident. This is on the basis that it would be reasonable to replace the damaged car with another car, rather than to spend more on repairing the old car. This principle would not, of course, apply were the damaged car irreplaceable, for example, a vintage car. Some guidance is given on this subject in *Dodd Properties (Kent) Limited and Others* v. *Canterbury City Council and Others* (1980) where it was said:

> 'The general object underlying the rules for assessment of damages is, so far as is possible by means of a monetary award, to place the plaintiff in the position that he would have occupied if he had not suffered the wrong complained of, be that wrong a tort or a breach of contract. In the case of a tort causing damage to real property, this object is achieved by the application of one or other of two quite different measures of damage, or, occasionally, a combination of the two. The first is to take the capital value of the property in an undamaged state and to compare it with its value in a damaged state. The second is to take the cost of repair or reinstatement. Which is appropriate will depend on a number of factors, such as the plaintiff's future intentions as to the use of the property and the reasonableness of those intentions. If he reasonably intends to sell the property in its damaged state, clearly the diminution in capital value is the true measure of damage. If he reasonably intends to continue to occupy it and to repair the damage, clearly the cost of repair is the true measure.'

The proper measure of damages will usually be the cost of the remedial work at least where the injured party wishes to continue to enjoy the property. However, it may be that diminution in value can be claimed in addition to the cost of the remedial work. This situation could arise where remedial works are carried out but, notwithstanding the fact that the defects are remedied, the property is worth less by reason of those remedial works. For example, brickwork subjected to differential settlement and repaired may detract from the value of the property. In such circumstances, there may be considerable difficulties in proof and evidence from expert valuers would be essential. An example of an award of damages for diminution in value, in addition to the cost of remedial works, is to be found in *Thomas and Others* v. *T. A. Phillips (Builders) Limited and the Borough Council of Taff Ely* (1985).

In a case where surveyors had been instructed by a lessee to see that very extensive building works were properly carried out by the landlords, the landlords, the surveyors and the landlords' own architect were all found liable to the lessees in the same measure of damage: the full cost of repair: *Raybeck Properties Limited* v. *County and Nimbus Estates Limited* (1983).

The basis of diminution in value was taken in respect of defects in *G.W. Atkins*

Limited v. *Scott* (1990) in the Court of Appeal. Here the finding of the judge was upheld. He had considered the defects not to be of a serious character and that that was a good reason in law for using a different basis of assessment than the cost of repair. Diminution is more appropriate where the proportion of defective work is small in relation to the whole property; where the sale of the property is not in prospect and where the damage only affects the 'amenity value' of the property. It was said that the predilection of the building owner in wanting reinstatement is only one of the factors the court should consider in deciding what is reasonable.

Unless there are compelling reasons to the contrary, damages will usually be assessed without any regard to the fact that the materials replaced were used or worn and the plaintiff will have new materials. This proposition was emphasised in an Australian case, *Day* v. *O'Leary* (1992). It was held that the householders were entitled to new parquet flooring even though the floor which the contractor had agreed to re-surface had virtually reached the end of its useful life.

9.1.4   *Consequential loss*

The most important items of consequential loss are those caused by delay, loss of use, loss of profit and the costs of vacating premises whilst repairs are carried out. The tests as to whether these are recoverable are the usual tests in contract and tort. For example, where the designer could reasonably have foreseen (tort) or may reasonably have contemplated (contract) that the defective design would necessitate the vacating of the premises and the employer hiring other premises, then the reasonable costs of the removal and the hire of the other premises will be recoverable.

As to the consequences of delay, such as loss of profit, these will be dealt with in different ways according to the circumstances under which the loss is suffered. If the designer by his negligence causes a contractor to be delayed during the course of the works, then under the standard forms of construction contract (JCT 80 and ICE), the contractor will be able to obtain an extension of time for completion which will prevent the employer from recovering liquidated damages in respect of that delay from the contractor. In such circumstances, the employer would be entitled to claim the value of those liquidated damages from the designer, those damages being a genuine pre-estimate of the employer's loss should delay occur.

Where the loss of use of the property occurs after completion of the project, then the method of calculation of the damages will depend on whether the property is a profit making or non profit making asset. Where it is a profit making asset, such as a factory, then the employer will be entitled to recover loss of profits for the reasonable period that the remedial works take: *The Mediana* (1900). Where the property is non profit earning, such as a local authority swimming pool, there is no rule of law that damages cannot be recovered. Where a substitute building could be used, then the cost of hire would be appropriate damages. However, in such cases it is likely that no substitute building is available and the proper measure of damages may be interest on the capital value of the property for the period during which the repairs were carried out: *The Hebridian Coast* (1959); *The Greta Holme* (1897); *Birmingham Corporation* v. *Sowsbery* (1969). These principles as to both profit earning and non profit earning property will also apply to cases where there is delay during construction and there are no liquidated damages provisions in the construction contract.

Where a defect in a system designed to reduce fire risk, such as sprinkler systems, causes increased insurance premiums to be paid, then the cost of those increased premiums will be recoverable but only to the extent that the building owner carried out repairs within a reasonable time: *Rumbelows Limited* v. *A.M.K. and Another* (1980).

In *Richard Roberts Holdings Limited* v. *Douglas Smith Stimson Partnership and Others* (1988), it was held that the parent company owner of a dyeworks, let to a subsidiary company, could not recover the consequential losses of its subsidiary from architects who were in breach of contract. This case was decided before *St Martin's Property Corporation Limited and Another* v. *Sir Robert McAlpine* (1993), House of Lords, and it may be doubted that this point would have been decided in the same way if it had been heard after *St Martin's*.

In *T & S Contractors Limited* v. *Architectural Design Associates* (1992), a property developer recovered damages in respect of breach of contract by architects, being the reduced value of the development because of a fall in the property market during the period of delay created by the architects.

9.1.5 Distress

Where a design is negligently prepared, or there is negligent supervision, and the designer's client is an individual, rather than a company or corporation, then a great deal of distress and upset can be caused. A court can award damages for such mental distress and frustration in certain circumstances. This arises, for example, where the damage falls within the second branch of the rule in *Hadley* v. *Baxendale*: the parties had actual knowledge that a breach of contract might cause greater loss than would ordinarily result. The courts applied this test where a disappointed holiday maker succeeded in obtaining damages for mental distress from a tour operator: *Jarvis* v. *Swans Tours Limited* (1973). In the case of a designer's breach of duty, such damages will be recoverable by an injured individual provided that the building works were not being carried out for profit as a commercial venture: *Hutchinson* v. *Harris* (1978); *Perry* v. *Sidney Phillips & Son* (1982); *Murray* v. *Sturgis* (1981).

In *Franks and Collingwood and Another* v. *Gales* (1983) damages were awarded for distress which were less because the construction related to a holiday residence than they would have been had the house been a permanent home. Where there was a negligent survey resulting in a damages award of £4425, £500 was awarded for distress, worry and vexation (*Bolton* v. *Puley* (1983)), and £500 appears to be the sort of modest sum that is awarded for such a claim. For example, in *Haig* v. *London Borough of Hillingdon* (1980) the two plaintiffs were jointly awarded £1000 in respect of the failure of a bedroom floor. However, where there had been two years of very serious discomfort and distress during building works a single plaintiff was awarded £1500 per annum, a total of £3000, by Master Topley: *Mattia* v. *Amato* (1982). In a surveyor's negligence case, £600 was awarded in respect of anxiety and inconvenience: *Hooberman* v. *Salter Rex* (1984). In a case involving structural damage, with eight plaintiffs who were owners of dwellings in the block, the court awarded £1250 to the worst affected and £750 each to the rest: *Thomas and Others* v. *T. A. Phillips (Builders) Limited and the Borough Council of Taff Ely* (1985).

A most useful review of further cases on general damages is to be found in an article by Kim Franklin, Barrister: '*More Heartache – a Review of General Damages in Building Cases*', (1992) 8 Const LJ 318.

9.1.6   Betterment and elaborate repair

Where a building is repaired or replaced as a result of negligence by the designer, the designer will often seek to show that the new building or repairs provide a better building than the employer would have had if there had been no negligence. On this basis, the designer seeks to have the employer's damages reduced on the basis of betterment. It does not always follow that such contentions will be successful.

Where the employer chooses to rebuild rather than repair an old building which was rendered useless by designer's negligence, it does not follow that the damages will be assessed on the basis of the value of the old building before and after the damage caused by the negligent act. The employer will recover the cost of rebuilding at least where the new building is merely a replacement for the old building. In such circumstances, the employer will not be obliged to allow anything for betterment: *Harbutts Plasticine Limited* v. *Wayne Tank and Pump Limited* (1970). Although this case is overruled, it is submitted these principles are good law. Indeed, in the Court of Appeal in *Dominion Mosaics and Tile Co. Limited* v. *Trafalgar Trucking Co. Limited and Another* (1990), it was held, partly on reliance on *Harbutt's Plasticene*, that if business premises are negligently destroyed by fire and the owner reasonably moves to new premises, then *prima facie* the cost of the new premises is the amount of his loss.

It is the case that damages will usually be assessed without regard to the fact that the old materials, replaced by reason of defective workmanship, were virtually at the end of their working life: *Day* v. *O'Leary* (1992), Australia.

Where the new building does more than replace the old, then there may be an element of betterment for which an allowance should be given. The same will apply where there is an over elaborate repair of a defective building. There are two aspects to be considered: the first is causation; the question is whether the repair was necessitated by the breach of duty of the designer. If it was not, then a credit should be given. An example of this would be in a claim for hire of scaffolding to repair defectively designed windows where the employer had used the opportunity of having the scaffolding erected to repoint the brickwork, which was his own maintenance responsibility. If the scaffolding is on hire longer by reason of the brickwork repointing, then a credit should be given for the longer period of hire, for which the designer is not liable.

Betterment was considered by Judge Newey QC, Official Referee, in *Richard Roberts Holdings Limited* v. *Douglas Smith Stimson Partnership and Others* (1988). Here, architects contended that the remedial works carried out by the building owner would give them something better than that which they were entitled to expect under their contract with the architects. Judge Newey said:

'I think the law can be shortly summarised. If the only practicable method of overcoming the consequences of a defendant's breach of contract is to build to a higher standard than the contract had required, the plaintiff may recover the cost of building to that higher standard. If, however, a plaintiff, needing to carry out works because of the defendant's breach of contract, chooses to build to a higher standard than is strictly necessary, the courts will, unless the new works are so different as to break the chain of causation, award him the cost of the works less a credit to the defendant in respect of betterment.'

The second aspect is that of mitigation. The employer should not have over elaborate repairs carried out. His duty is to act reasonably in both his own and the designer's interest. The question as to whether the employer has been reasonable is a matter of fact to be decided by the court following expert evidence given on behalf of the parties. In circumstances where the employer has taken other professional advice and has carried out their recommendations, it may be very difficult to argue that he did not act reasonably, but each case depends on its particular facts. The designer's prospects of successfully arguing that the employer did not act reasonably will be improved if he is able to draw the employer's attention to a less expensive, adequate means of repair before the employer has made his final decision as to which method of repair to adopt; however, the employer is not bound to adopt the solution put forward by the designer. On the other hand, if the employer insists on carrying out repairs which are excessive or unwarranted he will not necessarily be able to recover the cost of so doing from the negligent designer. His recovery will be limited to such part of his loss as is properly to be regarded as being caused by the breach of duty: *Sotiros Shipping Inc. and Another* v. *Sameiet Solholt* (1983).

In a reported decision where a betterment argument was upheld, the plaintiff was required to give an allowance in respect of the betterment. The argument was in relation to defective tiling on the external elevations of two buildings. Tiling on the first complex had begun in July 1969 and was completed by July 1971; the first serious falls of defective tiles and backing occurred in June 1980. The interval between tiling and falls on Phase II was much shorter. Expert evidence given at the trial put the expected life of the tiles at ten years. Judge John Newey QC, Official Referee, said that if the employer had starting retiling in July 1980, they would have been doing so when the original tiling on that phase was coming to the end of its life. The tiles on Phase II at that time only had a few years left of their life. The judge formed the view, in the face of an allegation of betterment, that the plaintiff should give credit for betterment equal to four-fifths of their replacement value on Phase I and one half on Phase II: *Victoria University Manchester* v. *Hugh Wilson and Lewis Wormersley and Another* (No. 2) (1985). An element of betterment was conceded in *Imperial College of Science and Technology* v. *Norman and Dawbarn* (1986). In that same case, the value of VAT included by the plaintiff in the claim in respect of VAT properly chargeable but on a hypothetical scheme, was disallowed by the judge.

Where the proper initial design would have been more expensive than the negligent design that was, in fact, carried out, credit may be given in the claim for damages for a hypothetical additional cost of the proper initial design. In this way, credit will be given for what would otherwise be an element of betterment: *Bevan Investments* v. *Blackhall and Struthers* (1977), New Zealand.

9.1.7   *Date for assessment of damages*

Two factors have combined to make the date of assessment of damages of importance. Firstly, there is inflation which causes building costs to rise with the passing of time. Secondly, where an employer wishes to postpone the carrying out of the repairs until the designer has been found liable, there is inevitably a delay whilst the matter is pursued through the courts or arbitration. It follows that by the time judgment is obtained the cost of repair can be greatly in excess of the cost at the time that the breach of duty was first discovered.

It used to be the law that the employer could recover damages at the date when the repairs could reasonably have been carried out. In practice, this was shortly after the discovery of the breach of duty by the designer. However, this rule was reconsidered by the Court of Appeal in 1979 in a very important case which, although an action in the tort of nuisance, states principles equally applicable to claims in contract: *Dodd Properties (Kent) Limited and Others* v. *Canterbury City Council and Others* (1980).

Garage owners brought a claim against a council, a building contractor and a piling contractor in respect of repairs to their garage and prospective damage due to interruption of their business whilst the repairs were carried out. The piling contractors admitted, shortly before the trial in 1978, that they were liable for the damage that they had caused to the garage in 1968. However, they alleged that the cost of the repairs should be calculated at the date when it would have been reasonable for the garage owners to carry out the repair work, namely 1970. The garage owners contended that the cost of repairs should be calculated at the date of judgement, namely 1978 prices. There was some dispute during the proceedings as to whether the garage owners would actually carry out the repairs but the trial judge found that they would. The Court of Appeal found, amongst other things:

(1)   Where the cost of repairs is the measure of damage, the cost should be assessed at the earliest date that those repairs could reasonably be undertaken, having regard to all the surrounding circumstances.

(2)   The garage owners had decided to postpone the repair work, as a matter of commercial good sense, until it was decided whether or not the piling contractor was liable: it was, therefore, reasonable to assess the cost of repairs at the date of trial.

It follows from this case that damages may be assessed at the date of judgment in proceedings, at least in circumstances where it makes commercial good sense to delay the carrying out of the repairs. This should be contrasted with the position where the delay in carrying out the repairs is caused exclusively by the lack of funds of the employer (*The Liesbosch* (1933)) but the *Dodds* principle will apply where lack of funds was only one of a number of factors that produce the decision to delay the repairs. The *Dodds* case was followed in *William Cory and Son Limited* v. *Wingate Investments (London Colney) Limited* (1980), where Mr Justice Walton said that in assessing a date all the facts should be taken into account. In the same case, Lord Justice Ormrod said the problem should be seen as an aspect of the duty to mitigate.

In *T & S Contractors Limited* v. *Architectural Design Associates* (1992), property developers employed architects in connection with the construction of a housing development in Leigh-on-Sea. There were problems with planning. The judge found the architects had been negligent. The effect of their negligence was that the development reached a condition when it could be sold on 1 August 1989, whereas without the negligence, it would have been in that condition on 1 June 1988. The property market fell dramatically between those dates and continued to fall thereafter. The question arose as to what was the proper date for assessment of damages. The judge decided that the proper date was to be found by an analysis of the contract and the breach determining the point at which the developer could fairly be said to be in a position where money could compensate him for the effect of the breach. On these facts, it was held that damages should be assessed at 1 July 1989 and not any other date such as the date of trial.

9.1.8   Cost of managerial and supervisory resources

An employer may spend considerable sums of money in dealing with, and putting in hand, remedial works resulting from a design failure. Provided the employer has kept proper records of the time spent by his staff, he will be able to recover the cost of his managerial time as a head of damage: *Tate and Lyle Food and Distribution Limited and Another* v. *Greater London Council and Another* (1982). Although this case has subsequently been to the House of Lords, the issue of managerial time did not arise and the Court of Appeal remains good authority.

9.1.9   Planning permission

Surveyors who have obtained planning permission for project managers of a residential development, on the basis that the permission was subject to an application being made for approval of certain reserved matters within three years, will be liable in negligence if they fail to make the necessary application such that the planning permission for the land was irrevocably lost. In such a case the measure of damages will be diminution in value, that is to say the difference between the value of the land with detailed planning consent and the value of the land without any planning consent: *Hatchway Properties Limited* v. *C. Henry Bonds & Co.* (1983).

9.1.10   Assignment

For a discussion of damages recoverable by an assignee, see section 7.2.4.

9.1.11   Interest

The High Court has power to award interest in proceedings. The court's power to award interest is given by statute, the Supreme Court Act 1981, section 35A (introduced into that Act by the Administration of Justice Act 1982 which provisions superseded the previous provisions under the Law Reform (Miscellaneous Provisions) Act 1934). The court is given power under this section to award interest in respect of any debts and/or damages which are outstanding when the proceedings are commenced even if the principal sums are paid after the proceedings are commenced but before judgment. The old rules only permitted interest to be given on such sums in respect of which judgment was given. The new rules therefore are wider. The rate of interest can be whatever rate the court thinks fit, or is expressly provided by the Rules of the Court, and different rates can be applied for different periods. The court's discretion extends to all or any part of the debt or damages and runs for all or any part of the period between the date when the cause of action arose and the date of judgment or, where payment is made before judgment, the date of payment. Once judgment has been given, the rate of interest on the judgment debt is that fixed by statutory instrument from time to time. Where two judgments are given in an action, one on liability and the other on quantum, the latter is the relevant 'judgment debt' from which interest runs under the Judgments Act 1838, section 17: *Lindop v. Goodwin Steel Castings* (1990).

In arbitration the position used to be very different. It was said that an arbitrator had an implied right to exercise the same power as a court in respect of the awarding of interest: *Chandris v. Isbrandtsen-Moller* (1950). There are now statutory provisions in the Arbitration Act 1950 at section 19A (a section that was added to the Act by the Administration of Justice Act 1982). This statutory provision has had effect since 1 April 1983. This section gives the arbitrator power (unless a contrary intention is expressed in the arbitration agreement) to award simple interest at such rate as the arbitrator thinks fit. The sum to which the arbitrator applies the interest is one of two sums or a combination of both. The first is any sum which is the subject of the reference but which is paid before the award, in which case he can award interest for such period as he thinks fit ending on the date of payment. The second is on the sum which he awards, in which case he can award interest for any period that he thinks fit ending not later than the date of his award. The powers in the Act are expressly made to be without prejudice to any other power to an arbitrator to award interest; the effect of that is that the common law implied right still exists.

After the award, interest is payable at the same rate as a 'judgment debt: section 20, Arbitration Act 1950. This rate of interest varies from time to time and it has been held that the rate to be applied is that in force at the date when the order is made and not the rate as it varies from time to time: *Rocco Giuseppe & Figli v. Tradax Export S.A.* (1983).

The House of Lords have held that it is not possible to claim interest as damages for a breach of contract to pay money on time in circumstances where the money has been paid late but before proceedings were started: *President of India v. La Pintada Compania Navigacion S.A.* (1984); however, it is possible to recover such interest as damages where they are special damages and not general damages: *Wadsworth v. Lydall* (1981), a Court of Appeal decision expressly approved by the House of Lords in the *President of India* case.

9.1.12   Example of principles

Many of the general and particular principles set out above were applied in the Australian case of *Bevan Investments v. Blackhall and Struthers* (1977), which is set out by way of example.

Bevan wished to build a speculative recreation centre. He engaged an architect who in turn engaged an engineer in relation to the structural work. There was no contract between Bevan and the engineer. The engineer adopted a method of construction of the structure called the 'lift slab technique', which involved precast prestressed concrete. It transpired during construction that this system for the floor slabs could not be proceeded with because the design was defective. Bevan could not finance the continuation of the project on the basis of a new scheme and he could not be certain as to whether any damage would be recovered from the engineer who persistently denied his liability. The trial judge found that the engineer had been negligent. The action went to the Court of Appeal as to damage. The Court of Appeal held:

(1) Bevan was entitled to be put into the position that he would have been in had the contract been performed.
(2) The damages should be the amount required to put right the defects so as to give Bevan the equivalent of the building that he had wished to have under the contract. This rule should be applied unless the court could be satisfied that there should be some basis on which less compensation should be awarded.
(3) On the facts, the only practicable solution was to complete the project on the new design and the cost of doing that was the reasonable measure of damages.
(4) An allowance should be made in respect of the hypothetical extra cost of a proper initial design, in order to avoid the question of betterment.
(5) Damages should be assessed at the date of trial.
(6) Although there was difficulty in assessing the proper measure of damages for loss of profit on this speculative venture, it was probable that the company would have made some profit and it was awarded \$10,000.

9.2 Contributory negligence and contribution

Rights to contribution are those rights that exist between persons who are liable in respect of the same damage to some innocent party. This is to be contrasted with contributory negligence by which the damages paid to a plaintiff can be reduced by his own contributory negligence. This section is concerned only with contribution between wrongdoers.

9.2.1 Contributory negligence

The Law Reform (Contributory Negligence) Act 1945 permits a court to reduce the damages recoverable by a person in circumstances where the damages result partly from his own fault and partly from the fault of another person. It has remained, until relatively recently, an open question as to whether or not a party liable under a contract can have the damages reduced by reason of the partial fault of the plaintiff where the claim arises in contract. In other words, does the Law Reform (Contributory Negligence) Act 1945 apply to contracts?

In *Basildon District Council* v. *I. E. Lesser (Properties) Limited and Others* (1984), the court considered whether the job architect and the clerk of works' conduct in failing to ensure that the foundations were taken to the appropriate depths and failing to detect the lack of support on seeing the contractors' initial drawings was a matter that should be taken into account under the Act. The court was referred to the New Zealand authority of *Rowe* v. *Turner Hopkins & Partners*

(1980), in which a similar provision in the New Zealand statute was considered. The court concluded that the Act only applied to contracts when the plaintiffs' cause of action was in respect of some act or omission for which the defendant was also liable in tort. The court adopted the reasoning in *Rowe's* case and decided that contributory negligence was not applicable to the particular claim. A like conclusion was reached in *A. B. Marintrans* v. *Comet Shipping Co. Limited* (1985).

However in *Forsikringsaktieselskapet Vesta* v. *Butcher and Others*, both at first instance (1986) and in the Court of Appeal (1988), it was held that the court was empowered to apportion blame under the Law Reform (Contributory Negligence) Act 1945 in certain circumstances. In the House of Lords, this issue did not fall to be considered. The approach in the *Marintrans* case was disapproved and the approach in the *Basildon* case was said to be concerned with a different category of case. The circumstances in which the *Vesta* case says that there can be contribution in contract cases are where the defendant's liability in contract is the same as his liability in the tort of negligence, independent of the existence of any contract.

This case should be compared with the reasoning in *Kensington and Chelsea and Westminster Area Health Authority* v. *Wettern Composites and Others* (1984), although the 1945 Act point is not expressly considered, where the damages claimed by an employer against the contractor were reduced by reason of the vicarious liability of the clerk of works.

9.2.2   Contribution

By the Law Reform (Married Women and Tortfeasors) Act 1935 it was made possible for the courts to apportion liability between persons jointly liable in tort. That apportionment of damages between tortfeasors does not affect the amount of damages receivable by the plaintiff. The contribution is such as the court finds just and equitable taking into account the extent of the responsibility for the damage. In some cases, the contribution could be 100%, that is to say a complete indemnity. However, this statutory right to contribution is limited to tortfeasors liable in respect of the same damage and there are no provisions for contract breakers. This Act applies only where the relevant damage occurred before 1 January 1979.

The Civil Liability (Contribution) Act 1978 deals with contribution between persons liable in respect of any damage, whether tort, breach of contract or otherwise (section 6(1)). It follows that under the provisions of this Act, two persons who are in breach of separate contracts with a third person producing the same damage can claim contribution against each other – for example, where an architect in breach of his conditions of engagement with his employer in respect of supervision can claim contribution from a contractor who is in breach of the JCT Contract, provided the damage to the employer is the same (section 1(1)). The Act provides for contribution only in respect of damage that occurred on or after 1 January 1979 and only applies to contracts made on or after that date (sections 10(2) and 7(2)).

In order to succeed in a claim for contribution, it must be shown that the party from whom the contribution is sought is liable in respect of the same damage (section 1(1)). It follows that, if that person is not liable in respect of the same damage, no contribution can be recovered. As to that liability, a judgment given in other proceedings is conclusive evidence in the contribution proceedings (section 1(5)). So that, for example, where an employer has sued an architect and the architect was found not liable, that judgment will be conclusive in proceedings brought by a contractor to recover a contribution from the designer. On the other hand, the fact that there has been judgment in other proceedings does not prevent the recovery of contribution (section 1(2)).

The Act also deals with the position where one of the wrongdoers settles the proceedings against him by providing that a contribution can be recovered (section 1(2)). However, there is no right to contribution from a party who is not liable because the limitation period between him and the person who has suffered the damage has expired (section 1(3)). On the wording of section 1(3) contribution could not be recovered from a party who has settled the action with the person who suffered the damage at a date which is outside the limitation period, unless the contribution proceedings were commenced within the limitation period.

The assessment of the amount of the contribution is subject to principles. Firstly, the contribution is required to be just and equitable having regard to the extent of the person's responsibility for the damage in question (section 2(1)). Secondly, where the amount of the damages that have been awarded is subject to a limit in an agreement or by reduction under the Law Reform (Contributory Negligence) Act 1945, the person from whom the contribution is sought cannot be required to make a contribution of greater amount than the amount of those limited damages (section 2(3)). An example of this occurs in the JCT with Contractor's Design Contract which provides, by clause 2.5.3, for the limitation of the contractor's liability to the employer in respect of loss of use, loss of profit and other consequential loss arising out of breach by the contractor of his design warranty. Where, for example, such a contractor has sub-let the design to an architect, he will not be able to claim contribution from the architect in excess of the limit of liability set out in the contract between the contractor and the employer, assuming that clause is itself a valid limitation of liability.

A claim for a contribution or an indemnity in the High Court can be made by notice under the Rules of the Supreme Court, Order 16, Rule 1 or Rule 8. A Rule 8 Notice does not require the leave of the court but can only be issued against an existing defendant. In a case where a Rule 8 Notice had been served by one defendant on another but thereafter the claim against that other defendant had been discontinued by the plaintiff, it has been held that the notice remained effective; the court also found that if that was not right and it was found that leave was needed to serve a notice under Rule 1, that leave would be granted: *Harper* v. *Gray and Walker and Others* (1984).

Some points bear emphasis in relation to these apportionments carried out by the courts. Firstly, they tend to be a broad assessment in units of 10%, or occasionally 5%. They are not accurately or obsessively examined in great detail. Secondly, each party found liable in respect of the same damage is liable to the plaintiff for the whole of the damages – the contribution is a matter *between* the defendants. It follows that, if one defendant cannot pay his share, the other defendants have to pay the plaintiff. This arises because all the defendants are jointly and severally liable to the plaintiff for the loss that he has suffered. Thirdly, it follows that the effect of *D & F* and *Murphy* is to remove local authorities, quite often, from the frame of liability with the consequence that they will not be making contributions to damages as they did before. Fourthly, those who have tried to persuade the Court of Appeal to interfere with contribution percentages decided by the judge have not fared well (see, for example, *Adcock* v. *Norfolk Line Limited* (1993)). The Court of Appeal are clearly loathe to interfere with decisions of the judges on these issues – after all, the judge has heard the witnesses and been closer to the issues affecting contribution than the Court of Appeal could ever hope to be.

Some examples of apportionment are set out below (but many were before *D & F* and *Murphy* and should be read in that light – for example in many of these cases the local authority might well have been found not liable at all).

In *Acrecrest* v. *W.S. Hattrell & Partners and Another* (1983), the Court of Appeal refused to disturb the judges apportionment of the designer 75% and the local authority 25%.

In *Eames London Estates Limited and Others* v. *North Hertfordshire District Council and Others* (1981) the Official Referee apportioned 32½% to the architect, and 22½% each to the local authority, the original owners of the land at the time of construction and the specialist sub-contractor.

In *Worlock* v. *Saws and Rushmore Borough Council* (1982), the judge had apportioned 60% to the contractor and 40% to the local authority on the basis that the local authority knew of the builder's inexperience. However, the Court of Appeal said that the builder's inexperience was not a relevant factor and adjusted the apportionment to 75% to the contractor and 25% to the local authority.

In *Equitable Debenture Assets Corporation* v. *William Moss Group Limited and Others* (1984), the Official Referee gave separate apportionments of liability in respect of the design and workmanship problems arising from curtain walling. In respect of design, he apportioned 25% to the architect and 75% to the specialist sub-contractor. In respect of workmanship, he put 5% against the architect, 15% against the main contractor and 80% against the sub-contractor.

Although not strictly a case of 'contribution', the decision in *Kensington and Chelsea and Westminster Area Health Authority* v. *Adams Holden & Partners and Another* (1984) is of interest. It seems that the Official Referee took the view that the supervision responsibility had been the job of the architect and the clerk of works and that, although the clerk of works was not a party to the proceedings, the damages awarded against the architect should be reduced by 20% to reflect the fact that the clerk of works had failed to carry out his duties properly.

In *Thomas and Others* v. *T. A. Phillips (Builders) Limited and the Borough Council of Taff Ely* (1985), contribution was ordered in the proportions 75% as to the builder and 25% as to the local authority.

The same sort of apportionments take place in Canada; for example, in *Roco Developments* v. *Permasteel Engineering and Took Engineering Services* (1983) where, in relation to inspection of foundations by engineers, the engineer was held 25% to blame, the developer 25% and the contractor 50% to blame.

Chapter 10

Professional indemnity insurance

10.1 Generally

A designer faced with a claim for professional negligence is unlikely to be able to make any payment in respect of the claim without serious financial consequences to his business or even bankruptcy. There is little point adopting the ostrich approach: 'It will never happen to me'. There are ways of spreading the risk and limiting the liability so that the consequences of a successful professional negligence claim are less severe. One method of spreading the risk is insurance whereby insurers collect a great many premiums in order to have the funds available to meet a relatively smaller number of claims. Although professional indemnity insurance can be expensive, it might properly be regarded as one of the expenses of running the designer's business. At present, the RIBA do not require their members to take out professional indemnity insurance, even where the practice is carried on as a limited company but the ACE do where there is an express or implied limitation of liability (see 11.1.2). The RICS do require their members to take out professional indemnity insurance and a check is made by the RICS to see that their members are complying with the requirement.

Professional indemnity insurance does not cover every contingency with which the designer may be faced; the usual policy provides cover in respect of any loss from a claim made against the designer in respect of any negligent act, error or omission. In other words, the cover is usually limited to professional negligence and would not provide cover in a case where there was a breach of duty but no negligence. Before considering what the contents of a policy should be, it is necessary to look at the principles that govern professional indemnity policies. Before that, however, there is one point to make that cannot be over-emphasised.

It is vital that the designer reads the policy to understand the cover (which may involve consideration with brokers), the restrictions on the cover (including the exceptions, the excess and geographical area covered) and the requirements as to claims notification. There should be one person responsible for this in every organisation.

10.2 Principles of professional indemnity insurance

10.2.1 Contract

Arrangements for insurance are made by contract but there are special rules in insurance law. For example, there is the duty of the utmost good faith (see

10.2.2); the terms of the policy are likely to turn the statements of the insured in the proposal form into warranties; there is widespread use of 'conditions precedent', that is to say, for example, conditions that must be complied with by the insured before the insurers have any liability; and there is extensive use of 'exceptions' to define the cover provided. Subject to that, the usual rules as to the *formation* of contracts apply to contracts of insurance. The usual procedure is for the designer to complete a proposal form, usually the insurers' standard form; that form will usually refer to the standard conditions of the insurers' policy and by signing the proposal form, the designer is offering to accept insurance on those terms. The terms themselves usually contain a provision that the proposal form is incorporated into and is the basis of the insurance contract. In this way, all the information given by the designer in the proposal form becomes part of the contract. Thus it becomes a warranty, breach of which enables the insurer to avoid the policy or bring it to an end. It follows that once the proposal form has been given to the insurers and the insurers have accepted the proposal, a contract will exist and the insurers will, and are obliged to, issue a policy in the terms agreed between the parties.

In the general law of contract, a warranty is a term collateral to the main purpose of the contract, breach of which gives the aggrieved party a right to damages but not rescission of the contract. In insurance law, a warranty is a condition of the policy, breach of which discharges insurers from liability under the contract of insurance from the date of breach. The requirements of a warranty are strict and even an unwitting infringement can have serious consequences for the insured.

Where the insurers, on receipt of the proposal, tell the designer that they wish to vary some of their standard terms, for example, because they wish to have an additional exclusion, then there will be no contract because the insurers have made a counter-offer which can only form a contract when the varied terms are accepted by the designer.

10.2.2   Disclosure and risk

In *Carter* v. *Boehm* (1766), a case that retains its seminal importance notwithstanding that it was decided so long ago, Lord Mansfield said:

> 'Insurance is a contract of speculation. The special facts upon which the contingent chances to be computed lie most commonly in the knowledge of the insured only; the underwriter trusts to his representations and proceeds upon confidence that he does not keep back any circumstances...'

Thus we see that the duty of disclosure is based upon the notion of inequality of information and includes at its very heart the obligation on the assured to disclose all material facts or circumstances which he knows (or ought in the ordinary course of business to know), prior to completion of the contract.

The proposal form that is completed by the designer is a document of the utmost importance. It will usually be made the basis of the contract; the truth of statements made by the designer in the proposal will often be made a condition precedent to the insurer's liability; that is to say, where the statements are untrue, the insurer can lawfully refuse to make payment in respect of a claim for which he would otherwise be liable. He may also be able to avoid the policy. The other aspect of the proposal form is that it enables the insurer to assess the risk so that he can decide whether or not to accept the proposal and on what terms. It follows that the insurer cannot make a proper evaluation unless the designer makes full disclosure to him of all those matters which are relevant to the risk. That will involve doing more than just answering the questions on the proposal form, if there are other matters of which insurers should be made aware. It is against this background that the common law developed the principle that a contract of insurance is based on the utmost good faith of the parties (known as the principle of *uberrimae fidei*).

The principle of the utmost good faith applies to both parties to the insurance contract (*Banque Keyser Ullman SA* v. *Skandian (UK) Insurance Co. Limited and Others* (1987), which was not overruled on this point in the Court of Appeal or the House of Lords) and where the utmost good faith has not been shown by one party, the other party can avoid the contract (see section 10.2.3). In such a case, the contract would be at an end and the insured would have no insurance cover. It does not necessarily follow that any premium paid has to be returned. In the absence of fraud, the premium will be returned but if there is fraud, it is not refundable. In any event, the most important aspect of the principle of the utmost good faith is the duty imposed on the designer when making his proposal to the insurer:

(1)   to disclose all facts that are material, and
(2)   not to make a statement that amounts to a misrepresentation of a material fact.

Such non-disclosure or misrepresentation enables the insurer to avoid the policy *ab initio*; existing claims will not be met. Similarly, if the designer fraudulently conceals a material fact, the insurer will equally be entitled to avoid the policy. Non-disclosure and misrepresentation are now considered separately.

10.2.3   Non-disclosure

A designer has a duty to disclose all facts that are material. Moreover, it is the fact and not the significance of the fact which must be disclosed. If there is a leak through a roof it must be disclosed even though the designer may not know that the whole roof is defective. Where there is a breach of this duty, the insurer has a common law right to avoid the policy. The duty involves consideration of two matters.

Firstly, the designer must disclose all material facts that are actually within his knowledge. However, he cannot necessarily assume that matters that are not within his knowledge are not disclosable. The principle of the utmost good faith probably requires that the designer should include material facts that he could discover by making reasonable enquiries.

Secondly, the duty is limited to those facts that are 'material'. A designer should be aware that whether or not a fact is material is not to be limited by what the designer thinks is relevant. Section 18(2) of the Marine Insurance Act 1906 states that a fact is material if it would 'affect the judgment of a prudent insurer'. The approach to this matter by the courts indicates that a fact can be material even if it would not have affected the decisions of a prudent insurer as to taking the risk or fixing the premium.

There have been some developments in this area of the law. In *CTI* v. *Oceanus Mutual Underwriting (Bermuda) Limited* (1984), the Court of Appeal decided that the prudent insurer test was the sole test; prior to that, it had been thought that there was a two stage test: first, was the insurer misled; second, would it have influenced his judgement? After *CTI*, it became only the second test. Further, that test meant that it was enough that the actual insurer wanted the information, not that he would have acted differently if he had it. This tipped the balance on this point almost wholly in favour of insurers against the insured.

That decision came in for much criticism and has now been restricted to some extent by the Court of Appeal in *Pan Atlantic Insurance Co* v. *Pine Top Insurance Co. Limited* (1993). The court looked again at the test in *CTI*, noting that only the House of Lords could change the substantive decision. However, they did feel able to look at the phrase 'affect the judgement of a prudent insurer.' Lord Justice Steyn suggested that the phrase was capable of at least three meanings:

(1)   A fact is material only if it would have a decisive influence on the mind of a prudent insurer.
(2)   A fact is material if it would cause a prudent insurer to appreciate that the risk was different from that actually presented to him.
(3)   A fact is material if a prudent insurer would wish to be aware of it.

In *CTI*, (1) was rejected and it had been thought that (3) was taken as the test. However, in *Pan Atlantic*, the Court of Appeal held that there had been no clear choice in *CTI* between (2) and (3). They decided that the matter was open to that extent and adopted (2) as the correct test of materiality. Clearly this is such an important area for the insurer and the insured that further clarification of the law in *Pan Atlantic* itself or some other future case in the House of Lords is both likely and desirable.

Where information is known to the insured but discoverable by the insurer on making inquiry this raises difficulties. Does the insurer have a duty to carry out his own investigations? For example, if the insurer is told things by the insured that put the insurer in a position where he should make further enquiries of his own, he cannot do nothing: the insurer must make further enquiries. The insurer also cannot rely on non-disclosure of matters that are public knowledge. This point was canvassed in the Supreme Court of Canada in *Coronation Insurance Co.* v. *Taku Air Transport Limited* (1992). The court decided that an insurer could not rely on a failure on the part of the insured to disclose information that was already held in the insurer's own files. Indeed, in this case, the information was a matter of public record (an air crash) which the court held the insurer could have discovered on reasonable investigation. Justice Cory said the effort required on the part of the insurer to discover the information was 'light and minimal'. The Canadian court relied heavily on the English authority of *Carter* v. *Boehm* (1766) in coming to their view. This case shows that in certain circumstances an insurer is obliged to undertake his own investigations, although the boundary of that obligation may not be very wide.

The designer has a duty to disclose material facts, not only in the proposal form, but also any further material facts which come to his knowledge before the contract of insurance is concluded. For example, where a designer is negotiating with a new insurer and, on having completed a proposal form a claim comes to his attention, he has a continuing duty to inform his proposed insurers of that claim. It should be noted that the date of the contract is unlikely to be the same date as the date of commencement of the insurance cover. The test is when there is a contract.

10.2.4   Misrepresentation

As part of his duty of disclosure, the designer must not only make accurate statements as part of his general duty to disclose all material facts, but must also see that any particular questions asked by the insurers are answered accurately. This precludes making statements which are true but by reason of the fact that they are incomplete are misleading: *Aarons Reefs* v. *Twiss* (1896). If a statement is untrue, it does not matter that the designer thought that it was true when he made it. The insurer will still be able to avoid the policy if the misrepresentation was material. However, where the insured adds a qualification to his statement by saying that it is true to the best of his knowledge and belief, then he may be afforded some protection provided he did so believe his statement to be true and that belief was reasonable: *Wheelton* v. *Hardisty* (1858). That is the position at common law but where the conditions of the insurance provide that the truth of the statements is a condition precedent to the insurer's liability, then honest belief will not assist and the insurer will not be liable.

The test as to whether a misrepresentation is material is the same as that for non-disclosure; the duty to state facts accurately, as with non-disclosure, also continues to the date that the contract is made.

10.2.5   Renewal

Professional indemnity policies are usually written for a period of 12 months. The policy can only, therefore, be renewed where both parties consent. They often do by the insurer sending out a renewal notice and the designer paying a renewal premium. There is not necessarily a new proposal form, particularly where brokers are involved. However, the duty of the utmost good faith arises on every renewal because it is, in fact, a new contract of insurance. The basis of the new contract will be the same as the old contract. It follows that the designer has a duty to the insurer to check that the proposal for the old insurance is still applicable and, if not, to notify the insurer before renewal of any additional relevant facts or any other matters which make any of the statements in the original proposal misleading in any way. If a material fact had not been disclosed in the previous year, it is worthwhile considering notifying it on renewal.

It is not uncommon, particularly in the volatile insurance market that has existed over the last few years, for an insured to change insurer on renewal. The difficulties that can arise where a writ is issued but the extent of the claim was not known until after a new insurer came on risk were considered by the Court of Appeal in *Thorman and Others* v. *New Hampshire Insurance Co. (UK) Limited and the Home Insurance Co.* (1987). In this case, the architects had been designers on a project that had been completed in 1977. They were covered by New Hampshire ('NH') up to 30 September 1983. From 1 October 1983 they were covered by the Home ('H'). There were terms requiring notification of claims and occurrences which might give rise to a claim in both policies. In 1976, complaints had been made about cracking of brickwork. The owners took possession of the properties between November 1976 and November 1977. In 1978 and 1979 the owners required remedial works to be carried out to the brickwork and the architects informed NH of a claim for the cost of the remedial works. By 1979 NH had filed their papers. In May 1982 the architects were told of further problems and in June 1982 the owners issued a writ indorsed in general terms alleging professional negligence. The statement of claim, which was not served by the owners until January 1984, contained allegations going to a variety of defects beyond the brickwork. NH claimed they were only on risk as to the brickwork and nothing else, saying that the other claims were only made after they had ceased to be the relevant insurer. On this point, the court was much influenced by a letter written by the owners' solicitors to the architects in June 1982, which was while NH were on risk and which letter they saw. It said in part:

'Serious problems have arisen in this development, *inter alia*, with regard to cracking and defective brickwork, for which we hold you responsible.'

Sir John Donaldson, Master of the Rolls, said of that passage:

'Note the words '*inter alia*'. This is the clearest possible claim in respect of all serious problems which had arisen by that date and is not confined to brick-work. The fact that it was unparticularised and uninformative is nothing to the point. All matters listed in the Scott Schedule [in the proceedings] are in this category and it follows that all were the subject matter of a claim before New Hampshire came off risk.'

The court found that the true test was: what was the claim being put forward by the claimant – not, what the proposed defendant thought it was? The writ subsequently issued merely particularised a claim that had been made in general terms before and did not constitute new or different claims.

10.2.6   Waiver

An insurer who discovers a non-disclosure or a misrepresentation that entitles him to avoid the policy does not have to do so. He can elect whether to avoid the policy or not. An insurer can waive his right to avoid the policy by his conduct, for example, by taking over the conduct of the defence of the proceedings. Sometimes, insurers who are aware of their right to avoid the policy may proceed on the clear understanding that by so proceeding they are not waiving their rights subse-quently to avoid the policy. Insurers who have paid a claim, not knowing at the time that they were entitled to avoid the policy, can subsequently recover sums paid to the designer. The most common waiver by insurers is accepting a premium after they are aware of a non-disclosure or misrepresentation.

10.2.7   Subrogation

Where the insurer pays the amount of the loss to a designer, the insurer has a right to be placed in the position of the designer and avail himself of all the rights and remedies of the designer against third parties. Where there is no condition in the policy dealing with this matter, the right of subrogation is not exercisable until the insurers have paid the loss to the designer: *Castellain* v. *Preston* (1883); *Page* v. *Scottish Insurance Corporation Limited* (1929). There is much old legal authority on implied terms as to subrogation but the House of Lords have considered the modern position in *Lord Napier and Ettrick* v. *N.F. Kershaw Limited* (1993). The implied terms were classified as follows by Lord Templeman:

(1)   an obligation on the assured to initiate proceedings in order to reduce his loss;
(2)   a promise by the assured to account to the insurer for monies received by him from the third party;
(3)   a promise by the assured to allow the insurer to exercise his right of action against the third party wrongdoer in the event that the assured fails to do so himself;
(4)   a promise by the assured to act in good faith when proceeding against the third party.

However, it is likely that the policy will have express provisions dealing with the equivalent of subrogation rights as contractual terms. It will usually be provided that the insurer will be entitled to take over and conduct any proceedings brought in respect of a claim. Nevertheless, although the conduct of the proceedings may be taken over in this way, the designer will remain as the party named in the proceedings.

10.2.8   Premium and duration of policy

The amount of the premium is assessed by insurers on the basis of their experience of claims in the relevant sphere of activity. In any particular case, the average premium based on the claims experience of the insurers may be increased or decreased by reason of a variety of factors including the matters set out in the proposal. The agreement of the premium (or the basis upon which it is to be calculated) is an essential ingredient in the formation of the contract. Once a valid contract has come into being, the insurer may be liable on the policy, notwithstanding the fact that the premium has not been paid. In practice, however, insurers will avoid that position arising by making payment of the premium a condition precedent to their liability under the policy.

The duration of the policy will usually be expressly stated both as to commencement and expiry. The policy will usually contain a condition entitling the insurer to cancel the policy on giving a specified number of days' notice in writing to the insured. The insurer's risk will continue until that period has expired and, where the condition also provides that the designer shall be repaid a proportionate part of the premium, the insurer will remain at risk until that proportionate part of the premium has been repaid: *Bamberger* v. *Commercial Credit Mutual Assurance Society* (1855).

10.2.9   Claims

There will usually be a condition requiring the designer to give written notice to the insurer of claims made against the insured. The precise wording of this condition is of fundamental importance because observance of the procedure in the policy for giving notice to the insurers is often made a condition precedent to the insurers' liability. However, there are insurers who accept that wording requiring 'immediate' notice or that claims must be notified 'forthwith' are not fair on the insured. It is therefore worthwhile negotiating this part of the policy wording to try to obtain wording that is not a condition precedent. Designers should read the condition setting out the procedure for notification of claims carefully to be certain that they comply with it. The usual wording requires the written notice to be given when the designer becomes aware of circumstances which may give rise to a claim. Such wording means that the designer cannot wait until a claim is actually made against him but rather as soon as he knows of circumstances which may lead to such a claim, he has a duty to inform insurers. If the condition requires the notification to be in writing, then it should be done in writing and to the person specified in the policy, so as to avoid any arguments as to the precise date of notification that might arise if the notification was given at a meeting or in a telephone conversation.

Once a claim has been made, it will be necessary for the proceedings against the designer to be defended. On the usual policy terms, the insurer then has three options; he can:

(1) pay the designer the amount for which the dispute can be settled but not exceeding the limit of the indemnity; or

(2) take over and conduct the defence of the action in the name of the designer, in which case, the insurers will probably be unable to dispute that they are liable to indemnify the designer up to the limit of indemnity under the policy: *Soole* v. *Royal Insurance Co.* (1971); or

(3) permit the designer to conduct his own defence, in which case the policy will usually provide for the designer to be paid his legal costs provided the insurer has so agreed in writing before the costs were incurred.

Where the insurer conducts the proceedings himself in the name of the designer, the insurer owes a duty to the designer to see that the proceedings are properly conducted and, in particular, the insurer should see that the designer agrees with the proposed defence: *Groom* v. *Crocker* (1939).

The question of who starts proceedings where the insurer has given a payment of part of the losses can give rise to problems. This is illustrated by *Insurance Company of the State of Pennsylvania Limited* (1989) v. *IBM UK Limited* and *IBM UK Limited* v. *Henry Boot Scotland Limited and Robert Matthew, Johnson-Marshall & Partners* (1989). Here, IBM had employed RMJM as architects and Boot as contractor for an extension to a factory. Following problems with the works, IBM claimed to have suffered losses of about £4.25 million. IBM were indemnified as to part of that sum by their property insurers, Pennsylvania. IBM began proceedings against Boot and RMJM. Two days later, Pennsylvania, acting in IBM's name, issued a writ against Boot, with RMJM added later as second defendants. The statements of claim in the two actions were substantially the same, although Pennsylvania's claim was for the amount they had paid to IBM. Boot and RMJM applied to court to stay Pennsylvania's claim or strike it out as vexatious or an abuse of process. Pennsylvania sought a declaration that they could bring an action in their own name or that of IBM. Judge John Newey QC had to consider the position under New York law and English law. He then decided:

(1)   Pennsylvania's rights remained those of subrogation.
(2)   Pennsylvania had been entitled to bring their action in IBM's name but they were not entitled to commence fresh proceedings, or be co-plaintiffs, in their own name.
(3)   Pennsylvania's action was not dismissed because they had been entitled to bring it in IBM's name.
(4)   It was oppressive for Boot and RMJM to face two actions in relation to the same matters at the same time. The judge ordered a stay of the Pennsylvania action because the IBM action was more advanced.
(5)   Pennsylvania were given liberty to apply to remove the stay in case IBM discontinued its action or there was some other unexpected development.

Where the policy gives the insurer the right to settle the proceedings, the insurer can settle the proceedings without discussing the matter with the designer and the insurer is entitled to recover from the designer the excess under the policy and any other sums which the designer has to bear under the policy: *Beacon Insurance Co. Limited* v. *Langdale* (1939). In practice, the insurer will usually involve the insured in negotiations, particularly where there is a large excess. All policies will contain a provision requiring a designer to make no admission or offer of settlement or the like. The observance of such a provision is usually made a condition precedent to the insurer's liability and, accordingly, any such offer to settle made by the designer, without the consent of the insurers, will have the effect of enabling the insurer to repudiate liability under the policy.

Where the insurer pays in respect of a claim, he will ask for a form of discharge to be signed. The insured should be careful to see that the wording of the form of discharge does not go wider than the matters that are being settled. For example, in *Kitchen Design and Advice Limited* v. *Lee Valley Water Co.* (1989), a form of discharge signed in respect of a claim for physical damage caused by flooding referred not only to claims advanced but also to any that might be advanced; the discharge prevented recovery of later claims for consequential loss.

There is developing authority for the proposition that an insured owes a duty of good faith to the insurer when making an insurance claim: a duty to disclose material facts. For example, in *The Litsion Pride* (1985), Mr Justice Hirst held that the duty of utmost good faith extended to a time after the making of the contract and would be breached by a claim submitted containing fraudulent mis-statements. This reasoning was followed in *The Captain Panagos DP* (1986) and approved by Lord Jauncey in *La Banque Financière de la Cité* v. *Westgate Insurance Co. Limited* (1990). As to the consequences of fraudulently mis-stating material facts, or fraudulently omitting material facts, it has yet to be decided whether this breach of the duty of good faith entitles the insurer to avoid the policy *ab initio* or not. This issue will be a red herring unless the insurer is also trying to avoid other claims because there will, in any event, be an implied term not to submit fraudulent claims. The issue as to whether fraud is a necessary ingredient, which it is not generally in relation to good faith, has been considered in an English case: *Bucks Printing Press Limited* v. *Prudential Assurance Co* (1991).

In that case the insured asserted in his insurance claim that machinery had been properly packed in circumstances where he did not know whether the machinery had been properly packed. Mr Justice Saville found the insured had been reckless, rather than fraudulent, in making the statement and he said:

'... the making of fraudulent or reckless material misrepresentations by an insured to an insurer in support of a claim under the insurance amounts to a failure to observe the duty of the utmost good faith ... and gives the insurer the right to repudiate liability under the insurance.'

Mr Justice Saville was asked whether negligence, as opposed to fraud or recklessness, was enough but he felt it was not. That part of the judgment is, in any event, *obiter dicta* (not binding). It may be that the position as to the submission of false or misleading claims is rather that there is an implied obligation not to submit such claims. However, the consequence would be that the insurer could avoid the claim and claim damages for breach but could not treat the policy as void *ab initio*.

However, the law in Canada appears to be ahead of England in this respect. In *Re Ontario Securities Commission and Osler Inc.* (1982), there was neither fraud nor recklessness, just a failure to disclose information and this was held to be a breach of the duty of good faith. In the United States of America, these matters are treated as matters of good faith (see for example, *Golden* v. *Pacific Indemnity Co.* (1993). English law and American law have been following divergent paths for some time.

10.2.10   Rights against insurers

A person who brings a claim against designers has no cause of action against the designers' insurers. However, there is one exception to this rule which is provided by statute. Where the designer becomes bankrupt or makes a composition or arrangement with his creditors, or in the case of a company, a winding-up order is made or a resolution for voluntary winding-up is passed, or a receiver or manager is appointed, then the injured party has the right to bring an action against the insurers: Third Parties (Rights Against Insurers) Act 1930, section 1. The effect of the Act is to try to put the injured party in the position that the designer would have been *vis à vis* the insurer. The insurer is only liable to the injured party to the same extent that he would have been liable to the designer.

Unfortunately for those seeking to avail themselves of this Act, the path now has a serious stumbling block in the way of success. In *Bradley* v. *Eagle Star Insurance Co. Limited* (1989), Doris Bradley, who had worked at the mill of Dart Mill Limited for many years on and off, had contracted byssinosis. Dart Mill Limited had been voluntarily wound up and the company dissolved in 1976. The issue before the court was whether she had a reasonable prospect of making a successful claim against the defendant insurer, who had insured Dart Mill Limited, under section 1 of the Third Parties (Rights against Insurers) Act. She did not succeed. The Court of Appeal decided that she did not have a right under the Act because that right did not arise unless she had already obtained judgment against Dart Mill Limited. She could not obtain that judgment because the company no longer existed in law. In these circumstances, she had no claim against the insurer direct. Lord Brandon, agreeing with the decision in an earlier case, put it this way:

> '... the reasoning ... in the *Post Office* case ... on the basis of which they concluded that, under a policy of insurance against liability to third parties, the insured person cannot sue for an indemnity from the insurers unless and until the existence and amount of his liability to a third party has been established by action, arbitration or agreement, is unassailably correct.'

It follows that the Act can only be used where the third party has proven the liability of the insured by way of judgment, arbitration or agreement. Without that, there is little benefit in this Act to third parties. However, it is possible to have a company that has been struck off the Register of Companies reinstated and then pursued to judgment so as to obtain the benefits of the Act.

Under section 2(1) of the Act, the liquidator of an assured is to 'give at the request of any person claiming that the [assured] is under a liability to him, such information as may reasonably be required by him for the purpose of ascertaining whether any rights have been transferred to and vested in him by this Act'. The application and effect of this section was tested, following *Bradley*, in *Nigel Upchurch Associates* v. *Eldridge Investment Co. Limited* (1993). An architect had entered into a voluntary arrangement with his creditors on grounds of insolvency. Proceedings were brought in the architect's name by the administrator of the scheme of arrangement in respect of unpaid fees, breach of contract and remuneration for other work. The defendant denied liability and counterclaimed; he also sought details under the Act of the architect's insurance. As the rights under section 2 could only arise when section 1 was satisfied, the court decided that in the light of *Bradley*, the defendant had no right to see the insurance documents.

It follows from all this that the usefulness of the Act is severely restricted and that its apparent benefits are largely illusory.

In different circumstances, the Court of Appeal has considered the effect of the Third Parties (Rights Against Insurers) Act 1930 in *Normid Housing Association Limited* v. *Ralphs and Others* (1989). In this case, the clients of a firm of architects brought claims against the firm in respect of defects to the refurbishment of the clients' properties. Shortly before the hearing of the action, the architects paid into court a sum of £150,000, which sum was not acceptable to the clients. When the hearing of the action began, counsel for the architects advised the architects' clients that the architects' insurers had offered to pay a further £100,000 in addition to the payment into court of £150,000 on condition that the architects accepted that payment in full and final settlement of all their claims against the insurers. Counsel for the architects also told the architects' clients' counsel that the architects had in mind to accept the offer and to give the insurers a release in respect of any further liability under any policy of insurance.

The following day, an application was successfully made for an injunction to restrain the architects from entering into the proposed settlement of their claims with the insurers. In the Court of Appeal, the injunction was discharged. The Court of Appeal took the view that the architects were under no statutory duty or contractual duty to take out professional indemnity insurance that was entirely a matter for their own judgment and if so in what form and for how much cover.

Furthermore their contractual duty to exercise professional skill and care did not oblige them to effect any such insurance. If they did effect such insurance, then they had no duty to deal with the policies in any particular way – those policies were their own assets and they were as free to deal with their rights under them as with any other of their assets. In the absence of any bankruptcy, the clients of these architects had no rights by reason of the Third Parties (Rights Against Insurers) Act 1930 to restrain such a settlement as was proposed. The question as to whether or not the clients of these architects could successfully apply for a *Mareva* injunction to freeze the proceeds of the insurance policies pending the outcome of the trial was left open. As to that possibility, see *Lubenham Fidelities and Investment Co. Limited* v. *South Pembrokeshire District Council and Others* (1985) at section 9.1.2.

10.2.11   Unfair contract terms

The main provisions of the Unfair Contract Terms Act 1977 do not extend to contracts of insurance (Paragraph 1(a) of Schedule 1 of the Act). It follows that there is no possibility of a designer seeking to challenge, by reference to the provisions of the Act, provisions in a policy requiring certain contract terms to satisfy the test of reasonableness. The Commission of the European Union have a document under discussion at present that could affect this area of the law in due course if action is taken by the EU.

10.3   The professional indemnity policy

The purpose of this section is to set out some practical considerations that are relevant to the selection of an appropriate policy.

10.3.1   The cover

The usual cover is against the designer's legal liability for damages and costs in respect of claims for breach of professional duty by reason of any negligence, error or omission on the part of the designer. The usual policy wording will not provide indemnity in respect of breach of a fitness for purpose obligation. Generally, terms provide cover solely for 'negligent act, error or omission'. Thus, where the designer has given an express or implied warranty that his design will be fit for the purpose required, there is no cover for breach of that warranty. Typical policy wording is:

> 'The Insurer agrees to indemnify the Insured up to the limit specified in the Schedule in respect of any sum or sums which the insured may become legally liable to pay as damages for breach of professional duty as a result of any claim or claims made upon the Insured during the period of insurance arising out of the conduct of the practice described in the Schedule as a direct result of any negligent act, error or omission committed by the Insured in the said practice or business.'

In *Greaves* v. *Baynham Meikle* (1975), if there had been only a finding of liability for breach of warranty alone, a policy, if it were on these terms, would not have covered the insured. The cover will be limited to liability incurred in connection with the particular business of the designer and the nature of that business will usually be defined in the policy. The usual legal and insurance interpretation of the words 'negligent act, error or omission' is that, whilst there is cover for breach of a contractual duty as to reasonable skill and care, there has to be negligence and that the words 'error or omission' are to be interpreted only in the context of negligence. However, a different view has been expressed in one case in 1984 where it was said that cases habitually relied upon to support an assertion that the words 'negligent act, error or omission' were apt to cover only negligence did not in fact support that contention. On the other hand, it was said that not every loss caused by an omission or error was recoverable under the policy: it must be one which in principle could create liability and must not be a deliberate error or omission: *Wimpey Construction (UK) Limited* v. *Poole* (1984). In *Wimpey*, Mr Justice Webster said:

> 'A professional indemnity policy does not necessarily cover only negligence. In my view I must give effect to the literal meaning of the primary insuring words and construe them as to include any omission or error without negligence, but not every loss caused by an omission or error is recoverable under the policy. In the first place, which is common ground, it must not be a deliberate error or omission.'

It is important to see that the description of the business and the work it carries out is properly described either in the policy or in the proposal. The precise wording of the liability that is covered will vary from policy to policy and the designer will only be covered for liability that falls within the description of the cover in the policy. For those who wish to consider the scope and significance of particular policy wordings, the following cases may be helpful: *Davies* v. *Hosken* (1937); *Goddard and Smith* v. *Frew* (1939); *Simon Warrender Pty Limited* v. *Swain* (1960); *Whitworth* v. *Hosken* (1939); *Walton* v. *National Employers Mutual* (1974).

The basis of a professional indemnity policy is that it provides an indemnity, that is to say, the insurer agrees to indemnify the designer against his legal liability; if there is no liability, there will be no indemnity: the designer has to suffer a loss before he can claim against the insurers.

10.3.2   Exceptions

The designer should be aware of the exceptions or exclusions in the policy. These will vary from policy to policy but typical exceptions are:

(1) the excess/deductible
(2) a claim brought about by any dishonesty, fraud or criminal act on the part of the designer
(3) any claim brought outside a specified geographical area, such as the United Kingdom
(4) libel and slander
(5) personal injuries caused to a third party unless they arise out of a breach of professional duty
(6) the usual war and atomic radiation exclusions.

There may also be an exclusion in respect of surveys of existing buildings unless the survey is carried out by someone with a qualification specifically stated in the policy. Another exclusion often found is in the following typical form:

'Any claim arising out of a specific liability assumed under a contract which increases the Insured's standard of care or measure of liability above that normally assumed under the Insured's usual contractual or implied conditions of engagement of service.'

It is essential to check that none of the exclusions contained in the insurer's conditions exclude a liability which the designer wishes to insure. Of those referred to above, three are likely to be more important than the others. The first is the exclusion of claims arising under a contract. It is clear that such an exclusion would be likely to exclude from cover not only fitness for purpose (undertaken either by an implied or an express term in conditions of engagement) but also liability arising out of a collateral warranty. Prior to *D & F* and *Murphy*, it was possible to argue that all that was achieved by a collateral warranty was to put in writing obligations that already existed in tort. It followed that this insurance exclusion did not affect cover. However, that argument is no longer available. It is vital to agree policy wording to deal expressly with this issue. Typical available policy wording is:

'Notwithstanding Exclusion 'X' above, indemnity provided by this policy shall apply to collateral warranties or similar agreements provided by the Insured but only in so far as the benefits of such warranties are not greater or longer lasting than those given to the party with whom the Insured originally contracted and subject to the following exclusions, unless specifically otherwise agreed by the Company:
(i)   acceptance of or guarantee of fitness for purpose where this appears as any express term
(ii)   any express guarantee including any relating to the period of a project
(iii)   any express contractual penalty
(iv)   any acceptance of liability for liquidated damages
(v)   any assignment of a collateral warranty or similar agreement to:

(a)   more than two parties in respect of assignments to funders, financiers and bankers
(b)   more than one party in respect of assignments to any other parties.

These exclusions shall not apply to liability which would have attached to the Insured in the absence of such collateral warranties or agreements.'

It is to be noted that this wording does not appear to exclude from cover a fitness for purpose obligation as an *implied* term (see (i) above). However, consideration would then have to be given to the meaning of 'not greater or longer lasting' in the opening paragraph.

The second important exclusion is the geographical limit and the wording of this exclusion should be carefully checked against the work that the designer has and the work that he hopes or intends to take on. The third is the exclusion in respect of personal injuries. The designer should check that he is covered in respect of death or personal injuries which may be caused to a third party who in using the building or structure that the designer has designed is injured *as a result of negligent design or breach of duty*: see for example *Clay* v. *A.J. Crump & Sons Limited* (1964); *Kelly* v. *Frank Mears & Partners* (1981). Public liability and employer's liability policies will not necessarily provide cover in this respect.

10.3.4   Limit of indemnity

The policy will have a stated limit to the indemnity that is to be provided by the insurer. In some policies, the limit is on the basis of a global maximum in any period of insurance and in other policies, the indemnity is on the basis that it will apply to each and every claim. In the former case, all claims will be met by the insurers provided they do not in total exceed the limit of indemnity. On an each and every claim basis, the limit of indemnity applies to each claim usually on the basis that the excess is met by the designer on each and every claim. An each and every claim basis will usually be the better proposition for the insured but will be more expensive in premium.

As to the limit of indemnity, this will be selected by the designer and its level is a matter of balance between cost of premium, the likelihood of claims at any particular value, the value of the construction projects on hand, and the commercial judgment of the designer.

Neither the RIBA nor the ACE (except where there is a limitation of liability: see 1.1.2) require professional indemnity insurance but the RICS does require insurance for members. This arises under Bye-Law 24(9A), which states:

'Every Member shall, in accordance with the Regulations, be insured against claims for breach of professional duty as a surveyor.'

There are detailed provisions in the Regulations, including defining 'Member' for this purpose. Briefly, it includes a member held out to the public to be practising as a surveyor, including sole principals, partners, directors, consultants and, significantly, members who have retired from practice after 1 January, 1986. The policy has to be 'no less comprehensive than the [policy] issued by RICS Insurance Services Limited'. The minimum amount of cover has to be:

'(i)   £100,00 for each and every claim where the gross income of the practice, firm or company in the preceding year did not exceed that amount; or
(ii)   £250,000 for each and every claim where the gross income of the practice, firm or company in the preceding year exceeded £100,000.'

The minimum cover applies irrespective of the number of employees. The uninsured excess is not permitted to exceed 2½% of the sum insured.

Although these figures are of interest, each designer must decide the level of the limit of indemnity which suits his own particular circumstances and needs to bear in mind that he will have to find the excess of any successful claim brought against him to the extent that it exceeds the level of the limit of indemnity in the policy. It should be observed that the limit applies to the year in which the claim is made and not to either the year in which the work was done or to the year in which the claim is settled.

10.3.5   Employees

Where an employee has been negligent in the firm's business, it is likely that the injured party could, if he so chose, bring an action in tort against the employee directly. It is, therefore, essential that the policy wording should provide indemnity for any employee in respect of such liability incurred on the firm's business.

Where an employee has been negligent, and the insurer indemnifies the firm, the insurer can recover the full amount of his loss from the employee (*Lister* v. *Romford Ice and Cold Storage Co. Limited* (1957)) by using his rights of subrogation to bring an action against the employee in the employer's name, though such procedure has been judicially criticised (*Morris* v. *Ford Motor Co. Limited* (1973)). Although there is an agreement between the government and the insurance industry that the insurers will not exercise rights of subrogation under employer's liability policies, that agreement does not extend to professional indemnity policies. This difficulty is easily overcome. The policy can contain a provision such as that set out in the first paragraph of this section or, alternatively, the policy can contain a waiver of the rights of subrogation against employees who have been negligent.

10.3.6   QC clause

Professional designers are quite properly jealous of their reputations. Any litigation, particularly litigation with a bad outcome, can be damaging to reputations. Clearly, where an insurer has the right to take over and conduct such proceedings, his interests may be in conflict with the professional interests of the designer. It is for this reason that a QC clause should be included in professional indemnity policies. Such a clause provides that the designer will not be required to contest proceedings brought against him except where a Queen's Counsel has advised that the proceedings could be contested with the probability of success. Such a clause is of benefit both to the designer and to the insurer because it is protective of both their interests.

10.4   Avoiding disputes with insurers

Having paid the premiums to secure the benefits of a professional indemnity policy, it clearly makes sense for a designer to do everything in his power to see that he does not lose the benefit of his insurance cover because the insurer has avoided the contract or repudiated liability on the grounds of some inadvertent act or omission by the designer. For this reason, someone in the designer's organisation should be responsible for reading the proposal and the policy conditions and understanding them. A short check list is set out below which should not be considered as covering every matter that needs to be dealt with.

10.4.1 *When completing a proposal form*

(1) Answer all the questions fully and honestly and, where appropriate, state that they are accurate to the best of the designer's belief.

(2) Consider whether there are any matters which a prudent insurer would wish to take into account in deciding whether to provide cover: if so, disclose them. This should include asking insurers if they want details of collateral warranties entered into.

(3) Ask for a copy of the full policy conditions. Do not rely on advertising brochures. Having obtained the conditions, read them and check that the conditions and the exclusions correspond with what is required. Check, in particular, the items set out earlier in this chapter under the heading above 'professional indemnity policy' (see 10.3).

(4) Keep a clear record of any representations made by the insurer or the broker. The principle of utmost good faith applies to the insurer as well. Brokers can incur liability to the insured.

(5) Insofar as it is possible, satisfy yourself that the proposed insurer has status in the professional indemnity field.

(6) Decide whether extensions are required to the policy: for example, to cover collateral warranties, the previous business of any partners; persons who are no longer partners and that such cover extends to their estates should they die; loss of documents; libel and slander; dishonesty of employees.

(7) Make enquiries in writing to senior staff, requiring answers in writing, as to any matters of which they are aware that should be disclosed to insurers. Check that each addressee responds. It is not necessary to ask every employee, merely those who should be aware of such matters: *Australian and New Zealand Bank Limited* v. *Colonial and Eagle Wharves Limited and Boag* (1960).

(8) Decide on the limit of indemnity.

10.4.2 *During the currency of the policy*

(1) Notify any changes in the partnership, such as new partners/directors/consultants or retiring partners/directors/consultants.

(2) Obtain insurer's agreement to cover any new matters that were not contemplated initially, for example, a contract outside the geographical limit of the policy.

(3) Ensure not only that any claims received are notified extremely promptly, in accordance with the policy provisions, but also anything that might later develop into a claim e.g. complaints of any kind of defects. Where that provision is to notify on becoming aware of circumstances which might give rise to a claim, it is better to be over cautious and notify all such matters promptly.

(4) Do not in any circumstances agree to compromise or admit liability in respect of any claim or any possible claim.

(5) Do not enter into collateral warranties which have terms that are at variance with the cover provided by the policy.

10.4.3 *On renewal of policy*

Before paying the premium, read the proposal, if any, the policy and any schedule or schedules, and check every item to see whether insurers should be notified of any changed material facts or changed requirements or any other matters. Make enquiries of staff as set out at (7) above.

10.5   Design and build contracts

10.5.1   *Generally*

This section, which relates to professional indemnity insurance for design and build contracts, should be read in conjunction with the information at 10.3 above for the simple reason that design and build contractors face all the problems of a consultant designer with many additional difficulties.

There is no doubt that contractors and sub-contractors engaged in the design and build field should have professional indemnity insurance, which should be regarded as an essential feature of the design and build process. The design and build contractor is not only constructing the works but also designing them. This is of course a fundamentally different position for the contractor than the traditional contracting arrangements. A design failure is a potential source of major financial loss and indemnity insurance can help to mitigate financial loss resulting from the failure; however, it should not be regarded as a panacea.

Employers who are not professionally advised may not even consider the insurance aspect of design and build contracts and may, accordingly, fail to take any steps to protect their interests. If they do consider the matter, they will wish to raise the question of professional indemnity insurance with potential contractors, in order to ascertain whether or not their arrangements are satisfactory. For example, the JCT Design and Build Contract does not require the contractor to insure the design obligation. Nor does the ACA Form.

Many contractors believe that their other insurance policies provide them with sufficient protection in respect of design work. This is not so. The usual contractors' all risks policy normally excludes design risks entirely. 'All Risks' does not mean all risks that the contractor undertakes. The usual policy is quite restrictive in its cover. Policies may provide indemnity in respect of damage caused by negligent design but limited to work which is not of itself defective and give no indemnity in respect of the actual defective part itself. Even if the cover does provide that sort of indemnity, the cover often ceases at the end of the construction period or the defects liability period. Design errors do have a habit of showing themselves many years after completion of the building. Furthermore, such a policy usually provides no indemnity in the absence of physical damage or in respect of consequential loss.

Some difficult points of legal construction arose on a contractors' all risks policy in *Cementation Piling and Foundations Limited* v. *Aegon Insurance Co. Limited and Commercial Union Insurance Co. plc* (1993). Cementation sought to recover losses suffered in rectifying gaps and voids in diaphragm walls, forming part of the construction of a series of quays within the existing dock at Barrow-in-Furness which they had contracted to carry out. There were admitted defects in design, materials and workmanship. Commercial Union's policy indemnified Cementation in respect of '... physical loss or damage to the property insured'. This was subject to an exception in respect of '... the cost of replacing or rectifying defects in design, materials or workmanship unless the property insured suffers actual loss, destruction or damage as a result of such defect'. It was common ground that the costs of removing escaped sand and filling the gap left where the sand had escaped was 'physical damage'. The parties differed as to whether the making good of the gaps between the concrete sections was 'physical damage'. Aegon argued that it was not possible to fill the gaps left by the sand without also making good the gaps between the concrete sections. Commercial Union's position was that the cover was merely property cover and not intended to cover liability. It would follow, CU said, that if the policy was held to cover repairs rendered necessary by negligence, the policy would extend to a scope beyond that agreed by the parties at the outset. Whilst the deputy judge accepted that his construction of the policy did involve an element of guarantee, that was consistent with the plain words of the policy. His decision was that Commercial Union were liable to indemnify Cementation.

The contractors 'public liability' policy is usually of no assistance in respect of design failures. The wording of such policies varies considerably from policy to policy and design risks are normally expressly excluded or there is limited cover as described above in relation to contractors' all risks policies. Indeed, by its very nature, such a policy will not generally apply to the contract works themselves but rather to personal injury or damage to property other than the contract works. It follows that the usual contractors' policies are not adequate to provide for indemnity in respect of design liability.

10.5.2 *The cover*

The principle of professional indemnity insurance for design and build contractors is the same as that for architects and engineers. The cover usually provided will only be in respect of the 'negligent act, error or omission' of the contractor in the performance of his 'professional activities'. The policy wording for the main operative clause for design and build contractors and other parts of the construction industry is often different to the policies of the construction professions. One policy wording, for example, is in the following form:

> 'We ... agree to indemnify the Assured for any sum or sums which the Assured may become legally liable to pay ... as a direct result of negligence on the part of the Assured in the conduct and execution of the professional activities and duties as herein defined.'

It has long been argued whether 'negligence' is properly to be construed as meaning claims in tort or for breach of a contract term as to reasonable skill and care or both. The word 'negligence' can have a particular meaning in law. That meaning is negligence as a tort. If it had that meaning in this clause, then the designer would not be insured for breach of a reasonable skill and care obligation in a contract, although he would be insured if he were also liable in tort. It is possible that a court might give this wording a legal construction, liberal to the insured, covering breaches of contract. However, the converse is a real possibility. The word 'negligence', in circumstances where a limitation statute was being construed, was said by the court to only apply to tort: *Iron Trades Mutual Insurance Co. Limited and Others* v. *J.K. Buckenham Limited* (1989) at first instance and in *Société Commerciale de Réassurance* v. *E.R.A.S.* in the Court of Appeal. Those cases probably have no direct application to this policy wording but given the difficulties and uncertainty of the law at present as to the circumstances in which there can be concurrent liability in contract and tort, a contractor offered this policy would be well advised to consider whether he should seek to have the wording changed. If that is not possible, then he may seek to have the word 'negligence' defined for the purposes of the policy to include, say, breach of any obligation at common law to use reasonable skill and care and/or breach of any obligation to exercise reasonable skill and care whether arising under a contract (by reason of either an express or implied term) or under statute or otherwise.

Policy wording sometimes found in construction, for example in product liability policies, is as follows:

'... against all sums which the Insured shall become liable at law to pay as damages and such sums for which liability in tort or under statute shall attach to some party or parties other than the Insured but for which liability is assumed by the Insured under indemnity clauses incorporated in contracts and/or agreements. ...'

The words 'liability at law' in this policy were considered in *M/S Aswan Engineering Establishment Co.* v. *Iron Trades Mutual Insurance Co. Limited* (1988) where the court found it was not limited to tort. Mr Justice Hobhouse said:

'... the meaning of "liability at law" was to be ascertained by reference to the ordinary use of language. The court should not strain to put an artificial construction on the phrase, especially when it was the insurance company which was seeking to rely on the strained construction of one of their own standard forms. The meaning of the relevant words was plain. It was not restricted to liability in tort, especially having regard to the express reference to such liability in the second half of the clause.'

The court was referred to two Canadian cases, where a different view was formed, but declined to follow those decisions: *Canadian Indemnity Co.* v. *Andrews and George Co.* (1952); *Dominion Bridge Co. Limited* v. *Toronto General Insurance Co.* (1964)

10.5.3   Terms and fitness for purpose

Two fundamentally important points for design and build contractors arise from the basis of the insurance. Firstly, the contractor's 'professional activities' must be carefully and adequately stated in the policy so that all the contractor's design activities fall within the scope of the policy. If the contractor has any doubt as to whether part of his design operation falls within the policy he should clarify the position with his insurers forthwith and, if necessary, a suitable endorsement should be provided to the policy.

Secondly, there is usually to be implied into design and build contracts a term that the design will be fit for its purpose. If such an obligation is to be implied or is expressly provided for in the contract, then the professional indemnity policy will not provide an indemnity in respect of a breach of the fitness for purpose obligation unless there is also negligence; the reason for this is that the usual indemnity provided is on the basis of any 'negligent act, error or omission' and not for breach of some absolute obligation undertaken by the contractor under his contract. The JCT Design and Build Contract seeks to avoid the imposition of a fitness for purpose obligation (clause 2.5.1 see 8.2.7), whereas the ACA Form expressly requires it.

The mere fact that a design and build contractor engages independent architects and engineers to provide the whole or part of the design will not affect his liability under his contract to the employer – the contractor's duty is to the employer and it is on him that the primary liability will fall when there is a design defect. Whether or not the contractor can recover from the independent architects or engineers is irrelevant to the contractor's duty to the employer; it follows that, even in circumstances where the contractor sub-lets his design, he should still have professional indemnity insurance cover and he should see that the cover provided by the policy extends to sub-letting the design, if necessary, by an appropriate endorsement to the policy.

One of the difficulties of design and build projects in the United Kingdom is the professional indemnity insurance position. The policy will usually provide indemnity in respect of claims that are notified during the period of the policy, usually 12 months. This does not pose a problem to those contractors who regularly engage in design and build work and renew every year their professional indemnity policy because the indemnity will usually apply irrespective of when the original design error took place.

Those contractors who do not regularly engage in design and build work have three options. Firstly, they do not take out insurance at all. Secondly, if they take out an annually renewable policy, they should continue to pay the premium for a great many years: actions can be brought against negligent designing contractors very many years after completion of the work (see Chapter 12) and it is not possible to say with any degree of certainty when a contractor could safely cease renewing the policy. Thirdly, although it is not at all common, it is possible to arrange professional indemnity insurance on a single project basis and this could prove to be a more economic course for a contractor who only rarely engaged in design and build projects. However, these policies have a severe handicap in that they will usually have a short life, often only up to a fixed period of time after practical completion. It may be that the insurance market would be prepared to extend that period, but if they did so agree, it would be likely to be a relatively short period. It follows that such a policy would provide no indemnity outside the specified period. However, it might be possible by a combination of such a policy and a limitation of liability clause in the design and build contract to limit the contractor's liability by agreement; but there is no way in which a design and build contractor can limit his liability to those with whom he is not in contractual relations.

10.5.4   *Proposal form*

Insurers will usually ask more questions of design and build contractors in the proposal form than they would of architects and engineers in private practice. Indeed, the amount of the premium can be affected by the professional qualifications and experience of the contractors in-house design team, the insurance cover carried by any firms to whom design is sub-let, the percentage of work value involved in design as opposed to the total project value and, above all, the type of work undertaken to be designed. It is of the utmost importance that these, and all the other questions in the proposal form, are fully and accurately answered in order to prevent the risk of insurers avoiding the policy for non-disclosure or misrepresentation (see 10.2.3 and 10.2.4).

10.5.5 Claims

As with architects and engineers in private practice, there is little point in paying premiums and then losing the benefit of the insurance cover because the insurer has avoided the contract or repudiated liability; design and build contractors should have regard to the suggestions in the procedure for seeking to avoid disputes with their insurers set out at 10.4. Additionally, they should have in mind the following three points.

Firstly, claims or alleged defects should be notified immediately. It is particularly difficult in a design and build contract to say whether a defect is due to design or workmanship: in many cases it may be a mixture of the two. It is clearly of the utmost importance for the contractor to err on the side of caution and notify insurers immediately of any matter which may involve an allegation of design defects. Secondly, a design and build contractor must not make good any defects without his insurer's consent. Thirdly, difficult issues can arise as to whether the design defect is the responsibility of the contractor or whether it is in fact the responsibility of the employer by reason of some requirement of the employer. In particular, the JCT Design and Build Contract provides no machinery for resolving discrepancies between the Employer's Requirements and the Contractor's Proposals. Clearly, the contractor's insurers would have to be satisfied that the fault lay with the contractor and not with the employer before agreeing to indemnify the contractor.

A system developed in France and, through France, in many parts of Africa and the Middle East provides for there to be a pool of money available immediately a serious construction failure comes to light, so that the building owner can get on with his remedial works without delay. In due course the parties can sort out who is liable for what, but at least whilst that is going on the building owner has had his building repaired. This is the decennial insurance of construction works. The provisions in France are for the works to be insured for ten years after handover and this is usually provided on the payment of a single premium at the time when the structure is first at risk. Such insurance is now available in the United Kingdom.

A typical policy would be taken out by the owner of the building and could optionally extend to the successors in title of the building and would cover the cost of repairs and certain other costs such as architects' and surveyors' fees. The policy will not cover every repair; it will be limited to major and serious problems such as latent defects in materials, construction or design which result in actual collapse or a threat of collapse or total prevention of the use of the building by some statutory order such as a dangerous structures notice in London. In other words, this is a major disaster type of insurance and will not usually extend to less severe construction problems.

The insurance premium is likely to be a sum of about 1½% of construction cost but, in addition, it will usually be a condition of the insurance that the building owner employs at his own expense the services of an inspector approved by the insurer. That inspector will have the duty of examining and verifying the design and the method of work, workmanship and materials used during the construction. This inspection function can of course add enormously to the cost of the construction process and there is a tendency for an over-cautious design in such circumstances which can also increase cost.

10.6   BUILD

The Construction Industry Sector Group of the National Economic Development Council published a report in 1988: 'Building Users' Insurance against Latent Defects', known as BUILD. One major recommendation was that there should be insurance taken out by the developer at an early stage, well before work starts on site. This would be a non-cancellable material damage policy against specified latent defects and damage lasting for ten years from practical completion. They suggested it should cover at least the structure, the foundations and the weather-shield envelope. It should be transferable to successive owners and tenants of the whole building. Where there were multiple tenants, the landlord would indemnify tenants on a back-to-back basis with the policy benefits. It was also suggested that insurers should waive their rights of subrogation against the party liable to the developer, such as the architect or the engineer.

Some insurers have taken to providing this type of cover in the UK, although its use is not widespread and there is, generally, no waiver of subrogation rights, leaving it open to the insurer to pursue the negligent designer. The designers have to continue to maintain their own professional indemnity cover because of that and also because, even if there were a waiver of subrogation on building defects cover on particular projects, they would still have projects where there is no building defects insurance. The costs (premium and independent verification) are of the order of 1.3% to 1.7% of the rebuilding costs but in certain circumstances the cost can be considerably lower. By way of example, a £10,000,000 building would produce a premium and other costs of the order of £150,000. Although small in the context of total development cost, this is a substantial sum in a commercial property marketplace where, even in recessionary times, developers still seem to obtain tenants on a full repairing covenant with collateral warranties from the contractor and the design team. It remains customary for collateral warranties to be given free of charge; the climate for more widespread use of insurance might change if architects, engineers and contractors were to charge for warranties. Such a change is not likely when there is a shortage of work in construction, although the Royal Incorporation of Architects in Scotland recommend their members to charge 10% of their fee value for a warranty, with a minimum of £1000.

However, as insurers' experience widens, the scope of the available cover is increasing, although the excesses remain fairly high (a minimum of £25,000). In practice, insurers usually require independent verification of the project, not only the design but also the construction, at the expense of the insured. Insurers will consider the giving of cover on completed buildings but because they will not have had the opportunity of that verification process, the premiums will be higher. Insurers active in this field include Allianz, Norman, SCOR and Sun Alliance.

10.7   Professional indemnity – changing insurers

There is benefit in continuing to renew cover with the same insurer in the professional indemnity field. Indeed, the consequences of failing to do so can be horrific. It is good advice not to change insurers unless the terms and/or premium are wholly unacceptable. Loyalty and track record do count for something when issues such as non-disclosure or late notification arise. There may be different policies from insurer to insurer in relation to collateral warranties – the position agreed with one insurer, at the time a warranty is given, will not bind a different insurer at a later date when a claim arises under that policy.

There can also be difficulties in ascertaining under which policy a claim falls. An example is where defects arise. Defects of a minor nature do arise regularly in construction. When do they become a matter to be notified to insurers? Take a situation where minor defects are known about, but not notified to insurers because they are regarded as routine construction defects. The defects then appear to be more serious and are notified, after a new insurer has taken over. There is the risk that the old insurer will seek to avoid liability by reason of late notification and the new insurer will seek to avoid liability by non-disclosure (saying that he should have been told before he took on the risk).

Other difficulties can arise where a specific allegation of negligence is made against say, an architect, by his client and, later, after a new insurer has come on risk, other allegations of negligence are made in relation to other matters on the same or a different project for the same client. This is discussed at 10.2.5 where the case of *Thorman and Others* v. *New Hampshire Insurance Co. Limited and the Home Insurance Co.* (1987) is considered.

Chapter 11

Limitation of liability

Insurance is, of course, the classic means of spreading risk; the designer can also protect his position to some extent by practising as a limited liability company or by excluding liability or the consequences of liability in his contract of engagement. Both these methods of limiting liability have to be subject to the relevant rules of professional conduct and these are considered below in respect of architects, engineers and chartered surveyors. Furthermore, designers can evolve a system of risk management aimed at reducing the likelihood of professional negligence.

11.1 Relevant rules of professional conduct

11.1.1 Architects

Architects are subject to some statutory regulation (see 1.4.2) but the practice of architects as limited liability companies is expressly provided for by section 17 of the Architects (Registration) Act 1931 which states:

'Nothing in this Act shall prevent a body corporate, firm or partnership from carrying on business under the style or title of Architect:

(a) if the business of the body corporate firm or partnership, so far as it relates to architecture is under the control and management of a superintendant who is a registered person and who does not act at the same time in a similar capacity for any other body corporate, firm or partnership; and

(b) if in every premises where such business as aforesaid is carried on and is not personally conducted by the superintendant such business is bona fide conducted under the direction of the superintendant by an assistant who is a registered person.'

The effect of this provision is that where a limited liability company is carrying on business and calling itself 'architects' then the architectural business of that company must be under the control of a registered architect, subject to the detailed provisions of sub-sections (a) and (b) of section 17.

The position under the Rules of Professional Conduct of the RIBA up to the end of 1980 was that members were forbidden to practise as limited liability companies. From 1 January 1981, new rules applied. These rules came into being after some argument within the profession as to ethics. The Council of the RIBA accepted a proposal to change the rules, subject to consultation of the members at its meeting in October 1979. One member in ten, chosen at random, was then sent a questionnaire on the proposed changes. However, at a special general meeting held in April 1980, resolutions were passed criticising the changes and requiring the Council to poll all the members. Of the 26,869 papers that were sent out, 10,799 were returned, and on the question of limited liability practice, 8,633 were in favour and 2,024 against. That result was binding on the Council who then proposed that the by-laws should be changed to require professional indemnity insurance in respect of architects practising under limited liability in respect of sites in the United Kingdom. A special general meeting was called in April 1981 at which the proposal was rejected at a meeting where the number of members present was only slightly in excess of the quorum required. (See the *RIBA Journal* for November 1979; January, February and September 1980; and February 1981.) The position is, therefore, that since 1 January 1981 architects are no longer forbidden to practise as limited liability companies by the rules of the RIBA and they are not required to take out professional indemnity insurance. However, it is inherent in the wording and in the Preface to the Code of Professional Conduct that an RIBA member who practises as a limited liability company is still subject to the Code of Professional Conduct and the disciplinary regulations (By-law 5). The same applies to professional accountability under the Architects (Registration) Act (see 'Advice to Architects', issue number 1, 17 June 1981, ARCUK).

ARCUK published a document 'The Standard of Conduct for Architects (approved on 17 June 1981) which concerns all architects, whether or not they are members of the RIBA. Whilst the Standard does not have the force of law, it is a guide to the attitude that is likely to be adopted by the Disciplinary Committee when considering whether or not an architect should have his name removed from the register for disgraceful conduct. The Standard provides, amongst other things, that a registered person:

> 'Will before making an engagement whether by agreement for professional services by a contract of employment or by a contract for the supply of services or goods have defined beyond reasonable doubt the terms of engagement including ... any limitation of liability ...'

The standard requires any limitation of liability imposed by the architect's contract to be 'defined beyond reasonable doubt'.

11.1.2   Engineers

The Association of Consulting Engineers publish a Code of Professional Conduct (June 1983) which contains rules for professional conduct and in respect of limited liability the rules provide:

'3.4   Members shall maintain accounts separate from their parent companies, shareholders, owners and any affiliated firms such that all costs whether direct or indirect are brought into account...

4.2   Any Firm whose constitution (whether expressly or by its effect) limits the liability of its members or partners shall ensure that this fact is not concealed from its clients and is apparent from all business stationery of the Firm. Such a Firm shall also maintain professional indemnity insurance.'

Insofar as work on sites outside the United Kingdom is concerned, the rules provide:

'Members shall order their conduct according to the Rules in whatever country they are working save that in a country where there are recognised standards of professional conduct laid down by a competent body recognised by the Council they may choose instead to order their conduct according to such standards. While the Association remains a member of the International Federation of Consulting Engineers (FIDIC) a Member operating in a country where there is a competent body which is also a member of FIDIC shall order his conduct according to the Rules and Standards of that body': (Rule 6.3).

It follows that in respect of work on sites outside the United Kingdom, a member of the ACE can choose to be governed by the standards of the appropriate body in the country in which he is operating. It follows that if those standards permit the limiting of liability, then the ACE member will be free to do so whether or not English law applies to his contract of engagement.

The bye-laws of the Institution of Civil Engineers forbid the use of the designation 'Chartered Civil Engineer' by a company (Bye-law 31(c), Royal Charter, By-laws, Regulations and Rules, the Institution of Civil Engineers, 1992). Clearly, an engineer wishing to avoid disciplinary problems who is subject to the rules of more than one professional body, should comply with those rules that are the most restrictive.

11.1.3   Chartered quantity surveyors

The Rules of Conduct of the Royal Institution of Chartered Surveyors (as amended 1991) provide that: 'No Member shall carry on practice as a surveyor through the medium of a company except in accordance with the Regulations' (Bye-law 24 (4)). The previous version of this rule was worded in a way that may have prevented any limitation of liability by a contract term. That restriction appears to have been removed. There are Regulations governing a member practising as a company with limited liability:

'Incorporation with Limited or Unlimited Liability
10(1)   A Member may carry on practice as a surveyor through the medium of a company provided he complies with these Regulations.

(2)   No Member shall carry on practice as a surveyor as aforesaid in any case where he is a director of the company concerned unless:

(a)   a provision to the following effect is included in the Memorandum of Association or equivalent constitutional document of that company and in such a way that it qualifies those powers of that company enabling it to offer surveying services:

"Any business of surveying for the time being carried on by the company shall at all times be conducted in accordance with the Rules of Conduct for the time being of the Royal Institution of Chartered Surveyors";

(b)   a provision to the following effect is included in the Articles of Association or equivalent constitutional document of that company:

"It shall be the duty of the Directors to ensure that any business of surveying for the time being carried on by the company shall at all times be conducted in accordance with the Rules of Conduct for the time being of the Royal Institution of Chartered Surveyors."

12(1)   The restrictions imposed by Regulation 10 shall apply only in the case of a company which undertakes or seeks work in any one or more of the United Kingdom, the Republic of Ireland, the Channel Islands, the Isle of Man and Hong Kong.

(2)   No Member shall carry on practice as a surveyor as aforesaid in any country other than the United Kingdom, the Republic of Ireland, the Channel Islands, the Isle of Man or Hong Kong if to do so would conflict with the laws of that country or with the rules of the relevant professional society, if any, in that country.'

It follows from these rules, that provided they are complied with, surveyors who are RICS members can operate through limited liability companies.

11.2   Modes of practice

11.2.1   Partnership

The law relating to partnerships, other than limited partnerships, is to be found in the Partnership Act 1890. A partnership is the relationship that exists between persons carrying on a business in common with a view to profit (section 1(1)). The Act has provisions governing the relationship between the partners themselves and also the position between third parties and the partners. Whilst the partners can vary the statutory provisions governing their internal relationships, they cannot vary the provisions of the Act that govern the relationship between the partners and third parties (section 19). It follows that the relationship between partners and a third party in a case of professional negligence is governed by the relevant provisions of the Partnership Act. The most important of these are as follows:

(1)   The partnership has unlimited liability in respect of any transaction entered into by any partner in the ordinary course of the business; this includes debts and contractual obligations (sections 5 and 8). Likewise, all the partners are liable for any tort committed by any partner in the ordinary course of the firm's business or with the authority of all the partners (section 10), although the partners have a right to an indemnity from the negligent partner. Where a partner makes an admission or a

representation in the ordinary course of business, that will be treated as evidence against all the partners (section 15).

(2) The liability to meet a claim falls on the partnership. Where the partnership has insufficient funds and is insolvent, then resort can be had to each individual partners private assets.

However, creditors of the firm cannot claim their debts against the assets of individual partners until the private, that is to say not the firm's, creditors have been paid in full. Likewise, where an individual partner is bankrupt, his creditors cannot claim against that partner's share of the partnership's assets, until the firm's creditors have been paid in full (Article 10, Insolvent Partnerships Order 1986, SI 1986 No. 2142).

(3) Every partner is entitled to share equally in the profits, unless the partnership agreement specifies otherwise. Equally every partner is required to meet the liabilities of the partnership, usually in the same share that applies to profits (section 44).

(4) A person who holds himself out as being a partner is at risk of being liable as a partner, whether he is or not (section 14). This principle applies to a partner who retires so that while he remains apparently a partner, for example by his name appearing on the notepaper, he will be liable for the debts of the partnership incurred after his retirement and will be liable to any creditor who has not been notified of his retirement (section 36(1)). Where the retirement is advertised by means of a notice in the *London Gazette*, this will be effective to prevent the retiring partner incurring liability to any person who did not deal with the partnership before he retired (section 36(2)). However, a partner who dies or becomes bankrupt does not incur liability through his estate for debts of the partnership incurred after his death or bankruptcy (section 36(3)). On the other hand, the estate of a partner who has died is liable in both contract and in tort for any wrong done or debt incurred while he was a partner (sections 9 and 12).

There is another species of partnership called the limited partnership and this was created by the Limited Partnership Act 1907, although the provisions of the Partnership Act 1890 largely apply to a limited partnership. The main feature of a limited partnership is that it has two types of partners: general and limited partners. The general partners are liable for the firm's debts whereas a limited partner is liable only to the extent of the capital that he contributes to the partnership. The Registrar of Companies has to register a limited partnership (Limited Partnership Act 1907, section 8). The limited partner cannot participate in management and has no power to bind the partnership (Limited Partnership Act 1907, section 6(1)). The limited partner can only transfer or assign his share with the consent of the general partners and the transfer has to be published in the *London Gazette* otherwise the assignment or transfer will not be effective (Limited Partnership Act 1907, sections 6(5) and 10(1)). The limited partnership is not extensively used and the reason for this is that it has many of the disadvantages of both partnership and unlimited liability companies and does not have any of the advantages of a limited liability company.

Trying to hide assets from creditors can give rise to problems. An accountant, faced with negligence actions, sold his practice and made gifts to his wife. These gifts included his interest in the family home and £65,000 (of which £40,000 was used to pay off the mortgage on the house). At the time of these transactions, he knew that there was doubt about his professional indemnity insurance cover. The court made an order that the wife must not dispose of the house or the remainder of the money pending the outcome of the negligence actions in order to preserve the property for the claimants. The gifts were said to be transactions '...at an undervalue ... for the purpose of putting assets beyond the reach of a person who is making...a claim against him' under the Insolvency Act 1986: *Moon and Others* v. *Franklin and Another* (1990).

11.2.2   Sole practitioner

The position of a sole practitioner is that his professional contracts and obligations are those which are his personally. It follows that there is no segregation of the assets of his 'business' from his personal assets (such as that under Article 10, Insolvent Partnerships Order 1986, see above). It follows that a sole practitioner is personally liable to the full extent of his personal assets for any liabilities that he incurs.

11.2.3   Companies

As with partnerships there are two types of companies, those with limited and unlimited liability, and they are governed by the Companies Act 1985. In the following section, references are to the 1985 Act, unless otherwise stated.

11.2.3.1   Limited companies

The overwhelming majority of all companies are companies limited by shares. Companies may also be limited by guarantee, but these are rare. The liability of members to a company limited by guarantee is to meet the amount which they have undertaken to pay in the event of the company going into liquidation and being unable to pay its debts. Since 1980, no such company can be formed with, or require, a share capital, and so the majority of such companies are formed to incorporate professional trade or charity associations or clubs supported by subscriptions.

The fundamental difference between a company limited by shares and a partnership is that the liability of the shareholders is limited to paying to the company the full amount payable on their shares. The scheme is that there are members of the company (shareholders) who own and ultimately control the company. The day to day management of the company will be in the hands of its directors and employees, who may or may not also be members.

A person having a claim against the company has to recover the amount of the claim from the company itself. In the event that the company is unable to meet the claim, the creditor may petitition for an administration order under section 8 of the Insolvency Act 1986, if the court is persuaded that the making of the order would be likely to achieve the survival of the company. A creditor owed at least £750 may petition to have the company wound up by the court. Alternatively, the company itself may seek a voluntary scheme of arrangement with the creditors under sections 1 to 7 of the Insolvency Act 1986, or it too may petition for an administration order, or it may put itself into liquidation, which, if the company is insolvent, is known as a creditors' voluntary winding-up. In the event of the company going into liquidation, whether as a result of a compulsory winding-up or a voluntary winding-up, the only liability that a member of the company incurs is to contribute to the company's assets to the amount, if any, unpaid on his shares (section 1(2)(a)). It follows that a limited liability company enables business to be carried on in such a way that neither the members who have provided capital as shares, nor those engaged in day to day mangement of the business, usually incur personal liability for the debts of the company.

Companies formed under the Companies Act may be either public or private. Public companies are defined by the Companies Act 1985 as companies which are limited by shares or by guarantee, which state in the memorandum that they are to be public, and which comply with the requirements of the Act as to registration, including a requirement that the share capital stated in the memorandum is to be not less than the 'authorised minimum', which is currently £50,000. The name of a public company must end with the words 'Public Limited Company', which can be abbreviated to 'plc'. The vast majority of limited companies are private and a private company uses the traditional 'Limited' or 'Ltd' at the end of its name.

There are exceptions to the general rule of limited liability which need to be set out. Amongst the most important are:

(1)   The minimum number of members for both public and private companies is two (section 24), but a private limited company may have one member: Companies (Single Member Private Limited Companies) Regulations 1992, SI 1699. A public company must have at least two directors whereas a private company need only have one director (section 282). If a company carries on business having only one member and does so for more than six months, that member, who for the whole or any part of the period that the company carries on business after those six months, is liable, jointly and severally with the company, for the payment of the company's debts contracted during the period or, as the case may be, that part of it so long as he knows that the business is being so carried on. Limited liability companies do not give any protection, therefore, in such circumstances.

(2)   Where a company is being wound up, the liquidator may discover that there has been either fraudulent trading or wrongful trading within the meaning of the Insolvency Act 1986. In either case, the protection of limited liability may be lost. By section 213 of the Insolvency Act 1986, relating to fraudulent trading, the court can order any person knowingly a party to carrying on the business of the company with a view to defrauding creditors or for other fraudulent purposes to make such contribution if any to the company's assets as the court thinks proper. Fraudulent trading is also a criminal offence. By section 214 of the Insolvency Act 1986, relating to wrongful trading, the court may declare a director of an insolvent company personally liable to contribute to the assets of the company, if satisfied that the director knew, or ought to have concluded, that there was no reasonable prospect that the company could avoid going into insolvent liquidation and thereafter failed to take every step to minimise the loss to the company's creditors.

Under section 214 it has been decided that a director can be ordered to make a substantial contribution to the assets of a company which has traded whilst insolvent even though no fraudulent intent was proved, provided he knew or ought to have known of the likely insolvency. The test of a director's knowledge was what could be expected of a reasonably diligent director of the particular company and its business: a large company with sophisticated procedures may result in a higher expectation of directors than a small company with simple accounting methods. The amount of the contribution is the amount by which the assets of the company have been depleted by the director's wrongdoing but the court has a discretion: *In Re Produce Marketing Consortium Limited* (1989).

(3)   Employees will not necessarily escape liability in tort in respect of a breach of duty committed in the course of the company's business. It may be easy for a person who has a defective design to identify the person or persons who carried out the design on the company's behalf. It may be possible for that person to establish that the designer owed a duty of care in tort independently of the company's obligations in contract and tort.

Furthermore, any clause in the contract between the company and its client excluding or limiting liability would not benefit the employee who had carried out the design.

> 'In *Adler* v. *Dickson* (1935), the plaintiff's contract with the defendant's employers, although excluding all liability for negligence, nevertheless did not preclude her from recovering damages in negligence from the defendant, a servant of the company with which she had contracted, because he owed her a personal duty of care apart from his contractual obligations to his employers and because he was held to be in breach of that duty. That was a case of personal injury but I cannot see why a case of damage to the plaintiff's property must be regarded differently in law': *Fairline Shipping Corporation* v. *Adamson* (1975).

(4)   Directors of companies are not normally liable for the torts of the company. However, there may be, in exceptional circumstances, cases where they can incur liability because they owe a duty of care independently of the company's contract or duty in tort.

The British Columbia Court of Appeal considered the position of a director giving advice owing a duty of care in tort to the company's client in the case of *Sealand of the Pacific* v. *Robert C. McHaffie Limited* (1975). In that case Robert C. McHaffie was a director and employee of Robert C. McHaffie Limited. The plaintiffs brought the action against him as well as the company on the ground that he had made a negligent statement to them about the qualities of a certain kind of cement. Judge of Appeal Seaton, giving the judgment of the court, said:

> 'An employee's act or omission that constitutes his employer's breach of contract may also impose a liability on the employee in tort. However this will only be if there is a breach of a duty owed independently of the contract by the employee to the other party. Mr McHaffie did not owe the duty to Sealand to make inquiries. That was a company responsibility. [T]he duty in negligence

and the duty in tort may stand side by side but the duty in contract is not imposed upon the employee as a duty in tort.

More recently in England, the case of *The Thomas Saunders Partnership* v. *Harvey* (1989) considered the possibility of a director owing duties in tort to his company's customer. A letter had been written to architects by a director of a company confirming that the company's proposals met the required specification. He knew it did not meet the specification when he wrote the letter, which was written to procure a contract for the company. He was found liable in the tort of deceit and in negligence. Judge Thayne-Forbes QC, Official Referee, sitting as a deputy High Court judge, said:

> 'I agree with [counsel] that, in making the representation that he did in the letter... Mr Harvey owed a duty of care to both [the architect] and the [employer] to take reasonable care to see that the representation was correct under the principles of *Hedley Byrne & Co.* v. *Heller & Partners* (1963). Mr Harvey had special knowledge and skill in the field of design and manufacture of raised access flooring and the approach to him by [the architect] on behalf of themselves and [the employer] was for information in the area of his specialist knowledge and skill. Although Mr Harvey was acting in the course of his duties as a director of Cavco and on Cavco's business when he made the representation, the words and the information were his and his alone and, at least by implication, he assumed responsibility for what he was saying. The present case seems to me to be the same sort of situation as that which was given by Ralph Gibson LJ as an example of the *Hedley Byrne* type of case in his judgment in *Pacific Associates* v. *Baxter* ... [and] falls squarely within the principles enunciated in *Esso Petroleum Co. Limited* v. *Mardon* ... there is no reason in principle why Mr Harvey should not be personally liable in negligence ... I do not agree that such an approach is to drive a coach and horses through the principle of the cloak of incorporation...'

This issue has also occupied the Court of Appeal in New Zealand: *Trevor Ivory Limited* v. *Anderson* (1991). Here, a company director advised the owner of an orchard, which included a raspberry plantation, to use a particular herbicide to control couch grass which was threatening the raspberry crop. He failed to give advice as to precautions to be taken and the raspberry crop was severely affected with the result that the plants had to be dug up. It was held that an officer or servant of a company, no matter his status in the company, might in the course of his activities on behalf of the company come under a personal duty to a third party, breach of which might entail personal liability. The test as to whether such liability had been incurred was whether there had been an assumption by the director or employee of the company of a duty of care, actual or imputed. Liability depends on the facts. The court was referred to *Adler* v. *Dickson, Sealand of the Pacific, Thomas Saunders, Fairline Shipping, C. Evans & Sons Limited* v. *Spritbrand Limited* (1985) and many other relevant cases, all of which were reviewed. Mr Justice Hardie Boys said:

> 'The question ... is ... whether in giving advice pursuant to his company's contract with the respondents, Mr Ivory assumed a personal responsibility. It

is not enough that it was a one-man company. Indeed that fact may rather tell against personal responsibility, for use of a company to carry on a one-man business may be seen as itself a personal disclaimer. That this was a one-man company is of course by no means conclusive, but it made it necessary for the respondents to adduce clear evidence that in his dealings with them Mr Ivory was not simply acting as the company performing his contractual obligations towards them. . . .'

It was the assumption of a personal duty of care that led to a finding of liability on the director of a one-man company in *Fairline Shipping Corporation* v. *Adamson* (1975):

'Generally speaking, if an employer is liable to a plaintiff in tort on the basis of the doctrine respondent superior, the servant can also be held personally liable, though in practice it is, of course, usually more convenient and worthwhile to sue his employers. If this is the law as regards servants, it cannot logically be more favourable to company directors.'

In that case the director was the owner of the cold store in which the limited company carried on its business. He sent out invoices on his own private note-paper and not the company's and he took goods personally into the store at a time when the company had become dormant.

Additionally, company directors may find that they have inadvertently contracted on their own account rather than entering into a contract on behalf of the company. This may not usually pose a problem but where the company is insolvent, the other party may bring an action against the director on the basis of his personal contract in order to obtain payment from the director personally, in full knowledge that the company is unable to meet the claim. Directors should, therefore, be careful to see that the company's contracts are properly entered into in the name of the company.

The right of a company to sue its directors is beyond the scope of this book. However, such a right does exist although, paradoxically, such a right may not be as strong as the ability of a company to sue its employees. However, it is often the case that directors of companies are not only directors but are also employees.

11.2.3.2   Unlimited companies
The Companies Act also makes provision for companies to be registered as unlimited in which case the word 'limited' must not appear in the company name. In such companies, the members are liable without limit for all the debts of the company but such liability does not arise unless and until there is a winding-up. Such companies are exempt from filing profit and loss accounts, balance sheets and auditors' and directors' reports (unless they are subsidiaries of limited companies or the holding company of a limited company).

11.2.3.3   Partnerships and companies contrasted
On the basis of the matters set out above, in order to provide some limitation of liability, limited companies are to be preferred, at least in circumstances where this is permitted by the relevant rules of professional conduct. Where the rules of

conduct permit unlimited liability companies, these have certain advantages, particularly in relation to retiring designers and secrecy of the financial accounts.

There are other factors which would influence adoption of the mantle of either a limited or unlimited liability company which have nothing to do with limiting liability. These are strictly outside the scope of this book but for the sake of completeness, they are mentioned very briefly. The partners in a partnership pay income tax on all the profits; in companies, corporation tax is payable on the profits left after allowances which include the salaries of employees and directors. There can be considerable tax savings as a company, but each case is different and should be considered on its merits. There are considerably more difficulties with changes in a partnership, through death, retirement and new partners than is the case with a company which provides a continuing legal entity.

A company may find it easier to finance its operations because it is able to borrow on a debenture and create a fixed and floating charge on its assets. On the other hand, there are many more formalities to be complied with in the case of companies which include the filing of annual returns, and in the case of limited companies, accounts. There is no limit on the number of partners in a partnership of consulting engineers and building designers (Companies Act 1985, section 716 and regulations made thereunder). Additionally, there may be many non-legal reasons for adopting the structure of a company whether limited or unlimited. Large partnerships can become difficult to manage because every partner is entitled to take part in the management of the firm (Partnership Act 1890, section 24). The management structure of a company may enable this problem to be overcome and also to facilitate the bringing in of non-shareholding directors – in partnerships this presents difficulties.

In any event, designers should not assume that operating as a limited liability company will solve all their liability problems. Firstly, there is the possible liability in tort of employees and directors referred to above; in this respect the professional indemnity insurance policy should provide waiver of subrogation or indemnity to directors and employees in respect of duties that they may owe in tort arising out of the company's business so that employees and directors are indemnified in the event that the injured party does not sue the company, or the company is sued but is unable to meet its liabilities. Secondly, Parliament has decided to limit the possibility of setting up strings of companies which can be put into liquidation should they get into difficulties. The Company Directors Disqualification Act 1986 has provisions that enable a court to order that a person be disqualified from acting as a director or taking part in the management of a company where he has been, *inter alia*, a director of a company which has at any time become insolvent and his conduct as a director of *that* company makes him unfit to be concerned in the management of another company.

11.3   Limiting liability by contract

The law has always recognised the freedom of the parties to a contract to agree whatever terms they think fit. This freedom has been modified by both the common law and statute. It is commonplace nowadays to find extensive and detailed exclusion clauses in many everyday contracts, particularly in conditions that are printed in an order form or an acknowledgement of order form; the purchaser trying to incorporate his terms on the one hand and the seller trying to override those terms and incorporate his own. This has been referred to as the 'battle of the forms' and it can become particularly important where one of the parties has sought by a term to exclude or restrict his liability in the event that he is in breach of contract or negligent. Such exclusion clauses only affect the parties to the contract; for example, where a company incorporates an exclusion clause into its contract, that exclusion clause will not benefit an employee of the company who is sued in negligence by the other contracting party: *Adler* v. *Dixon* (1955). Furthermore, the extent to which a company can rely on the exclusion clause, if it were sued in negligence by a third party who was not a party to the contract, is now a matter of debate in cases. It may be that the party so sued cannot have a more extensive liability than that under his contract. This area of law continues to develop.

Whilst commercial organisations have no restrictions, other than legal requirements, on the exclusion clauses that they can incorporate into their contracts, designers are subject to further restraint of their conduct. The first part of this chapter explains how some professions in the construction industry are forbidden to limit their liability in this way. Others, whilst not being expressly forbidden to incorporate exclusion clauses, are not given express freedom to incorporate exclusion clauses. For example, each profession has its own general obligation in its rules of conduct imposing a duty on its members to uphold the dignity and reputation of the profession. It may well be that wide exclusion of liability would be a breach of that general obligation. It may, therefore, be that in any particular case, where a designer proposes to exclude liability, he should seek the advice of his professional body. The Council of the RIBA have indicated, for example, that members can limit their liability to the cost of remedial work and exclude liability for consequential loss (*RIBA Journal*, September 1971, page 424) and see the comments on SFA/92 below.

In order to be effective, exclusion clauses must, of course, be incorporated into the contract between the parties. Where it is desired to add an exclusion clause or clauses to standard printed conditions of engagement, it will be necessary to make appropriate amendments to the printed form or, alternatively, to incorporate the exclusion clauses by express reference.

There are some exclusion clauses that are robbed of their effectiveness by statute; there are others upon which statute imposes conditions as to their effectiveness; there are aspects of the common law that need to be considered in relation to exclusion clauses because it is a fact of life that courts do not generally look favourably on parties who, having committed a wrong, are seeking to escape their liability. For this reason, the courts have traditionally used many devices to overcome the effectiveness of exclusion clauses.

11.3.1   Common law

11.3.1.1   *Meaning of exclusion clauses*
In order for exclusion clauses to be effective, they must be very carefully drafted. If the words used are too wide or general, then they may not be effective in excluding a particular and specific liability. In particular, very clear words are required to exclude liability for negligence. The reason is that it must be clear that the parties intended to exclude liability for the particular loss that has arisen.

Accordingly, the wording of the clause must be such that the loss that has arisen falls within that meaning.

Where the wording is such that it has two or more meanings, the law has evolved means to resolve such ambiguities. Of these means, two are particularly important in the context of exclusion clauses. Firstly, exclusion clauses are construed against the person who seeks to rely on them. For example, where a party seeking to exclude liability relies on a meaning of an exclusion clause that is capable of bearing another meaning, that other meaning will be adopted by the court. Exclusion clauses are, therefore, said to be construed *contra proferentem*. Secondly, where there are particular words in a document that are followed by general words, the meaning of the general words is cut down so that it covers only the classes of meaning of the particular words. This is called the *ejusdem generis* rule.

11.3.1.2   Fundamental breach

One of the devices that courts have adopted in the past to overcome the effect of exclusion clauses was the doctrine of fundamental breach. It was said that, where a breach was so fundamental that it brought a contract to an end, the exclusion clause came to an end with the contract so that the exclusion clause could not be relied upon.

However, the House of Lords in 1980 decided that this principle does not exist and that, where a contract comes to an end by one party accepting the repudiation of the contract by the other party, then exclusion clauses were not necessarily thereby defeated; each exclusion clause in such circumstances should be applied subject to the usual rules of construction and any relevant statutory provisions: *Photo Production Limited* v. *Securicor Transport Limited* (1980). In that case, a company had been engaged to provide security services at a manufacturer's factory. The security company's employee started a fire (whether intentionally or not was never discovered) which destroyed the majority of the manufacturer's factory causing a loss of some £615,000. The House of Lords held, overruling the Court of Appeal, that the security company was entitled to rely on a clause in the contract which provided that the company would not be responsible in any circumstances for the default of its employees.

11.3.1.3   Oral terms

Where, at or before the time of contracting, the party who wishes to insert an exclusion clause tells the other party that it is intended only to apply in certain circumstances, he will not thereafter be entitled to rely on that exclusion clause unless those particular circumstances arise. For example, a wedding dress trimmed with beads and sequins was taken for cleaning to dry-cleaners whose terms of trading sought to exclude liability for any damages. The dry-cleaners explained to their customer that the terms were only intended to apply to damage to the beads and sequins. When the dress was returned with a stain, it was held that the dry-cleaners could not rely on their exclusion clause because they had represented that it only applied to the beads and sequins: *Curtis* v. *Chemical Cleaning and Dyeing Company* (1951).

11.3.2   Defective Premises Act 1972

This Act applies only to dwellings. In respect of dwellings, any term in a contract which purports to exclude or restrict any liability arising under the Act is void (section 6(3)). It follows that a designer is prevented by a statutory provision from limiting the liability or restricting the duty that is owed, for example, under section 1 of the Act to see that the work 'which he takes on is done in a work-manlike or, as the case may be, professional manner' so that the dwelling will be fit for habitation on completion.

11.3.3   Unfair Contract Terms Act 1977

This Act is of great importance in that it renders some contractual terms totally ineffective and subjects some other terms to a test of reasonableness. It is clearly of the utmost importance to clauses that seek to exclude liability for breaches of contract and torts, including negligence. The following discussion is based on the law in England, Wales and Northern Ireland. It should be noted that the law in Scotland is different.

11.3.3.1   Negligence

The Act renders totally ineffective a term that seeks to exclude or restrict liability for death or personal injury resulting from negligence (section 2(1)).

'Negligence' has a wide meaning for the purposes of this Act (section 1(1)) and includes:

(1)   any obligation, arising from the express or implied terms of the contract, to take reasonable care or exercise reasonable skill in the performance of the contract;
(2)   any common law duty to take reasonable care or exercise reasonable skill (but not any stricter duty).

For the purposes of this Act, therefore, there is no doubt that negligence includes failure by a designer to exercise reasonable skill and care in his design, irre-spective of whether that obligation arises from an express term of the designer's contract or is implied by law. Furthermore, the meaning of negligence is to include the duty owed to third parties on the *Donoghue* v. *Stevenson* principle and this will include users of the completed building who may suffer personal injury or death as a result of the designer's failure to exercise reasonable skill and care (see, for example, *Kelly* v. *Frank Mears and Partners* (1981)).

Liability for loss or damage, other than death or personal injury arising from negligence, cannot be excluded or restricted except where the contract term satisfies the requirement of reasonableness (section 2(2)). As to claims in tort, the test provides that the disclaimer notice must have been fair and reasonable having regard to all the circumstances obtaining when the liability arose or, but for the notice, would have arisen.

11.3.3.2   Contract

Insofar as seeking to exclude or restrict liability in respect of breach of contract, or render performance substantially different from that which was reasonably expected of him, or to render no performance at all (in whole or in part), the Act provides that such terms shall be subject to the requirement of reasonableness but only where one of the parties deals as a consumer or on the other's written standard terms of business (section 3(1)). It should be noted that the Act applies only to contracts made on or after 1 February 1978 (section 31(1) and (2)).

The Act does give rise to considerable difficulties in interpretation. For example, if a businessman buys a car, which is ancillary to his business, is he dealing as a consumer or in the course of a business? If it is the former, the Act applies; if it is the latter, the Act does not apply because it is excluded from operation where a contract is made in the course of business (section 12(1)(a)). There is some case law to help with this issue.

The Act does not, as is sometimes thought by non-lawyers, deal with unfair contract terms in general. Its scope is restricted. In a case in which the Act did not apply to the contract under consideration, *Photo Production Limited* v. *Securicor Transport Limited* (1980), Lord Wilberforce said:

> '[The Act] applies to consumer contracts and those based on standard terms and enables exemption clauses to be applied with regard to what is just and reasonable. It is significant that Parliament refrained from legislating over the whole field of contract. After this Act, in commercial matters generally, when the parties are not of unequal bargaining power, and when risks are normally borne by insurers, not only is the case for judicial intervention undemonstrated, but there is everything to be said, and this seems to be Parliament's intention, for leaving the parties free to apportion the risks as they think fit and for respecting their decisions.'

Themes in the development of the law in this field are becoming clearer. The courts will seek to avoid reliance on unreasonable clauses and will permit reliance on reasonable clauses. For example in two cases, to neither of which the Unfair Contract Terms Act applied, a greater distinction has been drawn between clauses which seek to exclude liability altogether and clauses which simply seek to restrict the consequences of liability. In *George Mitchell (Chesterhall) Limited* v. *Finney Lock Seeds Limited* (1983), the Court of Appeal refused to permit seed merchants who had negligently supplied defective seed to rely on a printed contractual term which sought to exclude all liability for any loss or damage; the limit of the seedman's obligation in respect of defective seed was replacement of the seed or repayment of payments made for the seed. On the other hand, in the House of Lords in *Ailsa Craig Fishing Co. Limited* v. *Malvern Fishing Co. Limited and Another* (1983), reliance was permitted on a clause that limited liability. In that case, there had been breach of an obligation to provide a continuous security service in a harbour such that a boat sank and became a total loss. The owners of that boat sought to claim their loss, £55,000, from the security firm. The security firm had two clauses limiting liability such that one claim was not permitted to exceed £1000 with an aggregate of all claims not exceeding £10,000. There was lengthy discussion in that case as to whether the contract term was sufficiently clear and unambiguous to limit the liability of the security firm in respect of its own negligence and that of its employees. It was held that it was.

The effect of these cases is in fact reflected by the provisions of the Act which states at section 11(4):

> 'Where by reference to a contract term or notice a person seeks to restrict liability to a specified sum of money and the question arises whether the term

or notice satisfies the requirement of reasonableness regard shall be had in particular to:

(a)   the resources which he could expect to be available to him for the purposes of meeting the liability should it arise and

(b)   how far it was open to him to cover himself by insurance.'

It would appear to follow that designers might be able successfully to limit their liability, rather than exclude it, to some reasonable sum and that a reasonable sum might be the limit of indemnity in their professional indemnity policy.

11.3.3.3   'Dealing as a consumer'

The Act does give greater protection to those who deal as consumers when compared to others. Section 12 of the Act says that a party deals as a consumer if:

(1)   he neither makes the contract in the course of a business nor holds himself out as doing so, and

(2)   the other party does make the contract in the course of a business, and

(3)   in the case of a contract for the sale of goods or hire-purchase, or a contract for the supply of goods, the goods passing under the contract are of a type ordinarily supplied for private use or consumption.

Whilst (1) and (2) could apply to a designer's contract, (3) rarely will apply because goods do not normally pass under the contract. Most designers' contracts will not give rise to the 'dealing as a consumer' issue and therefore will not fall under the Act for that reason.

Those who have sought to argue 'dealing as a consumer' in commercial arrangements have not fared well. In *R & B Customs Brokers Co. Limited* v. *United Dominions Trust Limited* (1988), the Court of Appeal decided that the purchase of a car by a company, for use in his work by a director of the company, did not involve the company in dealing as a consumer. The same approach was taken in *The Chester Grosvenor Hotel Limited* v. *Alfred McAlpine Management Limited* (1992) where clauses in a construction management contract limiting McAlpine's liability fell to be considered. The approach of the judge was that Grosvenor were not dealing as a consumer because their luxury hotel required constant refurbishment and that this contract was an inherent part of their business.

11.3.3.4   'Written standard terms of business'

The term 'written standard terms of business' is not defined in the Act and there is little judicial authority. Many questions arise. Does it include the standard forms of building contract negotiated by, for example, the constituent members of the JCT, which members, it might be said, represent many competing interests? Does it apply to standard forms of engagement of designers produced by their professional bodies? Does it apply to amendments to standard forms? Does it make any difference if those amendments are not always used? Most of these issues are discussed in what follows.

In the version of this Act that applies in Scotland, section 17 uses the term 'standard form of contract' and this phrase has been judicially considered in *McCrone* v. *Boots Farm Sales Limited* (1981). Lord Dunpark said:

'...the section is designed to prevent one party from having his contractual rights, against a party who is in breach of contract, excluded or restricted by a term or condition, which is one of a number of fixed terms or conditions invariably incorporated in contracts of the kind in question by the party in breach, and which have been incorporated in the particular contract in circumstances in which it would be unfair and unreasonable for the other party to have his rights so excluded or restricted. If the section is to have its purpose, the phrase "standard form of contract" cannot be confined to written contracts in which both parties use standard forms. It is, in my opinion, wide enough to include any contract, whether wholly written or partly oral, which includes a set of fixed terms or conditions which the proponer applies, without material variation, to contracts of the kind in question.'

It appears to follow from this (assuming that this interpretation also applies to 'written standard terms of business') that even though terms are not always used or are varied, but not materially, they may nevertheless be standard terms. It would also appear to follow that standard amendments to standard form contracts could also fall to be considered under the Act. In *The Chester Grosvenor Hotel Limited* v. *Alfred McAlpine Management Limited* (1992), the court was referred to that passage from *McCrone* and applied it. The judge felt that the passage was applicable because if it were otherwise, the application of the Act could be avoided by simply making minor amendments to clauses or, on occasions, not using them at all. He said:

'What is required for terms to be standard is that they should be regarded by the party which advances them as its standard terms and that it should habitually contract in those terms. If it contracts also in other terms, it must be determined in any given case, and as a matter of fact, whether this has occurred so frequently that the terms in question cannot be regarded as standard, and if on any occasion a party has substantially modified its pre-pared terms, it is a question of fact whether those terms have been so altered that they must be regarded as not having been employed on that occasion.'

Using the Act and these two cases, it seems highly likely that the use by designers on a regular, but not necessarily exclusive, basis of the conditions of engagement produced by their professional bodies will give rise to those conditions being 'written standard terms of business'. If that is right, then clauses in them will fall to be considered under the Act.

A much more difficult issue is whether the 'negotiated' standard forms of construction contract (such as the JCT 'family' and the ICE contracts) are one party's written standard terms. In the case of ICE, the 6th Edition is a joint effort by the ICE, the Association of Consulting Engineers and the Federation of Civil Engineering Contractors who have set up a 'permanent joint committee' to receive suggestions and keep it under review (see inside front cover of the contract). In like manner, the JCT comprises: the RIBA, the Building Employers Confederation, the RICS, the Association of County Councils, the Association of Metropolitan Authorities, the Association of District Councils, the Confederation of Associa-tions of Specialist Engineering Contractors, the Federation of Associations of Specialists and Sub-contractors, the Association of Consulting Engineers, the

British Property Federation and the Scottish Building Contracts Committee. Those representatives cover a wide range of potentially vested interests. It might be said that this family of contracts is an industry standard form and cannot possibly be said to represent the standard terms of one party to a particular contract but under the Act that may not be conclusive because the Act does not prevent, of itself, such a contract being considered under the Act. However, these contracts are freely negotiated and it may be said that Parliament did not have such contracts in mind when creating this Act – it intended to prevent a specific mischief, namely, the imposition of clauses seeking, unfairly or unreasonably, to restrict or exclude liability. There is some judicial support for the view that there can be 'industry forms' that do not fall under the Act in *Walker* v. *Boyle* (1982), a case on the standard Law Society Conditions of Sale, and in *Tersons Limited* v. *Stevenage Development Corporation* (1963). *Tersons* was, of course, decided long before the Act and cannot be considered as a direct authority on the point, but the judge said of the ICE Conditions:

> 'It is not drawn up by one party in its own interests and imposed on the other party. It is a general form, evidently in common use, and prepared and revised jointly by several representative bodies including the Federation of Civil Engineering Contractors.'

In conclusion, it is very hard to see that a court is likely to come to any other view than that such forms of contract do not fall for consideration under the Act. However, employers who regularly, but not necessarily always, make standard amendments (even with non-material changes from time to time) to standard forms of building contract run the risk that any such provisions seeking to exclude or restrict liability will fall to be considered under the Act.

11.3.3.5   *The requirement of reasonableness*
There is a list of matters in Schedule 2 of the Act that are to be taken into account in relation to exempting liability for the implied terms in non-consumer contracts for the sale and supply of goods. However, in relation to contract terms, the Act provides only that:

> '...the term shall have been a fair and reasonable one to be included having regard to the circumstances which were, or ought reasonably to have been, known to or in the contemplation of the parties when the contract was made': (section 11(1)).

Three cases illustrate the approach of the courts to the requirement of reasonableness: *Rees-Hough Limited* v. *Redland Reinforced Plastics Limited* (1984), *The Chester Grosvenor Hotel Limited* v. *Alfred McAlpine Management Limited* (1992) and *Edmund Murray Limited* v. *BSP International Foundations Limited* (1992). Each of these is considered separately.

11.3.3.6   *Rees-Hough*
In *Rees-Hough Limited* v. *Redland Reinforced Plastics Limited* (1984), Judge John Newey QC, Official Referee, formed the view that the exclusion clause in the contract between the parties was 'clear and unequivocal' and was effective to

exclude liability, but had to be subject to the reasonableness test, which applied in this case by reason of the terms being one party's standard terms of business. The term in this case was in the following form:

> 'The company warrants that the goods shall be of sound workmanship and materials and in the event of a defect in any goods being notified to the company in writing immediately upon the discovery thereof which is the result of unsound workmanship or materials, the company will, at its own cost at its option, either repair or replace the same, provided always that the company shall be liable only in respect of defects notified within three months of delivery of the goods concerned. Save as aforesaid, the company undertakes no liability, contractual or tortious, in respect of loss or damage suffered by the customer as a result of any defect in the goods (even if attributable to unsound workmanship or materials) or as a result of any warranty, representation, conduct or negligence of the company, its directors, employees or agents, and all terms of any nature, express or implied, statutory or otherwise, as to cor-respondence with any particular description or sample, fitness for purpose or merchantability are hereby excluded.'

The judge applied his mind to the matters set out in Schedule 2 of the Act which he summarised as follows:

(a) the strength of the bargaining position of the parties
(b) whether the customer received an inducement to agree to the term or had an opportunity of entering into a similar contract with others without such a term
(c) whether the customer knew of the term
(d) where the contract excludes or restricts liability for breach of condition, whether it was reasonable to expect compliance with it
(e) whether the goods were manufactured to the special order of the cus-tomer.

The standard terms under consideration were those of Redland and the judge using the shorthand of 'RH' for Rees-Hough said in summary in relation to the facts and the guidelines:

> '...as to (a) and (c), I have already referred to the parties' bargaining position and to RH's knowledge of the terms; (b), RH did not receive an inducement to agree to the terms – they received a normal trade discount – there was no evidence as to whether they could have purchased the pipes from another supplier without the terms but at a higher price; (d), at the time of the contract Redland, as experienced pipe manufacturers could have been expected to produce satisfactory pipes; and (e), the pipes were ordered by RH, but they did not prescribe the design, which the guideline seems to require.
> Obviously some considerations carry much more weight than others; for example that RH did not lack the ability to look after themselves is probably the weightiest in favour of upholding the terms; and, for example, that Red-land have never in the past sought to rely upon the terms in its dealing with RH may well be the weightiest against.

Doing the best that I can, I reach the conclusion that Redland have failed to prove that their standard terms were reasonable; indeed, I think that the balance of the considerations is strongly against the terms being reasonable.

I therefore hold that Redland cannot rely upon the standard terms of sale to invalidate the express and implied terms between themselves and RH.'

11.3.3.7   The Chester Grosvenor Hotel Limited

In *The Chester Grosvenor Hotel Limited* v. *Alfred McAlpine Management Limited*, clause 17 of two contracts between the parties entered into in 1984 and 1985 sought to restrict the liability of McAlpine. McAlpine were 'project managers' and their functions extended to appointing the designers, planning and cost control, employing, supervising and inspecting the work of construction contractors. Clause 17 purported to restrict McAlpine's liability for the default of construction contractors. In finding that the provisions did satisfy the requirement of reasonableness, the judge said that the following were relevant:

(1)   The parties were of equal bargaining power (relying on *Stag Line Limited* v. *Tyne Shiprepair Group Limited and Others* (1984)).
(2)   The contracts were entered into between substantial commercial organisations who had bargained at arm's length and effected a division of risks between them.
(3)   The contracts could have been on other forms.
(4)   Grosvenor had plenty of time to consider the terms before signing.
(5)   Although McAlpine were being retained for their expertise, there was no reason why they should not seek to restrict their liability in respect of that expertise. This was merely one factor.
(6)   The availability of insurance was relevant. Either party could have obtained insurance. Grosvenor did not obtain it.

11.3.3.8   Edmund Murray Limited

Edmund Murray, a small firm, bought a drilling rig from BSP which was built to a specification (compliance with which was a contractual term) provided by Edward Murray. The contract contained terms excluding and restricting BSP's liability in various respects. In the event, the rig was unsuitable for the functions for which it had been expressly ordered. The Court of Appeal found that the clauses did not satisfy the requirement of reasonableness because:

(1)   The rig had been specially ordered.
(2)   The specification contained detail of the precise technical performance required.
(3)   Edmund Murray made known to BSP the precise purpose for which they required the rig; (c.f. *Chester Grosvenor* where this reliance on expertise seems to have been a much less important factor, in that McAlpine were permitted to restrict their liability in respect of their expertise).
(4)   The guarantee was restricted to faulty workmanship or materials.

This decision might be seen as akin to the doctrine of fundamental breach, which was found to have no application in English law in *Photo Production Limited*. If, as a result of *Edmund Murray* it is not possible to exclude liability for a fundamental breach of contract, then the Court of Appeal has in effect reinstated the doctrine through the medium of the Act.

11.3.4 Architect's standard terms

The Architect's Appointment and SFA/92 are likely to be regarded by the courts as the 'other's standard terms of business' and will therefore fall to be considered against the requirement of reasonableness insofar as there are terms seeking to exclude or restrict liability.

The Architect's Appointment seeks to exclude liability for the performance of 'consultants' under clause 3.6, irrespective of whether they are employed by the architect. Under clauses 3.8 and 3.9, similar exclusions appear in respect of specialist contractors, sub-contractors and suppliers, as well as the main contractor. These clauses fall to be considered under the Act as to their reasonableness and hence whether or not they can be relied upon by the architect. However, little general guidance can be given because the cases show that so much will depend on the facts of the particular case.

It is hard to see how an exclusion of liability for the 'competence, general inspection and performance of the work entrusted to that consultant' can be a fair and reasonable term where the consultant is employed by the architect direct, particularly where the architect failed to advise of the need for a direct contract or a warranty agreement to avoid the loss of rights to the client. If it were effective, it would deprive the client of all his rights in respect of that consultant's work by breaking the chain of liability through the contracts. The position may be different where the other party is engaged by the client direct, such as a direct consultant or a main contractor – the client will have direct recourse against that party. However, where design work is being carried out by a nominated sub-contractor, there should be a direct warranty agreement with the client in the form of NSC/W. It might be argued that the exclusion was a fair and reasonable one to include at the time of contract by reason of the knowledge that NSC/W would come into existence at a later date.

In relation to SFA/92, similar points arise to those above. However, SFA/92 does not envisage the architect appointing consultants himself – the client is to appoint them (clause 4.1.2). On the other hand, SFA/92 contains other provisions, in the Memorandum of Agreement, that fall to be looked at in the light of the Act:

> '5 No action or proceedings for any breach of this Agreement shall be commenced against the Architect after the expiry of ____ years from completion of the Architect's Services, or, where the Services specific to building projects Stages K–L are provided by the Architect, from the date of practical completion of the Project.'

The agreement contains an arbitration clause and it is not clear whether 'proceedings' covers arbitration. If it does not, then this clause (and clause 6.2) may be robbed of effectiveness in an arbitration. Limitation statutes provide two main periods: six years for a contract under hand and 12 years for a deed from the date on which the cause of action arises. The date on which a cause of action arises can be much later than the dates provided for in this clause. For that reason alone, this clause is likely to be considered under the Act. If the period inserted by the architect is very short, this clause is perhaps more likely to be held unreasonable but a great deal would depend on the particular facts. The same applies to inserting six years in a deed where, but for the insertion, the limitation period would be 12 years. The phrase 'practical completion of the Project' is not related to the provisions of any particular form of building contract. Its meaning therefore may give rise to some difficulty. Finally, it is not entirely clear that this provision will be effective where the project is for dwellings (see Defective Premises Act, sections 1(5) and 6(2)).

'6.1   The Architect's liability for loss or damage shall be limited to such sum as the Architect ought reasonably to pay having regard to his responsibility for the same on the basis that all other consultants, Specialists, and the contractor, shall where appointed, be deemed to have provided to the client contractual undertakings in respect of their services and shall be deemed to have paid to the Client such contribution as may be appropriate having regard to the extent of their responsibility for such loss or damage.

6.2   The liability of the Architect for any loss or damage arising out of any action or proceedings referred to in clause 5 shall, notwithstanding the provisions of clause 6.1, in any event be limited to a sum not exceeding £____.

6.3   For the avoidance of doubt the Architect's liability shall never exceed the lower of the sum calculated in accordance with clause 6.1 above and the sum provided for in clause 6.2.'

These provisions will be void and of no effect where the project was dwellings. The Defective Premises Act renders void such provisions: section 6(3).

There are two purported restrictions here on money liability. The first is an attempt to avoid the effects of the joint and several liability rules and the Civil Liability (Contribution) Act 1978 (clause 6.1). This is discussed under collateral warranties at 7.3.6.11.

The second is a money cap on damages (clause 6.2). The smaller the sum, the more likely in general it will be to be unreasonable. If, however, the risk of high damages is very great compared to the amount of the fees, then that will be a positive factor. Provided the amount of an architect's professional indemnity insurance is itself reasonable in all the circumstances, then it may well be this clause will be held to be reasonable where the figure inserted is the limit of indemnity in the policy (see section 11(4) of the Act). The amount of resources generally available to the architect, including insurance, is a relevant factor in forming a view as to the sum to be stated (section 11(4) of the Act).

11.3.5 Engineers

Condition 5.2 of the ACE Conditions seeks to limit the consulting engineer's liability in respect of specialist suppliers and contractors and any other persons who are engaged to carry out additional services under condition 7.4. The wording of condition 5.2 in respect of specialist suppliers and contractors differs from that in respect of persons performing additional services. In the former case, the consulting engineer is 'relieved of all *responsibility*' for the design, manufacture, installation and performance of the specialist work. Does this wording have the effect of excluding the consulting engineer's liability or is it merely that he does not have to carry out the design for that part of the work? If it does exclude liability, does it also exclude negligence, which is not mentioned? The position in respect of additional services is clearer because it is said that the consulting engineer is under 'no liability for any negligence, default or omission of such persons' and condition 7.4 provides that the client 'shall be responsible to any person or persons providing such services for the cost of them'. However, will these provisions exclude the consulting engineer's liability where he is in contract with the person providing additional services? See the discussion above under 'Architects'.

11.4   Risk management

It is, of course, naive to think that claims for professional negligence can be avoided because such negligence is, by its very nature, usually inadvertent. However, there is always scope for a designer to manage his business so that (a) the possibility of a claim is minimised, and (b) in the event of a claim, the effect on the business is limited. It may well be worthwhile considering an assessment of the business as a risk management exercise – for example, a check of the designer's office procedure with a view to minimising the possibility of circumstances that could give rise to a claim. Consider whether the designer sufficiently involves the client in decisions, particularly those that may involve risk. Consider the adequacy of site supervision by making conscious decisions as to the level of supervision that should be given. Specialist designers should be employed directly by the client to minimise the designer's risk. When recommending contractors or sub-contractors, consider doing so 'without responsibility'. Consider the professional indemnity insurance policy and whether there is scope for improvement of the cover. Those designers who are permitted by their professional bodies to do so, should consider whether there is any benefit in changing from a partnership to a limited liability or unlimited liability company and the incorporation of clauses limiting their liability in their contract of engagement.

The RIBA publish a handbook which architects, if not all designers, may find useful in the context of risk management: *Handbook of Architectural Practice and Management*, 4th Revised Edition, 1980, RIBA.

Chapter 12

Limitation of actions

12.1   Generally

The period after which a party is prevented from pursuing a designer for breach of contract and negligence has been determined by statute. The philosophy is that the person who has committed a wrong should not have the possibility of legal proceedings hanging over him like a sword of Damocles forever and that people injured by a wrong should be encouraged not to delay in bringing their proceedings. The method adopted by statute to achieve these aims is to fix a period after the expiry of which an action cannot be pursued. The period itself is a matter for Parliament and the present law fixes various periods that apply to different circumstances.

The injured party can stop time running against him in proceedings in the High Court by issuing (but not necessarily serving) a writ within the specified period of limitation. However, the Court of Appeal has decided that it is an abuse of the process to issue a writ without any present intention of serving a statement of claim and in circumstances where there was no evidence or ground upon which one could be reasonably served: *Steamship Mutual Underwriting Association Limited and Another* v. *Trollope & Colls (City) Limited and Others* (1986). For an example of the difficulties that are caused where there is inordinate delay in progressing proceedings, see *City of Westminster* v. *Clifford Culpin & Partners and J. Jarvis & Sons plc* (1987).

In the case of proceedings brought in arbitration, the injured party stops time running by serving on the party against whom he wishes to claim a notice to concur in the appointment of an arbitrator (Limitation Act 1980, section 34). The issuing of a writ or the giving of a notice to concur in the appointment of an arbitrator does, therefore, fix the dates on which time stops running for limitation purposes. The question then arises whether these actions were taken within a period specified by statute. To decide that question, the date on which the period of limitation started to run has to be fixed. It is in this area of the law that cases have made the fixing of that date an extremely complex matter, particularly in claims in tort. Before considering those difficulties in detail and contrasting the position in claims in contract and tort, it is necessary to set out the periods of limitation and the definition of when that period starts to run that is fixed by statute.

12.2   Statutory periods

12.2.1   Simple contract

A claim under an oral contract and a written contract under hand (i.e. not a deed but merely signed by the parties) will be statute barred six years after the time when the cause of action accrues (Limitation Act 1980, section 5).

12.2.2 Contract under seal or a deed

A claim under a contract under seal or a deed will be statute barred 12 years from the time when the cause of action accrues (Limitation Act 1980, section 8).

12.2.3 Tort

A claim in tort will be statute barred six years from the accrual of the cause of action (Limitation Act 1980, section 2).

12.2.3.1 Latent Damage Act 1986

As a result of the work of the Law Reform Committee the Latent Damage Act 1986, has come into force. It deals with latent damage, not including personal injuries.

The first point to consider is to what types of claim the Act applies. The main provisions of the Act apply only to actions for 'negligence'. However, negligence is not defined anywhere in the Act. The Act is intended only to apply to tortious negligence and not to any breach of duty under a contract. This point was considered in *Iron Trade Mutual Insurance Co. Limited and Others* v. *J.K. Buckenham Limited* (1990). The Commercial Court decided (in relation to section 14A of the Limitations Act 1980, inserted by the 1986 Act) that it did not apply to claims in contract because 'any action for damages in negligence' in section 14A meant any action for damages for the tort of negligence and could not be construed as meaning any action for damages, including an action for breach of a contractual duty, founded on an allegation of negligent or careless conduct. The 1980 Act expressly preserved the distinction between actions in tort and actions in contract and provided that the different forms of action were to be treated separately even though the time limits specified might be the same. The court said that section 14A could not be construed in isolation from that expressly preserved distinction in the 1980 Act. On that basis, a claim for breach of a duty under a contract to take reasonable skill and care will not be governed as to limitation by section 14A. This has now been confirmed by the Court of Appeal in *Société Commerciale de Réassurance* v. *E.R.A.S. (International) Limited* (1992).

In relation to a cause of action for damages for negligence (other than personal injury or death), the action is not allowed to be brought after the expiration of the later of two periods:

(1) six years from the date on which the cause of action accrued, or
(2) three years from the 'starting date, if that period expires later than the period in (1): Section 14A, Limitation Act 1980.

For the purposes of that provision, the 'starting date' is the earliest date on which the plaintiff, or any person in whom the cause of action was vested before him, first had both the knowledge required for bringing an action for damages in respect of the relevant damage and a right to bring such an action (section 14A(5), Limitation Act 1980). The effect of that provision is to incorporate into the law of negligence a similar test in latent damage cases to that which applies in personal injury cases. As to the knowledge required for bringing an action, that means knowledge both of the material facts about the damage in respect of which the damages are claimed and of the other facts which are relevant:

(1) that the damage was attributable in whole or in part to the act or omission which is alleged to constitute negligence, and
(2) the identity of the defendant, and
(3) if it is alleged that the act or omission was that of a person other than the defendant, the identity of that person and the additional facts supporting the bringing of an action against the defendants: section 14A(8), Limitation Act 1980.

There are further qualifications in relation to the definition of knowledge for the purposes of the three year period of limitation created by this Act. Firstly, knowledge that any acts or omissions did or did not, as a matter of law, involve negligence is irrelevant; further, a person's knowledge includes knowledge which he might reasonably have been expected to acquire (a) from facts observable or ascertainable by him, or (b) from facts ascertainable by him with the help of appropriate expert advice which it is reasonable for him to seek, but he is not to be taken by virtue of these provisions as having knowledge of a fact ascertainable only with the help of expert advice so long as he has taken all reasonable steps to obtain, and where appropriate, to act on that advice (section 14A(10) Limitation Act 1980).

The 1986 Act also created a 15 year 'long stop'. This is in section 14B of the Limitation Act 1980. An action in for damages in negligence cannot be brought:

'... after the expiration of fifteen years from the date (or, if more than one, from the last of the dates) on which there occurred any act or omission

(a) which is alleged to constitute negligence; and
(b) to which the damage in respect of which damages are claimed is alleged to be attributable (in whole or part).'

It follows from this that an action could be prevented even where the injured party remains unaware that he has the right to bring a claim. It prevents reliance on the other periods at section 14A if the 15 year period expires first. In relation to the 15 year long stop provision, it is important to remember that it can expire before the other two periods, namely, six years from the damage occurring or three years from discoverability – all three periods run from different starting dates. Furthermore, the effect of the long stop may be restricted in cases where there is a continuing duty to check and revise design or a duty to warn – see Chapter 4.

These time limits do not apply where there is deliberate concealment (section 32 of the Limitation Act 1980 and see discussion at sections 12.3.2 and 12.4.7).

In *Perry* v. *Tendring District Council and Others* (1984), it has been held that by reason of the *Pirelli* decision, where a property was already damaged on sale to a subsequent owner, that subsequent owner had no right of action by reason of the fact that he did not have an interest in the property at the time when the damage occurred. This mischief has been sought to be corrected by section 3 of the Latent Damage Act 1986. The effect of section 3 is to seek to provide that a fresh cause of action accrues on the date on which the interest in the property is acquired.

12.2.4   Indemnity

An indemnity provision contained in a contract is subject to the rules relating to contract so that the cause of action will be statute barred six years (or 12 years if under seal) from the accrual of the cause of action. However, the words 'accrual of the cause of action' have been given a wide interpretation by the courts in the case of indemnities. The position is that the cause of action does not accrue until the liability of the person seeking to be indemnified has been established: *County and District Properties* v. *Jenner* (1976); *Green and Silley Weir* v. *British Railways Board* (1980). On the other hand, it is submitted that clauses 20.1 and 20.2 of JCT 80 do not constitute indemnities for the purposes of bringing proceedings relating to defects in the works.

12.2.5   Contribution

A claim to recover contribution under the Civil Liability (Contribution) Act 1978 will become statute barred two years from the date on which the right to contribution accrued (Limitation Act 1980, section 10). The meaning of the accrual of the right to recover contribution is defined as either:

(1)   Where there is a judgment in civil proceedings or an award in arbitration the relevant date is the day on which the judgment is given, or the date of the award in the arbitration.

(2)   Where (1) does not apply and where the person seeking contribution makes or agrees to make a payment (whether admitting liability or not) the relevant date is the date on which the agreement to make the payment was made.

Where an architect claimed contribution from a firm of consulting engineers and the architect subsequently died, the engineers contended that his claim did not pass to his personal representatives. However, the Court of Appeal held that the right to a contribution created by the Law Reform (Married Women and Tortfeasors) Act 1935 survived the death and passed to the architect's personal representatives: *Ronex Properties Limited* v. *John Laing Construction Limited* (1982).

12.2.6   Personal injuries

There are special rules for actions where there are personal injuries and none of the other rules apply (Limitation Act 1980, section 11(2)). The time limits fixed by the Act for personal injury actions apply to, amongst other things, damages for negligence or breach of duty, whether or not the duty arises under a contract, a statute or independently of contract (Limitation Act 1980, section 11(1)). A claim for damages in respect of personal injuries will be statute barred three years from either the date on which the cause of action accrued or the date of knowledge, if later, of the injured person. Where the injured person dies the cause of action survives the death for the benefit of his estate (Law Reform (Miscellaneous Provisions) Act 1934, section 1) and a claim will be statute barred three years after the date of death or the date of the personal representative's knowledge, whichever is the later (Limitation Act 1980, sections 11(4) and (5)). There are detailed provisions defining the date of knowledge and the courts are given a discretionary power to allow an action to proceed notwithstanding the periods that are fixed by statute (Limitation Act 1980, section 33).

12.2.7   Defective Premises Act 1972

A claim for breach of duty under section 1 of the Defective Premises Act, which only applies to dwellings, is deemed to have accrued at the time that the dwelling was completed or at the time when further work, needed to rectify the original work, is finished (Defective Premises Act 1972, section 1(5)). The effect of this provision, when read with the Limitation Act 1980, is that a claim for breach of duty under the Defective Premises Act will be statute barred six years after completion of the work or the completion of rectification work, whichever is the later.

This period set down by statute is to be contrasted with the period during which the NHBC will meet claims for major structural defects, which is ten years. The latter period is a period that arises by reason of a contract, not a statute.

12.3   Limitation and contract

12.3.1   Generally

This section deals in a little more detail with the limitation position in contract. The same principles apply whether the contract is a simple contract with a six year limitation period or a deed (or under seal) with a twelve year limitation period (see 12.2.1 and 12.2.2 above). The period runs from the date of accrual of the cause of action. In contract, it is usually accepted that the cause of action accrues when there is a breach of contract or a breach of duty, not from the date of its discovery. In many cases, therefore, the date will not be difficult to find. For example, where there is a contractual obligation to pay a fixed sum of money on a fixed date and the money is not paid, the cause of action will arise on that fixed date.

However, there are other factors that need to be considered. Where there is any doubt about a cause of action having expired, the courts are not inclined to remove the injured party's remedy and they tend to look favourably on an analysis of the position that will give a later date for limitation purposes. For example, in the case of contractors, the relevant date will not necessarily be the date on which the defective work was built and it will usually be the date when the works were completed. This is because the contractor has an overriding obligation to complete the works in accordance with the contract and it is, therefore, to the completion date rather than the date of construction of the defective part that regard should be had. Furthermore, where there is a provision in the contract for making good defects and a defects liability period, it may be possible to argue that time does not begin to run for limitation purposes until that period has expired.

A designer's breach of duty in relation to his design will usually arise at the time that he prepares the defective drawing, specification or instruction. However, it has been held that a designer has a continuing duty to check his design and correct errors: *Brickfield Properties* v. *Newton* (1971) and by reason of this principle, it will usually be possible to argue for a later date than the date of the breach. Indeed, it has been said that a professional man is engaged to see the work through, and if errors emerge he has a duty to correct them such that, where a writ was issued less than six years after practical completion of a building but more than six years after the breach complained of, an application to strike out the proceedings by reason of limitation failed and the proceedings were permitted to continue: *Chelmsford District Council* v. *T.J. Evers Limited and Others* (1983).

There is also the possibility of arguing for a later date by reason of the duty to warn (see section 4.11). In the case of supervision, the architect's duties will be spread throughout the construction period but, again, it will usually be possible to argue for a later date by reason of the designer's duties under the JCT and ICE contracts in respect of certification. For example, under JCT 80, the payment on interim certificates is in respect of 'work properly executed'; certifying payment in respect of work not properly executed, will be negligence and will take place at a date later than the negligent inspection.

12.3.2   *Fraud and concealment – contract*

However, all this discussion is subject to an extremely important statutory exception. Section 32 of the Limitation Act 1980 provides that the limitation period does not even start to run where the designer or contractor has been guilty of fraud, or has concealed any relevant facts from the injured party, or the action arises from a mistake (section 32, Limitation Act 1980). Furthermore, concealment includes the circumstances where there is a deliberate breach of duty which is unlikely to be discovered for some time (Limitation Act 1980, section 32(2)). Additionally, 'fraud' is not limited to the meaning that it has in the criminal law and includes deliberate concealing of a breach of duty: *King* v. *Victor Parsons & Co* (1973). The fact that the employer had engaged a clerk of works or inspectors to supervise the work will not prevent the employer relying on section 32: *The London Borough of Lewisham* v. *Leslie & Co Limited* (1978). However, it is clear that simply getting on with the building work and covering up shoddy or incompetent work may not be enough to establish deliberate concealment. In a case on the Limitation Act 1939, where the words were 'fraudulent concealment' as opposed to deliberate concealment in the 1980 Act, the Court of Appeal found that there ought to be more evidence than simply getting on with the work and that it may be necessary to show concealment from the clerk of works or the architect or the building owner himself: *William Hill Organisation Limited* v. *Bernard Sunley & Sons Limited* (1982). In that case, Lord Justice Cumming Bruce said:

> '[Counsel] submitted that, whenever a builder under a contract did shoddy or incompetent work, which was covered up in the due succession of the building construction work, so that when the building was complete the bad work was hidden from view, such facts constituted fraudulent concealment within the well known line of cases on equitable fraud. We do not accept this

proposition. Simply getting on with the work after something shoddy or inadequate has been done or omitted does not necessarily give rise to a legal inference of concealment or of equitable fraud. As Edmund-Davies LJ... put it in *Applegate* v. *Moss* (1971):

> "It is a truism that not every breach of contract arising from a defect in the quality of materials or workmanship justifies a finding of fraud. Some breaches can be so fundamental that, if deliberately and knowingly committed, they properly give rise to an inference of fraud by the parties in breach. Furthermore, the special relationship between the parties may facilitate such a finding."

As Lord Evershed MR said in *Kitchen* v. *Royal Air Force Association* (1958) referring to what Lord Hardwicke had said a long time before in relation to equitable fraud:

> "...it is I think, clear that the phrase covers conduct which, having regard to some special relationship between the two parties concerned, is an unconscionable thing for the one to do towards the other."

...The question always resolves itself into this issue: in all the circumstances were the facts such that the conscience of the defendant or of the subcontractor, for whose acts and omissions the defendant is vicariously liable, should have been so affected that it would have been unconscionable to proceed with the works so as to cover up the defect without putting it right?'

In *E. Clarke & Sons (Coaches) Limited* v. *Axtell Yates Hallet and Others* (1989), Judge Esyr Lewis QC, Official Referee, referred to the above passage from *William Hill* and concluded that, although that passage was concerned with the 1939 Act, the observation in that case 'simply getting on with work after something shoddy or inadequate has been done does not necessarily give rise to a legal inference of concealment or equitable fraud' applied also in relation to section 32 of the Limitation Act 1980.

In *Gray and Others (The Special Trustees of the London Hospital)* v. *T. P. Bennett & Son, Oscar Faber & Partners and McLaughlin and Harvey Limited* (1987), the application of building defects to section 32 of the Limitation Act 1980 was considered by Sir William Stabb QC, sitting as a Deputy Official Referee. A hospital had been built in 1962 and 1963. In 1979 a bulge was noticed in a panel of brickwork. Investigation revealed that inaccuracies in setting out concrete panels had resulted in a lack of fit of the brick cladding and, further, during construction concrete nibs had been severely hacked back to try to fit in the brickwork. The employer brought proceedings against the architect, the engineer and the contractor. Judgment was eventually given for the employer against the contractors but the allegations in negligence against the architect and the consulting engineer were held by the judge not to have been made out. It is to be noted that approximately 25 years elapsed between the construction of the building and the judgment of the judge and the tracing of witnesses had proved extremely difficult – indeed, the contractor was unable to call any witnesses at all.

In relation to the assertion by the employer that there was here a clear case of deliberate concealment, under section 32 of the Limitation Act 1980, the judge said that the facts were very different to those in *William Hill Organisation Limited* v. *Bernard Sunley & Sons Limited* (1982). In this case, the wrongful and destructive action had been deliberately concealed from the supervisors of the employer and it followed from the Act that the limitation period did not begin to run until the employer had discovered the concealment. That was November 1979 when the bulge in the brickwork was discovered. Further, the judge held that the effect of the deliberate concealment was to amount to fraudulent concealment and thereby to prevent the contractors from relying on the final certificate as conclusive evidence that the works had been properly carried out – the final certificate was rendered invalid on the principle that fraud unravels all.

In a case on the proper legal construction of section 32, the court has held that a deliberate concealment can have the effect of preventing the limitation period from running even when the deliberate concealment occurred after a date on which the plaintiff's cause of action arose: *Sheldon and Others* v. *R. H. M. Outhwaite (Underwriting Agencies) Ltd* (1993).

12.4   Limitation in negligence

12.4.1   Generally

This section deals with all claims in negligence, excepting those that result in personal injuries for which there are special rules (see 12.2.6).

A claim in negligence will be statute barred six years after the accrual of the cause of action. Although that definition is the same as that in contract, the effect is very different because the general rule in tort is that the cause of action accrues when the damage is caused and not from the date of the breach of duty. It may, of course, happen that in some cases the breach of duty and the damage occur at the same time and that will pose no problem. The difficulties arise where the breach of duty occurs many years before the physical damage, which is the consequence of the breach of duty, manifests itself. The breach of duty is unknown and lies dormant until physical damage appears. It is the consideration of this area of the law by the courts in recent years that has led to considerable difficulty.

The present position in relation to limitation in tort in building cases has been set out by the House of Lords in *Pirelli General Cable Works Limited* v. *Oscar Faber & Partners* (1982) although the effect on this case of *Murphy* has yet to be worked out in the courts. However, in order to understand the development to the position in that case, it is necessary to see how the law has developed since 1963. There are therefore three sections that follow, the first dealing with the history of the law, all of which has now been overtaken by *Pirelli*, then a second section dealing with the *Pirelli* test itself and the subsequent cases that have applied in *Pirelli*, and finally the effect of *Murphy* on *Pirelli*.

12.4.2   History of development of the law prior to Pirelli

In *Cartledge* v. *E. Jopling & Sons Limited* (1963), a personal injury case, the House of Lords decided that

'. . . a cause of action accrues as soon as a wrongful act has caused personal injury beyond what can be regarded as negligible, even when that injury is unknown to and cannot be discovered by the sufferer, and that further injury arising from the same act at a later date does not give rise to a further cause of action': (Lord Reid).

In other words, whether the injured person knew that he had been injured or not, time for limitation purposes began to run against him from the time that the personal injury was caused whether or not the damage could have been discovered. The result of that case was perceived as a mischief and in 1963 Parliament passed a Limitation Act to deal with that mischief. It extended the time limit, in personal injury actions only, for the bringing of actions where the material facts were outside the knowledge of the plaintiff.

In *Sparham-Souter* v. *Town and Country Development (Essex) Limited* (1976). The owners of two houses which had suffered damage as a result of faulty foundations brought actions against the builders and the local authority. Most of the local authority's breaches of duty, but not all, had occurred more than six years prior to the issue of the writ at a time when the house owners were not the owners of the property. It was held that the cause of action accrues when the damage is discovered by the injured party, or when he should with reasonable diligence have discovered it. It was said:

'When building work is badly done – and covered up – the cause of action does not accrue, and time does not begin to run, until such time as the plaintiff discovers that it has done damage, or ought, with reasonable diligence, to have discovered it': (Lord Denning MR).

This decision was therefore inconsistent with the finding of the House of Lords in *Cartledge* and was overruled in *Pirelli*.

The next case was *Anns* v. *London Borough of Merton* (1978), since overruled in *Murphy*. This was another claim against a local authority in negligence in relation to inspecting foundations. Limitation was not directly in point in this case but it was considered by the House of Lords. Lord Wilberforce said:

'In my respectful opinion, the Court of Appeal was right when, in *Sparham-Souter* v. *Town and Country Developments (Essex) Limited*, it abjured the view that the cause of action arose immediately on delivery, i.e. conveyance of the defective house. It can only arise when the state of the building is such that there is present or imminent danger to the health or safety of persons occupying it.'

It appeared to follow from this judgment that the *Sparham-Souter* decision was explained by saying that the cause of action is only complete when the damage is such that there is 'present or imminent danger to the health or safety of persons' occupying the building. This view was not accepted in *Pirelli*.

There was, therefore, a conflict between the view that the cause of action in tort accrues when the damage is suffered, whether or not the plaintiff knows of it, and the view that it only accrues when the plaintiff discovers the damage or ought, with reasonable diligence, to have discovered it. This was the issue that the House of Lords had to consider in *Pirelli*.

12.4.3 The Pirelli decision

The facts of *Pirelli* were that they had had a chimney built which was about 160 feet high. The chimney was made of precast concrete and had four flues. The refractory inner lining was made of a material which was unsuitable for its purpose. Cracks developed and eventually the chimney had to be partly demolished and replaced. The chimney had been designed by a nominated sub-contractor who was in liquidation but the trial judge had found that the defendant engineers had accepted responsibility for the design and that finding was not challenged in the House of Lords. The facts were such that the date upon which Pirelli had discovered the cracks was within six years prior to the issue of the writ and on the basis of the decision in *Sparham-Souter* there would be no limitation defence available to Oscar Faber. However, the engineers contended that the cause of action accrued at an earlier date and they suggested three possibilities:

(1) when Pirelli decided to act on their advice to install a chimney;
(2) the date on which the building of the chimney was completed; and
(3) the date on which the cracks occurred.

All those dates were more than six years before the issue of the writ and, accordingly, if any of those contentions were successful Pirelli would not be able to pursue their claim by reason of limitation.

The House of Lords found themselves unable to agree with the decision in *Sparham-Souter* and, in particular, Lord Fraser said that he could not agree with the distinction drawn in *Sparham-Souter* between personal injury which was clinically unobservable and latent damage in a building. He said:

> 'It seems to me that there is a true analogy between a plaintiff whose body has, unknown to him, suffered injury by inhaling particles of dust, and a plaintiff whose house has unknown to him sustained injury because it was built with inadequate foundations or of unsuitable materials. Just as the owner of the house may sell the house before the damage is discovered, and may suffer no financial loss, so the man with the injured body may die before pneumoconiosis becomes apparent, and he also may suffer no financial loss. But in both cases they have a damaged article when, but for the defendant's negligence, they would have had a sound one.'

The House of Lords therefore held, in the words of Lord Fraser:

> 'The plaintiff's cause of action will not accrue until *damage* occurs, which will commonly consist of cracks coming into existence as a result of the defect even though the cracks or the defect may be undiscovered and undiscoverable.'

It therefore follows that the House of Lords resolved the inconsistency between *Cartledge* and *Sparham-Souter* in favour of the former. The House of Lords found that the apparent approval of *Sparham-Souter* and the date of discoverability in Lord Wilberforce's speech in *Anns* was more apparent than real, and that Lord Wilberforce had not said, and did not imply, that the date of discoverability was the date when the cause of action accrued.

The Irish Court has refused to follow *Pirelli* by distinguishing various matters including finding that it would be unconstitutional to permit an action to be barred before the plaintiff knew he had one; discoverability remains the test in Ireland: *Brian Morgan* v. *Park Developments Limited* (1983).

12.4.4   *Pirelli and 'doomed from the start'*

Lord Fraser in *Pirelli*, having set out the test that the cause of action will not accrue until damage occurs, went on to say:

> 'There may perhaps be cases where the defect is so great that the building is doomed from the start, and where the owner's cause of action will accrue as soon as it is built, but it seems unlikely that such a defect would not be discovered within the limitation period. Such cases, if they exist, would be exceptional.'

He also said:

> 'It seems to me that, except perhaps where the advice of an architect or consulting engineer leads to the erection of a building which is so defective as to be doomed from the start, the cause of action accrues only when physical damage occurs to the building.'

The phrase 'doomed from the start' appeared as long ago as 1978 in *Batty* v. *Metropolitan Property Realisations* but there does not appear to be any direct connection between Lord Fraser's remarks in *Pirelli* and the remarks of the Court of Appeal in *Batty*. The effect of Lord Fraser's 'doomed from the start' phraseology appears at first sight to suggest that a designer should do his utmost to show that his design was doomed from the start because that is likely to give the earliest possible limitation date and hence the greatest likelihood of defending such an action on a limitation basis. In other words the more negligent the designer was, the better his position will be for the purposes of limitation. Unfortunately for those who have sought to rely on this *dictum* of Lord Fraser, the path has proved to be far from smooth.

Firstly, it should be said that Lord Justice Lawton has said in the Court of Appeal that Lord Fraser's reference in *Pirelli* to buildings that were doomed from the start was not necessary for the decision he made:

> 'I would regard it as a cautionary dictum so as to leave for future consideration problems which might arise in exceptional cases': *Ketteman and Others* v. *Hansel Properties Limited and Others* (1984).

In the *Ketteman* case, the Court of Appeal had found that the facts were broadly similar to those in the *Pirelli* case and that they were not exceptional – 'if anything, all too common'. When *Ketteman* reached the House of Lords, they also rejected the doomed from the start argument.

In another post *Pirelli* case, a specialist security firm had carried out work for the installation of a security gate at a private home in 1967. The house was later sold to a subsequent owner and in 1979 that house was burgled; the burglar had been able to break through the security gate without enormous difficulty. The new house owner brought an action against the specialist security firm and that firm sought to argue that their installation had been doomed from the start and that, accordingly, the action was statute barred. However, it was held that the security firm had installed the gate negligently in breach of a duty of care they owed to the subsequent purchaser and that the cause of action accrued when the damage occurred, namely, when the burglar broke down the security gate. It was said that this case was on all fours with the *Pirelli* case: *Dove* v. *Banhams Patent Locks* (1983).

In two cases, the court have had regard to the facts of *Pirelli* in assessing the doomed from the start argument on the particular facts of the case before them. The fact was that the cracks in the *Pirelli* chimney were the product of faulty materials and had developed within a year of construction, and yet even in that case the House of Lords has been unable to regard the design as doomed from the start. If the House of Lords did not regard those facts as being doomed from the start, then most cases will not be an exception to the general rule: *Kensington and Chelsea and Westminster Area Health Authority* v. *Adams Holden & Partners and Another* (1984) and *Ketteman and Others* v. *Hansel Properties Limited and Others* (1987). The Court of Appeal in a unanimous judgment took the view that Lord Fraser's dictum was to be limited to extreme cases: *Jones* v. *Stroud District Council* (1986).

Doomed from the start was also argued in *London Congregational Union Incorporated* v. *Harriss and Another* (1986). This was a case where there was inadequate drainage to deal with surface water and floodings and dampness had occurred. The Court of Appeal said that the concept of 'doomed from the start' had been very frequently invoked but rarely applied and that it would not be wise or useful to attempt to define the kinds of cases which would qualify for inclusion within the dictum. For a rare case where a building was found to be doomed from the start, see *Kaliszewska* v. *John Clague & Partners* (1984).

12.4.5 Pirelli *after* Murphy

Some difficulties have been created to the *Pirelli* decision in the light of the decision in *Murphy* in 1990, some seven years after *Pirelli*. *Pirelli* was classified in *Murphy* as a case of negligent advice falling under the principle set out in *Hedley Byrne* v. *Heller & Partners Limited*. Lord Keith, in *Murphy*, said:

'It would seem that in a case such as *Pirelli*, where the tortious liability arose out of a contractual relationship with professional people, the duty extended to take reasonable care not to cause economic loss to the client by the advice given. The plaintiffs built the chimney as they did in reliance on that advice. The case would accordingly fall within the principle of *Hedley Byrne*....'

The obvious difficulty with this approach is that it would mean that the decision in *Pirelli* as to the date on which the cause of action accrues is different to that found in *Pirelli*, namely the date on which Pirelli relied on the advice of Oscar Faber as to how to build the chimney; that is certain to be a date earlier than the date on which 'damage occurs, which will commonly consist of cracks coming into existence ... even though the cracks ... may be undiscovered and undis-

coverable'. *Murphy* was not a limitation case so care is needed in drawing conclusions from that analysis.

However, this issue was considered further in *Nitrigin Eireann Teoranta and
Another* v. *Inco Alloys Limited and Another* (1991). This case was concerned with a
specialist supplier, not a professional man, so it should be considered in that
light. It remains to be seen if the decision will be the first tentative step in this
dichotomy being resolved by the House of Lords, which is where it will have to
be resolved. A specialist pipe, containing explosive gases, had burst causing
damage to the plant around the pipe. Inco had manufactured and supplied the
pipe under a contract made in about 1981. It was accepted that the claim in
contract was statute barred and the case concerned only a claim in tort. The
parties agreed facts for the purposes of the trial on the preliminary issues, one of
which was whether, if there was a cause of action in tort, it was statute barred:

(1)   The pipe was manufactured by Inco and supplied in the summer of 1981.
(2)   'Damage' in the form of cracking occurred in the pipe itself in or before
      July 1983, and was discovered by Nitrigin that month.
(3)   Despite reasonable investigation, Nitrigin were unaware of the cause of
      the cracking, but took steps to repair it by grinding out the crack.
(4)   On about 27 June 1984 the pipe again cracked and burst causing damage
      to the structure of the plant around the pipe.
(5)   The writ was issued on 21 June 1990 alleging negligent manufacture and
      Nitrigin asserted it was issued within the period of limitation in tort.
(6)   It was assumed for this hearing (although denied) that the pipe in 1983
      and 1984 was defective and cracked by reason of negligence in manu-
      facture, namely inadequate distribution of titanium.

Nitrigin asserted that they did not acquire a cause of action in 1983 when the pipe
cracked but that the appropriate date was when the pipe burst on 27 June 1984.
Inco, on the other hand, said that the cause of action accrued in 1983 when the
pipe cracked and that the claim was statute barred. Mr Justice May decided that
Nitrigin did not acquire a cause of action in 1983 when the pipe cracked. The
cracking was damage to the 'thing itself' (as discussed in *D & F*), constituting a
defect of quality producing economic loss which was irrecoverable in negligence. He found that the cause of action accrued in June 1984. In coming to this
view, he distinguished *Pirelli* on the basis that the relationship between Inco and
Nitrigin was not one of a professional man and a client, that is to say that it did
not fall within *Hedley Byrne*. The judge said of *Pirelli*:

> 'The relevant damage was, however, damage to the chimney itself and *Pirelli*
> cannot, in my judgment, now be read as a wide general authority that cracking
> damage to a chimney itself affords a cause of action against anyone concerned
> with its supply, manufacture or construction. That would be plainly incon-
> sistent with *D & F* and *Murphy*. *Pirelli* remains the leading authority on the
> limitation point which it decided and it also remains, as Lord Keith explained
> in *Murphy*, as an example of a case where tortious liability arose from a con-
> tractual relationship with professional people. Although ... it might be pos-
> sible to argue in the House of Lords that the law as now understood should not
> afford a cause of action in negligence against a professional man in favour of a

client with whom the professional is also in contract, such a conclusion is not open to a court of first instance. [Counsel for Inco] urges me to find that the relationship between Nitrigin and Inco can be equated with that between the plaintiff and defendant in *Pirelli*. I am not so persuaded.

In *Pirelli* the defendants were a firm of professional consulting engineers engaged to advise and design. Here [Counsel] can glean no more from the pleadings than that Inco are alleged to be specialist manufacturers who knew or ought to have known the purpose for which their specialist pipes were needed. In my judgment, that is neither a professional relationship in the sense in which the law treats professional negligence nor a *Hedley Byrne* relationship.'

Unless and until this dichotomy is resolved in the House of Lords, it would appear to follow from this case that in limitation cases, *Pirelli* will govern the position where there is cause of action in negligence arising out of a relationship between a client and a professional man but that *Pirelli* may be distinguished in other cases, such as a supplier/client relationship. The law will no doubt be developing in this area.

12.4.6   *Other cases since* Pirelli

Cases based on *Pirelli*, and decided before *D & F* and *Murphy* now have to be read with some caution, particularly in the light of *Nitrigin*. However, the following cases are of interest subject to that caveat.

The question as to when damage occurs (rather than when the damage was discovered or ought reasonably to have been discovered) will usually be a matter for expert evidence. That is to say, expert evidence will have to be called to try to establish when the damage did occur. That is of course easier to say than it is to establish in practice and particular difficulties arise where there is a progressive problem which may have been minor to start with and grows more serious as time goes by. In *Kensington and Chelsea and Westminster Area Health Authority* v. *Adams Holden & Partners and Another* (1984), an Official Referee had to consider movement in artificial stone mullions which were part of an extension to Westminster Hospital. He took the view that damage occurred when movement occurred because by then the mullions were no longer safe and keeping the building weatherproof. The Official Referee went on to find that if movement was to constitute damage it had to be more than negligible and he was able to ascertain a date from the evidence upon which substantive movement occurred.

Immediately following the decision in *Pirelli*, a great many defendants were trying to decide whether they could prevent actions that had been started against them going any further. The issue arose as to what procedure in the courts was appropriate. This was considered in *Ronex Properties Limited* v. *John Laing Construction Limited and Others* (1981). This issue arises because a limitation point has to be taken by way of defence in proceedings and it can be argued that this therefore is a matter upon which a judge should hear evidence at trial and that it would not be right in any interlocutory proceedings before the trial to pre-empt what a judge might find. On the other hand, there is provision in the Rules of the Supreme Court in Order 18, rule 19(b) for a defendant to apply to the court to strike out the claim on the grounds that it is frivolous, vexatious, and an abuse of the process of the court. In the *Ronex* case, Lord Justice Donaldson said that such an application could be made in a very clear case and that the application could be supported by evidence in affidavit. Lord Justice Stephenson in the same case said:

> 'There are many cases in which the expiry of the limitation period makes it a waste of time and money to let a plaintiff go on with his action ... the right course is therefore for a defendant to apply to strike out the plaintiff's claim as frivolous and vexatious and an abuse of the process of the court, on the ground that it is statute barred.'

It was precisely this that happened in *National Graphical Association* v. *Thimbleby* (1983). The learned editors of *Building Law Reports,* in their commentary on this case, suggest that four features were present in that case and that it is these features that would be essential for a successful application to strike out:

'(1) The damage relied on by the plaintiffs and its cause or causes must have been identified in the pleadings (or be very clearly identifiable from them or from uncontroverted evidence).

(2) There must be clear and uncontroverted or uncontrovertible evidence that such damage in a material form arose prior to the commencment of the relevant limitation period.

(3) There must also be clear evidence that such damage was not attributable to any cause other than the cause or causes relied on by the plaintiffs.

(4) The defence of limitation must have been pleaded or otherwise clearly raised.' (See 25 BLR 92 and 93.)

There have been two cases where Official Referees have held that time begins to run in negligence from the time when a building is handed over. The first in time was *Tozer Kemsley and Millbourn (Holdings) Limited* v. *J. Jarvis & Sons Limited and Others* (1983). In that case, Judge Sir William Stabb QC, Official Referee, said of a defective air conditioning plant:

> 'It is a damaged article in the sense that it is not a sound one ... a building is a manufactured thing, and if it is unsuitable or defective when it is handed over it seems to me that the cause of action arises when the person acquires it in its defective state.'

That passage was adopted by Judge Smout QC, Official Referee, in *Chelmsford District Council* v. *Evers* (1983) where he said of the duty in tort:

> 'I think that an engineer who is concerned with designing and supervising the erection of a building owes a duty of care to the building owners and that the duty must continue until the building is completed.'

It does seem that the *Tozer* and *Chelmsford* cases have tended to equate what is said to be the *Pirelli* test with the date on which the damage could reasonably have been discovered. It is difficult to see how the strict application of the *Pirelli* test could produce such a result. It may be that the justification of these decisions is in the argument that architects, engineers and contractors have the opportunity to put defects right until the building is handed over; if that be the justification, then the relevant date would not necessarily be the date of practical completion but could be a later date running into the defects liability period. This approach was considered in *University of Glasgow* v. *W. Whitfield and John Laing Construction Limited* (1988), where the judge distinguished *Tozer* and *Chelmsford*.

Difficult questions arise in relation to an assessment of the date of accrual of a cause of action where there are limitation issues. An example of the application of the *Pirelli* case is *London Borough of Bromley* v. *Rush and Tompkins Limited* (1985). The plaintiff took occupation of an office block under a lease with a full repairing covenant in 1968. In 1975, cracks to the exterior of the reinforced concrete structure were noticed. Investigation revealed that the cause was corrosion of steel reinforcement. A writ was issued on 5 March 1980 against the builders and the consulting engineers, both of whom pleaded that the cause of action arose outside the six year limitation period before the issue of the writ. Three expert witnesses gave evidence to the effect that corrosion in the concrete would have been rapid and that hairline cracks would have appeared three to four years before the spalling occurred which was estimated to have been in or about late 1976 or early 1977. On the basis of this evidence, it seems likely that hairline cracks in the concrete came into existence during 1972 or 1973 and certainly before March 1974, being six years before the writ was issued. The judge found that the hairline cracking, even though not discovered, was the first manifestation of the existence of relevant and significant damage in the building. On this basis, the judge was able to find that the cause of action of the plaintiff came into existence more than six years prior to the issue of the writ in March 1980 and the plaintiff's claim was statute barred.

In *Secretary of State for the Environment* v. *Essex Goodman and Suggitt* (1985) the plaintiff, who had leased a large office block, was irrevocably committed to the lease by the end of July 1975. The building had been constructed in 1974 and 1975. On discovering defects, he sued the architects, engineers and surveyors. The surveyors had been engaged by the plaintiff to survey the premises in relation to the then proposed lease. In relation to the surveyors, a preliminary issue was heard as to whether the limitation period began to run from the date when the plaintiff became irrevocably committed to leasing the premises. In other words, the surveyors were contending that the cause of action was complete on the date on which the plaintiffs acted on the allegedly negligent survey, which in any view could not have been later than July of 1975 – the writ being issued on the 6 January 1982. The court found that the cause of action did arise on the date on which the plaintiffs acted on the surveyors report and, accordingly, the plaintiffs' claim was statute barred.

12.4.7   Fraud and concealment – negligence

In addition to all these problems, the provisions of section 32 of the Limitation Act 1980 also apply to claims in negligence so that where there is fraud, concealment or mistake, the limitation period does not begin to run until the injured party has discovered the fraud, concealment or mistake or could with reasonable diligence have discovered it (see 12.3.2).

12.5   Reform of the law

The reform of the law in the area of professional liability has been much discussed, particularly in relation to limitation of action. The EU have produced discussion documents as to the harmonisation of construction liability in Europe. One of the recommendations was a uniform period of limitation throughout the EU running from the date of completion of the project. At the time of writing this Fourth Edition, the Commission appear to be having second thoughts by inviting further discussion (by the end of 1993) as to whether any harmonisation is necessary. In the UK, the Department of Trade and Industry commissioned a report: 'Professional Liability: Report of the Study Teams', published by HMSO (April 1989). In respect of limitation, the Construction Professions Study Team proposed:

> '... to amend the Limitation Act 1980 (and thus the provisions introduced into the 1980 Act by the Latent Damage Act 1986) to achieve the following:
>
> - a limitation period for negligent actions in tort and in contract (whether or not under seal) of ten years from the date of practical completion or effective occupation (staged if necessary);
> - the ten years limitation period acting as a longstop extinguishing the right;
> - substituting for the term "deliberate concealment" some other term such as "fraudulent concealment".'

No action was taken by the government. However, it now seems that a report is to be presented to the Department of the Environment dealing with similar issues, probably as a result of the Commission's decision to seek further views as to whether or not harmonisation is necessary. Time will tell whether government will act this time on a report being prepared by distinguished people in the field.

Chapter 13

Arbitration or litigation or alternative dispute resolution

13.1 Proceedings and inspection

There are some general points that should be made as to what a designer should do when he first discovers that there is a problem which may lead in due course to litigation. The first step he must take, if he has professional indemnity insurance, is to notify the insurers of the problem. Most policies require that the insurers be notified as soon as circumstances likely to give rise to a claim come to the notice of the designer. If the designer delays in notifying his insurers, the insurers may have the right to avoid liability under the policy. The designer should not usually at this stage admit liability or offer any compromise, and he must not do so in any event without the written consent of his insurers.

What does the building owner intend to do? He may be about to uncover some work on site with a view to investigating the problem. He may have decided to proceed with remedial work. It is clearly desirable that the designer should attend any investigation on the site to try to establish the cause of the problem and to inspect during remedial works. It may be, for example, that the designer, by such inspection, is able to establish that a defect is directly attributable to bad workmanship. He should, therefore, keep detailed and careful notes of his site visits and take photographs which identify clearly the location at which they were taken and the date. It may be that it is necessary, in order to analyse the cause of the defect, to take samples of materials for analysis by specialist laboratories or materials testing engineers. Usually, there will be no difficulty in arranging all these matters with the building owner. However, where the building owner refuses facilities for inspection, a designer has two choices. He can accede, in which case the court or arbitrator are likely to draw conclusions from the building owner's refusal.

Alternatively the designer can seek an order from the High Court under section 33(1) of the Supreme Court Act 1981, requiring the building owner to give facilities for inspection. Such an order can be obtained whether or not there are other proceedings pending (Rules of the Supreme Court, Order 29, rule 7A). On such an application, the court has power to order any one or more of the following: 'inspection, photographing, preservation, custody or detention of property', 'the taking of samples' or 'the carrying out of any experiment on or with such property' which may become the subject matter of subsequent proceedings in the High Court. Where an arbitrator has been appointed, an application for an order for inspection can still be made to the High Court (Arbitration Act 1950, section 12(6)(g) although the arbitrator almost certainly has power to make such an order himself: *The Vasso* (1983)). It may be that all these inspections should be carried out by an independent expert, that is to say independent of the designers and, as to this, see below 'Experts' at 13.6.

Furthermore, the building owner has a duty to mitigate his loss; if he seeks to adopt a scheme for remedial works that is over elaborate and more extensive than that which is reasonably necessary, he may be failing in his duty to mitigate. It follows that where a building owner delivers his proposals for remedial works to the designer, the designer should be particularly careful to examine the proposals in great detail, usually with the benefit of the advice of his expert so that if it is necessary, a detailed criticism of the proposed scheme can be prepared. On the whole, courts are disinclined to pay too much heed to a negligent designer who argues that the building owner is spending too much money to rectify the defects caused by the designer's negligence; however, where the designer has the opportunity to raise these issues before the building owner has embarked on his remedial work scheme, the court may be inclined to give weight to the designer's view. In any event, it should be made clear in such correspondence that by giving his views, the designer is not, thereby, admitting any liability. For a careful consideration of the issues that arise where there are allegations of over elaborate repair see *Governors of the Hospital for Sick Children and Another* v. *McLaughlin and Harvey plc and Others* (1987) and also 9.1.1.4 and 9.1.6. Where there are professional indemnity insurers, all these matters should be considered with them and their consent obtained; it may be, of course, that they will exercise their right to appoint solicitors in which case, the designer has a duty to assist those solicitors in every way.

13.2   Arbitration or litigation

An arbitration can only take place where the parties to the dispute have expressly agreed to refer their dispute to arbitration. Such arbitration agreements are commonly found in building contracts and conditions of engagement. For example, the JCT with Contractor's Design Contract contains an arbitration clause at clause 39; as do the Architect's Appointment, SFA/92 and the ACE Conditions of Engagement. In order to be effective, these clauses must be part of the contract. In the case of the JCT Contract, SFA/92 and the ACE Conditions of Engagement, this will not usually be a problem: there are Articles of Agreement to be signed by the parties and these Articles incorporate the arbitration clauses. Unless the arbitration clause and the other conditions are expressly incorporated into the contract, the arbitration clause will be ineffective: see for example *Sidney Kaye, Eric Firmin Partners* v. *Leon Joseph Bronesky* (1973). The arbitration agreement does not need to be signed: *Excomm Limited* v. *A. A-Q. Bamaodah* (1985).

If there is no effective arbitration clause, then the dispute can be resolved by the High Court. The mere fact that there is an arbitration agreement does not mean that the dispute must go to arbitration.

Is arbitration to be preferred to litigation? There are many factors to consider.

13.3   Comparison

13.3.1   *Power of courts*

It has been held that the power given to an arbitrator under the JCT Standard

Form of Building Contract to open up, revise and review certificates is the procedure that the parties have agreed and that no court can open up, revise or review certificates or decisions of the architect: *Northern Regional Health Authority* v. *Derek Crouch Construction Co. Limited and Another* (1984). Although this had been common practice for Official Referees, the decision of the Court of Appeal in *Crouch* brought it to an end. It has been argued that if the parties choose to litigate rather than arbitrate, then the court should have the same power as the arbitrator. However, the Court of Appeal refused to imply such a term on the grounds that it was not necessary and said that, in view of the agreement that the parties had made as to the powers of the arbitrator, it would not be right to substitute machinery of that kind for the machinery of the courts. In building contract cases, this issue may be an overriding consideration in deciding whether litigation is to be preferred to arbitration.

Crouch was distinguished by an Official Referee in *Partington & Sons (Builders) Limited* v. *Tameside Metropolitan Borough Council* (1985) but was extended, by another Official Referee in *Oram Builders Limited* v. *Pemberton* (1986), to a JCT Minor Works Contract where there is no power given to the arbitrator in the arbitration clause to open up, revise and review certificates. Indeed, *Crouch* has even been extended to a situation where there was no arbitration clause at all: *Reed* v. *Van Der Vorm* (1985).

The Court of Appeal had another opportunity to look at the *Crouch* decision in *Benstrete Construction Limited* v. *Angus Hill* (1987). It may be that this case means that the court will not have jurisdiction only in cases where the arbitration clause expressly gives to the arbitrator power to open up, revise and review certificates. The report of the *Benstrete* case runs to only two pages and it may be that it would not be appropriate to place too much reliance on the *Benstrete* decision. *Crouch* will remain a deciding factor as to the choice between litigation and arbitration in many cases.

There had always been some doubt as to whether an arbitrator had power to grant rectification for mistake and award damages for misrepresentation and negligent mis-statement. However, the Court of Appeal in *Ashville Investments Limited* v. *Elmer Contractors Limited* (1987) decided that the arbitrator did have such power, at least on the basis of the widely worded jurisdiction in the arbitration clause in JCT 63.

However, in a case on different wording of an arbitration clause, the Court of Appeal said that negligent mis-statement, misrepresentation and collateral warranty claims did not fall under the jurisdiction of an arbitrator: *Fillite (Runcorn) Limited* v. *Aqua-Lift (A Firm)* (1989). The clause here read: 'Any dispute or difference or question arising under these Heads of Agreement shall be referred to a single arbitrator...' This was contrasted with cases with a wider scope of words, such as 'arising under, out of or in any way connected with'.

13.3.2 Technical disputes

One of the reasons that is often given for preferring arbitration to the courts is that a technically qualified arbitrator will be more readily able to understand the points at issue in a technically complex dispute. There are three things to be said about that. Firstly, High Court judges are used to dealing with complex technical matters. In particular, those judges in the High Court known as Official Referees grapple every day with complex technical matters, many of which are disputes relating to designers and contractors in the construction industry. Given adequate expert evidence and reasonable advocacy by counsel, there will be no problem dealing with technical disputes before a judge sitting on Official Referee's business.

Secondly, there is always the risk with a technically qualified arbitrator that he might prefer to have regard to his own knowledge rather than the evidence that is put before him by the parties. It has been said that a technically qualified arbitrator must use his own expertise to understand the evidence put before him and not to provide it. If he does otherwise, it is the equivalent of hearing evidence in private and the arbitrator is liable to be removed for misconduct by the High Court: *Fox* v. *P. G. Wellfair* (1981). This case was followed in two further cases: *Zermalt Holdings SA* v. *Nu-Life Upholstery Repairs Limited* (1985) and *Top Shop Estates Limited* v. *C. Danino* (1985).

Thirdly, an arbitrator is in a judicial position and is subject to many rules governing the practice of hearings such as the rules of evidence and natural justice. It is not unknown for arbitrators to err. For example, an arbitrator was removed for misconduct by the High Court after he had delivered an interim award when he had only heard one party's opening on a point of law, without hearing the other party's submissions. It was said that he had misconducted the proceedings by a clear breach of natural justice and because he had thereby lost the confidence of the parties, he should be removed: *Modern Engineering (Bristol) Limited* v. *C. Miskin & Son Limited* (1981). The Commercial Court has said that, where there is an issue of bias in the arbitrator, the test is whether an objective observer would have concluded that there was a significant risk of bias: *Tracomin SA* v. *Gibbs Nathaniel (Canada) Limited and Another* (1985). However, in another case this approach was doubted and it was suggested that the test might be whether a reasonable and fair minded person, sitting in court and knowing all the relevant facts, would have a reasonable suspicion that a fair trial would not be possible: *Cook International Inc.* v. *BV Handelmaatschappij Jean Devaux and Others* (1985). See also 'Point of law' at 13.3.5.

13.3.3   *Publicity*

Arbitration hearings are private and not open to the public. The hearing of a trial in the High Court is open to the public, but the preliminary hearings before the trial are in private known as 'in chambers'. It follows that in theory a party shunning publicity might prefer arbitration. In practice, the press do not take a great interest in the complexities of construction litigation in the High Court. Very few construction cases are reported in detail as news items in the national press, although it is more likely that reports will appear in the professional and trade press. It follows that the supposed advantage of arbitration in this respect is often much exaggerated. On the other hand, where there are allegations of professional negligence that are said to have caused death or personal injury, then it is likely that there will be publicity; there was considerable publicity in relation to the Abbeystead case: *T. E. Eckersley and Others* v. *Binnie & Partners and Others* (1987).

13.3.4 *Procedure and speed*

It is often thought that arbitrations are much less formal and the procedure is much less restrictive so that this enables a dispute to be disposed of more quickly than would be the case in court. Whilst arbitration can sometimes be faster, this is not always the case for a variety of reasons.

The procedure up to the hearing, whilst conducted in a slightly less formal atmosphere, is not necessarily any faster. There will usually have to be written pleadings and these can, and usually do, take as long to prepare in an arbitration as in the High Court, so there is no advantage in that respect. Furthermore, where one party is delaying an arbitration, arbitrators are less inclined to take draconian action than the courts would be in similar circumstances. Additionally, the House of Lords has indicated that the courts should be loath to interfere with an arbitration where there is delay: *Bremer Vulkan* v. *South India Shipping Corporation* (1981), *Paal Wilson & Co.* v. *Partenreederei Hannah Blumenthal* (1982). Since 1 January 1992 section 13A of the Arbitration Act 1950 has been in force. It was introduced by the Courts and Legal Services Act 1990 (section 102) as an aid to an arbitrator to deal with delay and reads as follows:

'13A(1) Unless a contrary intention is expressed in the arbitration agreement, the arbitrator or umpire shall have power to make an award dismissing any claim in a dispute referred to him if it appears to him that the conditions mentioned in subsection (2) are satisfied.

(2) The conditions are

(a) that there has been an inordinate and inexcusable delay on the part of the claimant in pursuing the claim; and
(b) that the delay
(i) will give rise to a substantial risk that it is not possible to have a fair resolution of the issues in that claim; or
(ii) has caused, or is likely to cause or to have caused, serious prejudice to the respondent.

(3) For the purpose of keeping the provision made by this section and the corresponding provision which applies in relation to proceedings in the High Court in step, the Secretary of State may by order made by statutory instrument amend subsection (2) above.'

This section gives arbitrators a power (so long as the parties have not excluded it by agreement) that they have not had before and it remains to be seen how it will be used in practice. However, it seems that delay prior to 1 January 1992 can be taken fully into account: *Yamashita-Shinnihon Steamship Co. Limited* v. *L'Office Chérifien des Phosphates Unitramp SA, The Boucraa* (1993). Such delay is relevant background so that it may be sufficient to show only modest delay and prejudice after 1 January 1992 in circumstances where there was delay and prejudice prior to that date.

Although the Arbitration Act 1950 provides a legal framework within which arbitration can take place, the precise procedure for the conduct of a particular arbitration has historically had to be decided by the parties and the arbitrator at the outset of each arbitration. That remains the position in relation to the standard forms of engagement of architects and engineers. However, in relation to disputes between the employer and the contractor, detailed arbitration rules now apply to disputes arising under the ICE Conditions of Contract and under the JCT forms.

13.3.4.1   *Institution of Civil Engineers Arbitration Procedure (1983)*

In the case of the ICE Conditions of Contract, 6th Edition, the rules are incorporated into the contract by express reference in condition 66(8)(a) of the contract. The rules are the Institution of Civil Engineers Arbitration Procedure (1983). This procedure has many useful aspects, as well as dealing with the important matters such as the preliminary meeting, pleadings and discovery, procedural meetings, preparation for the hearing and evidence. There is an option, for example, to opt for the Short Procedure which is designed to provide for as quick a resolution of simpler disputes as is possible, while trying to strike a balance between the need for natural justice and speed of procedure.

There are provisions setting out the power of the arbitrator in relation to the control of the proceedings, the ordering of protective measures (say, in relation to materials, documents and money) as well as power to deal with security for costs in favour of one or more of the parties and security for his own costs. A useful rule permits additional disputes under the same contract to be referred to the same arbitrator.

Express provision is also made for the arbitrator to make summary awards in a procedure which is on similar lines to the procedure for an interim payment in the High Court (under Order 29 of the Rules of the Supreme Court). Rule 14 permits the arbitrator to award payment by one party to another of a sum representing a reasonable proportion of the final nett amount which, in his opinion, that party is likely to be ordered to pay after determination of all the issues in the arbitration, and after taking into account any defence or counterclaim relied on by the other party. These rules do not seek to set out a definitive statement of procedure for each and every arbitration but rather to provide useful guidelines (some of which are flexible) which can form the basis of the particular detailed procedure of a particular dispute.

13.3.4.2   *JCT Arbitration Rules 1988*

In contrast, the Arbitration Rules published by the Joint Contracts Tribunal, adopt a less flexible approach. By amendments to most of the JCT contracts (but not the Prime Cost Fixed Fee Form), these Arbitration Rules will be incorporated into the arbitration agreement and will, unless they are deleted, form the procedure to be adopted in arbitrations arising under those forms. The contracts incorporating these Arbitration Rules (from 18 July 1988) include:

- The Standard Form of Building Contract 1980 Edition (and NSC/W, NSC/C)
- The Standard Form of Building Contract with Contractor's Design 1981 Edition
- The Intermediate Form of Building Contract for Works of Simple Content, 1984 Edition (including NAM/SC)
- The Standard Form of Management Contract, 1987 Edition (including Works

Contract/1 and Works Contract/2 and the Employer/Works Contractor Agreement)

- The Agreement for Minor Building Works, 1980 Edition.

As with the ICE Arbitration Procedure, these Rules set out a framework for the conduct of arbitrations but the framework is structured and in many respects rigid. The Rules deal with the preliminary meeting, separate provisions for a procedure without a hearing on documents only or a full procedure with a hearing, or a short procedure with a hearing, inspection by the arbitrator of work, goods and materials, a provision for the parties to be jointly and severally liable to the arbitrator for the payment of his fees and expenses, interim payment provisions for the arbitrator's fees, and an obligation on the claimant to take up the award of the arbitrator and pay his fees within ten days of the notification given by the arbitrator of the publication of his award. As with the ICE procedure, these rules set out that the arbitrator is to have certain powers and, in particular, what his powers are when a party is absent.

The mechanism for choosing which procedure is to apply is set out in Rule 4 which also deals, to some extent, with the conduct of the preliminary meeting. This Rule requires a preliminary meeting to be held within 21 days of the date on which the arbitrator has accepted the reference. At that preliminary meeting or within 21 days of the arbitrator's agreement to act, the parties have to decide whether the procedure without hearing, full procedure with hearing or the short procedure with hearing are to be used. Subject to some detailed rules, a short procedure with hearing arbitration can only take place where both parties accept that this procedure is to apply. If it does apply, then each party is to bear its own costs of the arbitration, unless the arbitrator thinks otherwise for special reasons; no guidance is given as to what this means and there is no express provision for the payment of the arbitrator's fees.

There is a very strict timetable set down so that the hearing has to take place within 21 days of the date when this procedure has been adopted as being appropriate. No evidence is permissible at the hearing, except such documents as have been delivered to the arbitrator by either or both parties not later than seven days before the hearing. At the end of the hearing, the arbitrator either gives his award forthwith orally (subsequently confirmed in writing) or publishes his award within seven days of the date of the hearing.

While the intended speed of this procedure is admirable, the quality of the justice achievable may turn out to be less than that attained under the usual procedure. It should not be forgotten that this procedure is not an interim procedure (of the adjudicator type) pending a full hearing of the arbitration, but rather a final arbitration. The mechanism for the choice of this procedure is in Rule 4 and the detailed procedure is in Rule 7.

The procedure without a hearing (on documents only) is found in Rule 5 and this procedure can only be adopted where the parties consent or where the arbitrator, after considering representations by the parties, directs that it should be used. This procedure requires that a statement of the claimant's case is to be served within 14 days after the date on which this procedure is adopted and within 14 days thereafter the other party has to serve a statement of defence and counterclaim if any. Within 14 days thereafter, the claimant can serve a statement of reply to the defence and a defence to the counterclaim. All those documents

are required to include a list of all the documents either party considers necessary to support any part of its statements and copies of those documents are also
required to be appended.

Subject to certain other matters, the arbitrator has to publish his award within
28 days after receipt of the last of the statements. There is no express right to
discovery of the other party's documents or to inspection or, indeed, any provision as to expert evidence. There are strict provisions as to time limits for
various steps (the implications of which are similar to Rule 6, and are discussed
below in relation to the full procedure). Here again, while the attempt at speed is
admirable, the quality of the justice achievable in anything but the simplest of
cases may be less than that attainable under the usual procedures.

The full procedure arbitration is to be found in Rule 6. It is this Rule that is
likely to be the Rule that will apply to anything but simple disputes. Again, time
limits are set out for taking various steps which apply (unless it is otherwise
agreed or the arbitrator otherwise directs). There are 28 days from the date when
Rule 6 applies for the service of a statement of case; 28 days thereafter for the
service of a defence and counterclaim, if any; and 14 days thereafter for the
service of a reply to the defence and defence to the counterclaim.

Further, the Rule requires that each of the parties' statements shall include a
list of the documents that they consider necessary to support their statements,
and with their statements they are required to serve a copy of the principal
documents on which reliance will be placed by them, identifying clearly in each
document the relevant part or parts on which reliance will be placed.

No doubt by reason of this provision, it is intended that generally there will be
no orders made for discovery. In the Rule there is no requirement on any party to
produce any documents which are embarrassing to their own case or helpful to
the other party. Bearing in mind that the procedure under this Rule will be the
procedure to be adopted in complex disputes, it is envisaged that most parties
will in fact be asking the arbitrator for an order for discovery in the usual way,
otherwise there is a serious risk of injustice.

Under this full procedure, there is no longer power for the parties (or their
solicitors on their behalf) to agree extensions of time for the service of any
documents that have to be served. If the parties agree to such an extension, it has
no effect until the arbitrator has approved that extension of time in writing. If any
time limit has not been complied with, the arbitrator has to deliver an 'unless'
notice, giving the offending party seven days to comply. If the party failing to
comply with such a notice is the claimant, then the arbitrator is required to make
an award dismissing the claim and ordering the claimant to pay the arbitrator's
fees and expenses and the costs incurred by the respondent. The arbitrator is not
obliged to make such an award where he is satisfied there is good and proper
reason why an application for an extension of time was not made. On the other
hand, if the defaulting party is the respondent, the effect is to disallow the
statement of defence. It will therefore follow that the respondent cannot put
forward any positive case but the claimant will still have to prove his case.

Although there is no provision in the JCT Rules for a summary award, there is
provision for an interim award. If such an interim award has been published in
favour of the claimant, then the arbitrator is given power to direct that the
respondent shall deposit money in respect of that award with a trustee-
stakeholder, pending a direction from the arbitrator as to who shall be paid the

money, or a joint direction of the parties (if the arbitrator has ceased to act), or directions of a court.

In all of these JCT procedures there is an attempt at speed and reduction of cost, both of which are to be welcomed. The use of these procedures over a period of time, if they are not extensively deleted from standard form contracts, will determine whether or not that speed and reduction in cost are achieved at the expense of the quality of the justice that will be provided. However, the step of taking away from the parties and giving to the arbitrator the final decision as to whether there should be an oral hearing, and the absence of standard directions in relation to discovery and inspection of the other parties' documents, are potentially dangerous in the context of achieving justice. Some devices that could have been used as an attempt to save cost, such as the ordering of exchange of proofs of evidence of witnesses of fact, have not been incorporated into the Rules.

Furthermore, although the arbitrator is given express power to take legal or technical advice after consultation with the parties, he is not expressly obliged, after having taken that advice, to give the parties the opportunity to make submissions to him in relation to that advice – arbitrators' failure so to do has resulted in several arbitrators being removed for misconduct (see e.g. *Fox* v. *P. G. Wellfair* (1981)).

There is no doubt that parties who are not legally advised may not understand the exceedingly strict time limits the Rules seek to impose, and that failure to comply with them can have very serious adverse consequences to both a claimant and a respondent. Although there are good arguments for giving the arbitrator powers to deal with unreasonable and unjustified delay by one party, it is questionable whether those powers need to be as draconian or to be operated in such a short space of time as those envisaged in these Rules.

One of the factors that will influence whether arbitration or litigation is ultimately faster is whether an early date for a hearing before the arbitrator or before the court can be fixed. Where a hearing is likely to last only a few days, there will probably not be much difference between arbitration and the courts; however, where the hearing is likely to last many weeks, the position may be different. Experienced arbitrators often have such long cases allocated in their diaries many months ahead and whilst they can fit in shorter hearings, it may be a long time before they can deal with a long hearing. The same position applies in the courts but it can be less severe.

It can, therefore, be seen that arbitration is not necessarily any faster than the High Court. However, where there is a very short point to be decided, there is little doubt that arbitration will be quicker if it is technical and the High Court will be quicker if it is a legal point. For example, it is now possible to deal very quickly with the legal issue of the meaning of a contract term in the Commercial Court.

13.3.5 Point of law

Where the issue in dispute between the parties is a point of law, there will not usually be any advantage in going to arbitration. This is particularly so where the point of law is difficult and appeals to higher courts are likely to result. Furthermore, the Arbitration Act 1979 restricts the appeals that can be brought to the court from an arbitrator's award.

13.3.6   Appeal to court

The guidelines that the court should adopt in deciding whether to give leave to appeal from an arbitrator are to be found in *Pioneer Shipping Limited* v. *BTP Tioxide Limited (The Nema)* (1982). Where the arbitrator is a judge of the High Court (appointed under section 4 of the Administration of Justice Act 1970), the court is required to adopt the same approach as if the appeal were from an arbitrator who was not a judge: *Seaworld Ocean Line Co. SA* v. *Catseye Maritime Co. Limited* (1988).

Further, the Court of Appeal has had to consider what the court's approach should be to granting leave to appeal from a decision of an arbitrator where a point of law was not argued in the arbitration but was sought to be argued on the application for leave to appeal under section 1(3) of the Arbitration Act 1979. In essence, the Court of Appeal found that the fact that a point which it was proposed to argue had not been argued before the arbitrator was not an absolute bar to the grant of leave to appeal, but it was to be taken into account in the exercise of the discretion provided by section 1(3). In circumstances where the failure to argue a point before the arbitrator had had the result that all the necessary facts were not found, this would be a powerful factor against the granting of leave, but that even in such a case, it might, in very special circumstances, be right to remit the award to the arbitrator for further facts to be found with a view to the granting of leave. Otherwise, if all the necessary facts had been found, the judge should give such weight as he thought fit to the failure to argue the point before the arbitrator and, in particular, he should have regard as to whether the point sought to be argued was similar to points that had been argued or, alternatively, whether it was a totally new point: *Petraco (Bermuda) Limited* v. *Petromed International SA and Another* (1988).

The usual practice in construction cases where application is made to the Commercial Court for leave to appeal is that the Commercial Court will transfer the case to an Official Referee for the substantive hearing. This practice was confirmed in *Tate and Lyle Industries v. Davy McKee (London) Limited* (1988).

13.3.7   Third parties

Unless the arbitration agreement expressly provides for it, or possibly where the parties agree, or in wholly exceptional circumstances (*Abu Dhabi Gas Liquefaction Co. Limited* v. *Eastern Bechtel Corporation and Another* (1982)), third parties cannot be joined into arbitration proceedings. Thus, where a designer wishes to claim contribution from a contractor, he will not be able to do so in his arbitration with the building owner; he can, of course, do so in separate proceedings but this would result in added and probably unnecessary expense. On the other hand, the High Court has rules providing for the joining in of other parties so that all the issues in dispute between all the parties can be resolved at the same trial. Accordingly, where there is a multiplicity of parties in a designer's dispute, the High Court is the only realistic option. It should be noted that the arbitration clause in the JCT with Contractor's Design Contract does not provide for multi-party arbitration. It follows that, where the contractor's sub-contractor has carried out his design negligently, unless the employer agrees, the contractor cannot join the sub-contractor into the arbitration proceedings. In such circumstances, there is now likely to be a multiplicity of proceedings with a building contract dispute in arbitration and an employer's dispute with his designer in another arbitration or before the High Court.

13.3.8 *Expense*

Most people in the construction industry believe that resolving a dispute by arbitration is considerably cheaper than proceeding in the High Court. The reality is exactly the opposite. At the end of the hearing, when the arbitrator has made his award, he has to deal with costs in the same way as the High Court. The general principle is that the party who wins has his costs paid by the party who loses. Insofar as the parties' costs of the hearing are concerned, they are likely to be much the same in arbitration as in court: these include the cost of preparing pleadings, making any necessary applications to the arbitrator or the court, discovery of documents, preparation for trial and the hearing itself. However, the use of a courtroom and the judge's time is free to the parties and is an expense of government. In an arbitration, the parties are responsible for appointing the arbitrator; it is a private arrangement and the arbitrator charges for his services. Additionally, a room has to be found for the hearing of the dispute. These two items of expense can be very substantial indeed in a lengthy hearing. Furthermore, nowadays it is not at all unusual for arbitrators to seek a payment on account of their fees in advance and to stipulate their entitlement to be paid for any period that they have set aside for a hearing whether or not it takes place. The reason for this is that so many disputes are settled near to the hearing date that it would be unfair to expect an arbitrator to set aside a considerable period of his professional time, and then find at the last minute that he will not be gainfully employed for that period. Sometimes these cancellation fees are on a sliding scale so that the nearer the parties are to the hearing date when they settle, the greater the payment to the arbitrator.

13.4 Where the designer prefers arbitration

If the building owner starts an arbitration, then there will be no problem because the designer has what he wants. However, what happens where the building owner starts a High Court action and the designer prefers arbitration?

Section 4 of the Arbitration Act 1950 provides a procedure whereby a designer served with a High Court writ can apply to the court for an order that the dispute be referred to arbitration and the High Court proceedings be stayed. In this context, the 'staying' of High Court proceedings means that they are to all intents and purposes at an end. The application has to be made to the court before the designer has taken any 'steps' in the High Court proceedings. In practice, this means that the designer must make his application to the court for a stay and do nothing further in the High Court proceedings. In non-domestic (i.e. international) arbitrations, the court has no discretion and must order a stay of the High Court proceedings (section 1, Arbitration Act, 1975). Domestic arbitration agreements are defined in section 1(4) of the Arbitration Act 1975:

'(4) In this section "domestic arbitration agreement" means an arbitration agreement which does not provide, expressly or by implication, for arbitration in a State other than the United Kingdom and to which neither –

(a) an individual who is a national of, or habitually resident in, any State other than the United Kingdom; nor

(b) a body corporate which is incorporated in, or whose central management and control is exercised in, any State other than the United Kingdom;

is a party at the time the proceedings are commenced.'

The court is not obliged to stay High Court proceedings in relation to a 'domestic dispute'; the power is discretionary and the court will take many factors into account in deciding whether or not to send the dispute to arbitration. For example, the designer must be ready and willing both when the High Court proceedings were commenced and at the time of his application to stay, to do everything necessary to the proper conduct of the arbitration (Arbitration Act 1950, section 4). There must be a dispute because if there is no dispute, there is nothing that can be referred to arbitration. Under section 4, the court has power to impose terms if it decides to order a stay and one such term that is sometimes imposed is security for costs: *C. M. Pillings & Co. Limited* v. *Kent Investments Limited* (1985).

The courts are given powers under section 24 of the Arbitration Act 1950 to make an order that the arbitration agreement shall cease to have effect and for the revocation of the authority of the arbitrator in circumstances where there is any question as to whether 'any such party' has been guilty of fraud. It was thought until recently that the court would usually make such an order where there is an allegation of fraud – fraud having its ordinary meaning and not having its meaning extended into calling into question the professional reputation or integrity of the designer: *Attorney General of Hong Kong* v. *Aoki Construction Co. Limited* (1981). However, in *M. & D. Cunningham-Reid* v. *I. Buchanan-Jardine* (1987), the Court of Appeal decided that section 24 was not restricted to situations where the stay was being opposed by the party charged with the fraud and further that, although there was in this case a serious charge of fraud (the defendant it was alleged had arranged for dummy invoices to be made up by suppliers and had used monies received from the other party for personal expenses), there was no good reason why the matter should not be permitted to proceed to arbitration and a stay was granted. A particularly important matter to which the court will give much weight is whether the dispute is substantially concerned with a point of law; it is unlikely that a stay would be granted where a mere point of law is involved. The court ought to exercise its discretion by refusing to stay proceedings to arbitration where there are allegations of incompetence, negligence and impropriety against a professional man such that his reputation is at stake: *Turner* v. *Fenton and Others* (1982), *Binnie & Partners* v. *Swire Chemsyn Limited* (1982), High Court of Justice of Hong Kong.

Where there are three or more parties to the High Court action, and one or more of the agreements between those parties contains an arbitration clause, the court is likely to refuse to send any part of the dispute to arbitration. The reason is that where the court grants a stay, substantially the same disputes would be litigated in separate proceedings with the result of increased cost and the risk of different findings in the court and in the arbitration. The leading case is one where a building owner brought an action in the High Court against his architect and his contractor. The contractor sought to have his dispute with the building owner referred to arbitration and the High Court proceedings stayed. The court refused to order a stay: *Taunton-Collins* v. *Cromie* (1964). However, the established views on these matters are changing. For example, the High Court was quite prepared to permit various parts of the disputes referred to in *Northern Regional Health Authority* v. *Derek Crouch Construction Co. Limited and Another* (1984) to be heard in arbitration and in the High Court. Indeed, the decision in that case that the courts did not have power to deal with certain matters reserved to the arbitrator under the standard JCT contract makes it inevitable that such a position will arise.

Furthermore, the Hong Kong courts have refused to be bound by the *Taunton-Collins* v. *Cromie* approach. In *Wharf Properties Limited and Others* v. *Eric Cumine Associates and Others*, the owner of a large development was involved in proceedings with his contractor relating to delay and defects and the contractor had claims for payment. The architects and various other parties (20 in total) were in the proceedings. The contractor and some of the sub-contractors (who had tripartite arbitration agreements) sought a stay under the Hong Kong equivalent of section 4 of the Arbitration Act. The employer argued that it should be allowed to disregard the arbitration clauses because all the claims and cross-claims arose out of the same facts and should be heard at the same time in order to avoid multiplicity of proceedings. However, the court emphasised that there is now a presumption in favour of the enforcement of arbitration agreements and ordered a stay of the court proceedings against the main contractor and the other defendant who had applied for a stay. It was said that the employer, having entered into an arbitration agreement, had created the difficulties which were of his own making: *Bulk Oil (Zug)* v. *Trans-Asiatic Oil Limited SA* (1973).

A particular difficulty arises where there is a limitation problem. Consider the position where a building owner has issued a writ against his architect and contractor within the limitation period but has not delivered a notice to concur in the appointment of an arbitrator in circumstances where his High Court proceedings are not statute barred but arbitration proceedings would be statute barred. (The same can happen vice versa.) This often arises where the building owner has issued his writ in time and then waited to serve the writ. (A writ has to be served within four months of its issue.) In these circumstances, a contractor might apply to the court for an order seeking a stay of the High Court proceedings. If he were successful, the building owner's claim against him would be statute barred and the architect would be unable to claim contribution from the contractor: Civil Liability (Contribution) Act 1978, section 1(3); *Wimpey* v. *BOAC* (1955). The fact that the building owner's proceedings in the arbitration would be out of time is no good reason to refuse the stay: *Bruce* v. *Strong* (1951). In these circumstances, in one case a stay has been granted and in another case it has been refused: *The Jemrix* (1981); *The Eschersheim* (1974). The report of the case in which a stay was granted – *The Jemrix* – does not indicate that the court was referred to *Taunton-Collins* v. *Cromie* and it was held that the fact that identical issues might be litigated in the court and in arbitration should not prevent a stay being granted. However, in that case there was likely to be a multiplicity of proceedings in any event because there was an international element and in such cases, the court has no discretion and must order a stay (Arbitration Act 1975, section l(4)).

13.5   Where the designer prefers a court

Where the building owner starts proceedings in the High Court, the designer is not obliged to go to arbitration simply because there is an arbitration agreement; he can defend the High Court proceedings in the usual way.

Where the building owner wishes to arbitrate, the designer is in a more difficult position. Certainly, if he goes along with the arbitration and takes part in it, it will be almost impossible to then proceed in the court. However, when the designer first receives the notice to concur in the appointment of an arbitrator, he could at that stage, before the arbitrator has been appointed, start his own High Court proceedings; in such a case, he is likely to be met by an application to the court on the part of the building owner for a stay of the proceedings under section 4 of the Arbitration Act. The designer may defeat that application where there are a number of parties on the basis of *Taunton-Collins* v. *Cromie.*

13.6   Experts

The rules of evidence generally prevent a witness from giving evidence of his opinions; he is limited to giving evidence of facts that are within his own knowledge. Thus, a designer accused of professional negligence can give evidence as to what he did but he will not usually give evidence of his opinion as to what was the generally accepted practice of designers at the time. This rule against the giving of opinion evidence extends to witnesses not being permitted to give their opinion on the facts that have been established in other evidence. However, where a professional person intends to give expert evidence himself, or to call his employees or former employees to give such evidence, the court can require such evidence to be disclosed to the other party in the form of written reports: *Shell Pensions Trust Limited* v. *Pell Frischmann & Partners* (1986).

However, the rule is relaxed in the case of expert witnesses who are permitted to give evidence of their opinions. It is sometimes said that an expert is independent. Each party may have an expert and their views may differ. Indeed, they would not be called to give evidence by a particular party if their evidence did not support that party's position. To that extent, whilst their opinions are honestly held, expert witnesses cannot be said to be independent. A witness will be an expert if he has acquired by training or experience sufficient expert knowledge to express an opinion. In other words, he need not possess degrees or be a member of a professional institution provided he has the necessary experience.

In many cases involving the building industry, expert evidence will be given. However, in the field of professional negligence, expert evidence is essential in order to assist the court to ascertain whether reasonable skill and care has been shown by the designer. In the absence of such evidence, the claim will fail: *Worboys* v. *Acme Investments Limited* (1969). However, Judge Peter Bowsher QC, Official Referee, took a different view on particular facts and evidence in *University of Glasgow* v. *W. Whitfield and John Laing Construction Limited* (1988). In many cases, it will be appropriate for an expert to be instructed at an early stage of the dispute, even before litigation has started. His opinion is likely to be invaluable to professional indemnity insurers and lawyers and will be of great assistance in assessing at an early date the strengths and weaknesses of the designer's position. He can also advise on the remedial works proposed by the building owner and any tests or samples that should be taken before those remedial works are carried out. When he is acting in that position exclusively, or dominantly, on the instructions of solicitors, his advice, written opinions and reports will be privileged from production to the other parties.

As to the giving of expert evidence in court, there are detailed provisions in the Rules of the Supreme Court (Order 38) which are in accord with the Civil Evidence Act 1972. The first and most important point is that expert evidence cannot be given at a trial unless the party wishing to give it has obtained the leave of the court (Order 38, rule 36). In other words, the court has a discretion and in exercising its discretion it may impose terms. In particular, the court may, and usually does, give leave on the basis that the expert evidence should be disclosed to the other party in the form of a report on a fixed date before the trial (Order 38, rule 38). The usual order is that the parties will exchange expert's reports that is to say they will each disclose their reports to the other at the same time. The purpose of this rule is to enable the parties to see the other party's expert evidence and thus not be taken by surprise and to try to see if there are any areas where the experts agree so as to limit the evidence that needs to be given to the court. Sometimes, the court, in exercising its discretion to grant leave will also order that the experts' reports be agreed, if possible. This procedure means, in practice, that the parties need to consider the necessity for expert evidence at an early stage in the proceedings in order to obtain the necessary leave. The court may be loath to give leave at a late date but this is a matter of degree; an application six months before the trial will almost certainly be successful whereas an application made during the trial may be unsuccessful. Indeed in *Winchester Cigarette Machinery* v. *Payne* (1993), the Court of Appeal re-stated the position as to leave to call expert evidence where leave had been refused by the judge three weeks before the trial was due to start. The procedure set out above will also apply in arbitrations.

The expert's report prepared for the purposes of exchanging with the other party is an extremely important document. Its aim is not only to set out the evidence that that expert will wish to give at the trial but also it can serve a tactical use in persuading the other party, before the trial has started, that his case is weak. However, an expert should never overstate his client's position because he will only do him a disservice. The contents of the report and its presentation are important. Firstly, the expert must not deal with any legal issues. It will usually be necessary for him to set out some facts and probably a brief history of the problem but if none of these matters are within his own knowledge, he should say so expressly in the report. If there are allegations made that a design is defective then he should set out the documents prepared by the designer that he has looked at and then express his opinion as to whether the design shows an exercise of reasonable skill and care; in so doing, he may wish to refer to the general practice of designers in relation to that type of design.

If the claim against the designer relates to negligent supervision, the expert will wish to deal with various aspects of supervision, including whether it is his opinion that the visits made to the site by the designer were sufficiently often and sufficiently detailed; he will wish to deal with the usual practice of designers and the position of clerk of works and inspectors so as to enable him to form an opinion as to whether the designer fell short of the standards expected of a reasonably competent member of his profession. The expert will probably consider the contents of his report with solicitors and counsel before the final version is prepared; some consultation is, of course, entirely proper but there has been judicial criticism of lawyers who exert too much influence over their experts. It has been said that:

> 'Expert evidence should be, and should be seen to be, the expert's independent product uninfluenced by the exigencies of litigation as to form or content. Otherwise, it was likely to be not only incorrect but self defeating': Lord Wilberforce in *Whitehouse v. Jordan and Another* (1980).

Where the amount of damages claimed against a designer is also in dispute, expert evidence may be necessary in relation to that. To the extent that it is a matter of principle in that it is alleged the repairs were over elaborate or unnecessary, this will be a matter of the expert evidence of a designer. To the extent that the dispute relates to valuation of remedial works, particularly where the remedial works have not been executed at the time of trial, then that is a matter for an expert chartered surveyor. If diminution in value of the property is claimed then expert evidence will be needed from an expert estate agent (chartered surveyor).

13.7   Alternative dispute resolution

The main methods of settling disputes, other than litigation or abitration, are:

- negotiation
- alternative dispute resolution (ADR).

13.7.1   Negotiation

Negotiation is voluntary but is only likely to succeed where there is a willingness on the part of both parties to settle or one party has an important sanction against the other party; it is usually private and, more often than not, without prejudice. The parties control their input to the process. It is quick, cheap, uncomplicated and gives the parties control over what they are doing.

If parties are sensible commercial bodies, why is it that a substantial number of disputes reach an impasse without settlement? The usual reasons are:

- failure in communication – have they talked at all?
- lack of information – do they have all the facts?
- wrong people talking – they are not empowered to settle and/or are too involved in the issues and/or cannot see the wood for the trees.
- emotional involvement – is someone's job at risk, depending on the outcome?
- poor negotiating skills – these are widespread. They can be taught but rarely are.
- genuine disagreement, in good faith, about the legal/financial outcome.
- unrealistic expectation of the legal/financial outcome.

13.7.2   Litigation/arbitration

These are involuntary processes in the sense that once the process is started, the other party has to take part. This is a particular problem with multi-party disputes. The end result is an enforceable judgment/award which is binding on the parties, subject to appeal. The right of appeal from an arbitrator is limited. The decision reached is *imposed by a third party* judge/arbitrator who has no regard to anything other than the parties' legal rights.

The procedure in court is based entirely on an analysis within rigid rules of the *rights* of the parties: no regard can be given to the *interests* of the parties. The outcome is a decision based on principles and precedents supported by a reasoned opinion (not necessarily a reasonable opinion or an opinion which is 'fair'). The full hearing of a trial in the High Court is open to the public. Arbitration is private. The costs risk in both arbitration and litigation is very high – sometimes prohibitive.

13.7.3   Alternative dispute resolution (ADR)

Alternative dispute resolution is a generic expression for a variety of methods of resolving disputes as an alternative to litigation or arbitration. The most common types encountered are the 'mini-trial' and mediation. There are other variations on this theme but they are beyond the scope of this book. In a mini-trial, presentations are made to executives from each party. Those executives should not have been involved with the problem that now needs to be resolved. After listening and questioning the executives then try to settle the dispute with, or sometimes without, the aid of a neutral third party. This process is non-binding and without prejudice unless a settlement is reached. Mediation is used more frequently and a more detailed discussion now follows.

13.7.4   Mediation

Mediation is a principled negotiation with the assistance of a neutral third party who does not impose a solution but assists the parties to achieve consensus. The process of itself, if handled skilfully by the mediator, generates a desire to settle. Some of the main aspects of the process are:

- it is a voluntary process;
- if there is agreement, there can be enforcement as a contract;
- the mediator – selected by the parties;
- informal/flexible procedure;
- case presentation is flexible – can include *interest* based solutions;
- facilitative (the mediator assisting the parties), or, evaluative (the mediator stating a non-binding opinion on a point to assist in reaching a consensus); these can be as a combination of facilitative and evaluative approaches;
- there is no imposed solution;
- it is a private process;
- it is quick and relatively cheap;
- if mediation fails, arbitration/litigation can still proceed.

13.7.5   Comparison

LITIGATION/ARBITRATION	ADR
Protagonists – Adversarial with binding decision imposed.	Consensual – parties agree to seek business solution assisted by (advisers and) neutral.
Procedural rigidity – procedures, timetable, representation, evidence, costs.	Control – parties agree timetable, procedure, agenda. Outcome is contractual agreement.
Positional – 'win or lose'. Parties assert maximum claims. Boxed into positional stances by the process.	Cost-saving – emphasis on key issues, not on exploring every corner to substantiate case or meet other side's evidence.
Past-looking – analyse 'history' of issue and evidence and relate to legal precedent.	Continued business relations – emphasis on interests, on problem-solving, on business solutions.
Public domain – court hearing open to public and press. Arbitration private.	Confidentiality – private meetings to explore and agree settlement.
Pressure of costs, delay, adversarial postures, risks lead to late 'collapse' into settlement. Final arguments often on how to divide costs.	Creative – commercial/business solutions not limited by legal rules or precedent, nor by historical perspective.

13.7.6   Cases appropriate for ADR

The following indicate some reasons why ADR might be considered:

- the need to preserve business relations/reputation;
- having a 'final shot' at a settlement;
- concern about the costs/risks/stress of litigation/arbitration;
- the disputes are too complex to manage in negotiations;
- the need for privacy;
- difficulty in communication between the parties;
- the need for creative thinking/a fresh mind;
- a desire for an independent appraisal of the case (before the 'win/lose' outcome of formal proceedings);
- a desire for fairness, not power, in business relationships;
- the pursuit of business interests rather than adopting strict legal positions;
- where the negotiation needs third party assistance to move forward;
- a legal ruling will not solve the basic problems;
- and most importantly – the parties both wish to explore settlement.

13.7.7   When not to use ADR

It is sensible to reconsider the use of ADR from time to time during proceedings because the factors which previously caused a rejection of ADR may change with changes in circumstances. However, ADR is highly unlikely to be of any use in the following situations:

- one or both parties has no genuine interest in settlement (e.g. the party at fault has no money);
- one party requires legal precedent (e.g. an insurer with a point of principle extending to many thousands of insurance claims);
- one or both parties needs a public hearing (perhaps to clear a reputation);
- a need for an injunction (to preserve rights/property/money);
- where direct negotiations are likely to be effective;
- where legal action is needed to create a necessary sanction for negotiations.

13.7.8   What is the best time for ADR?

There is no 'best time' but the following are some pointers: mediation is non-binding. You can walk away at any time if it is not proving fruitful. Once proceedings are started, more often than not contact between the parties direct is reduced. If that is a possible bar to negotiations, ADR can remove it. The earlier the use of ADR, the greater the potential benefit in terms of cost, time saving and preservation of business relations, but all parties must have a genuine interest in seeing an end to the dispute.

13.7.9   How is the ADR process started?

It will not start, even if both parties think it is a good idea, if one party does not suggest it. The difficulty here is the natural concern, which also occurs in negotiation, of any approach being perceived as a sign of weakness. ADR is capable of being sold as a positive initiative to help both parties; putting ADR forward as a threat (e.g. the mediator will soon tell the other side what a bad case they have got) is unlikely to be productive. The Centre for Dispute Resolution (CEDR) do offer the facility of making contact with the other parties in a dispute if that were thought to be helpful.

A better way forward is to have a clause in the contract (i.e. from before the time when the dispute arose) obliging the parties to mediate. CEDR produce standard clauses. Even though there may be some doubt as to the certainty (and therefore the legal effect) of such clauses, they do at least create the basis for a discussion as to whether or not ADR is appropriate.

How are the standard forms of contract rising to the challenge of ADR? The answer is not very well, if at all.

The ICE Conditions of Contract, 6th Edition, contain a provision for 'Conciliation' (clause 66(5)). This provision gives a right to conciliation on the following basis:

(1)   Conciliation can only take place where no notice of arbitration has been given *and* the 'Engineer's Decision' has been given or the time for the giving of his decision has expired. These provisions limit the usefulness of conciliation.

(2)   The conciliation takes place under the 'Institution of Civil Engineers' Conciliation Procedure' – see below.

(3)   The conciliator's decision is deemed to have been accepted as a settlement unless arbitration is started within one calendar month.

(4)   The ICE conciliation procedure is fairly rigid; it envisages documents

(tantamount to pleadings) from each party with a right of reply in writing; the conciliator can hear both parties, hear evidence (but is not bound by the rules of evidence) and he can hear the parties separately. He has the power to express preliminary views but the whole thrust of the procedure is to arrive at a point where the conciliator makes a recommendation – in other words, this is substantially an evaluative process rather than a facilitative process.

In summary, the ICE procedure is better than nothing but an opportunity appears to have been lost to create a truly flexible process.

On the other hand, the RIBA, ACE and JCT have yet to take a serious step down the ADR route. Indeed, SFA/92 and the ACE conditions contain no mediation machinery.

13.7.10 *Choosing mediators*

The mediator's role is a skilful, dynamic process which should not be attempted by the untrained. CEDR maintains a list of approved mediators, all of whom have been through four days of intensive training and been assessed by CEDR during that training. They have to have been present at mediations (in an observer capacity) prior to being put forward as mediators by CEDR. Most importantly CEDR receive reports back from the parties as to the competence of the mediator. CEDR has the power to remove mediators from the approved list.

13.7.11 *Cost/time*

The main costs at November 1993 at CEDR were:

SMALL CLAIMS SCHEME

		Value of Claim	Mediation Fee Per Party Per Day
(1)	Mediation Fees	Up to £20,000	£350
		£20,000 to £35,000	£400
		£35,00 to £50,000	£450

(2)   Mediation Expenses such as room hire, mediator's travel expenses etc.

STANDARD FEE LEVELS

		Value of Claim	Mediation Fee Per Party Per Day
(1)	Mediation Fees	£50,000 to £250,000	£750
		£250,000 to £1 million	£1,000
		£1 million to £10 million	£1,250
		£10 million upwards	£1,500

(2)   Mediation Expenses such as room hire, mediator's travel expenses etc.

(3)	Arrangement Fee	Members of CEDR	No charge
		Non-members	£500
		Clients of member firms	£300

The average mediation is over in between one and two days; in order to have an effective mediation, there may well be considerable fees incurred in the preparation for mediation. Indeed, it would be pointless to arrive at the mediation either wholly unprepared or with inadequate preparation. Overall, CEDR's experience is that in successful mediations no more than two months on average elapses between the start and the finish of the whole process.

13.7.12   The way ahead?

ADR is catching on, but slowly in the UK. The Lord Chancellor talks about it but does not seem inclined to fund it. One Official Referee, Judge Fox-Andrews QC, is on occasions ordering ADR with a one month stay on the court proceedings. Presumably he is doing so by consent of the parties, otherwise he would not have the power to make such an order.

The factors that will affect how ADR proceeds are:

- a greater awareness of the process amongst lawyers and clients
- some firms of lawyers see ADR as PR – not as a really useful tool
- other lawyers see it, usually through ignorance, as a waste of time, effort and cost
- an acceptance that, in appropriate cases, there is little to be lost and, potentially, a lot to gain
- overcoming the 'fear of weakness' in suggesting it
- incorporating ADR clauses (widely drawn – not like the ICE, see 13.7.9) in contracts, particularly in standard forms
- the cost of litigation and arbitration
- the uncertainty of litigation and, particularly, arbitration
- whether there is any progress towards court-annexed ADR.

Table of Cases

Note The following abbreviations are used:

AC	Law Reports, Appeal Cases
ALJR	Australian Law Journal Reports
All ER	All England Law Reports
BCLR	British Columbia Law Reports
BLR	Building Law Reports
C & P	Carrington & Payne Reports
CB	Common Bench
Ch.	Law Reports, Chancery Division
CILL	Construction Industry Law Letter
CL	Current Law
CL & Fin.	Clark and Finnelly Reports
CLD	Construction Law Digest
CLR	Commonwealth Law Reports
CLY	Current Law Year Book
Co Law	Company Lawyer
Com Cases	Commercial Cases
Com. LR	Commercial Law Reports
Con LR	Construction Law Reports
Const LJ	Construction Law Journal
CPR	Canadian Patent Reporter
DLR	Dominion Law Reports
E & B	Ellis & Blackburn Reports
EG	Estates Gazette
EGLR	Estate Gazette Law Reports
EGCS	Estates Gazette Case Summaries
Ex.	Law Reports, Exchequer Division
F	Faculty Decisions, Court of Session
Fam Law	Family Law
Fin LR	Financial Law Reports
FLR	Family Law Reports
HLR	Housing Law Reports
ICLR	International Construction Law Review
IR	Irish Reports
IRLR	Industrial Relations Law Reports
JP	Justice of the Peace
JPL	Journal of Planning Law

Jur	Jurist Reports
KB	Law Reports, King's Bench Division
LGR	Local Government Reports
LJ	Law Journal Newspaper
LJCP	Law Journal, Common Pleas
LS Gaz	Law Society's Gazette
LT	Law Times Reports
LL. LR	Lloyds List Law Reports
Lloyd's Rep.	Lloyds Law Reports
NLJ	New Law Journal
NPC	New Property Cases
NSWLR	New South Wales Law Reports
NZLR	New Zealand Law Reports
OWN	Ontario Weekly Notes
P & CR	Property and Compensation Reports
PD	Law Reports, Probate Division
QB	Law Reports, Queen's Bench Division
RR	Revised Reports
RTR	Road Traffic Reports
SASR	South Australian State Reports
SLT	Scots Law Times
Sol. J	Solicitors' Journal
TLR	Times Law Reports
TrLR	Trading Law Reports
WLR	Weekly Law Reports
WR	Weekly Reporter

Table of Statutes

Index